# Tolkien's Shorter Works

PROCEEDINGS OF THE 4TH SEMINAR
OF THE DEUTSCHE TOLKIEN GESELLSCHAFT
& WALKING TREE PUBLISHERS
DECENNIAL CONFERENCE

edited by
Margaret Hiley & Frank Weinreich

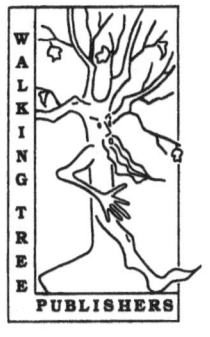

2008

Cormarë Series

No 17

Series Editors
Peter Buchs • Thomas Honegger • Andrew Moglestue • Johanna Schön

Library of Congress Cataloging-in-Publication Data
Hiley, Margaret and Frank Weinreich (eds.)
    Tolkien's Shorter Works. Proceedings of the 4th Seminar of the Deutsche Tolkien Gesellschaft & Walking Tree Publishers Decennial Conference
    ISBN 978-3-905703-11-5

Subject headings:
Tolkien, J. R. R. (John Ronald Reuel), 1892-1973 – Criticism and interpretation
Tolkien, J. R. R. (John Ronald Reuel), 1892-1973 – Language
Fantasy fiction, English – History and criticism
Literature, Comparative.

Cover artwork by Anke Eissmann.

All rights reserved. No portion of this book may be reproduced, by any process or technique, without the express written consent of the publisher.
Walking Tree Publishers, Zurich and Jena 2008.

for my grandparents
(1918 – 2007) (1914 - 2008)
(M.H.)

for Sannyu
(F.W.)

# Table of Contents

Introduction — Margaret Hiley & Frank Weinreich … i

"Tom Bombadil": Poetry and Accretion — Allan Turner … 1

Speaking With Animals: A Desire that Lies Near the Heart of Faërie — Guglielmo Spirito OFM … 17

Setting Things Right in *Farmer Giles of Ham* and *The Lord of the Rings*: Tolkien's Conception of Justice — Marek Oziewicz … 37

The Rout of the King: Tolkien's Readings on Arthurian Kingship – *Farmer Giles of Ham* and *The Homecoming of Beorhtnoth* — Vincent Ferré … 59

*Farmer Giles of Ham*: the Prototype of a Humorous Dragon Story — Friedhelm Schneidewind … 77

"... Until the Dragon Comes": Tolkien's Dragon-Motif as Poetological Concept — Patrick Brückner … 101

Theology and Fairy-Stories: A Theological Reading of Tolkien's Shorter Works? — Thomas Fornet-Ponse … 135

The "Meaning" of *Leaf by Niggle*     165
Bertrand Alliot

The Autobiographical Tolkien     191
Heidi Steimel

Leaf by Tolkien? Allegory and Biography in Tolkien's
Literary Theory and Practice     209
Fabian Geier

Redefining the Romantic Hero: a Reading of *Smith
of Wootton Major* in the Light of Ludwig Tieck's
*Der Runenberg*     233
Martin Simonson

*Smith of Wootton Major*, "The Sea-Bell" and
Lothlórien: Tolkien and the Perils of Faërie     251
Maria Raffaella Benvenuto

A Star Above the Mast: Tolkien, Faërie and the
Great Escape     263
Anna E. Slack

Journeys in the Dark     279
Margaret Hiley

*Smith of Wootton Major* Considered as a Religious Text     293
Martin Sternberg

Metaphysics of Myth: The Platonic Ontology of
"Mythopoeia"     325
Frank Weinreich

# Introduction

MARGARET HILEY & FRANK WEINREICH

Tolkien's Middle-earth and its legendarium have drawn extensive scholarly attention nearly from the first publication of *The Lord of the Rings* in 1955 (the harsh critique of Edmund Wilson comes to mind as well as W.H Auden's praise). These tales have also been appraised by the various audiences of the books as well as the audioplays, films and numerous other artistic interpretations of Tolkien's work. However, there is more to Tolkien than the history and legends of Middle-earth, and there has hitherto been a certain lack of academic criticism focused primarily on his shorter fictional works like *Farmer Giles of Ham, Smith of Wootton Major, Roverandom* and his poetry. Although scholarly evaluations of these works exist, they often deal with the shorter texts more as an afterthought, as footnotes to the "major" texts which seem to repeat themes and concerns of the major texts rather than demand attention in their own right. This dearth of studies seems to suggest it is time for a closer look at Tolkien's 'Shorter Works'.

With this in mind, in May 2007 Walking Tree Publishers and the German Tolkien Society (*Deutsche Tolkiengesellschaft, DTG*) held a joint conference at the Friedrich Schiller University in Jena, Germany, which made the shorter works the focus of scholarly interest. Academics and enthusiasts from all corners of Europe gathered to explore and discuss them, and various interesting aspects, details and connections were unearthed which are likely to broaden the understanding of said shorter works, but also of Middle-earth and Tolkien's overall fictional work and the man and author J.R.R. Tolkien himself. The findings of this conference are collected and presented in this volume.

In the first article Allan Turner examines the poems collected in *The Adventures of Tom Bombadil*. Although these are presented in the wake of *The Lord of the Rings* as a further selection from the Red Book, many of the individual pieces were written much earlier and with no apparent connection to Middle-earth at all. Turner demonstrates the ways in which much of Tolkien's earlier work was drawn into and incorporated by his secondary world. In the second essay, Padre Guglielmo Spirito examines the two "Tom Bombadil" poems and *Farmer Giles of Ham*, focusing on how each text deals with the speech of animals. Referring to Tolkien's essay "On Fairy-stories", which posits a deep-rooted human "desire to hold communion with all living things", Spirito shows how fantasy writing represents one way of addressing this desire.

Marek Oziewicz addresses the concept of justice to be found in *Farmer Giles of Ham*. In his reading, *Farmer Giles* exemplifies "compensational justice" that can satisfy on both an individual and a wider political level. This political dimension remains present in Vincent Ferré's article on kingship in *Farmer Giles of Ham* and *The Homecoming of Beorthnoth*. Ferré notes that in his criticism, Tolkien is frequently concerned with the ruler's failure to protect his people, as shown in medieval texts such as *Beowulf* and *Gawain*. This issue is taken up in Tolkien's fiction and, in the case of *Farmer Giles*, resolved.

Dragons form the focus of the next two essays. Friedhelm Schneidewind points out that while Tolkien had, in his own words, "desired dragons with an intense desire" since childhood, they feature more prominently in his shorter works than in his longer and better-known fiction. In his shorter works, Tolkien can be seen as participating in the long European tradition of dragon-tales. Patrick Brueckner examines how Tolkien uses the dragon motif as a poetological device to generate epic historicity. The dragon thus becomes the measure of different levels of reality, and Brueckner uses the example of *Roverandom* to show how dragons blur the boundary that divides fantastic from real and render it permeable.

In the next article, Thomas Fornet-Ponse looks at how Tolkien's essay "On Fairy-Stories" can be read as setting out not just a literary, but a theological programme. Tolkien's shorter fiction can be seen as reflecting various aspects of Recovery, Consolation and Escape and can thus be read theologically as an illustration of his theory.

Next follow three essays that focus on *Leaf, by Niggle*. Bertrand Alliot works out the "meaning" of this obviously, if not straightforwardly allegorical text. Alliot examines how in it, Tolkien attempts to reconcile the irreconcilable, namely what he termed "the laws" of artistic creativity. Heidi Steimel examines both *Niggle* and *Smith of Wootton Major* in the light of Tolkien's own biography, showing that parallels between life and fiction certainly existed despite Tolkien's own depreciation of biographical analysis. Fabian Geier's essay then shows how, far from being a contradiction, Tolkien's own use of allegory and autobiographical matter is consistent with his theoretical remarks once the theory of sub-creation (normally ignored in this regard) is taken into account.

The next esssays deal with the other autobiographical story Tolkien wrote, *Smith of Wootton Major*. Martin Simonson addresses the concept of the romantic hero in his essay. He contrasts the protagonist of *Smith of Wootton Major* with the hero of Ludwig Tieck's *Der Runenberg*, showing how Tolkien offers a redefinition of the more pessimistic Romantic hero by using his own elements of Escape and Consolation to effect the Recovery at which the Romantic hero fails. Maria Raffaela Benvenuto compares Smith's adventures in Faërie to those of the speaker of "The Sea-Bell" and the Fellowship of the Ring in Lothlórien. All three texts, in accordance to folk and fairy-tale tradition, show the "perils" of their respective magical realms and seem to posit that any mortal's involvement with Faërie will end in loss. Taking up this theme, Anna Slack notes how in Tolkien's works, *Faërie* is inevitably associated with *farewell*. Many of his shorter works, written under the threat of war or towards the end of his life, thus carry a note of valediction and bereavement.

Continuing the focus on *Smith of Wootton Major*, Margaret Hiley examines how both *Smith* and "The Sea-Bell" represent stories of quest. However, in Tolkien's modern version of the traditional quest motif, the hero sets out not to discover and master a new world, but to realise that the fantastic world is and will always remain unknowable. Martin Sternberg brings a theological dimension to his study of *Smith*. Faërie can be read as a representation of what Mircea Eliade termed the "holy time of creation", a place/time to which man must periodically return in order to regenerate both himself and the world. It is precisely the balance between the real and the fantastic that must be maintained for humanity to reach its full potential.

In the final essay, Frank Weinreich explores Tolkien's poem "Mythopoeia". While often linked to the essay "On Fairy Stories", "Mythopoeia" goes further than the essay in questioning traditional notions of reality, truth and fiction. Weinreich shows the similarities to Platonic philosophy evident in "Mythopoeia", and debates what relevance these ideas might have for Tolkien's *oeuvre* as well as for his personal beliefs in its entirety.

These essays reflect the breadth and depth of the discussion generated at the conference. From light-hearted to serious, from literary to philosophical to theological to biological, the debate was wide-ranging and, as such debates must, ultimately raised many more questions than it answered. We hope that the present collection will not only enlighten its readers as to many hitherto unconsidered aspects of Tolkien's shorter works, but also encourage them to further follow some of the lines of thought opened up here. The aim of both the conference and its proceedings is to show that "short" these works may be, but "minor" they are not – and as such, they merit even more attention than we have been able to give them. This volume marks a starting, not an end point.

A few final words to the editorial procedure. As is now traditional practice for Walking Tree Publishers, a more light-handed approach was adopted, that (while each contribution was carefully proof-read and suggestions for alterations and emendations made) aims to preserve the authors' own style and culture-specific scholarly traditions. This volume thus represents, as indeed the conference where it originated did, the truly diverse and international nature of contemporary Tolkien scholarship.

Margaret Hiley & Frank Weinreich<br>
Peterborough & Bochum, Winter 2008

# "Tom Bombadil": Poetry and Accretion

## Allan Turner

### ABSTRACT

The poems collected in *The Adventures of Tom Bombadil* are presented in the wake of *The Lord of the Rings* as a further selection from the Red Book. However, many of the individual pieces, which represent a cross-section of the types of verse that Tolkien wrote chiefly in the 1920s and 1930s, have a longer history of publication. What gives the collection its appearance of unity is on the one hand a series of revisions and accretions which draw the subject matter into the world of Middle-earth, and on the other hand the pseudo-scholarly Preface which offers a parallel to the Appendices of *The Lord of the Rings* and subsumes these texts within the same frame narrative.

*The Adventures of Tom Bombadil* must have been a puzzling book when it first came out. Seven years had passed since the publication of *The Lord of the Rings*, during which time the reputation of the author of the three-volume romance had quietly but steadily grown but no further works had appeared to build on his success. Now here, in place of a further epic based on the character whose memory spanned millennia, was a slim volume of apparently light verse, some of it even lifted straight from its predecessor. The reviewer in the *Times Literary Supplement*, although evidently well disposed to Tolkien's world, nevertheless finds very little to say other than to damn the poems with faint praise: Tolkien is "an ingenious versifier, rather than a discoverer of new insights", and the verses "do not grip a reader as did all the tales of hobbits and elves" (Duggan 892).[1] For those already devoted to Middle-earth it was a morsel to tide them over until something more substantial could

---

[1] The review is anonymous, but the *TLS* online index shows that it was written by Alfred Duggan.

appear; for others it must have been simply a confirmation that Tolkien was not to be taken seriously.

For the fans there was a further difficulty in that the world depicted in *Tom Bombadil* was not completely congruent with the immensely detailed background they had already gained from the Appendices. The Mewlips[2] did not fit anywhere into the lore of living creatures, and the Merlock Mountains were obviously a mere invention, quite unlike the Misty Mountains. Even the Shire of Perry the Winkle was not quite that of Frodo Baggins, in spite of the references to Michel Delving and the Lockholes. In particular the illustrations by Pauline Baynes, delightful though they were, were difficult to reconcile with the wider, more "factual" Middle-earth: hobbits in medieval or Elizabethan costume, or elven knights with wings riding among dandelions and marigolds that were almost as big as they were.

It is only through the publication (or re-publication) of works by Tolkien unavailable at that time that the verses from *The Adventures of Tom Bombadil* can be fitted into the complex context of the development of his oeuvre, showing his typical processes of assimilation and accretion at work. It can also be seen that the relationship between Tolkien's prose and poetry is not linear, but rather cyclical, with one literary genre feeding back into another, reflecting the cross-fertilisation between his scholarly and creative activity. The pseudo-scholarly Preface provides a clue to help the attentive reader to place the volume in context, although that was little remarked on at the time except as an example of scholarly wit. In particular, I shall argue that by utilising the conceit of the Red Book of Westmarch, it gives a new significance not only to the poems but also to the narrative framing device itself.

---

[2] The *TLS* reviewer, possibly under the unconscious influence of Shakespeare's *As You Like It*, II, vii, calls them "the Mewlings". Thankfully there is no reference to any Pukings.

Four questions in particular will be addressed here:
1) How do the poems in *The Adventures of Tom Bombadil* fit into Tolkien's poetic output overall?
2) How did the process of accretion come about?
3) How does it function in *The Adventures of Tom Bombadil*?
4) What is the literary effect of drawing these poems into world of *The Lord of the Rings*?

## TOLKIEN'S POETIC OUTPUT

So was the book, written at the suggestion of his 90-year-old aunt (*L* 308), just a pot-boiler? Certainly it is the slightest of the works that he published in book-form. Nevertheless I wish to argue that it is important in his output in that it represents one of the last phases in a process of assimilation and accretion which characterises Tolkien's method of composition, a process that he memorably allegorised in *Leaf by Niggle*.

Tolkien wrote most of his independent poems in the earlier part of his life, mainly from the beginning of his student days to the mid-1930s.[3] The ones which were chosen to appear in *Tom Bombadil* date mostly from his Leeds and early Oxford period. Two exceptions are *Cat*, written in 1956 for his granddaughter Joanna, and *Bombadil goes Boating*, which was composed specially for this collection to form a matching piece to the original Bombadil poem. His verse production seems to have petered out as he became more involved in writing the prose tales which form the major part of his work, although the embedded poems and songs represent an important part of his narrative technique in both *The Hobbit* and *The Lord of the Rings*.

---

[3] Concerning the genesis and development of all of Tolkien's individual poems, the most up-to-date information can be found in Scull & Hammond. Earlier versions of some of the *Tom Bombadil* collection, as well as other poems not previously published, can be found in the *History of Middle-Earth*.

It does not seem as if Tolkien had any particular publishing project in mind, since the poems were printed (if at all) in a variety of periodicals, sometimes under a pseudonym, and sometimes a considerable time after their composition. For example, an earlier version of *The Mewlips*, which appeared in the *Oxford Magazine* of February 1937 under the title of *Knocking at the Door* by 'Oxymore', was probably written ten years earlier according to Scull & Hammond (586). These periodicals were typically small-circulation magazines, often associated with educational establishments, notably Leeds and Oxford Universities.

Since a number of poems appeared in the *Oxford Magazine*, it is worth looking at a more or less contemporary characterisation of that periodical. *The Cambridge History of English and American Literature* (published 1907-21) compares it with its Cambridge counterpart:

> Resembling *The Cambridge Review* in general, it differs in being the organ of the don. [...] [T]he Oxford paper is more elaborately written than its contemporary. It is, in fact, almost too well written, and loses, sometimes, in irony and paraphrase, what it would have gained by naturalness. [...] The volume [i.e. a collection of re-printed articles] is also strong in that humour which comes from imitating in English the style and manner of an ancient author.

The overall picture suggests that much of Tolkien's poetry circulated in the world of dons rather than metropolitan literary circles. The readers would not be the poetic avant-garde; they were more likely to be highly educated people, sufficiently well-read to appreciate a subtle parody, but possibly rather conservative in their tastes. The probability is that in the club-like atmosphere of colleges and schools many of the authors and readers would have known one another well enough to spot an in-joke or an individual's predilections. The reference here to the parodying of ancient (i.e. Latin and Greek) authors is very reminiscent of what Tolkien was to do for, usually for more serious effect, with Germanic texts. In fact the pattern for a part of Tolkien's poetry may have been set by his earliest-known piece, *The Battle of the Eastern Field*, a parody in heroic verse of a rugby match which was published in his school magazine. This is also the first example of his use of the 'found manuscript' conceit (Scull & Hammond 75).

The poems can be divided loosely into six different categories, although there is inevitably a certain amount of overlapping, since a poem may have more than one characteristic. These categories are a) mysterious, b) philological (serious), c) philological (playful), d) metrical and phonaesthetic experiments, e) other parodies and satires, and f) miscellaneous.

a) The poems that I have described as "mysterious" set out to conjure up an atmosphere. This may suggest simply a quickening of the senses, a diffuse sense of the numinous as in *Habbanan beneath the Stars*, or it may bring a tingling of the spine, as in *A Song of Aryador* and *Goblin Feet*, with their suggestion of something slightly uncanny just behind a conventional landscape. Poems of this kind belong to the earliest period; the genre appears to have been abandoned as soon as the mythology took on a more definite shape. The only one that found its way into *Tom Bombadil* is perhaps *The Sea-bell*, although that is a later poem from 1932-33 which is on an altogether higher level of seriousness as an introspective exploration of the dangers of fantasy and imagination.

b) It is well known that Tolkien used his musings on words and phrases in the philological texts with which he dealt professionally as the basis for his imaginative creations. The poem originally known as *The Voyage of Éarendel the Evening Star*, which provides a mythological narrative context for the name found in Cynewulf's *Crist*, forms one of the imaginative germs of the whole legendarium. The representative of this category in *Tom Bombadil*, *The Hoard*, takes its idea and its original title from line 3052 of *Beowulf*, "Iúmonna gold galdre bewunden".

c) The impulse from philology could also be used in a playful vein, as with the two spoof Man in the Moon poems, which present purported lost "originals" of nursery rhymes, a concept which underlies several motifs in Tolkien's prose works too. Similar to these are the parodies of the Old English beast lore from the Exeter Book, two of which appear in *Tom Bombadil*, *Oliphaunt* and *Fastitocalon*. Something of the spirit in which they were written can be seen from their superscription in the Stapeldon Magazine: "Adventures in Unnatural History and Medieval Metrics, Being the Freaks of Fisiologus". *The Stone Troll*, originally one of the Songs for the Philologists compiled by Tolkien and Gordon as didactic amusement for their philology students at Leeds, also demonstrates linguistic principles such as metanalysis in "my nuncle" or metathesis in "axin'".

d) Although a number of the above poems make virtuoso use of techniques such as alliteration and internal rhyme, there is a category of Tolkien's poetry in which metrical experiments and sounds of words are almost an end in themselves. In particular he seems to have enjoyed trying to imitate in modern English the metres of other languages or earlier periods, as can be seen in his verse translations, for example *Sir Gawain and the Green Knight* or extracts from *Beowulf*. His poem *The Nameless Land* he claims to be an attempt to demonstrate that it was possible to re-create in modern English the extremely complicated verse form of the Middle English *Pearl* (*L* 317). However, in *Tom Bombadil* the firework of metrical experimentation is *Errantry*, written in a complicated verse form which Tolkien regarded as his own invention, although he wrote only one poem in it and "blew it out in a single impulse" (*L* 163).

e) Tolkien's fairly gentle satirising of the stupidity of people with limited outlook and imagination can be found in the group of poems which he called *Tales and Songs of Bimble Bay*, written around 1928 and set in an imaginary English seaside town. One of these poems, *The

*Bumpus*, is transformed in *Tom Bombadil* into *Perry the Winkle*, where the setting is transferred to the Shire, whose inhabitants are already well known for their small-minded rejection of anything that is new to them.

f) Finally there is a small category of miscellaneous poems which seem to be the doodles of Tolkien's idle moments, written for personal amusement. Examples that were included in *Tom Bombadil* are *Princess Mee* and *The Shadow Bride*.

It is clear from the above examples that in compiling the collection for publication, Tolkien had a very heterogeneous body to draw on. However, his choice was constrained by the problem of establishing some kind of unity. If the early Bombadil poem was to set the keynote for the whole volume, then the others had to be fitted into a context in which the figure of Tom Bombadil could exist. But how many of the poems that were chosen had their setting right from the start in the world of *The Lord of the Rings*? The answer to that is only one – *Bombadil goes Boating*, the only poem which was specially written for the collection. All of the others had to made to fit in some way. Either they had to be re-written, whether in small details or more radically, to serve their new function, or else the new context in which they were embedded could bring out in them a new significance. This was a process which was typical of Tolkien's Niggle-like method of composition, which might be called accretion.

## THE PROCESS OF ACCRETION

It is not possible here to give the complete textual history of the poems included in *Tom Bombadil*, an outline of which can be found anyway in the entries for the individual poems in Scull and Hammond. My intention is rather to illustrate the process of giving new significance to a poem by a relatively small change in the wording or by providing it with a new context. As an example I shall take a poem that does not appear in *Tom Bombadil*, but which demonstrates very clearly the types of transformation which Tolkien practised on his verse: *The Horns of Ylmir*, the history of which is given in *The Shaping of Middle-earth* (213-218).

According to Christopher Tolkien the earliest known manuscript is variously titled *The Tides* and *On the Cornish Coast*; it is dated 1914 and is associated with a visit to the Lizard Peninsula in Cornwall, although he adds that his father "remembered the origin of the poem to be earlier than that time". Indeed, Scull & Hammond (879) have identified what appears to be the earliest form, *The Grimness of the Sea*, composed in 1912 at St. Andrews in Scotland, almost at the other end of the country. But whichever part of Great Britain inspired it, it seems clear, although the precise text of this version is not reproduced, that Tolkien conceived it as pure nature poetry evoking the power of waves crashing against the cliffs, completely unconnected with his embryonic mythology.

By the time the next version was composed in 1915, this poem had been metamorphosed into *Sea Chant of an Elder Day*, with the Old English subtitle *Fyrndaga Sléop*. Two things have happened here: the setting has been withdrawn from the present into a remote past by the addition of lines referring to a time when "no sound of men's voices echoed in those eldest of all days", while the subtitle associates it with Tolkien's increased preoccupation with philology – the poem has, so to speak, been drawn into what Shippey (24) calls "asterisk reality".

However, it is still unclear when this remote time may have been and how the speaker comes to be contemplating it. The most radical recontextualisation comes in 1917, at the time when Tolkien was working on *The Fall of Gondolin*. It was at this time that the poem was extended both at the beginning and at the end to place the setting in the Land of Willows, with references to Ulmo (changed to Gnomish *Ylmir*) and Ossë interpolated, in effect changing a descriptive nature poem into a first person narrative of Ulmo's appearance to Tuor at Vinyamar. However, what is of particular significance is that at the same time a prose introduction was added in the voice of a third person narrator, explaining that this song was sung by Tuor to Eärendil to explain his sea-longing. Not only has the poem been assimilated in this way into the secondary world of the growing mythology, it has also become implicitly a document from a fictitious history. This document was in turn written into the 1930 *Quenta Noldorinwa* as "the song of Tuor that he wrote for his son Eärendel" (*SM* 142). However, the existence of a document presupposes a manuscript tradition and a historical context in which it could be known, that is to say the frame narrative which Tolkien never conceptualised to his own satisfaction, but which is constantly hinted at in fragmentary form. In this process of conferring a new significance can be seen not only a typical process in which isolated motifs became integrated into the texture of a vast legendarium, but also a method which could be consciously adopted by Tolkien in future.

RE-CONTEXTUALISATION IN *THE ADVENTURES OF TOM BOMBADIL*

To move forward almost half a century in time, we can see exactly the same procedures at work in the compilation of *Tom Bombadil*: the addition of references to people and places from what was by this time a well-known and highly detailed story, *The Lord of the Rings*, together with a certain amount of re-writing to improve the cultural fit, and as a framing device a prose introduction like a much more developed parallel to that of *The Horns of Ylmir*, which places everything within a manuscript tradition.

Of course, the very fact of anthologising the poems creates a context; readers will naturally try to relate them to one another and to what they know of Tolkien's world, in contrast to the original publication of a number of them as isolated pieces in magazines. However, the Preface, which is a minor narratological *tour de force*, plays a special role in the unifying effect and calls for a careful study, since it not only explicitly relates the poems to one another and to characters and places in *The Lord of the Rings*, but it also establishes an implicit parallel to the larger work through the literary and textual methods employed. Its key feature is that it stays entirely within the text world, just like the Prologue and Appendices to *The Lord of the Rings*, while its narrative voice is clearly the same as that of the editor/translator persona used there, which in itself has a strong integrative effect. However, there is a further similarity in that in *Tom Bombadil* too the apparently unnecessary detail gives the impression of a world that is solid and knowable, while at the same time the effect of verisimilitude is reinforced through the illusion of scholarly method. For example, we are told that Fíriel "was also the name of a daughter of Elanor, daughter of Sam (a glimpse of a new generation in the "then" of the narrative), but we are also given the linguistic information that the Hobbit name, if connected at all with that poem, "must be derived from it; it could not have arisen in Westmarch" (pseudo-authoritative philological detail seen from the "now" of the narrator and the reader). Similarly the highlighting of the new names *Grindwall, Breredon* and *the Mithe* with their etymological explanations helps to ground the events of *Bombadil goes Boating* in the historical geography of the Shire.[4]

This preface may be compared to that of *Farmer Giles of Ham*, which is also a fine piece of tongue-in-cheek writing. It too stays within its own text world, but that is a different, less complete one, with no connection to that of *The Lord of the Rings*. Besides, *Giles* as a whole is also more obviously parodistic and humorous, satirising academic activ-

---

[4] The *TLS* reviewer sounds a warning that "by too frequent use of invented names anyone can compose verses to rhyme and scan". However, as far as I can see the only new name used specifically for a rhyme is Tode (in *The Mewlips*, rhyming with "road"). *Grindwall* certainly rhymes (more or less) with "windfall" and "Withywindle", but as in the other cases (*Meel Shee*, the *Bay of Bel* and the pseudo-Elvish inventions in *Errantry*) the play with names is a deliberate part of the game, with the reader's attention drawn to it in the Preface. This seems to be another example of a critic picking out not what Tolkien actually did but what a less careful writer might have done in a similar situation.

ity, as for example when the narrator pokes fun at the *OED* definition of a blunderbuss. In comparison, *Tom Bombadil* achieves a much finer balance between what is to be felt as real, at least within the secondary world, and what is pure whimsy.

It is notable that the Preface to *The Adventures of Tom Bombadil* is the only one of Tolkien's narrative works other than *The Lord of the Rings* to use the device of the Red Book of Westmarch, to which the verses are here attributed. The Red Book is generally held to be Tolkien's final solution to the problem of accounting for the preservation of the (then still unpublished) 'Silmarillion' tales by regarding them as translations from the Elvish by Bilbo, preserved along with his and Frodo's personal accounts of the War of the Ring, although this is not made absolutely explicit either in the main narrative or in the Appendices. Here that somewhat mysterious document is made more concrete and realistic by reference to its layout: it contains loose leaves bearing poems, while other verses and doodles appear in margins or blank spaces. We are told that some verses in the Red Book are also found in the narrative of the *Downfall of the Lord of the Rings*. This cannot mean the published *Lord of the Rings*, which is never referred to by this title. In fact it is the heading provided by Frodo for his completion of Bilbo's account as told in the final chapter of *The Lord of the Rings*; the implication here is that the editor/translator has direct access to a manuscript, the putative original.[5] The brief glimpse that we as readers are allowed may suggest that the Red Book contains other things too; it was no doubt left open-ended in case Tolkien found an opportunity to publish any other small pieces which might be fitted into the same framework.

This outline may give an idea of how the Preface to *Tom Bombadil* works on a deeper literary level. On the surface level it brings an originally heterogeneous collection of poems into a common context by

---

[5] However, the second edition of *The Lord of the Rings*, published four years later, says that the original manuscript is *not* preserved ("Note on the Shire Records").

ascribing them to different sources in the secondary world, either individual characters or more general cultures such as Gondor. An obvious first step is the attribution of the animal poems to Sam Gamgee, since he recites *Oliphaunt* in *The Lord of the Rings*, although here a double anchoring in Hobbit culture is established by the careful caveat that in the case of *Fastitocalon* that "at most Sam can only have touched up an older piece of the comic bestiary lore of which Hobbits appear to have been fond". The poems about Tom Bombadil are from the Buckland, which we know is the part of the Shire nearest to the Old Forest. *Errantry* is by Bilbo, an earlier version of the Eärendil poem we have already heard in the Hall of Fire at Rivendell. The philological poems have their origins in Gondor or Rivendell, which we already know to be places of greater learning than the rustic Shire. Since the poems are in this way integrated with people, places and events in the greater narrative, readers are more likely to interpret them against the unifying background of the secondary world than might otherwise have been the case, so that they take on some of the added stature of the epic world.

The two Bombadil poems show a strange cyclical movement. It is well known that the original poem *The Adventures of Tom Bombadil* predates *The Lord of the Rings*, being published in the *Oxford Magazine* in 1934, and that subsequently Tolkien used characters from it (Tom and Goldberry, Old Man Willow, the barrow wight) as a source for some adventures on the way to Rivendell. Some readers have felt the whole Bombadil episode to be an anomaly which merely holds up the story, and it was left out in the radio and film versions by Brian Sibley and Peter Jackson respectively. Indeed, in a letter to Rayner Unwin (*L* 315) Tolkien claims that the poems "integrate" Tom with the world of *The Lord of the Rings* "into which he was inserted"; the use of the verb 'insert' suggests that he was aware of such a problem. The process to which he is referring is the composition of a completely new poem, *Bombadil goes Boating*, where through the account of a visit by Tom to

Farmer Maggot, with oblique references to Rangers and Ringwraiths in "Tall Watchers by the Ford, Shadows on the marches", the events of *The Lord of the Rings* are fed back into a collection of poems which otherwise have no direct connection with the tale. In this later poem ("later" in both the primary and the secondary world) it is made to appear that the Hobbits themselves have a literature, however rustic, that contains intertextual references to their own history (or perhaps even national epic, as the true tale of Frodo the Hobbit merged into myth over the course of time). If Tolkien's interpretation is correct, *Bombadil goes Boating* will motivate a retrospective re-interpretation by the reader of several chapters of *The Lord of the Rings*, in just such a way as the Appendices motivate a re-reading of the main text.

However, the integration of Tom Bombadil works on more than a motivic level. It is no coincidence that of all the characters in *The Lord of the Rings*, Bombadil originated as a poetic creation, since he is the one who consistently uses metrical diction, even when it is written as prose rather than verse. The underlying rhythm was already established in what appears to be Tolkien's transcription of an earlier note preserving the original sketch for a Tom Bombadil poem given in *The Return of the Shadow*, 115f.:

> Ho! Tom Bombadil
>   Whither are you going
> With John Pompador
>   Down the River rowing?

In the house of this "aborigine" (*RS* 117) who "remembers the first acorn and the first rain-drop", the Hobbits discover that singing is "easier and more natural than talking". This seems to be an echo of Barfield: if in pre-modern societies there was no differentiation between literal and metaphorical meanings, then at the same time verse was simply a heightened variant of prose. Consequently it seems a perfectly natural development for events from *The Lord of the Rings* to appear versified in the later Bombadil poem.

'The Hoard' is another poem which originally had no direct connection with the Middle-earth material, although the epigraph from *Beowulf* brings it close to the 'Northern' spirit. Interestingly, In the Preface the editor links it not with *The Lord of the Rings* but with the older (in two senses) tales of the then unpublished 'Silmarillion': "it seems to contain echoes of the Númenorean tale of Túrin and Mím the Dwarf". Túrin has been mentioned in passing in *The Lord of the Rings* as a great hero of old, but the reference to Mím is new, and is the only occurrence of the name in a work published in Tolkien's lifetime. Apart from awakening yet more desire for a world half glimpsed, it could also have been preparing the ground for the publication of individual stories from the 'Silmarillion' material as Tolkien seems to have been contemplating during the 1960s (*L* 360). It is impossible to say how these would have been presented, but they would certainly have required a frame narrative or text-world editorial preface to put them in context. At any rate he had established here that the tradition was to come from Númenor rather than directly from the Elves.

## THE LITERARY EFFECT OF THE PREFACE

The Preface actually works on several levels. Together with tackling the serious task of creating the integrative effect that supports secondary belief, Tolkien is at the same time having a joke with us, but also guiding our critical responses. The joke lies in the way that he fictionalises his actual process of composition. For example, we now know from the drafts published in *The Treason of Isengard* (81-109) what only a very few insiders knew at the time, that the relationship between *Errantry* and the *Eärendillinwë* is very much as in the fictive account, with one growing out of the other through the process of accretion outlined above: "In origin a 'nonsense rhyme', it is in the Rivendell version found transformed and applied, somewhat incongruously, to the High-elvish and Númenorean legends of Eärendil". Indeed, a large part of the joke is at Tolkien's own expense, since he admits the incongruity of what he is doing. But by pointing out these features explicitly, he is also defusing the criticism in advance.

Some readers may ask themselves whether this self-referentiality makes Tolkien a post-modern author. The obvious answer is that it does not, since if it were a central feature of the conception it would need to be made far more obvious. Here it is purely incidental; it remains on the level of an insider joke. And where Tolkien has his tongue most firmly in his cheek is in the ascription of the poems to perhaps his most enduring creation, the Hobbits. We are told: "They are fond of strange words, and of rhyming and metrical tricks – in their simplicity Hobbits evidently regarded such things as virtues or graces, though they were, no doubt, mere imitations of Elvish practices". For "Hobbits" read "Tolkien". This convenient fiction ultimately provided the excuse for publishing (or re-publishing) a heterogeneous collection of poems, some written many years before, as a further textual deepening of the world of *The Lord of the Rings*, a pendant to the comical rusticity of some of the scenes set in the Shire. If the literary level is not to the taste of critics, it is the fault not of the author but of the unsophisticated Hobbits.

Finally, it is a very legitimate question to ask if this joke does not undermine the whole effect of verisimilitude which the Preface seeks to achieve by integrating *The Adventures of Tom Bombadil* with Tolkien's major work. Again, for me the answer is no. Like any other part of his fantasy, it is real for as long as one stays within the secondary world, as Tolkien argues in *On Fairy-stories* (*TL* 36), but the reader is always aware that it is a fiction; that is the paradox of any work of literature that does not deliberately alienate the reader. One is always free to step outside; indeed, that is essential since otherwise there could be no recovery in the primary world. But at no point in the Preface is there any mockery of the secondary world as such. That remains intact, and indeed is only strengthened by the complex web of allusion that Tolkien has drawn around it.

ALLAN TURNER studied German, medieval studies and general linguistics. He wrote his doctorate on the problems of translating the philological elements in *The Lord of the Rings*, and is particularly interested in stylistic and narratological aspects of Tolkien's writing. At present he teaches English language and British cultural studies at the University of Marburg.

## Works Cited

Barfield, Owen. *Poetic Diction*. 3rd ed. Middletown, Connecticut: Wesleyan University Press, 1973.

Carpenter, Humphrey, ed. *The Letters of J.R.R. Tolkien*. London: George Allen and Unwin, 1981.

Duggan, Alfred Leo. "Middle Earth Verse". *The Times Literary Supplement* 23 November 1962: 892.

Scull, Christina and Wayne G. Hammond. *The J. R. R. Tolkien Companion and Guide: Reader's Guide*. London: HarperCollins, 2006.

Shippey, T. A.. *The Road to Middle-Earth*. 3rd ed. London: HarperCollins, 2005.

"The Oxford Magazine." *The Cambridge History of English and American Literature in 18 Volumes* (1907–21) Volume XIV, The Victorian Age, Part Two. [http://www.bartleby.com/224/0505.html, cited 9.2.2008]

Tolkien, John Ronald Reuel. *The Adventures of Tom Bombadil*. London: George Allen and Unwin, 1962.

---, *Tree and Leaf*. London: George Allen and Unwin, 1964.

---, *The Shaping of Middle-earth*. Ed. Christopher Tolkien. London: George Allen and Unwin, 1986.

---, *The Return of the Shadow*. Ed. Christopher Tolkien. London: Unwin Hyman, 1988.

---, *The Treason Of Isengard*. Ed. Christopher Tolkien. London: Unwin Hyman, 1989..

# Speaking With Animals:
# A Desire that Lies Near the Heart of Faërie

GUGLIELMO SPIRITO OFM CONV. (ASSISI)

### ABSTRACT

Beasts and birds often talk like men in fairy-stories. To some extent, this marvel derives from one of the primal 'desires' that, according to J.R.R. Tolkien, lie near the heart of Faërie: the desire of men to hold communion with other living things. But our language has little to do with that desire, and is often wholly oblivious of it. We desire instead the understanding of the proper languages of birds and beasts as such, and that is much nearer to the true purpose of Faërie. Fairy-stories are plainly not primarily concerned with possibility, but with desirability. This desire, as ancient as the Fall, reveals a sense of separation – or even severance – of ourselves from beasts. Man has broken off relations, and looks now only from the outside ... with a few who are privileged to travel abroad a little; others must be content with travellers' tales. 'Even about frogs '(Tolkien added in 'On Fairy-Stories'). What is this desire, this 'desirability' and even this 'possibility' to us? This article tries to find an answer through the dynamics that underlie a couple of the sub-creational Tales from the Perilous Realm, i.e., *The Adventures of Tom Bombadil* ( I and II) and *Farmer Giles of Ham* (or rather, Garm of Ham).

### INTRODUCTION

I remember discovering the echo of sound as a child. It was a fascinating discovery. I tried out my voice and the echo returned faithfully every time I did so. It was as if the solid limestone mountains had secret hearing and voice. To hear one's echo among the lonely mountains seems to suggest that one is not alone. Landscape and nature know us, and the returning echo seems to confirm that we belong with them. We live in a world that responds to our longing; it is a place where the echoes always return, albeit sometimes slowly. It is as if the dynamic symmetry of the echo comprises the radius of an invisible but powerful circle of belonging (O'Donohue XXI – XXII).

The hunger to belong is at the heart of our nature. Cut off from others, we atrophy and turn in on ourselves. The sense of belonging is the natural balance of our lives. Mostly, we do not need to make an issue of belonging – when we belong, we take it for granted. There is some innocent childlike side to the human heart that is always deeply hurt when we are excluded.

No one was created for isolation. When we become isolated, we are prone to become damaged. Our minds lose their flexibility and natural kindness and we become vulnerable to fear and negativity. The sense of belonging keeps one in balance amidst inner and outer immensities.

Wherever there is distance, there is longing. Yet there is some strange wisdom in the fact of distance. It is interesting to remember that the light that sustains life here on earth comes from elsewhere. Light is the mother of life. Yet the sun and the moon are not on the earth; they bless us with light across vast distances. We are protected and blessed in our distance. Were we nearer to the sun, the earth would be consumed in its fire; it is the distance that makes the fire kind. So, in a contrary fashion, nothing in creation is ever totally at home in itself. Nothing is ultimately at one with itself. Everything that is alive holds distance within itself.

This is especially true of the human self. It is the deepest intimacy which is nevertheless infused with infinite distance. There is some strange sense in which distance and closeness are sisters, the two sides of one experience. Distance awakens longing; closeness is be-longing. Yet they are always in a dynamic interflow with each other, and when we fix or locate them definitively, we injure our growth. It is an interesting imaginative exercise to change them about: to consider what is near as distant and to consider the distant as intimate. Our hunger to belong is the longing to find a bridge across the distance from isolation to intimacy (O'Donohue XXII).

As far as we know, cows are not burdened in this manner by ultimate questions (O'Donohue 172). Nevertheless, you often encounter such loneliness in animal presence; animals seem to receive it from elsewhere. It belongs somehow to the intimate pain of the world. An animal's face can often be an icon of profound lonesomeness. It is said that Nietzsche, before one of his major breakdowns, was walking down a street in Turin. Coming up the street in the opposite direction were horse and cart. He looked deeply into the horse's face and went up, put his arms around its neck and embraced it. The sadness in the old horse's face was a perfect mirror of his own torture. Every form of life participates in the light soul and also in the darkness of suffering.

Animals have always held a profoundly significant place in the human imagination in ways that have nothing to do with their actual existence as a particular animal of any kind. It is as if people see something of themselves and their own lives reflected in these creatures and their behaviour. In the world of allegory, fable and fairy-tale, animals serve as keys to human existence. They are given human characteristics and introduce people to worlds which they could never otherwise enter. They appear as symbolic figures in our dreams. Animals have something approaching a "second existence" in the human mind and fantasy. Children come to know animals frequently in books and cartoons and stuffed toys before they meet them as living creatures, and their acquaintance with these animal "characters" bears no relation to the living creatures they represent. An immense gulf separates the animals inhabiting the human psyche from those in the real world; indeed, these anthropomorphic figures can even block access to real animals (Birch and Vischer X).

Man is, ironically, the only animal that defines itself as the animal that it is not. Paradoxically, the animal is always invoked in defining the human in a way that says: we are not beasts. The animal is necessary to say what we are, but have forgotten and rendered invisible. We need the animals to be human, and we render them no thanks, and considerable scorn, in the bargain.[1]

What is outside in Nature is also inside in human nature – whether it be large rolling storms, Icelandic meadows flowering in a sudden spring, or underground artesian wells. All these are inside us in some way. Through Literature, we can discover some of these aspects. In their depicting of beasts as bearers of human traits while still letting the animal character dominate their being, beast fable and beast epic spring to mind. And this is were we finally turn to Tolkien's work.

We find a couple of examples, both in *The Hobbit* and in *The Lord of the Rings*, of animals acting or thinking like humans. One example is the fox who sees Frodo, Sam and Pippin walking through the woods and who then actually *thinks* to himself how strange that is; another is the scene in *The Hobbit* when Beorn's hall is described as peopled with animals who do ordinary housework.

In *Tree and Leaf,* Tolkien then leads us to the heart of the matter:

> There is another type of marvellous tale that I would exclude from the title fairy-story', again certainly not because I do not like it: namely pure 'Beast-fable'. [*TL* 15]
>
> The beast-fable has, of course, a connection with fairy-stories. Beasts and birds and other creatures often talk like men in real fairy-stories. In some part (often small) this marvel derives from one of the primal 'desires' that lie near the heart of Faerie: *the desire of men to hold communion with other living things But beast-fable, as developed into a separate branch, has little reference to that desire, and often wholly forgets it. The magical understanding by men of the proper languages of birds and beasts and trees, that is much nearer to the true purposes of Faerie.* [*TL* 40f.; emphasis added]

---

[1] Cf. Wockner and McNamee and Campbell p. 113: "No other animal that I know of evokes such intensity of feeling, for and against. It is the intensity of this passion that attracts me to wolves. They have helped me find myself, howling me back to myself."

And he continues:

> I had no special childish 'wish to believe'. I wanted to know. Belief depended on the way in which stories were presented to me, by older people, or by the authors, or on the inherent tone and quality of the tale. But at no time can I remember that the enjoyment of a story was dependent on belief that such things could happen, or had happened, in 'real life'. *Fairy-stories were plainly not primarily concerned with possibility, but with desirability. If they awakened desire, satisfying it while often whetting it unbearably, they succeeded.* It is not necessary to be more explicit here, for I hope to say something later about this desire, a complex of many ingredients. [*TL* 57; emphasis added]

This is the central point, or better the meeting point of all dynamics! We do not, or need not, despair of drawing because all lines must be either curved or straight.

Occasionally, the fog lifts. We catch a glimpse of what we hope are "things as they really are," and then the fog creeps over us again. I do not find this a gloomy prospect at all. The fog keeps us humble and compassionate, the flashes of light keep us hopeful and exhilarated (cf. Jones 66).

### COMMUNICATION

Often communication is like a dialogue between bird and fish, each calling from an element the other could not live in (cf. Renault *Mask* 221). Then, we feel somehow challenged. As Pawel and David felt:

> "Yes, and more than that. Spoken language and silence are keys."
> "Keys to what?"
> "To communion."
> "What do you mean by communion?"

"At-oneness." (O'Brien 265)

"More is needed. If we fail to speak with true voices, our language dies. In the great fabric of existence, a dead language is one that is no longer lived and acted upon ." (O'Brien 397)

David Abram (73, 75) says that

> Every attempt to definitively say *what language is*, is subject to a curious limitation. For the only medium with which we can define language is language itself. We are therefore unable to circumscribe the whole of language within our definition. It may be best, then, to leave language undefined, and to thus acknowledge its open-endedness, its mysteriousness. Nevertheless, by paying attention to this mystery we may develop a conscious familiarity with it, a sense of its texture, its habits, its sources of sustenance.
>
> [...]
>
> We do not, as children, first enter into language by consciously dying the formalities of syntax and grammar or by memorizing dictionary definitions of words, but rather by actively making sounds. [...] *We thus learn our native language not mentally but bodily.* We appropriate new words and phrases first through their expressive tonality and texture, through the way they feel in the mouth or roll off the tongue, and it is this direct, felt significance-the *taste* of a word or phrase, the way it influences or modulates the body-that provides the fertile, polyvalent source for all the more refined and rarefied meanings which that term may come to have for us.
>
> Language, then, cannot be genuinely studied or understood in isolation from the sensuous reverberation and resonance of active speech.

*It is the mark of little men to like only what they know,* said Mary Renault's Theseus (Renault *Bull* 110); one step beyond, and they feel the black cold of chaos. There are some stories which give us fine examples of people who accepted the challenge:

> The wolf's gaze melts into softness. Saints and angels must have eyes like these. The old woman beside me moves restlessly. "She knows you. They always know their own." I glance sideways, curiously, at the old woman, crooked like a broken branch. The little breeze lifts her hair, the colour of blood and snow, and blows it around her face. I am surprised at her words. "What do you mean?" I ask. "Mother Wolf knows you. She knows you are a wolf." Turning back to those golden eyes, listening to the old woman muttering beside me, the wolf and I speak in silence. (Martino 1)

Farley Mowat, in his *Never Cry Wolf,* tells about an Inuit who, he believed, learned "wolf-talk":

> Ootek had many singular attributes as a naturalist, not the least of which was his apparent ability to understand wolf language. In my notebooks I had recorded the following categories of sounds: Howls, wails, quavers, whines, grunts, growls, yips and barks. Within each of these categories I had recognized, but had been unable adequately to describe, innumerable variations. I was also aware that canines in general are able to hear, and presumably to make, noises both above and below the range of human registry; the so-called "soundless" dog-whistle which s commercially available being a case in point. I knew too that individual wolves from my family group appeared to react in an intelligent manner to sounds made by other wolves; although I had no certain evidence that these sounds were anything more than simple signals. My real education in lupine linguistics began a few days after.

> Ootek suddenly cupped his hands to his ears and began to listen intently. "Listen, the wolves are talking!" and pointed toward a range of hills some five miles to the north of us. I listened, but if wolf was broadcasting from those hills he was not on my wavelength. Ootek grabbed my arm and broke into a delighted grim. "Caribou are coming; the wolf says so!" [...] Some Eskimos, and Ootek in particular, could hear and understand so well that they could quite literally converse with wolves. (Mowat 93-95)

Also take Farmer Giles of Ham - or should we speak rather of Garm of Ham? Yes and no. Yes, for Garm uses the vulgar tongue, but remains dog-like, he communicates, but is not really "humanized". No, for we are here more interested in Giles *speaking with* Garm, than in the fact of Garm as a speaking animal? But perhaps both are true: for Giles speaks *with* Garm, and not only *to* Garm, doesn't he?

> Farmer Giles had a dog. The dog's name was Garm. Dogs had to be content with short names in the vernacular: the Book-latin was reserved for their betters. Garm could nor talk even dog-latin; but he could use the vulgar tongue. [...] Quite forgetting that he was out without leave, he carne and barked and yammered underneath his master's bedroom window. There was no answer for a long time. Farmer Giles was not easily wakened. 'Help! help! help!' cried Garm. The window opened suddenly and a well-aimed bottle carne flying out. Ow!' said the dog, jumping aside with practised skill. 'Help! Help! Help!' Out popped the farmer's head. 'Drat you, dog! What be you a-doing?' said he. 'Nothing,' said the dog. 'I'll give you nothing! I'll flay the skin off you in the morning,' said the farmer, slamming the window. 'Help! help! help!' cried the dog. Out came Giles's head again. 'I'll kill you, if you make another sound,' he said. 'What's come to you, you fool?' 'Nothing,' said the dog; 'but something's come to you.' 'What d' you mean?' said Giles, startled in the midst of his rage. Never before had

> Garm answered him saucily. 'There's a giant in your fields, an enormous giant; and he's coming this way,' said the dog. 'Help! Help! (TP, 5-8)

By the way, this "help! help!" is rendered nicely as a kind of barking, in the BBC radio play of it.

As we saw – as far we know – cows (and, we assume, mares) are not burdened by ultimate questions. Instead, perhaps, dogs, as wolves' relatives, are deeply skilled in 'talk-art'? It seems rather evident that Giles and Garm (and Giles's wife with both of them) have a good relationship, a nice partnership, and that they communicate and share events and feelings also through language (verbal and not verbal); and do not all these belong to our own deeper desires? Only one thing remains, I'm afraid, beyond our reach (if we are not English): only English dogs could have such sense of humour! Another example for the gift of communion in Tolkien is, of course, Gandalf.

Numerous also are examples told of the Christian saints. In *The Life of St. Paul, the First Hermit* by St. Jerome, St. Anthony hears that there is a man who has been in the desert longer than he has and is much holier. Seeking the hermit, Anthony wanders through the desert unsure of his goal. When he sees a she-wolf, Anthony guesses that Paul is providing the wolf with water and he enters the cave. The theme here again is relationship, not raw human power over nature. Reciprocity marks Paul's dealings with his neighbours. The wolf arrives seeking water and later his crow arrives bringing bread.

With St Ciaran other animals came from their lairs, a fox, a badger and a deer, and "they remained with him in the greatest docility, for they obeyed the orders of the holy man in everything like monks". One day however the fox, "who was more cunning and wily than the other animals", reverted to his former ways and, tired of his vegetarian diet, succumbed to the temptation, stole his master's shoes and took them to his old den in the wilderness, intending to devour them there.

The story then continues with its gentle and kindly account of his backsliding, his repentance and his restoration. "Learning this the holy father Ciaran sent another monk or pupil, namely the Badger, to the wilderness after the Fox to bring back the brother to his place. And the Badger, who was well acquainted with the woods, obeying at once the word of his superior, set out came straight to the cave of brother Fox" (cf. Gibbings and Waddell 91-95). And, of course, I should mention here St. Francis of Assisi [2] as well as Konrad Lorenz although he was not a saint (but he spoke with animals altogether).

Legends such as those mentioned above are endless and make delightful reading. But their charm should not be allowed to blind us to the profound truth which they reveal. In some mysterious way we see at work here mutual love, trust and sympathy which breaks down barriers between humans and animals, and brings about a glimpse of that common redemption which is promised to the world in Romans 8. Of all these stories none is more delightful than that account which we find in Bede of St Cuthbert's walk along the beach on the isle of Lindisfarne at night. He is watched by a hidden observer who reported that there followed in his footsteps two little otters who prostrated themselves on the sand, licking his feet, warming them with their breath and trying to dry them with their fur.[3]

As we read them we are taken into the timeless world of storytelling: truth perceived by way of the imagination. Here, we arrive at Tolkien's unique character of *Tom Bombadil*: "Tom the spirit that desires knowledge of other things, their history and nature, because they are 'other' and wholly independent of the enquiring mind" [*Letters*, 192]. He approaches each thing with attention, he never imposes himself, he allows each thing to communicate itself to him its own terms,

---

[2] Cf. Bell 59-61. Cf. also Guglielmo, SPIRITO, *Tra San Francesco e Tolkien una lettura spirituale del Signore degli Anelli*, Rimini, Il Cerchio, 2006, p.45-65 cap.3 *Il fascino di Tom Bombadil*.

[3] Cf. Bell, p. 87. Cf. *St. Cuthbert and the otters*, in Gibbings and Waddell o.c., p. 55-57.

and he gives it its own voice (*TP* 63). Here we find again badgers, otters and birds:

> Out came Badger-brock with his snowy forehead
> and his dark blinking eyes. In the hill he quarried
> with his wife and many sons. By the coat they caught him,
> pulled him inside their earth, down their tunnels brought him.
> Inside their secret house, there they sat a-mumbling:
> 'Ho, Tom Bombadil! Where have you come tumbling,
> bursting in the front-door? Badger-folk have caught you.
> You'll never find it out, the way that we have brought you!'
>
> 'Now, old Badger-brock, do you hear me talking?
> You show me out at once! I must be a-walking.
> Show me to your backdoor under briar-roses;
> then clean grimy paws, wipe your earthy noses!
> Go back to sleep again on your straw pillow,
> like fair Goldberry and Old Man Willow!'
> Then all the Badger-folk said: 'We beg your pardon!'
> ("The Adventures of Tom Bombadil" *TP* 67)

And also:

> Little Bird sat on twig. 'Whillo, Tom! I heed you.
> I've a guess, I've a guess where your fancies lead you.
> Shall I go, shall I go, bring him word to meet you?'
>
> 'No names, you tell-tale, or I'll skin and eat you,
> babbling in every ear things that don't concern you!
> If you tell Willow-man where I've gone, I'll burn you,
> roast you on a willow-spit. That'll end your prying!' [...]
>
> 'Tee hee! Cocky Tom! Mind your tub don't founder!
> Look out for willow-snags! I'd laugh to see you flounder'.

'Talk less, Fisher Blue! Keep your kindly wishes!
Fly off and preen yourself with the bones of fishes! (*TP* 75)
[...]
Rings swirled round his boat, he saw the bubbles quiver.
Tom slapped his oar, smack! at a shadow in the river.
'Hoosh! Tom Bombadil! 'Tis long since last I met you.
Turned water-boatman, eh? What if I upset you?'

'What? Why, Whisker-lad, I'd ride you down the river.
My fingers on your back would set your hide a-shiver.'

'Pish, Tom Bombadil! I'll go and tell my mother;
"Call all our kin to come, father, sister, brother!
Tom's gone mad as a coot with wooden legs: he's paddling
down Withywindle stream, an old tub a-straddling!"

'I'll give your otter-fell to Barrow-wights. They'll taw you!
Then smother you in gold-rings! Your mother if she saw you,
she'd never know her son, unless 'twas by a whisker.
Nay, don't tease old Tom, until you be far brisker!"

'Whoosh!' said otter-lad, river-water spraying
over Tom's hat and all; set the boat a-swaying,
dived down under it, and by the bank lay peering,
till Tom's merry song faded out of hearing.

Old Swan of Elvet-isle sailed past him proudly,
gave Tom a black look, snorted at him loudly.
Tom laughed: 'You old cob, do you miss your feather?
Give me a new one then! The old was worn by weather.
                    ("Bombadil Goes Boating" *TP* 73)

What is actually happening in the poem is anything but humorous. Tom Bombadil is in situations which for anyone else could represent mortal danger. He does not laugh them off, but escapes because he can command the creatures which threaten him. The combination of serious subject matter with comic metre is a curious one. Is it purely our expectations of what constitutes 'serious' poetry and what does not that make this seem funny? Was Tolkien perhaps deliberately exploiting the contrast for effect? It is possible, to say the least.[4]

## CONCLUSIONS

We must test each step, learning never to love opinion more than truth; never forgetting that men see as much truth as their souls are fit to see; always, till we pass through death and go forth to know ourselves, ready to go back to the start and look at all our premises, and begin again (Renault *Mask* 280). Behind the fantasy real wills and powers exist, independent of the minds and purposes of men (*TL* 14). Fantasy, the making or glimpsing of Other-worlds, was the heart of the desire of Faërie (*TL* 41). "And whatever he called every living creature, that was its name" (Gen. 2:9). By naming the animals, humans enter into a special relationship with them (Birch and Vischer 4).

So far, we have plainly concerned with *desirability* than with *possibility*. As Flannery O'Connor says,

> if the writer believes that our life is and will remain essentially mysterious, if he looks upon us beings existing in a created order to whose laws we freely respond, then what he sees on the surface will be of interest to him only as he can go through it into an experience of mystery itself. (O'Connor 41)

May we go a step forward, and have a glimpse of what could be, perhaps, possible? At least, we can try to share Tolkien's hope on the

---

[4] Cf. Lewis and Currie 163: "We believe it is quite clear that '*The Adventures of Tom Bombadil* is a poem which is deeply indebted to British folklore, with some influence from other Northern European traditions as well."

final *eucatastrophe*. So, switching from desirability to possibility (or trying to make desirable things, possible), we need to consider *hope* (theological *hope)*, or surrender "either to sadness or to wrath" (*TL* 65): we are saying, with Tolkien, that tales of communion with animals are not lies "and therefore worthless, even though breathed through silver" (*TL* 50).

May we say: *contra factum non est argumentum*? Some, as we have seen, *lived* both desirability *and* possibility. So, possibility is *open* also for us – if we choose not to follow Sandyman's scepticism!

"I will make for you a covenant on that day with the wild animals and I will make you lie down in safety" (Hosea 2:18)."I will make with them a covenant of peace and banish wild animals from the land, so that they may live in the wild and sleep in the woods securely" (Ezekiel 34:25). And this promise extends to the well-known vision of reconciliation between the world of humans and cattle on one hand and that of the wild animals on the other: "The wolf shall live with the lamb, the leopard shall lie down with the kid, the calf and the lion and the fatling together, and a little child shall lead" (Isaiah 11:6).

Creation is allowed to hope that it "will be set free from its bondage to decay and will obtain the freedom of the glory of the children of God" (Rom. 8:21). This state has not yet been reached. Creation is still "groaning in labour pains" (v. 22), but a new creation free from the rule of force has already been announced.

In Jesus peace with wild animals as foretold by the prophets becomes reality: "He was in the wilderness forty days, tempted by Satan; and he was with the wild beasts; and the angels waited on him" (Mark 1: 13). "At destruction and famine you shall laugh, and shall not fear the wild animals of the earth. For you shall be in league with the stones of the field, and the wild animals shall be at peace with you" (Job 5:22f.). The "community of the sixth day" is restored. It is certainly no accident that in the post-biblical period the ox and ass were introduced into the account of Jesus's birth (for the first time in the Gospel of Pseudo Matthew) for these are the animals capable of recognizing what human beings ignore. Recall again Isaiah's words: "The ox knows its owner and the donkey its master's crib; but... my people do not understand" (Is 1:3).

The doctrine that the whole world (and not just human beings and angels) is to be saved in *some* fashion occupies a key position in the theologies of many of the early Fathers, such as Justin, Irenaeus, Hippolytus, Mileto, Commodian, and Lactantius. For instance, in his impressive scheme of creation and redemption, Irenaeus understands the historical process from the Fall until the incarnation as a narrowing of the locus of salvation: after the Fall only one nation was chosen to carry the message and task of salvation, and then one person was chosen to represent that people. But from the single point of the incarnation, an ever—widening transmission of Christ's redemptive life has begun as the church grows to include all nations. This movement, Irenaeus believed, will not be completed until the whole universe has been 'recapitulated' and transformed (cf. Linzey and Yamamoto 191).

For centuries our search for wholeness has led us back to the animals, to our origins, to our history. Something mysterious happens when we look into the eyes of an animal, whether it be a panther or a poodle—we see something familiar looking back: ourselves. But we also see an "other". We see something that is in us and yet without us, something we recognize and yet is unfamiliar, something we fear but for which we long. We see the wild. The animals have always been a part of our survival and healing; and we, sometimes, theirs. At a time when our relationship to land and soil and place has been diminished, we still turn to our animals, domestic and wild, as a conduit to healing. And through our animals—those of our childhood, those in our homes, and those in the wild—we can begin to find our way back to being whole.

"This seemed the only good: to be one with the living mountain, with her birds and goats and wolves" (Renault *King* 341).

It was Christ's claim that a huddle of feathers on the ground was not unregarded by the Father of mankind. 'With Christ,' said Sulpicius Severus, 'every brute beast is wise, and every savage creature gentle'; and St. Kevin refused the levelling of the mountains about Glendalough to make rich pasture for his monks, because he would not have God's creatures disturbed. In the first paradise that lies behind the memory of the world there was no cruelty: and when Isaiah, sick of war, made his poem of the golden world, the climax-vision was a holy mountain where 'they shall not hurt nor destroy.' And whether these ancient ways of thought seem to us only the delusions sloughed by a wiser world, or whether 'those first affections, Those shadowy recollections are still the fountain-light of all our day. Are still a master-light of all our seeing' it matters very little (Cf. Gibbings/Waddell XVIf, XXIV, Ward 10, Murray 102).

The legends of saints will endure since they serve this deep need that we have: *to believe that what we long for is possible.* Here are men and women who, because they have first found God in themselves, can then encounter him in the world outside themselves. Here are lives in which miracle *is* commonplace and in which the world of present reality is absorbed into an all-encompassing, all-pervading world of grace, one above all which speaks to us of that harmony and unity of the whole of creation for which we all so deeply long (Gibbings and Waddell XXVIII).

There is no division into realms, the natural and the supernatural, but the two flow together into one: "The mutual enclosure of this world in the next and the next in this", as Charles Williams once put it. Or in Tolkien's words about humans and animals:

> The desire and aspiration of sub-creation has been raised to the fulfilment of Creation. The Birth of Christ is the eucatastrophe of Man's history. The Resurrection is the euca-

tastrophe of the story of the Incarnation. This story begins and ends in joy. It has pre-eminently the 'inner consistency of reality'. (*TL* 72)

Or in the words of Timothy Radcliffe (128):

> We go to literature in general, to be forwarded within ourselves. The best it can do is to give us an experience that is like foreknowledge of certain things which we already seem to be remembering.[5]

And Tolkien himself emphasizes:

> All tales may come true; and yet, at the last, redeemed, they may be as like and as unlike the forms that we give them as Man, finally redeemed, will be like and unlike the fallen that we know. (*TL* 73)

We need oases of leisure and silence and gratitude where we can, literally, come to our senses and clarify our sight, like the prodigal son, who 'came to himself' and remembered the truth of who he was, his father's son. And then, remembered too of being brother or sister of every living creature. Sharing. Communicating. Speaking. In wonder, delight and gratitude… *until we arrive beyond the circles of the world, where there is more than memory!*

> My eyes already touch the sunny hill,
> going far ahead of the road I have begun.
> So we are grasped by what we cannot grasp;
> it has its inner light, even from a distance –
> and changes us, even if we do not reach it,
> into something else, which, hardly sensing it, we already are;
> a gesture waves us on, answering our own wave …

---

[5] We can also see this in one of Martin Buber's hassidic tales: About Rabbi Arye and the Baal-Shem Tov, The Language of the Birds; in Buber 185-194.

but what we feel is the wind in our faces.[6]

GUGLIELMO SPIRITO OFM is a conventual franciscan friar (Minorit, in German) and works and lives in Assisi. He was born in Buenos Aires in 1958 and studied philosophy and egyptology before joining the Order of Saint Francis in the Eighties. In Rome he obtained the Degree (Licenza) in Pastoral Theology of Health Care at the *Camillianum* and the Doctorate in Theology with specialitation in Spirituality at the Pontifical Ateneum *Antonianum*. Since 1994 he is professor of Patristic and Franciscan Spirituality and of Theology and Literature (specially J.R.R. Tolkien) at the Theological Institute of Assisi and at the Pontifical Faculty of Saint Bonaventure in Rome. He gave courses in Croazia, Romania, Russia and Mexico, and lectures in England and Canada, Armenia and Egypt. On Tolkien he had published essays, articles and books, as *Tra San Francesco e Tolkien* and *Lo specchio di Galadriel with Il Cerchio*. He is also a member of the *Società Tolkieniana Italiana*. Contact by mail (fraguspi@itali.it) or through the Theological Institute of Assisi (http://www.chiesacattolica.it/teologiassisi).

## Works Cited

Abram, David. *The Spell of the Sensuous*. New York: Vintage Books, 1997.

Askins, Renée. *Shadow Mountain:* A memoir of Wolves, a Woman, and the Wild. New York: Anchor Books, 2002.

Bell, David N. *Wholly animals: a book of beastly tales*. Kalamazoo: Cistercian Publications, 1992.

Birch, Charles, and Vischer, Lucas. *Living with the Animals: The Community of God's Creatures*. Geneva: Risk Book Series, 1997.

Buber, Martin. *Legend of the Baal-Shem*. Princeton: Princeton University Press, 1995.

Gibbings, Robert and Helen Waddell. *Beasts and Saints*. London: Darton Logman Todd, 1995.

Jones, Alan W. *Soul making: the desert way of spirituality*. San Francisco: Harper & Row, 1989.

Lewis, Alex and Currie, Elizabeth. *The Uncharted Realms of Tolkien: A critical study of text, context and subtext in the works of J.R.R. Tolkien*. Oswestry: Medea Publishing, 2002.

Linzey, Andrew, and Yamamoto, Dorothy. *Animals on the Agenda questions about Animals for Theology and Ethics*. London: SCM Press LTD, 1998.

---

[6] Rilke, Rainer Maria, *"The Walk" selected Poems of Rainer Maria Rilke*, in Askins 52.

Lorenz, Konrad. *Er redete mit dem Vieh, den Vögeln und den Fischen.* Wien: Borotha-Schoeler, 1950.

Martino, Teresa Tsimmu. *The Wolf, the Woman, the Wilderness*: A true story of returning. Troutdale: NewSage Press, 1997.

Mowat, Farley. *Never Cry Wolf.* New York: Brown and Company, 1963.

Murray, Robert. *The cosmic Covenant*: Biblical Themes of Justice, Peace and the Integrity of Creation. London: Sheed & Ward, 1992.

O'Connor, Flannery. *Mystery and Manners.* New York:: The Noonday Press, 1997.

O'Donohue, John. *Eternal echoes. Celtic reflections on our yearning to belong.* New York:: Harper Perennial, 1999.

Radcliffe, Timothy. *What is the Point of Being a Christian?* London: Burns & Oates, 2005.

Renault, Mary. *The Mask of Apollo.* Toronto et. al.: Bantam Books, 1974.

---. *The King must Die.* London: Arrow Books, 2001.

---. *The Bull From the Sea.* London: Arrow Books, 2004.

Spirito, Guglielmo. "Il *Lupo "malvagio": un mito rivisitato"*. Convivium Assisiense VIII (2006): 61-86.

---. *Tra San Francesco e Tolkien: una lettura spirituale del Signore degli Anelli.* Rimini: Il Cerchio, 2006.

---. Ed. *Lo specchio di Galadriel: i francescani celebrano J.R.R. Tolkien.* Rimini: Il Cerchio, 2006.

Tolkien, John Ronald Reuel. *The Hobbit or There and Back Again,* London: Harper Collins, 1993a.

---. *The Lord of the Rings.* London: HarperCollins, 1993b.

---. T*ree and Leaf. The Homecoming of Beorhtnoth Beorhthelm's Son.* London: Harper Collins Publishers, 2001.

---. *Tales from the Perilous Realm.* London: HarperCollins, 2002.

Ward, Benedicta. *The Spirituality of St Cuthbert.* Fairacres: SLG, 1992.

Wockner, Gary and McNamee Gregory and Campbell, SueEllen. *Comeback Wolves: Western Writers Welcome the Wolf Home.* Boulder: Johnson Books, 2005.

# Setting Things Right in *Farmer Giles of Ham* and the *Lord of the Rings*: Tolkien's Conception of Justice

MAREK OZIEWICZ

ABSTRACT

One of the most fundamental assumptions of Tolkien's famous essay "On Fairy Stories" is that fairy-stories – mythopoeic fantasy, as I prefer to call the genre Tolkien had in mind – speak to our spiritual and psychological needs. One among these, and quite important for human well-being, is a thirst for justice. This paper is concerned with how Tolkien represents the working of justice in human relationships and in politics. By examples taken from *Farmer Giles of Ham* and from the last three chapters of *The Return of the King*, I argue that the relationship between customary and legal, social and political justice in Tolkien's work is structured on the principles of compensational justice. More satisfying to human spirit than legal justice, more psychologically desirable than the political justice known to his contemporaries in pre-WWII Europe, compensational justice is, I believe, presented by Tolkien as a viable concept on the individual as well as on the political level. As such, compensational justice constitutes an important part of Tolkien's appeal to modern readership.

*"It is useless to meet revenge with revenge: it will heal nothing"*
Frodo

INTRODUCTION

This paper grew out of an ongoing investigation of the notion of justice in mythopoeic fantasy. In brief, I believe that an important part of the appeal of the kind of fantasy as practiced by Tolkien, Lewis, and other mythopoeic fantasists lies in the fact that their novels employ a specific concept of justice, one I have elsewhere tentatively called compensational[1]. Far more satisfying to the human thirst for justice than its legal idea, compensational justice is grounded in the customary sense of fairness, applied to and expected of us in ordinary human relations. A multifaceted notion, compensational justice is structured around a set of assumptions about guilt, crime, compensation, and giving others their due. Inasmuch as the examination of this issue in the whole of Tolkien's fiction is clearly impossible here, I will look at two examples of how Tolkien presents the working of justice in human relationships and in politics.

Having outlined what I think constitutes Tolkien's understanding of right and wrong, I shall apply his own principles to *Farmer Giles of Ham* and to the last three chapters of *The Return of the King*. My focus in these two examples will be on the situation of "takeover," of restoring justice and order or, as Tolkien bluntly puts it in *The Return of the King*, of "setting the things right" (*RK* 242). A closer look at the takeover in those two works reveals, I think, not only that justice was for Tolkien an essential component of human relationships, but also, and specifically,

---

[1] See my "Let the Villains Be Soundly Killed at the End of the Book: C. S. Lewis's Conception of Justice in the Chronicles of Narnia" (in Amy Sturgis, ed., *Past Watchful Dragons*, Altadena, CA.: Mythopoeic Press, 2007). The concept of compensational justice consists of several elements that make it different from any of the four major conceptions of justice known today in the West. In contrast to the retributive approach which through punishment (the imposition of pain, alienation, and deprivation) attempts to make the wrong right, compensational justice aims at restitution and reconciliation that will reintegrate the offender and the community. Contrarily, again, to the utilitarian approach, which essentially sees punishment as a way to deter others from following in the footsteps of the offender, compensational justice does not instrumentalize individual cases in the service of any ideology or system, but focuses on the consequences of an action and on the ways of dealing with them. Compensational justice is also distinct from the rehabilitationist approach focused on compulsory treatment of offenders seen as medical cases; instead, it sees them as human beings truly capable of taking responsibility for their actions. Finally, in contrast to the restitutionist approach, which seeks to materially pay off the victim, compensational justice sees the process as essentially moral and emotional, rather than as a calculation of gains and losses, and focuses as much upon the victims as on the offenders. In all cases, compensational justice is part of the whole complex of values - compassion, truth, loyalty, dignity, and so forth - which collectively are the yardstick of a given character's humanity. As such, it is thus an understructure of principles that regulate the character's dealings with others and can be viewed as operating in minor as well as major cases.

that compensational justice is an apt term to describe what in his fiction is envisioned as an ideal relationship between customary and legal, and social and political justice.

## TOLKIEN ON JUSTICE

The closest I have come to Tolkien's understanding of justice, and thus of right and wrong, are his reflections in a note on W. H. Auden's review of *The Return of the King*. Jotted down, most likely, sometime in 1956, these thoughts offer a glimpse of certain fundamental principles that hold, I think, for all of Tolkien's writing and are inherent in his understanding of justice in its political, social and absolute dimensions. Within a five-page piece, Tolkien lays down six important principles.

The first is the difference between the political and the humane. In its context Tolkien questions the all-pervasiveness of politics and asserts that certain actions, such as Frodo's quest or Elrond's decision to destroy the Ring, are motivated by their interest in the good of the world and of all beings in it. Such actions are, by Tolkien's standards, humane and must be seen as different from political ones aimed at preserving or furthering any specific political entity or power structure[2].

The second is Tolkien's acknowledgment that "in 'real life' causes are not clear cut" and situations in which "*right* is from the beginning wholly on one side" are quite rare (*L* 242). However, he adds, this does not release anyone from making choices and from taking responsibility for them.

Stemming from this idea Tolkien's third principle evolves:

---

[2] Commenting on Frodo's duty, Tolkien claims it "was 'humane,' not political." He then adds an explanation: "the quest had as its object not the preserving of this or that polity, such as the half republic and half aristocracy of the Shire, but the liberation from an evil tyranny of all the 'humane'—including those, such as 'easterlings' and Haradrim, that were still servants of the tyranny" (*L* 240-241).

> [In] conflicts about things or ideas I am more impressed by the extreme importance of being on the right side, than I am disturbed by the revelation of the jungle of confused motives, private purposes, and individual actions (noble or base) in which the *right* and the *wrong* in actual human conflicts are commonly involved" (*L* 242).

Well said as it is, this imperative naturally calls for a definition of what right and wrong are. Tolkien's answer here is the fourth pillar of his thinking about justice:

> If the conflict really is about things properly called *right* and *wrong*, or *good* and *evil*, then the rightness or goodness of one side is not proved or established by the claims of either side; it must depend on values and beliefs above and independent of the particular conflict. [...] That being so, the *right* will remain an inalienable possession of the right side and justify its cause throughout. (*L* 242)

Like in his discussion of the humane, Tolkien here acknowledges the existence of certain universal standards and values which define the right: a universal moral law that Lewis called "the Tao" and defined as "the doctrine of objective value, the belief that certain attitudes are really true, and others really false, to the kind of thing the universe is and the kind of things we are" (Lewis *Men* 18). From this belief ensue the two remaining principles that Tolkien feels important to bring up. One, the fifth, is that "the rightness of the cause will not justify the actions of its supporters, as individuals, that are morally wicked"; the last and sixth is that "good actions by those on the wrong side will not justify their cause" (*L* 243). In a sense then, Tolkien's idea of right and wrong as expressed in these six principles is the following claim:

> The aggressors are themselves primarily to blame for the evil deeds that proceed from their original violation of justice and the passions that their own wickedness must naturally

(by their standards) have been expected to arouse. They at any rate have no right to demand that their victims, when assaulted, should not demand an eye for an eye or a tooth for a tooth. (*L* 243)

Assuming that this statement represents an accurate picture of what Tolkien thought about justice, I feel I should add that the intricacy of the issue makes it impossible to reduce Tolkien's opinions on the subject to facile statements. Tolkien's Christian worldview – with its conception of God's justice and mercy, the Last Judgment, the ideas of reward, punishment and desert – as well as his experience of the politically confused, war-torn and conflict-ridden world obviously shaped his conceptualizations of right and wrong, and of how they operate in human reality, into a complex vision which does not lend itself to simplifications.

For example, when I started to work on this paper, I thought there was an analogy between the crystallization of Tolkien's idea of justice in politics and the snowballing manipulation of the ideas of justice and right in European politics of the late 1930s. Especially when thinking about *Farmer Giles of Ham* – composed around 1937, extensively reworked throughout 1938 and submitted to Allen & Unwin at the time of the Munich conference in September 1938[3] – I was strongly inclined to see the story in the context of the events of the time: the Nazi seizure of Austria and Europe's betrayal of Czechoslovakia. It seemed to me quite likely that Giles's rebellion against the King and the ruler's increasing demands might be seen as somewhat reflecting the rising awareness of the British people – combined with a widespread anger and a crisis of conscience – of the abysmal discrepancy between justice as conceived by the politicians in totalitarian states, such as Nazi Germany, and justice as understood by the masses of people in countries

---

[3] See Tolkien's letter to C. A. Furth from February 2, 1939 in *L* 42.

such as Britain. However tempting the analogy between these events and Tolkien's story was, I was unable to find any evidence which would support that parallel. Whether there is one or not, however, does not invalidate my point. Since Tolkien was a man of strong opinions, especially on issues related to religion and morality, I think it is safe to assume that for him being human meant making choices. Those choices, Tolkien knew, necessarily have moral implications, either for right or for wrong.

## TOLKIEN'S IMAGINATIVE REPRESENTATION OF JUSTICE:
### *FARMER GILES OF HAM*

The standards of just and right action that Tolkien outlined in the Auden note can, I believe, be said to inform the way he envisioned "setting things right" in *Farmer Giles of Ham* and in the last three chapters of *The Lord of the Rings*.

A facetious little tale, *Farmer Giles of Ham* is, in Tom Shippey's words, unique in two ways: it is "Tolkien's only entirely successful published narrative outside the hobbit-sequence," and, unlike his other writings, it "shows Tolkien quite at ease with himself" (Shippey 289, 292). Although light-hearted, the story does make a strong point. Shippey considers it to be a serious evaluative comparison between the kind of folk culture of "vulgar tongue" which continues the legacy of songs, lays, romances and beliefs associated with them, and the court culture of book-Latin which no longer takes the old tales seriously and is devoted to "style at the expense of substance" (290). At the heart of the story, Shippey points out, the conflict is between these two types of social and cultural organization, rather than between the humans and Chrysophylax.

These are perceptive remarks, for indeed Chrysophylax and Giles eventually find themselves on the same side, allied against the King. The other strong point the story makes is what it has to say about doing the right thing, the takeover of power in this case. It is in this light that Giles's cause is the right one, although, in a very real sense, the story describes a subject's rebellion against the King and the resulting separation of an area – later known as the Little Kingdom – from the realm of the Middle Kingdom.

The legitimacy of this course of action derives from two factors. One is the narrator's implied republicanism, according to which many small kingdoms are a "happier" social organization than one large kingdom, for they allow villages to be "proud and independent" (*FGH* 125). More important still, Giles's rise to power is presented as a kind of natural consequence of a series of steps, each of which involves, to the same degree, taking responsibility with all the risks this involves but also enjoying the fruits of the outcome. In this sense, Giles is entitled to the fruits of his actions the way the King is not; as the story unfolds, Augustus Bonifacius is repeatedly shown to demand the outcome without input, to claim the benefits without investment.

The very hobbit-like Giles begins his half-serious, half-comic ascent with a defense of his own property – a motivation which is psychologically convincing. No matter how much the law has changed since Giles's times, a lot of modern people, upon hearing that someone is destroying their property, may just as well feel like loading a blunderbuss. "Property is property," says the narrator, adding that "Farmer Giles had a short way with trespassers that few could outface" (*FGH* 130). Although, as we come to know later on, "he seldom loaded it and never let it off" (131), the blunderbuss turned out to be an effective deterrent; in that event, Giles, "more anxious about his property than his skin" (132), not only caused the giant's retreat, but also became a local hero. Moreover, Giles's act communicates a message about private property.

> But even as they cheered they took note for their own profit that after all this blunderbuss could really be fired. There

had been some debate in the village inns on that point; but now the matter was settled. Farmer Giles had little trouble with trespassers after that (*FGH* 134).

Contrasted with Giles's action is the King's inaction. Inasmuch as the expulsion of a giant from the realm "seemed worthy of note and of some little courtesy" from the court (136), three months later Giles received a letter from the King, accompanied by the gift of a belt and a sword. "Plain heavy swords of that kind," the narrator wittily remarks, "were out of fashion just then, so the King thought it the very thing for a present to a rustic" (*FGH* 137). In this and other ways—like the description of traditional "dragon hunting" at court which culminates in eating Mock Dragon's Tail on Christmas Day – the narrator makes it plain that the King and his court fail to perform their traditional duties associated with the protection of the realm. The failure becomes even more glaring when Chrysophylax strikes.

At first, the King refuses to acknowledge the news, and as the King does, so do the knights. They abstain from action because "their knowledge of the dragon was still unofficial" (142). Even when the King brings the matter to their notice, the knights dally, presenting such excuses as the approaching Christmas, the already fashioned Mock Dragon Tail, the upcoming tournament, and the New Year Holiday. Ridiculous as these apologies sound, the serious subtext here is that of the failure of responsibility on the part of the King and his court.

Not that responsibility is easily taken. As soon as people start whispering behind his back and Giles finds himself facing their expectation that he should deal with the dragon, the Hero of Ham grows very uncomfortable. When verbal excuses are no longer accepted, when the hiding of the sword does not work, when he finds himself surrounded by villagers who repeat "we look to you, Master Aegidius" (*FGH* 145), Giles is "finding that a local reputation may require keeping up, and that may prove awkward" (144). The principle operating here is that with every social position goes its own responsibility. It is more important, Tolkien's narrator suggests, that Giles, the village hero, actually does go dragon-hunting, than that he does so only after much dallying and haggling, boosted not by a virtuous, knightly zeal but by "a deal of strong ale" and "a queer feeling of pride and encouragement [after learning] that his sword was actually Tailbiter" (148). The concatenation of lucky events which allow Giles to defeat the dragon does not diminish his victory. It is a victory and so much more spectacular, given that no knight took up the challenge.

What strikes the reader in this first encounter with Chrysophylax is that it involves a lot of negotiations on what is fair and right. Just as the dragon demands of Giles to make the encounter fair through a formal introduction (*FGH* 155), so, too, Giles and the villagers demand of Chrysophylax to be fair and compensate for the damage he had done. After the hilarious haggling episode, Tolkien has the parson set out just terms as follows:

> "Vile Worm!" he said. "You must bring back to this spot all your ill-gotten wealth; and after recompensing all those whom you have injured we will share it fairly among ourselves. Then, if you make a solemn vow never to disturb our land again, nor to stir up any other monster to trouble us, we will let you depart with both your head and your tail to your own home. And now you shall take such strong oaths to return (with your ransom) as even the conscience of a worm must hold binding." (*FGH* 160)

The quote above is the most succinct exposition of the principles of compensational justice in *Farmer Giles*. The corrective action proposed is intended to forestall further attacks by means of oaths, but also to compensate the injured parties by means of ransom. People's intentions notwithstanding, the dragon has no conscience and, once released, does not show up again.

Somebody else does, however. Deeply moved, clearly because of financial reasons, the King himself arrives in Ham to inspect the transaction. Having informed the people that "the wealth of the miscreant Chrysophylax all belonged to himself as lord of the land" (*FGH* 161-162), the King then promises that all citizens of Ham will receive "some token of our esteem" (162). While the Suzerain's appearance at that particular point strikes the readers and the villagers as a kind of cheating – a way to appropriate something the King had no hand in bringing about – the narrator strengthens the impression of the growing moral inadequacy of the King's power over Ham also in other ways: first, by suggesting that the tallies used to cover the King's expenses are void – thus the King is shown as purposefully cheating his subjects – and then by hinting at how ineffective the royal knights' expedition against the dragon is going to be.

And so it happens that Chrysophylax scatters the knights like straw before he is stopped, quite unexpectedly, by Giles. Another bout of bargaining follows, at the end of which a new deal is struck: the dragon will keep some of his treasures in exchange for carrying the ransom part back to Ham and helping Giles to keep it instead of handing it over to the King. This, clearly, is a pact which would have to be seen as a betrayal were it not for the fact that the King had actually asked for it by repeatedly neglecting his responsibilities while continuing to demand undeserved benefits. Giles, on the other hand, who is by now the victor over the dragon and the master negotiator, has taken responsibility and is now shown as enjoying the fruits of success. As the cavalcade travels back to Ham, Giles "is beginning to have ideas" (*FGH* 176) which soon flare up into an open conflict with the King.

Rather than any actual fighting, the conflict involves spelling out the redefined relationship between the King and Giles – a relationship which becomes apparent in the course of the narrative. Called for thrice, the hero of Ham does not report to the King, so the latter arrives in

Ham. Meeting on the bridge, both sides stake their claims: the King insists on obedience, apology, on the return of the sword and the dragon's hoard. Giles, refusing to satisfy any of these demands, replies that he has "wasted time enough on [the King's] errands" (*FGH* 180) and feels no obligation to him anymore. To the King's order "Give me my sword!" Giles responds with "Give us your crown!" – a declaration of local independence, and one wholly deserved, from what the narrative has shown so far. The rightness of this cause is sustained through the avoidance of bloodshed: Chrysophylax's appearance on the bridge scares the King's men-at-arms so successfully that no human bloodshed is necessary; in his hobbit-like fashion, Giles also waves off the King's challenge of a single handed combat, thus commenting on the inadequacy of a "solution" which – in the context of the whole situation – is nothing else than a chivalric shibboleth.

The idea of a just course of action in *Farmer Giles of Ham* can thus first be defined as the responsibility-based action, regardless of circumstances, combined with a recognition that one has to accept consequences of one's deeds; second that there are certain objective standards, such as freedom or mutual obligations of the ruler and the ruled, which define the *right* in this and other situations; third that the rightness of the cause does not justify actions that are morally questionable, such as unnecessary killing; and at last that the violators are "themselves primarily to blame" for whatever unpleasant consequences might result from "their original violation of justice," be it social or political (*L* 243).

## TOLKIEN'S IMAGINATIVE REPRESENTATION OF JUSTICE: *RETURN OF THE KING*

The takeover of power in the last three chapters of *The Lord of the Rings* is a restoration rather than a creation of a new order, as was also the case in *Farmer Giles*. A glance at the "The Scouring of the Shire" and the first part of "The Grey Havens" reveals, however, that the principles on which Tolkien's characters go about "setting the things right" (*RK* 242) are identical with those in *Farmer*: they recapitulate the imperatives of compensational justice. Being even more specific about justice than in Giles's tale, Tolkien in these chapters asserts that appropriate corrective action within the compensational justice paradigm must stop further perpetuation of injustice. Equally important, this should never disregard the possibility that the offender will at some time understand the wrong he has done and might turn to good.

On their way home, the hobbits are gradually prepared by hints, remarks, and scraps of recent news forewarning them that something is wrong with the Shire. They are also being gently familiarized with the thought that they will have to cope alone with whatever is wrong. Thus, on their departure from Bree, Mr Butterbur bids them farewell, saying: "you look now like folks can deal with troubles out of hand. I don't doubt you'll soon set all to rights" (*RK* 242) – which makes Frodo wonder, "what old Barliman was hinting at" (242). Gandalf, before he leaves the party for Bombadil's place, also makes it clear that he is not coming to the Shire: "You must settle its affairs yourselves. That is what you have been trained for. Do you not yet understand?" (242). What the hobbits must understand is that each of them has to take personal responsibility for the realization of a just law instead of relegating it to others and wishing for the best.

When the four hobbits reach the Shire, the gates are closed for the night and there are "lists of rules" everywhere (*RK* 246). There is a new governor who keeps the police force of big men, "ruffians out of wild" (245), and such laws that in no time the hobbits are arrested on charge of "Gate-Breaking, and Tearing up of Rules, and Assaulting Gatekeepers, and Trespassing, and Sleeping in Shire-buildings without Leave, and Bribing Guards with Food" (247). Although their typical hobbit-like common sense does not desert them, the four companions are devastated by what they encounter. At some point, Sam comments bitterly: "No welcome, no beer, no smoke, and a lot of rules and orc-talk instead" (246). Things look "ugly, damp, and cheerless" (248), which is what, according to Big Men who try to disperse the crowd in the village of Bywater, proper law and order mean. "Sharkey's come back," sneers the ruffian leader, "[… and since] this country wants waking up and setting to rights […] Sharkey's going to do it" (250). The travelers, however, are not as docile as their countrymen. They brandish their swords and assert that they will not be intimidated. " 'Go!' said Merry. 'If you trouble this village again, you will regret it' " (251). When the ruffians are gone, it dawns on the hobbits how bad things really are:

> "Well I am staggered!" said Pippin. "Of all the ends to our journey that is the very last I should have thought of: to have to fight half-orcs and ruffians in the Shire – to rescue Lotho Pimple!"
> "Fight?" said Frodo. "Well, I suppose it may come to that. But remember: there is to be no slaying of hobbits, not even if they have gone over to the other side. Really gone over, I mean; not just obeying ruffian's orders because they are frightened. No hobbit has ever killed another on purpose in the Shire, and it is not to begin now. And nobody is to be killed at all, if it can be helped. Keep your tempers and hold your hands to the last possible moment!" (*RK* 251-2)

Frodo's command, on the eve of possible war, sounds so unreal that Merry can do nothing but exclaim: "You won't rescue Lotho, or the Shire, just by being shocked and sad" (*RK* 252). Still, they all know that there is deep wisdom in Frodo's words. No matter how difficult it seems, the principle of just action articulated here – that is, good ends do not justify evil means – is a practical and effective way to deal with the problem of evil. On a smaller scale, it reflects the spuriously impractical but ultimately correct imperative that motivated the decisions of Aragorn, Elrond and Gandalf not to use the Ring and Frodo's continuous objection to killing Gollum, no matter how much Gollum seemed to deserve to die. This conduct also reflects the deep respect for life and everlasting hope inscribed in the conception of compensational justice.

Eventually, Merry and his companions raise the Shire. A bonfire is lit in the middle of the village, "just to enliven things, and also because it was one of the things forbidden by the Chief" (*RK* 254). The hobbits set up barriers across the entrance roads, and most of the populace wholeheartedly joins the rebellion. This is also true of the Shirriffs who "were [initially] dumbfounded; but as they saw how things were, most of them took off their feathers and joined in the revolt" (254). During an extempore council on the same evening, Frodo learns from Farmer Cotton that the Tooks from the Green Hills and the Great Smials have never submitted to the Chief, that they shot three of Sharkey's men for prowling and robbing, and have not allowed them on their land ever since. This confirms Merry's recognition that the hobbits are already at war which must entail losses. Yet, Frodo still does not want to legitimise killing: "I wish for no killing; not even of the ruffians, unless it must be done, to prevent them from hurting hobbits" (255). After that, Merry, who takes charge of the military action and treats Frodo as an authority, wins his approval for doing whatever must be done, if only he stays true to the principles of compensational justice.

In a sense, then, the story of the Shire's submission to the "law" describes the transition from the community laws informed by common sense and customary justice to the alien, faceless legal law imposed on the community by the mercenary police force. On that same night, Farmer Cotton recounts the events which confirm Tolkien's view that selfishness, greed and foolish pride, all fed by an individual's desire to rule others, get legitimized through the creation of legal law concerned with power, not with justice. First, Lotho Pimple "wanted to own everything himself, and then order other folk about" (*RK* 257). Then he began trading with strange foreign folks to the effect that "things began to get short" (257), and the rapacious ruffians started to colonize the Shire. The next step was a local coup during which the mayor Old Will was locked up, Pimple took over, declared himself Chief Shirriff, and "everything except Rules got shorter and shorter" (257). These developments from bad to worse were, however, in Cotton's eyes only a prelude and an invitation to the real destruction brought about with the coming of Sharkey. This mysterious stranger easily took over from Pimple, imprisoning him and his old mother, and sped up the worst type of devastation the Shire had known: industrialization. He set up a few factories which stole the remnants of peace from the Shire by their smoke, stench, noise, and their fouling of the countryside. Sharkey's was the vision of progress most abhorred by the hobbits and Tolkien himself, which, to be stopped, called for a united action of the community.

In the first skirmish, the leader of the ruffians is killed when, ignoring the warning and call to surrender, he attacks Merry. Also, the major battle of Bywater on the following day involves killing, but it, too, starts with a warning and Merry's call for surrender. Eventually, the battle turns out to be the greatest victory in the history of the Shire with nearly seventy ruffians killed. Nineteen hobbits die as well, though. About the main character it is said: "Frodo had been in the battle but he had not drawn sword, and his chief part had been to prevent the hobbits in their wrath at their losses, from slaying those of their enemies who threw down their weapons" (*RK* 261).

The apex of the chapter is Frodo's discovery of Saruman's presence in Bag End and of the fact that he is known as Sharkey. Throughout the whole of *The Lord of the Rings*, the treatment of Saruman is an excellent illustration of what compensational justice consists of. In the evil and the destruction he brought, Saruman looms large, though on a smaller scale, next to the devilish Sauron and acquires a status of a criminal against humanity. Yet, surprisingly, he is repeatedly allowed to live, even though one might expect executions for crimes lesser than his.

Upon the fall of Isengard, Saruman is deprived of his magical powers by Gandalf, but is still allowed to stay in the Orthanc tower. When he escapes, barely two weeks later, Saruman is overtaken by the hobbits' party returning north from Gondor when the war is over. It is then that Gandalf tells Saruman, "if you had waited at Orthanc, you would have seen [the king] and he would have shown you wisdom and mercy", but the fallen wizard is certain that the party has taken this road "to have the pleasure of gloating over [his] poverty" (*RK* 230) and refuses to accept help.

After the successful uprising in the Shire, Frodo finds his and other houses in the neighborhood in filthy disorder. "This is Mordor," he comments to Sam, "Just one of its works. Saruman was doing its work all the time, even when he thought he was working for himself. And the same with those that Saruman tricked, like Lotho" (*RK* 262). It is exactly at that point that Saruman appears at the door, "looking well-fed and well-pleased; his eyes gleamed with malice and amusement" (262). The wizard is overjoyed at having been able to ruin the Shire to the extent that, as he says, "you will find it hard to […] undo [it] in your lives" (263). Saruman's idea of justice is revenge, for he envisions that "it will be pleasant to think of [what I have done here] and set it against my injuries" (263). Likewise, most of the hobbits – surprised just as Saruman by Frodo's expression of pity towards the villain – demand justice-as-revenge, murmuring angrily, "Don't let him go! Kill him! He's a villain and a murderer. Kill him!" (263). Saruman defends himself by lying that whoever will kill him will be accursed and that his blood will turn the Shire into a desert. But Frodo knows better: "Do not believe him! He has lost all power, save his voice that can still daunt you and deceive you, if you let it. But I will not have him slain. It is useless to meet revenge with revenge: it will heal nothing. Go, Saruman, by the speediest way!" (263). The extent to which Frodo has understood what true justice is can be seen a moment later when he again forbids hobbits to kill Saruman – the person who just attempted to assassinate him:

> "No, Sam!" said Frodo. "Do not kill him even now. For he has not hurt me. And in any case I do not wish him to be slain in this evil mood. He was great once, of a noble kind that we should not dare to raise our hands against. He is fallen, and his cure is beyond us; but I would still spare him, in the hope that he may find it."
> Saruman rose to his feet, and stared at Frodo. There was a strange look in his eyes of mingled wonder and respect and hatred. "You have grown, Halfling," he said. "Yes, you have grown very much. You are wise, and cruel. You have robbed my revenge of sweetness, and now I must go hence in bitterness, in debt to your mercy. I hate it and you!" (*RK* 263-4)

In this passage, both Frodo and Saruman recognize the ultimate power of uncompromising respect for life, compassion, hope and love which lie at the roots of the conception of justice that Frodo administers. The denouement of the episode is Frodo's attempt to save Wormtongue from the hypnotic slavery to Saruman. Frodo offers Worm food and lodging till he is strong enough to fend for himself. This glimmer of hope for redemption is, however, immediately extinguished by Saruman who reveals Wormtongue as the murderer of Lotho. Although the slaying was committed on Saruman's command, it seems to have ruled out Worm's hope for asylum in the Shire. Having been offered an undreamt of chance and having lost it at the very same moment, Wormtongue breaks down in despair:

> Suddenly Wormtongue rose up, drawing a hidden knife, and then with a snarl like a dog he sprang on Saruman's back, jerked his head back, cut his throat, and with a yell ran off down the lane. Before Frodo could recover or speak

a word, three hobbit-bows twanged and Wormtongue fell dead. (*RK* 264)[4].

Tolkien's vision of compensational justice in the final chapter of *The Return of the King* involves a series of "liberation acts," such as freeing the prisoners from the Lockholes, hunting out the last remnants of the ruffians – not by killing but by capturing them and showing them off to the borders – pulling down ugly industrial plants, and restoring the countryside and villages. The old family feud between the Pimples and Bagginses is resolved. Lobelia, the hag, hobbles out of prison leaning on Frodo's, her former enemy's, arm. She is won over by Frodo's kindness and his offer of Bag End, which she returns to him. She is also won over by other hobbits who treat her as a martyr for the cause and give her "such clapping and cheering [...] that she was quite touched and drove away in tears" (*RK* 266). When she dies next year, "Frodo [is] surprised and much moved: she had left all that remained of her money and of Lotho's for him to use in helping hobbits made homeless by the troubles" (266). Thus, the end of a long feud is accomplished on the principles of compensational justice – in this case as simple as just showing each other respect. Lobelia's act of empowering Frodo to act as charity foundation for victims of the fighting in the Shire is an even better example of the application of compensational justice. It is her recognition of the fact that her and her son's actions may have been instrumental in bringing down the avalanche of trouble that swept through the Shire and affected so many hobbits. The bequest can thus be treated as Lobe-

---

[4] The fact that the two villains, Saruman and Wormtongue, die suggests Tolkien's use of retributive justice. A villain murdering his accomplice and then shot dead when escaping seems a neat, "Deux-ex-machina" way chosen by the author to eliminate the dangerous pair. And yet, I think that Tolkien presents these deaths as not really intended. If retributive justice is somewhat enacted, it is not suggested as a desirable solution. Rather, the two deaths are a kind of unfortunate conclusion to something that might have ended on a slightly more positive note.

lia's way of apologizing to the community for the hurts that she and her son had, though unintentionally, made possible.

## CONCLUSION

What these two examples suggest is that Tolkien believed in the need for human actions to be right. He never claimed it to be easy. I am convinced, however, that at the heart of what we so much long for in human relations are, in his opinion, justice, repentance, forgiveness, the healing of the wounds, of fear and mistrust – processes that enable both sides to put the past behind and start anew. Moreover, if Tolkien is right about the four functions that fantasy offers, I would argue that part of the psychological appeal of mythopoeic fantasy consists in the conception of compensational justice which it employs. Compensational justice, I think, is far more satisfying to men than any legal type of justice known in our world. Although it operates on the principle of "getting what one deserves," compensational justice is neither vengeance itself, nor is it vengeance-driven. Built into a theistic worldview, compensational justice involves a whole complex of values which regulate the characters' dealings with others and with the world. Contrarily to faceless legal justice which depersonalizes human relations, compensational justice fosters them by making characters face up to the hurts they brought about to others, recognize their offences and learn not to repeat their mistakes. In a larger social perspective, compensational justice is poignantly relevant to our conflict-torn, post-Holocaust world still driven, especially in politics, by the ideas of retribution, punishment, and "military solutions." It is a viable alternative to the vicious circle of "violence for violence" attitudes, discredited by the events in the Middle East, Ireland, India and Pakistan, Rwanda, the former Yugoslavia and, recently, Afghanistan and Iraq.

The idea of compensational justice does not solve the moral dilemma of what right one may have to forgive the "unforgivable," especially on somebody else's behalf; it does, however, point to the fact that without forgiveness there is no future. As Frodo says: "It is useless to meet revenge with revenge: it will heal nothing" (*RK* 263). Compensational justice – educational and preventive towards evildoers – is restorative by nature, promoting such qualities and attitudes as the obligation to do good, compunction, respect for life and freedom, common sense, holism and giving others their due. In mythopoeic fantasy, this conception of justice, with all its implications, is not just imposed on the readers, but gently brought to their consciousness by means of mythic narratives. In an essay "Tolkien's *Lord of the Rings*," C. S. Lewis writes:

> The value of the myth is that it takes all the things we know and restores to them the rich significance which has been hidden by "the veil of familiarity." [...] By putting bread, gold, horse, apple, or the very roads into a myth, we do not retreat from reality: we rediscover it. As long as the story lingers in our mind, the real things are more themselves. This [...] applies [...] not only to bread or apple but to good and evil, to our endless perils, our anguish, and our joys. By dipping them in myth we see them more clearly. (Lewis *Tolkien* 120-121)

This comment, I believe, is equally pertinent to our dream of justice which through "dipping in myth," that is through the prism of mythopoeic fantasy, becomes even more prominent. This realization may sometimes be so strong as to convince us that Tolkien and other mythopoeists present this kind of justice not as a utopian construct, but as an attainable ethical and political ideal to be sought for and realized in actual life.

---

MAREK OZIEWICZ is Assistant Professor of Literature and Director of the Center for Children's and Young Adult Fiction at the Institute of English Studies, University of

Wrocław, Poland. He holds a PhD in English Literature from this University. He has taught courses on literature and mythopoeia since 1997, with a break in 2005-2006 to research American fantasy on a Fulbright and then Kosciuszko fellowships. He is the author of numerous publications on fantastic literature. His main interest lies in the mythopoeic constitution of consciousness and the role of myth-making in cultural practices, especially literature.

## Works Cited

Carpenter, Humphrey, ed. *The Letters of J. R. R. Tolkien*. New York: Houghton Mifflin, 2000.

Lewis, Clive Staples. "Tolkien's *Lord of the Rings*." *Of This and Other Worlds*. Ed. Walter Hooper. London: Collins, 1982. 112-121.

---, "Men without Chests." *The Abolition of Man*. Ed. Walter Hooper. San Francisco: HarperCollins, 2001. 1-26.

Oziewicz, Marek. "Let the Villains Be Soundly Killed at the End of the Book: C. S. Lewis's Conception of Justice in the Chronicles of Narnia." *Past Watchful Dragons*. Ed. Amy Sturgis. Altadena, CA.: Mythopoeic Press, 2007. 41-63.

Shippey, Tom. *J. R. R. Tolkien: Author of the Century*. New York and Boston: Houghton Mifflin, 2000.

Tolkien, J. R. R. *The Return of the King*. London: Allen&Unwin, 1974.

---, "Farmer Giles of Ham." *The Tolkien Reader*. New York: Ballantine Books 1966. 121-187.

# The Rout of the King: Tolkien's Readings on Arthurian Kingship – *Farmer Giles of Ham* and *The Homecoming of Beorhtnoth*

## VINCENT FERRÉ

*For Mark Burde and Thomas Honegger*

### ABSTRACT

For a reader of *The Lord of the Rings*, it would be a mistake to remember only the *return* of the king, for this event only shows the long absence of a king and the vacancy of power. These motifs – echoes of *Beowulf* are the most obvious signs of a political crisis which seems to be general in Middle-earth, affecting leaders, and kings especially. My paper addresses the criticism found in shorter works by Tolkien, *Farmer Giles of Ham* and *The Homecoming of Beorhtnoth*, and refers to the political analysis, developed in Tolkien's critical texts, which underlines the failure of the king: in *Beowulf* (in 1936) and *Sir Gawain* (in 1953). Tolkien's main target appears to be Arthur, the centre of a *triumvirate* with Beowulf and Beorhtnoth: in a political reading of the medieval texts, Tolkien accuses the three leaders of failure in their leadership and responsibilities, of *hubris*, while he suggests – in his fiction – another model for a king.

To speak of "the rout of the king" and to give such importance to Arthur may seem paradoxical, when the reader of Tolkien's most famous work, *The Lord of the Rings*, is likely to remember the *return* of the king; and when Arthur seems to play a minor part in Tolkien's works, apart from an obvious 'Arthurian side' or 'atmosphere' in *The Lord of the Rings*. Still, it would be a mistake not to see, in the very event of his *return*, the sign of the long absence of a king in Gondor and Arnor, of the vacancy of power for a thousand years. These motifs – which recall

*Beowulf* – are not mere *topoi*, but the most obvious indices of a political crisis, a general crisis in Middle-earth affecting leaders and kings especially – one may also remember the senility of Rohan's king, Théoden.

Tolkien's "Fall of Arthur", left unfinished in the 30's, has not yet been published[2]. This fact can be ssen as a symbol: Arthur is present in Tolkien's fiction, but not at the forefront; and this presence is not limited to the well known fact that *The Lord of the Rings* has 'something Arthurian' because - to use a Tolkienian expression - it is "founded on earlier matter" (*L* 201), on medieval literature. Indeed, Tolkien regularly mentions Arthur in his nonfictional texts: in his letters[3], in his essay "On Fairy Stories", about the books he read in his youth; and he produced both an important edition and a translation[4] of the Arthurian *Sir Gawain and the Green Knight*, on which he lectured in 1953.

I would like to address the political analysis, developed in Tolkien's academic texts, which explicitly underlines the failure of the king in *Beowulf* (in 1936) and *Sir Gawain* (in 1953): this sheds some light on his fiction, and on the implicit criticism found especially in *Farmer Giles of Ham* and *The Homecoming of Beorhtnoth*. Beyond the differences between these two texts, between fiction (a tale and a dramatic dialogue) and nonfiction (conferences and essays), I will try to show that Tolkien's main target appears to be Arthur, the centre of a *triumvirate* with Beowulf and Beorhtnoth. In a political reading of the medieval texts, expressed in his conferences, Tolkien accuses the three kings (or leaders) of failure in their leadership and responsibilities, of

---

[1] See *Beowulf*'s prologue: "God [...] had perceived the cruel distress they once suffered when for a long time they lacked a king" (35).

[2] See Carpenter, ch. IV.

[3] See for instance *L*, 194 : about an anachronism in *Farmer Giles*, Tolkien evokes him: "[it is] not really worse than all mediaeval treatments of Arthurian matter". See also 144, 199, 241.

[4] *Sir Gawain and the Green Knight, Pearl and Sir Orfeo* (1975), transl. J.R.R. Tolkien, ed. Ch. Tolkien, London, HarperCollins, 2006.

excess, of *hubris*, while he suggests - in his fiction - another model for a king.

Among Tolkien's fictional works, *Farmer Giles* is a 'shorter work', but is it a 'minor work' as well? It is parodic and comic and its setting is England, not Middle-earth: this is precisely why *Farmer Giles* is interesting here, for it explicitly relates to the Arthurian legend. The foreword refers to Monmouth's *Historia Regum Britanniae* (a major source for Arthurian literature) and even to Arthur, to contextualize the tale: "Somewhere in those long years, after the days of King Coel maybe, but before Arthur" (*FGH*, 8). But it contextualizes the tale in a ludic way, since these "'mythological' Middle-Ages [writes Tolkien] blends unhistorically styles and details ranging over 500 years, and most of which did not of course exist in the Dark Ages of c. 500 A.D." (*L*, 280). It shares many common points with the Arthurian tradition: to name one, the establishment of "a new order of knighthood" (*FGH*, 76), or the reference to Arthur's genealogy in two of the king's names, *Aurelius Ambrosius*[5]. It was even more obvious in the first versions of the foreword, which contained a quote from *Sir Gawain*[6]. This might explain why Pauline Baynes does not need to underline this influence: for Tolkien, who agreed with her illustrations[7], "Pauline Baynes drew her inspiration for *F. Giles* largely from mediaeval MS. drawings – except for the knights (who are a bit 'King-Arthurish')"[8].

It is Tolkien's choice not to openly exhibit the presence of the Arthurian tradition in his works[9], but Arthur remains "the king of

---

[5] In Monmouth's text, *Aurelius Ambrosius* is the name of Arthur's uncle; it is also mentioned by Tolkien in his edition of *Sir Gawain* (Kocher, 179, 182).

[6] See Hammond and Scull's commentary, *FGH* 110-1.

[7] See *L* 133.

[8] Letter to Rhona Beare, October 4th 1958, *L*, 280.

[9] Elsewhere I made a few remarks about *The Lays of Beleriand* (the name *Broseliand*, the first colour of Lúthien's hair), see "De Tristan à Tolkien: Beren, Túrin et Aragorn" (article in two parts, online [http://www.modernitesmedievales.org/articles/articles.htm; cited 8.1.2008].

Faerie" ("On Fairy Stories", *MC,* 126), present inside Tolkien's works, though hidden, in a way like Arthur's name in Aragorn's father's name, Ar*ath*or*n*.

### ARTHUR AND 'ANTI-ARTHURIAN' CHARACTERS

Arthur is the centre, the heart of Arthurian medieval texts[10]; and this very heart is the target of a political criticism in Tolkien's fiction, of in subversion of his traditional features: his generosity (*largesse* in Old French), the devotion of his knights, justice, to name only a few. *Farmer Giles* depicts a king who is the exact contrary of the perfect king embodied by the 12th century Arthur, and is closer to the 13th century Arthur, the less known figure.

First, the magnificence of Arthur's court has been famous at least since Monmouth or Wace's *Roman de Brut* ; and it goes with the loyalty of his knights (let us think of Launcelot saving the queen in *The Knight of the Cart*) and it also goes with a generosity that Chrétien de Troyes depicts as higher than Alexander's and Caesar's. For example *Erec and Enide* (the first novel we know by Chrétien, from the end of the 12th century) recounts a dubbing ceremony of four hundred knights, richly endowed by the King:

> Avant que none fût sonnée
> A chacun, il fit don de trois chevaux
> le roi Arthur avait adoubé
> Et de deux paires de robes
> quatre cents chevaliers et plus
> Afin de rehausser l'éclat de sa cour.

---

[10] See for instance Charles Méla: "[…] everything begins with Arthur's court, which means that everything must come back to it" (47).

tous fils de comtes et de rois.
Le roi étala sa puissance et sa largesse[11]

By contrast, in *Farmer Giles*, the king Augustus Bonifacius is more preoccupied with his money (he has little) than with gifts he could make: his name is, thus, a lie, since *bonifacius* means in Latin 'he that does good'. In the tale, he leaves his castle only twice, not to rescue the people and protect them against the dragon, but to claim the treasure of the dragon when the latter is defeated by Giles. On this occasion, he wastes the food he receives from his subjects and lives on credit (*FGH*, 49-51, 70).

The attitude of his knights is a consequence of his miserliness. In the French narrative *Perlesvaus* (first half of the 13th century), Arthur is left by his knights when he ceases to make gifts with *largesse*[12]; in the same way, Augustus Bonifacius is not supported by his retainers: no Launcelot, no Gawain to help him, but a few knights trying to use feasts and tournaments as pretexts to avoid fighting the dragon (*FGH*, 28). And he is not a knight-maker: there is no dubbing ceremony in *Farmer Giles*, while Arthur's court attracts all the young men who wish to become knights, for example Perceval who wants to be dubbed by 'the best king on earth, the most generous and noble'[13]. Bonifacius only sends a sword to Giles; and an apparently old-fashioned sword, whose powers and history he doesn't know (21).

Thirdly, a sense of justice is a feature of the ideal king. In Béroul's text, Arthur is the warrant of Yseut's oath in front of Marc, allowing her

---

[11] Chrétien de Troyes, *Erec et Enide*, 273, l. 6652-6659. I will evoke a "European" Arthur – through diverse "Arthurian" works, such as Chrétien's or Beroul's –, to take into account the way characters and motives were in circulation at the time.

[12] "Mais un jour, sa volonté se trouva comme paralysée, et il perdit le désir de se montrer généreux. […] Voyant ses bienfaits se raréfier, les chevaliers de la Table Ronde se dispersèrent et commencèrent à délaisser sa cour." (*Perlesvaus*, 125).

[13] "Le meilleur roi vivant, le plus généreux et le plus noble" (Chrétien de Troyes, *Le Conte du Graal*, 1025).

to exonerate herself[14]; in *The Knight with the lion*, he arbitrates between two sisters[15] and his judgement goes against his own interests[16]. Again one notes a contrast with the depiction of Augustus Bonifacius: by the orders he gives to his subjects, he literally deserves his title, *tyrannus* (20),[17] and reminds us of another king in a 'short work' by Tolkien, or at least an unfinished work, the *Lay of Leithian*[18]. In this poem, Thingol, who has sworn not to kill Beren, tries to "twist [his] oaths" (*LB*, 191, l. 1084), acting like Celegorm and Curufin but, also, like Morgoth. For instance, the latter lies to Blodrin, who hopes to see his wife again in exchange for Beren's secret lair. The similarity between Thingol and Morgoth is very clear in the lay, and made explicit by Beren who compares Thingol to "faithless Morgoth" (l. 1085).

It would be easy to show, finally, that the relation between the king and God, an essential feature of medieval works[19], is absent in Tolkien, even in *The Silmarillion* or the *History of Middle-earth* texts, with the exception of King Elessar. There is no mention of God in *Farmer Giles*, although the king is supposed to be *pius* (20).

So, the image of the king that appears in Tolkien, especially in *Farmer Giles*, is the exact opposite of that of an ideal king – an ideal referring, I think, to the 12$^{th}$ century Arthur. This is the Arthur of *Erec et Enide*, who declares :

Je suis roi, je ne dois donc pas mentir
Il appartient à un roi loyal

---

[14] Tristan et Iseut, 187-217.
[15] Chrétien de Troyes, *Le Chevalier au lion*, 866.
[16] See Boutet and Strubel, 87.
[17] Regarding titles, it is difficult not to see an analogy (and thus an indirect criticism of the king) in the mention of the "imperial lineage" of the dragon (48, 67), an evil creature in most of the tale; especially since the narrator underlines its absence of "conscience", impossible to understand for "the simple" people of Ham (48).
[18] This poem is not *beyond Middle-earth*, and I mention the text only to show that this feature is (of course) not limited to *Farmer Giles*.
[19] See for instance Boutet, *Charlemagne et Arthur*, 53 sq.

> ni permettre la malhonnêteté,
> de maintenir la loi,
> l'iniquité ou la démesure:
> la vérité, la bonne foi et la justice. [...]
> il me faut garder raison et droiture.
> je dois être irréprochable[20].

In *Farmer Giles*, the satire of Augustus Bonifacius - to speak only of him for the moment - is aimed at Arthur, for two reasons: he is at the same time, obviously the *exact* opposite of the 12$^{th}$ century Arthur, *and* an image of the 13$^{th}$ century Arthur, analyzed by Marie-Luce Chênerie as a "weak" and even "perverted" king (i.e. "perverted" in the etymological meaning; cf. Chênerie, 86). Thus, Augustus Bonifacius is both an 'anti-Arthur' and an Arthurian figure, but the previous reference to *The Lay of Leithian* shows that this ambivalence is very common among Tolkienian kings. It is very telling that Thingol and Morgoth are often referred to by their title of *king*, and not by their names, and symbolized by their crown: as the first line goes, "A king there was in days of old" (*LB*, 1[21]).

### RESPONSIBILITY AND EXCESS

*Farmer Giles of Ham*, originally invented for Tolkien's children, was rewritten several times before its publication in 1949. In its final form, it is not longer a tale for children in the traditional meaning; all the more so, since it reveals Tolkien's tendency to replace academic writings by fiction. In February 1938, he read the third version of *Farmer Giles* to the Lovelace Society "*in lieu* of a paper 'on' fairy stories" (*L* 39). This fusing of fiction and academic research may explain the double levelled narrative and the pseudo-philological and onomastical remarks; it is also

---

[20] Chrétien de Troyes, *Erec et Enide*, 116-117.
[21] See also l. 355, 1012, etc. There is only one exception in the poem, Felagund, the lord of Nargothrond; but he dies and is replaced by wicked lords

a point *Farmer Giles* has in common with another text, combining essay and fiction (and which hence may be called "hybrid"): *The Homecoming of Beorhtnoth*, published in 1953, in which Tolkien also comments upon *Beowulf*, and *Sir Gawain and the Green Knight*, two central points of reference in his academic work as well as in his fiction.

What needs to be underlined here[22] is the *triumvirate* that Tolkien creates in *The Homecoming* with Beorhtnoth, Beowulf and Arthur, tying the threads of a reflection he began in his texts on *Beowulf* and on *Sir Gawain and the Green Knight*. In his discussion of the meaning of the Old English term *Ofermod*, which he translates with "overmastering pride", and not only with "overboldness" (like W. P. Ker), Tolkien makes a distinction between the lord Beorhtnoth and his companions, who follow him. It is essential to take this distinction into account when one reads Tolkien's fiction[23], but I will focus here on the three lords and kings. Contrary to his men who are his subordinates, Beorthnoth is responsible for a group of people; though he is not a king, strictly speaking, he is a duke, a *dux bellorum* (a 'lord of war') very similar to the first images of Arthur that we find in literature[24]. And his fault, claims Tolkien in the afterword, when he "yield[s] ground to the enemy, as he should not have done" (to quote *The Battle of Maldon*, l. 89-90) announces Arthur's fault in the 14<sup>th</sup> century poem *Sir Gawain*. There, Arthur is challenged by the Green Knight, and his honour and life are saved by Gawain's sacrifice, who confronts the fairy knight. According to Tolkien, in his lecture, king Arthur is at fault: his "rashness" is re-

---

[22] Important articles on *The Homecoming* have been published by Tom Shippey ("Tolkien and *The Homecoming of Beorhtnoth*", in *Leaves from the Tree*) and Thomas Honegger (in *Tolkien Studies, IV*). On the relation between fiction and nonfiction in this text, see also V. Ferré, "Tolkien, the author and the critic: *Beowulf, Sir Gawain and the Green Knight, The Homecoming of Beorhtnoth* and *The Lord of the Rings*", to be published in *The Ring Goes Ever On, Proceedings of the 2005 Conference in Birmingham*, The Tolkien Society.

[23] See *ibid.*7

[24] It is telling that Jane Chance, for instance, chose "the Anglo-Saxon King" (133) as a subtitle of her analysis of *The Homecoming*.

sponsible for the situation – one may add: like Beorhtnoth's *ofermod* is responsible for the rout of his army – and he is criticized in the poem, by the narrative voice and by the audience (*MC* 75). The relevant point is not to decide whether Arthur is really rash[25], but the distinction that Tolkien makes (the same as in *The Homecoming*) between the king and his retainers: Gawain protects Arthur against the Green Knight, sacrificing himself to protect the king, "his elder kinsman, of his king, of the head of the Round Table" (*MC*, 75). Tolkien praises Gawain: "[his] motive is not pride in his own prowess, not boastfulness", it is "a matter of duty and humility and self-sacrifice". And he symmetrically criticizes Arthur.

This is essential in Tolkien's analysis of medieval literature, as it is shown by the fact that he quotes the same passage from *Sir Gawain*, a condemnation of Arthur's *arrogant vaunt* by the audience, in his lecture on *Gawain* and in *The Homecoming*'s postscript (*TL*, 149). The resemblance between Arthur and Beorhtnoth becomes clear; but a third man appears. When Tolkien draws a line between "excess" and heroism in *Maldon*, he refers to Beowulf (*TL*, 144) to oppose the young hero (in the first part of the poem), without political responsibilities, and the king that he becomes in the second part. For Tolkien, Beowulf is not to blame when he confronts Grendel bare-handed: it is extremely bold, but he is not yet a leader, no subordinate depends on him; on the contrary, when he fights against the dragon and perishes because of his decision to fight without his retainers, almost alone, this choice is a disaster for his people and is to be condemned. *Sir Gawain* is close to *Beowulf* in this regard: Beowulf's courage and fault are distributed between a knight and his king; "Gawain's conduct is made more worthy, and more worth considering, again because he is a subordinate" (*TL*, 149) while Arthur

---

[25] None of his knights accepts the challenge, and Arthur is cut to the quick: "With that he [the Green Knight] laughed so loud that their lord was angered, / the blood shot for shame into his shining cheeks and face;/ as wroth as wind he grew,/ so all did in that place. / Then near to the stout man drew the king of fearless race." (*GPO*, 26).

does not act as a king should, as Hygelac does in *Beowulf* when he tries to stop the young hero (*TL*, 150).

Similarly, Beowulf and Beorhtnoth share the same desire for glory. Tolkien underlines its importance when he comments upon *lof* and *dom* (glory) in *Beowulf*:

> At the beginning of the poem, at the end of the first section of the exordium, the note is struck: *lofdædum sceal in mægþa gehwære man geþeon*. The last word of the poem is *lofgeornost*, the summit of the praise of the dead hero: that was indeed *lastworda betst*. For Beowulf had lived according to his own philosophy, which he explicitly avowed: *ure æghwylc sceal ende gebidan worolde lifes; wyrce se ðe mote domes ær deaþe: þæt bið dryhtguman æfter selest*, 1386 ff. The poet as commentator recurs again to this: *swa sceal man don, þonne he æt guðe gegan penceð longsumne lof: na ymb his lif ceara*ð, 1534 ff. (*MC*, 36)

Still, Tolkien opposes two forms of heroism (the king's and his retainers'), not only in his lecture on *Gawain* and his postscript on *Ofermod*, but also in his fiction.

In *The Homecoming*, the excessive pride of the duke is obvious through his desire to imitate Beowulf: "so keen was he/ to give minstrels matter for mighty songs" (*TL*, 137)[26]. Since he knows Beowulf through the literary tradition, the problem at stake here is the relation to literature, in a *mise en abyme*: Beorhtnoth is not different from Don Quixote, a fictional character reading fiction and anxious to act like his models. But reality destroys fiction, when Beorhtnoth literaly loses his head - as Don Quixote does, metaphorically - and is beheaded. This is a very strong symbol, since the head wears the crown (see Thingol and Mor-

---

[26] See also p. 146: Beorhtnoth is "moulded also by 'aristocratic tradition', enshrined in tales and verse of poets".

goth) and is the symbol of Beorhtnoth as a chief: for Torhthelm, "His head was higher than the helm of kings" (130).

Leaving aside *The Lord of the Rings*, not so 'short' a work[27], I shall mention the fight between Fingolfin and Morgoth as told in "The Quenta", written in the 30s and published in *The Shaping of Middle-earth*. Fingolfin reminds us of Beorhtnoth, for he is driven by a kind of folly: "his own death he sought in rage and anguish seeing the defeat of his people"; but he also reminds us of Beowulf fighting the Dragon, in his choice: "For he went to the gates of Angband alone and smote upon them with his sword, and challenged Morgoth to come out and fight alone" (*SME*, 107). But the outcome of the challenge is even more disastrous, for Fingolfin dies without defeating Morgoth, contrary to Beowulf, who kills the dragon with the crucial help of young Wiglaf; and Fingolfin's failure is all the more obvious since the Quenta relates, a few pages after this event, Túrin's glorious victory over the dragon, as a responsible leader. Túrin's story appears as a synthesis of Beowulf's and Fingolfin's, since he fights a *dragon-king* (129, my emphasis), both a creature of Morgoth's and a reminder of *Beowulf*'s dragon. Leader of a people of woodmen, Túrin accepts his responsibilities and transcends his status: even though he is still a young hero, he will not act rashly, like Beowulf facing Grendel. Instead of a blind heroism and a search of glory in a solitary fight, he only "ponder[s] how the horror could be warded from his people" (129), allows companions to come with him (they finally flee) and uses a trick to attack the dragon by surprise and defeat him. Still, in "The Quenta" Túrin is unquestionably a hero.

Thus, Beowulf, Beorhtnoth and Arthur share the same flaw, the tendency to *excess* and pride which is present in many royal characters, in Tolkien's fiction or academic texts. Even a minor character like Dior, Beren and Lúthien's son, in "The Quenta" (134-5), shows pride when

---

[27] V. Ferré (Tristan à Tolkien) addresses the similarity with Denethor, Boromir, Saruman and Sauron's excess, which I leave aside here.

he recovers his throne in Doriath. Are Aragorn and the Túrin of "The Quenta" the only exceptions, or can we find, even in a comic tale like *Farmer Giles*, which contains an acerbic satire of royal power, another model for a king?

## ENNOBLEMENT AND MERIT, ANOTHER MODEL FOR KINGSHIP

One cannot limit Tolkien's vision of kingship to this analysis of the failure and faults of Arthur, Beowulf and Beorthnoth, for his vision is also expressed in fiction, in the image of a kingship based on ennoblement and merit, which gets rid of the pomp of the court.

Since Wace's *Brut*, Arthur's court is conventionally not only magnificent, but is also an absolute reference, a symbol of civilization: in Chrétien de Troyes's romances, every character needs to join the court if they want to be reputed as courtly - or to "lerne to be a knyght" as Malory says (II, 745).[28] The contrast to Tolkien's texts is striking, where real heroism may only exist outside and *against* the court and the king; heroes do not wish to be integrated in the court but to escape from it. The movement is centrifugal; heroes want to reach a state of autonomy, to invent another centre of values, and finally create another court. The most exemplary characters in this regard are Aragorn and Giles[29].

Of Aragorn, who encapsulates several Arthurian (the 12th century Arthur, this time) features, one may say (in brief) that he remains a reference, an example of an apparently humble character, living outside the 'courts' (Gondor, Rivendell) as long as he has not proved his value. Very telling for this argument, his accession to the throne coincides with the disappearance of Denethor and the decline of Rivendell, which is the equivalent of a court – let us remember Elrond's departure at the end of

---

[28] See Alexandre and Cligès in Chrétien de Troyes's *Cligès* (293, 417).
[29] On Frodo and his difference with Arthurian knights who always come back to court once they are acknowledged as heroes, see V. Ferré, *Sur les Rivages de la Terre du Milieu*, 263, 281, referring to Erich Köhler's analysis.

*The Lord of the Rings*. This development, from outside the court to the centre of another court created around him, is a common feature between Aragorn and Giles, who is seemingly Aragorn's exact opposite while he also offers a rich reflexion on heroism.

The importance of this last question appears as early as the first version of *Farmer Giles*, in which the real hero is supposed to be Giles' mare; the second version ends with a question to the audience to determine who the hero is– and there are several answers, this time[30]. The third one shows a conception of heroism that is temperate, reasonable, as opposed to Beorhtnoth's folly – "Too foolish to be heroic" (*TL*, 146). In the successive versions, Giles is more and more heroic when he confronts the dragon[31]; but once the latter is defeated, Giles chooses a limited amount of money for its ransom: had he been too greedy, he might have caused the dragon to fight to the death, and lost everything. The narrator even praises this decision, with a humorous allusion: "Then 'Done with you!' he said, showing a laudable discretion. A knight would have stood for the whole hoard and got a curse laid upon it" (64).

Politically, Giles shows the same wisdom when he declines king Augustus Bonifacius' challenge (73): because he refuses excess, stays very cautious during fights, Giles is indeed an "anti-Beowulf" as Shippey (*Author of the Century*, 289) put it – see also Jane Chance (*Tolkien's Art*, 127). The parallel structures also invite the reader to this comparison since – very schematically[32] speaking – Giles and Beowulf fight two monsters, a giant (Grendel possesses nonhuman strength) and a dragon, and become kings[33]. But Giles is also an "anti-Beorhtnoth": it is true that part of his courage and inspiration comes from tradition, "popular

---

[30] On the previous versions, see Hammond and Scull's introduction, *FGH* ix-xv.
[31] See *FGH* 134 (note on p. 62).
[32] See Rayner Unwin's note on *Giles*, quoted in *FGH*, xi.
[33] Jane Chance compares the monsters in *Beowulf* with Gollum and the dragon in *The Hobbit* on one hand, with the giant and the dragon in *Farmer Giles* on the other hand (127).

romances", "songs and tales" (33-4) about Bellomarius's deeds (the previous holder of his own sword, Caudimordax / Tailbiter) – like Beorhtnoth. But part of it also comes from ... alcohol[34]: the irony is patent, here; and there is no sign of imitative desire in Giles.

His relation to literature and poetry is opposed to the knights', when they go dragon-hunting with a minstrel "singing a lay". Which one? It is not specified, but it is surely a heroic lay, since "the song [...] had been made long before in days when battles were more common that tournaments" (57); and its consequences are the same as in *The Homecoming*: because of the song (which the dragon overhears), the knights are killed.

Giles's heroism is of a different kind than Beowulf's and Beorhtnoth's; he is also a different leader, closer to Aragorn. But his kingship is founded only on merit, not at all on heredity, and it is the result of a process of ennoblement, announced by the title of the manuscript fictitiously found, *The Rise and Wonderful Adventures of Farmer Giles...* It is a progressive rise, not a *coup:* after the final victory over the dragon, Giles comes back with it, its treasure and a small group of people that he hires as soldiers. At this moment, he becomes aware of his dignity: "Giles began to feel like a lord" (65); and this consciousness finally expresses itself when he orders Augustus Bonifacius to resign: "Give us your crown" (71). The difference to the latter is strong, it is clear in Giles's the use of the *pluralis majestatis*, and in Giles's legitimacy, which has grown page after page and is confirmed by the *vox populi*: "from that day the power of the Middle Kingdom [that is Augustus Bonifacius's] came to an end in that neighbourhood. For many a mile round about men took Giles for their lord" (73). Contrary to Augustus Bonifacius, who was born a king and boasts with all his titles, Giles climbs up the

---

[34] When opposing the importance of popular songs for Giles and the attitude of the knights, T. Shippey (*Author*: 290) overlooks the importance of the lay for the latter and of alcohol for the former.

ladder: he is successively "Lord of the Tame Dragon", "Earl", "Prince", and "King" (74). Only in the end does he look like the traditional king, as the illustration by Pauline Baynes shows: with a sceptre, a crown and a sword, then (as time goes by) with a beard like Charlemagne – contrasting with the poor king Augustus's picture, a few pages above (75, 77 and 73).

*Farmer Giles* tells the story of a man who gains a throne but does not narrate much of his reign once he is a king – this is the same as Elessar in *The Lord of the Rings*. The few elements recorded are, thus, of great importance to show what kings they are: the principle upon which the kingship and court are based appears in another rise, parallel to Giles's - the rise of his first retainers, who become captains, then knights, of "a new order of knighthood" (76). Is this promotion fair? It seems logical, within the story, as well as deserved, especially compared with the indignity of Augustus Bonifacius's knights. And the narrator agrees to it, when he explains that in Giles' court, "merit was often rewarded" (76). The happy ending is not that naïve, for Giles is treated with a touch of irony, and his ennoblement is more literal (he becomes a king) than spiritual (contrary to the hobbits's ennoblement in *The Lord of the Rings*). But Giles, like Aragorn, promotes another model of kingship, not based upon birth (or not only), but on merit.

The examples of *Farmer Giles* and of *The Homecoming of Beorhtnoth*, but also of *The Lord of the Rings* and *The Lay of Leithian*, as well as Tolkien's analysis of *Sir Gawain*, *Beowulf* and *Maldon* show that a great part of his work *is* a 'fall of Arthur', as Arthur (at least, *Tolkien's* vision of Arthur) is an embodiment of a vision of Middle Ages that Tolkien rejects. And he offers a counter-model for a kingship based upon merit, with noble characters like Aragorn or comic ones, like Giles, which is exemplary and coherent with Tolkien's essays on medieval literature.

Auerbach's political distinction between medieval epics and romances may be useful here. The latter are supposed to lack any "economic and political foundations": in romances, the characters, contrary to epic ones (who defend the empire against Infidels, according to a feudal ethic), have no political side: the feudal ethic has become an "absolute" (Auerbach 130; my translation). If we follow Auerbach, Tolkien's rewriting of medieval *matter*, especially Arthurian, shows a strong inflection towards a more political reading of the text. *Farmer Giles* is exemplary, but more generally, the image of the king is dual, in Tolkien's works: the old king, like Augustus Bonifacius or Denethor the substitute (who believes in heredity), is criticised and replaced by a new king, who shows his virtues and a kind of heroism that one might almost call *revolutionary*, given the contrast with the old political regime.

VINCENT FERRÉ teaches comparative literature in Paris (University Paris 13) and works on modernist writers, especially Proust, Dos Passos, Broch; he has also published two books on J.R.R. Tolkien (*Sur lesRivages de la Terre du Milieu*, on death in *The Lord of the Rings*; *Tolkien, 30 ans après*, a collection of 17 articles), as well as articles and translations of Tolkien's works in French. He is in charge of the French editions of Tolkien's works for Christian Bourgois Editeur. He has delivered many lectures on Tolkien in France, England, Germany, Switzerland and Italy, and worked as an advisor on John Howe's exhibition *Sur les terres de Tolkien* (2002-2007), on John Howe and Alan Lee's exhibition *De l'imaginaire à l'image* (Bibliothèque nationale de France, 2003-2004) and for the French translation of the first film by Peter Jackson.

## Works Cited

### Works by J.R.R. Tolkien

FGH: *Farmer Giles of Ham* [1949]. London: HarperCollins, 1999.

GPO: *Sir Gawain and the Green Knight, Pearl and Sir Orfeo* [1975], transl. J.R.R. Tolkien, ed. Ch. Tolkien. London: HarperCollins, 2006.

HBBS: *The Homecoming of Beorhtnoth*, in *Tree and Leaf.* London, HarperCollins, 2001.

LotR: *The Lord of the Rings*. London: HarperCollins, 1999, 3 v.

MC: *The Monsters and the Critics and Other Essays* [1983]. ed. by Ch. Tolkien, London: HarperCollins, 1997.

## Medieval Works

*Beowulf,* ed. by M. Swanton. Manchester-New York: Manchester University Press, 1978.

*Beowulf,* in *Poèmes héroïques vieil anglais,* transl. A. Crépin. Paris: UGE, 1981.

*The Battle of Maldon AD 991,* ed. by D.G. Scragg. Oxford-Cambridge: B. Blackwell ; Manchester: Manchester University Press, 1991.

*Perlesvaus,* in *La Légende arthurienne: le Graal et la Table ronde,* ed. by D. Régnier-Bohler. Paris: Robert Laffont, 1989.

*Tristan et Iseut. Les poèmes français, la saga norroise,* ed. by D. Lacroix and Ph. Walter. Paris: L.G.F., 1989.

Chrétien de Troyes. *Erec et Enide, Cligès, Le Chevalier au lion, Le Conte du Graal,* in *Romans,* ed. by M. Zink. Paris: Librairie Générale Française, 1994.

## Secondary Works

Auerbach, Erich. *Mimesis: Dargestellte Wirklichkeit in der abendländischen Literatur* (1946). Tübingen, Basel: Francke, 1994.

Boutet, Dominique, *Charlemagne et Arthur ou Le roi imaginaire.* Paris: H. Champion, 1992.

Boutet, Dominique, and Armand Strubel. *Littérature, politique et société dans la France du Moyen âge.* Paris: PUF, 1979.

Carpenter, Humphrey, *J.R.R. Tolkien, A Biography* (1980), new edition. London: HarperCollins, 2002.

Chance, Jane. *Tolkien's Art: a Mythology for England,* rev ed. Lexington: the University Press of Kentucky, 2001.

Chênerie, Marie-Luce. *Le chevalier errant dans les romans arthuriens en vers des XII$^e$ et XIII$^e$ siècles.* Genève: Droz, 1986.

Ferré, Vincent, *Sur les rivages de la Terre du Milieu.* Paris: Christian Bourgois, 2001.

---, *De Tristan à Tolkien: Beren, Túrin et Aragorn,* online: [http://www.modernitesmedievales.org/articles/articles.htm; cited 8.1.2008]; published in two parts: "I- Fonder la comparaison", in *Otrante,* 19-20, Rosny aîné et les autres formes, Paris: Kimé, 2006, 281-290; and "II- L'amour fatal", in Anne Besson, and Myriam White ed., *Fantasy : le merveilleux médiéval aujourd'hui,* Paris: Bragelonne, 2007. 17-30.

---, Tolkien, the author and the critic: Beowulf, Sir Gawain and the Green Knight, The Homecoming of Beorhtnoth and The Lord of the Rings, *The Ring Goes Ever On,* Proceedings of the 2005 Conference in Birmingham. The Tolkien Society, 2007 [in print]

Honegger, Thomas. "*The Homecoming of Beorhtnoth*: Philology and the Literary Muse", *Tolkien Studies 4,* ed. D.A. Anderson et al. 191-201.

Kocher, Paul. *Master of Middle-Earth: the fiction of J.R.R Tolkien.* Boston: Houghton Mifflin 1972.

Méla, Charles. *La Reine et le Graal: la conjointure dans les romans du Graal de Chrétien de Troyes au Livre de Lancelot.* Paris: Seuil, 1984.

Malory, *The Works of Sir Thomas Malory*, 3 vols, ed. by E. Vinaver, revised bv P.J.C. Field. Oxford: Clarendon Press, 1990.

Shippey, Tom. "Tolkien and The Homecoming of Beorhtnoth", *Leaves from the Tree, J.R.R. Tolkien's Shorter Fiction.* The 4$^{th}$ Tolkien Society Workshop. London: The Tolkien Society, 1991.

---, *J.R.R. Tolkien, Author of the Century* [2000], London: HarperCollins, 2001.

Oziewicz, Marek. "Let the Villains Be Soundly Killed at the End of the Book: C. S. Lewis's Conception of Justice in the Chronicles of Narnia." *Past Watchful Dragons.* Ed. Amy Sturgis. Altadena, CA.: Mythopoeic Press, 2007. 41-63.

Shippey, Tom. *J. R. R. Tolkien: Author of the Century.* New York and Boston: Houghton Mifflin, 2000.

Tolkien, J. R. R. *The Return of the King.* London: Allen&Unwin, 1974.

---, "Farmer Giles of Ham." *The Tolkien Reader.* New York: Ballantine Books 1966. 121-187.

# *Farmer Giles of Ham*: the Prototype of a Humorous Dragon Story

## Friedhelm Schneidewind[1]

### ABSTRACT

Tolkien was interested in dragons since childhood. In Middle-earth they occupy minor roles; however, in his other fictional work they appear more often, even playing crucial roles, as in *Farmer Giles of Ham*. Beginning with an introduction to the history and mythology of dragons in Western culture (since Tolkien refers to this general picture of dragons) an overview of dragons in Tolkien's work will follow. The article then focusses on "Farmer Giles of Ham", presenting the editions of *Farmer Giles* and giving an introductory survey of its topics and myths. An evaluation of Tolkien's humour in the story, and of the tradition he takes part in with it, sums up the analysis of the story. Further thought is then given to the impact *Farmer Giles* had on modern dragon fiction. Some observations on how *Farmer Giles* can be seen as typical for Tolkien's work conclude the article.

> "*Never laugh at live dragons, Bilbo you fool!*"
> Bilbo in "The Hobbit" (J. R. R. Tolkien)
> *Draco dormiens nunquam titillandus*
> *– Never Tickle a Sleeping Dragon! –*
> Hogwarts' Motto (Joanne K. Rowling)

### INTRODUCTION

Tolkien took a lively interest in dragons ever since childhood[2]. While they play a rather subordinate role in the stories published in his lifetime and set in Middle-earth in other works of Tolkien's they appear more

---

[1] translated by Julia Bachale (www.jbachale.de)
[2] "I desired dragons with a profound desire. Of course, I in my timid body did not wish to have them in the neighbourhood, intruding into my relatively safe world, in which it was, for instance, possible to read stories in peace of mind, free from fear. But the world that contained even the imagination of Fàfnir was richer and more beautiful, at whatever cost of peril." (*OFS* 135)

often. To which extent he occupied himself with these creatures can be seen, for instance, in his art as in the beautiful painting "Glorund setting forth to seek Túrin"[3] (1927, Hammond and Scull 51) and in the rather amusing sketches "Untitled (Dragon and Warrior)" (1928) and "Ringborta Heorte Gefysed" (1929, both Hammond and Scull 52). In 1923, Tolkien published a first version of the poem "The Hoard" (*ATB* 107-109) which includes a very "traditional" dragon[4]. Dragons also appear in the story of "Roverandom" and in one of the five sketches belonging to it that are supposed to have been created around 1927. A dragon also plays a role in the "Letters from Father Christmas" (*FC* 1927).

The profound and humorous story *Farmer Giles of Ham* with its dragon Chrysophylax was already written in 1936, but as it was only published in 1949, the first dragon with which Tolkien became famous was Smaug from *The Hobbit* (1937). On January 1st 1938, shortly after *The Hobbit* was published, Tolkien held a Christmas lecture about dragons for children in the natural science (!) museum, during which he also showed some of his sketches. In his academic work, too, Tolkien was occupied with dragons now and then, for instance in his lecture "Beowulf: The Monsters and The Critics"[5], and in the essay "On Translating Beowulf"[6].

The focal point of this article is *Farmer Giles of Ham*. We begin with a short introduction to the mythology and history of dragons in Western culture, to which Tolkien refers in the first place, and a general

---

[3] Glórund is one of several early forms of Glaurung, whom I will discuss later on. Even if Glórund's story was only published posthumously in *The Silmarillion*, it was finished in its most important features around 1919 ("Turambar and the Foalóke", *CH* 9).

[4] Concerning the context of the story and characteristics of the dragon described, see Part 3 of the present paper: "Tolkien's Dragons".

[5] Held in 1936 before the British Academy, published in 1937 in the "Proceedings of the British Academy 22" (*MC* 5 – 48).

[6] "Prefatory Remarks on Prose Translation of *Beowulf*" about "Beowulf and the Finnesburg Fragment: A Translation into Modern English Prose", revised edition of the Beowulf translation by John R. Clark Hall (1911 by C. L. Wrenn, 1940) (*MC* 49 – 71).

overview of dragons in Tolkien's works. After a look at the various editions of *Farmer Giles* we will take a closer look at the topics and motifs from myths, sagas and tales used therein as well as at Tolkien's humour in this story and the tradition in which he participates. After a survey of the influence which the story has had on modern dragon stories, we will conclude by showing in how many different regards *Farmer Giles* is a prototype of the dragon story, and that it is typical for Tolkien's way of storytelling and humour in more than one sense.

## WESTERN TRADITION BEFORE TOLKIEN

Following the same pattern as he did in other areas, Tolkien united different myths and sagas for his dragons. For thousands of years dragons have been seen as mythological, mostly winged creatures that are usually equated with snakes. Often they are very mighty, such as the goddess Tiamat, a female dragon, that was killed by Marduk, the highest god of the Assyrians and Babylonians, god of light and life; according to the myth of creation *Enuma Elish* he formed heaven and earth from her corpse and mankind from her blood and clay. In Hindu belief Vishnu and his spouse Lakshmi rested in the "sea of milk", carried by the male dragon (or snake) Ananta with a thousand heads, the embodiment of all cosmic energies, who was left after heaven, earth and underworld evolved from the First Ocean. At the end of all times, Ananta will spit venomous fire and destroy all creation.

The Midgard Serpent from Norse mythology, Jormungand, clasps itself around the world; Tolkien refers to it by its Norse name *Miðgarðsormr* in his Beowulf lecture (*BUK* 154); like Hel and the giant wolf Fenrir it is a child of Loki. Thor fights against it three times, and at Ragnarök they will kill each other. After Ragnarök the carrion-eating Nidhöggr (dragon of envy) will die, too; since the beginning of the world he has been gnawing at the root of the world ash Yggdrasil.

The snake in Genesis is interpreted in very different ways by the Jewish and Christian religions, and is in no way always equated with the devil. The dragons Leviatan[7] and Behemoth[8] that appear in the Hebrew Bible mostly played a role in medieval imagination and are used as metaphors in political and sociological writings since then. The story of Daniel, who killed a Babylonian dragon (idol) by feeding it with flat blobs made of pitch, grease and hair (Dan 14, 23-27), can be read as an allegory as well as a tale about a very inventive prophet.

For Christian mythology and for Tolkien's ideas about dragons the Book of Revelations is of greatest importance, in which the dragon is equated with Satan. The fight between dragon and angel shows visible parallels to the fight between Eärendil and Ancalagon, also in that respect that on both sides entire armies fought (*S* 302 – 303): "And there was war in heaven: Michael and his angels fought against the dragon; and the dragon fought and his angels, And prevailed not; neither was their place found any more in heaven. And the great dragon was cast out, that old serpent, called the Devil, and Satan, which deceiveth the whole world: he was cast out into the earth, and his angels were cast out with him. " (Rev 12, 8-9).[9]

---

[7] Also *Leviathan*, from the Hebrew word liwyatan (serpentine animal): dragon of the ancient oriental mythology, described in Job 40 and 41 as a terrible flame-spitting, plated monster, symbol of chaos and the world powers that are hostile to god, and it is killed by god: "In that day the LORD with his sore and great and strong sword shall punish leviathan the piercing serpent, even leviathan that crooked serpent; and he shall slay the dragon that is in the sea." (Jes 27,1; King James' Bible).

[8] According to Job 40,15-24 it is a vegetarian counterpart to Leviathan that lives on dry land, and is sometimes taken to be a hippopotamus; in the apocryphal 1st Book of Henoch (Ethiopian book of Henoch) it appears as the male counterpart to the female Leviathan, together with her sent by god as a scourge for mankind and being Lord of the Desert (1st Hen 59,7fp.); in the Middle Ages often presented as a demon, servant of the devil and "cupbearer and cellarman of Hell".

[9] There are only few biblical books that can be (and are) interpreted so diversely. In art history the Book of Revelations has a high status. "The Apocalypse had an influence on hundreds of books and films. First and foremost it is complicated to interpret the relation between the dragon and the beast, which has the number 666 and is often equated with the antichrist and which is finally defeated by the lamb (Rev 13,1-18)."

Apart from this early Christian tradition ideas about dragons have been marked strongly in the Occident by Greek sagas and myths. Heracles has to defeat a dragon in order to gain the Golden Apples of the Hesperides (depending on the version he does this himself or he cunningly sends someone else), and he kills the seven-headed Ladon, a version of a dragon.

Typhon, son of Gaia and Tartarus, often described as giant with a hundred dragon or snake heads; he could not be killed, but was buried by Zeus under Mount Etna, where he spits fire even today. Perseus freed Andromeda before she was sacrificed to a dragon. Cadmus, founder and king of Thebes, killed a dragon and planted its teeth into the ground; they gave rise to the five ancestors of the Theban noble families. After his death the father of Europe is said to have been turned into a dragon.

From the early Middle Ages on, all these basic elements grew together to form different ideas and sagas, in which the dragonslayer is of higher importance than the dragon itself. One of the most famous literary versions of this in the German language is the *Nibelungenlied*[10] and in English it is the *Beowulf* epic.[11] In terms of Christian culture it is important to name the many holy dragon slayers, of whom St. George is the most outstanding example.[12] Only a few of them treat dragons in a

---

[10] Epic, written down by an unknown poet at the end of the 12th century with strong influence on modern art, for example on Richard Wagner and Tolkien.

[11] As mentioned before, Tolkien has occupied himself with this work very carefully; for him as a specialist in Anglo-Saxon language the Beowulf epic as an epochal work for English literature (the title has been added to the text only in 1805, named after the main character) was a target of scholarly approach as well as a source of inspiration from early childhood on. It is seen as the most important Anglo-Saxon heroic epic, the most extensive preserved Old Germanic epic song and the first big epic in verses, which has been written and handed down in a Germanic vernacular speech. It takes place in a later time than the "Nibelungenlied", in the Swedish Götaland in the first half of the 6th century. It is possible that this combination of Scandinavian history, antique examples, pagan mythology and Christian elements was written down during the 8th or 9th century by an educated monk. In *Beowulf* one can find some roots of parts of the Siegfried saga, the "Nibelungenlied".

[12] According to Markus Heitz, a German author of fantasy literature, the Austrian Museum of Folklore presented in an exhibition 83 different dragon saints, most of them

kind way, for instance Saint Martha, who tamed the sea dragon Tarasque in the 12$^{th}$ century; she is still commemorated annually today in Tarascon.

According to common lore, these dragons especially like to feed on virgins, that have to be sacrificed to them; this is also the case in antiquity such as in Perseus's and Andromeda's story. In his poem "Der Taucher" ("the Diver"), the German poet Friedrich Schiller describes dragons that dwell in the deep abyss. According to some myths, dragon blood is said to make invulnerable; this is the case for Siegfried in the Nibelung saga, who took a bath in the dragon's blood. Unfortunately, a leaf on his back prevented his whole body from becoming invincible. In the *Edda*, Sigurd can understand the speech of birds after tasting the blood (the "hürnen Seyfried" has to eat the heart of the dragon to be able to do so). But on the whole it is more common that dragon blood is venomous, which is the reason why Beowulf is not so much killed by the wound that he receives by the dragon but by the venom with which it is infected. Here, Tolkien sticks very closely to the sagas, for example with Glaurung[13], also considering the dangerous, even paralyzing gaze of dragons. In this regard the dragon is a close relative of the basilisk, feared in medieval times[14].

---

[13] men that had killed dragons; all of them were recognized as authentic by the catholic church.

This is similar in many other tales. In several tales of the Grimm Brothers the venom in the dragon's blood overwhelms and kills the heroes; and J. K. Rowling introduces at least 12 different forms of usage for dragon blood in her *Harry Potter* series.

[14] According to Hildegard of Bingen, the "King of Snakes" (Greek: basileus = king), hatches from the egg of a snake, which is bred by a toad. Even in the ancient world there were rumours about its all-petrifying gaze and its breath of pestilence, which created the desert. The sometimes winged monster with the head of a bird and the body of a snake could only be killed by the smell of a weasel or the crowing of a rooster. According to the *Malleus maleficarum* of 1487 the basilisk hatches from the egg of a seven to nine year-old rooster that has been bred by a toad, and it brings death, the plague and drought. It can only be killed by reflecting its gaze in a mirror. The monster in Terry Gilliam's film *Jabberwocky* is one kind of basilisk; the most popular basilisk nowadays is killed by Harry Potter in his second year at Hogwarts.

During the Middle Ages another dragon was of importance as a symbol for the cyclical nature of the universe: the writhing Ouroborus or Uroboros, that bit itself into its tail and is related to Oceanus and the Midgard Snake. It was also the symbol of the Dragon Order[15].

Until the early 19th century it was commonly agreed upon in the Western world that dragons existed. Conrad Gessner presented them in his famous *Schlangenbuch* (Book of Snakes, 1589), as did other famous zoologists like Ulisse Aldrovandi in his *Serpentum et Draconum historia* (1605) and the unknown author of the *Musaeum Hermeticum* (1678). The Lindwurmbrunnen (dragon well) in Klagenfurth, Austria (created around 1590) is just one example for the widespread dissemination of ideas about dragons; other examples are siege machinery formed as a dragon (around 1465) and the depiction of the "Kriegsfurie" (war fury) as a dragon on a copperplate print by Jacques Callot (around 1630). On the coat of arms of the Duke of Marlborough two dragons are shown and one can be seen on the Welsh flag. It is therefore no wonder that dragon stories were and are also common in literature. With *Farmer Giles of Ham* Tolkien became a member of a respectable tradition, to which we can, among many other stories, count the humorous dragon tales of the well-known author of children's books Edith Nesbit (1858 – 1924), an author of which Tolkien was fond.[16]

---

[15] The "gesellschaft mit dem trakchen" (society with the dragon), also called "ordo draconis" and "societas draconia/draconis", was founded in 1408 by Sigismund of Luxembourg (1368-1437, Hungarian king in 1387, German king in 1411, emperor in 1433) in order to fight the Pagans (the Turks) and the "im Verborgenen wütenden Christen" (Christians that rage in secret; i.e. the Hussites); its motto was: "O quam misericors est Deus justus et pius" ("Oh, the Lord is merciful, just and devout."). Among its members were Vlad Dracul the Second and his son, Vlad Tepes Draculea the Third, that have indirectly given the vampire Dracula his name.

[16] E.g. the book *The Seven Dragons* (1899) and the story *The Last Of The Dragons* (1925). The female author of over 40 children's books (1858 –1924) is seen as a both a classic and trailblazer of English children's literature; she influenced Tolkien (one of her characters was the base for the Psamathists, the sand sorcerors, in *Roverandom*) and besides C. S. Lewis she is the outstanding idol of Joanne K. Rowling. Nesbit, Tolkien and Rowling belong to the same tradition not only because of their use of dragons, but also because of their humour (see also footnote 31).

## TOLKIEN'S DRAGONS

Let us at first take a look at the dragons beyond Middle-earth (excepting, of course, *Farmer Giles of Ham*, which will be examined more closely later on).

In the earliest published work in which a dragon plays an important role, the poem "The Hoard"[17], a very typical young dragon kills a dwarf and takes his treasure. He guards his hoard greedily until he is very old and slain by a young warrior:

> "There was an old dragon under grey stone;
> his red eyes blinked as he lay alone.
> His joy was dead and his youth spent,
> he was knobbed and wrinkled, and his limbs bent
> in the long years to his gold chained;
> in his heart's furnace the fire waned.
> To his belly's slime gems stuck thick,
> silver and gold he would snuff and lick:
> he knew the place of the least ring
> beneath the shadow of his black wing.
> Of thieves he thought on his hard bed,
> and dreamed that on their flesh he fed,
> their bones crushed, and their blood drank:
> his ears drooped and his breath sank.
> Mail-rings rang. He heard them not.
> A voice echoed in his deep grot:
> a young warrior with a bright sword
> called him forth to defend his hoard.

---

[17] First published in 1923 in another version with the title "lúmonna Gold Galdre Bewunden" in *The Gryphon* (New Series, Vol. IV No. 4, January 1923, p. 130, Leeds University, Swan Press, Leeds), then in 1937 with the same title in *The Oxford Magazine* (Vol. LV No. 15, 4. March 1937, p. 473, Oxford, The Oxonian Press) and then in 1962 as 14th poem with the title "The Hoard" in *The Adventures of Tom Bombadil and other verses from The Red Book*; in 1970 again published with the title "The Hoard" in *The Hamish Hamilton Book of Dragons* (ed. Roger Lancelyn Green, p. 246–248, Hamish Hamilton, London).

His teeth were knives, and of horn his hide,
but iron tore him, and his flame died." (*ATB* 108)

This poem is a wonderfully melancholic and moral ballad about greed and the loss of magic and beauty in the world; the character of the dragon is, like all other protagonists, kept deliberately stereotypical.

The white dragon in *Roverandom*[18] comes from the moon, as all white dragons do according to this story. In olden times he lived on the earth and fought in Merlin and Arthur's time with the red dragon of Caerdragon ("Castle of Dragons"); here Tolkien refers to an old legend, in which the red dragon of the Celts was defeated by the white dragon of the Anglo-Saxons. The white dragon from the moon is able to breathe red or green fire with which he can dye the moon red; sometimes he also darkens it with his smoke. When it comes to such a lunar eclipse, the Man in the Moon has to fix the problem with strong magic charms. After the dragon was awakened by the moon dogs Rover and Roverandom and had chased them over the moon, the Man in the Moon manages to make him crash with a charm. Because of this charm, the white dragon has now black spots on his belly and is therefore called the Mottled Monster (*R* 43 – 45). We notice by means of this example, as in many other situations in *Roverandom*, how much Tolkien likes to unfold stories which explain reality through myths and tales, and phenomena of the primary world through events or conditions of the secondary world. We will also see this pattern later on in *Farmer Giles of Ham*.[19]

---

[18] Tolkien told this story to his children in 1925 intending to comfort his son Michael, who had lost his black and white toy dog at the beach during the summer holidays. It was written down in 1927 at the latest; in 1936 it was offered to George Allen & Unwin, but the publishing house rejected it. The story was finally published in 1998.

[19] Of course *The Lord of the Rings* can be read in this way, too. Many other authors liked to write in a similar vein; this pattern can already be found in texts from the ancient world. Nesbit had it mastered to perfection, Arthur Conan Doyle loved it and Rowling, too, is proficient in it; see also Section 4.2. The reliance on patterns of myth is also a distinguishing feature of the *Letters from Father Christmas*. In one of them Tolkien

Apart from the scholarly works on *Beowulf* and *On Fairy-Stories*, there are no other dragons outside of Middle-earth apart from the one in *Farmer Giles*. This is why we will take a brief look at the dragons in Middle-earth now. They are quite remarkable, as Tolkien developed a consistent overall concept with them. While the dragons examined previously, which were mostly thought up for children, are rather humorous and entertaining (except the dragon in "The Hoard", which fulfils a prototypical function), the ones of Middle-earth have to be taken absolutely seriously because they are thoroughly perfected in terms of mythology, biology and literature.

Tolkien developed an extended and conclusive evolutionary history for the dragons of Middle-earth. They were created by Melkor in Angband by breeding, magical manipulation and combination of different creatures, e.g. captured eagles.[20]

The first dragons in Middle-earth were the wingless Urulóki ("fire-drakes"), that looked like giant saurians. The most powerful of them was their progenitor, Glaurung the Golden. They could breathe magic fire; like in many sagas their excrement and their blood was poisonous (*S* 260, 266). They were intelligent, vain, malicious and able to talk; some of them also had magic at their disposal. Glaurung, for example, enchanted Túrin and Nienor with his gaze (*S* 255 – 256, 261, 267). Whether we should take his name "father of dragons" literally has to remain undecided, but it is still imaginable that the other dragons really were his descendants.[21]

---

[20] explains how it came to a lunar eclipse in 1927: The Man in the Moon had visited Father Christmas at the North Pole, where he had eaten and drunk too much and overslept, so he had not returned to the moon in time. The dragons of the moon had dared to come out and caused the lunar eclipse by producing too much smoke (*FC* 1927).

"Men dwelt in darkness and were troubled by many evil things that Morgoth had devised in the days of his dominion: demons, and dragons, and mishapen beasts, and the unclean Orcs that are mockeries of the Children of Iluvatar" (*S* 310). Further information on biology and evolutionary history of dragons, is found in Schneidewind, *Biology*.

[21] In *The Children of Húrin* Glaurung is introduced and described in more detail than in *The Silmarillion*, but regarding his main characteristics he stays the same.

Later on Melkor bred two other variations of dragons: cold-drakes, which could fly excellently but breathed no fire and the winged fire-dragons (like Smaug), which moved rather clumsily in the air and looked a bit like giant bats. The latter's fire was magical and so strong that it probably even could have destroyed the Rings of Power, except the One.[22] The mightiest Fire Dragon was Ancalagon the Black, vanquished by Earendil in the last battle of the First Age.[23] In the Second and the Third Age there were still cold-drakes[24] and fire-dragons like Smaug in existence.[25]

## FARMER GILES OF HAM

The subheading of the story alone shows through its language and layout that *Farmer* is a humorous story.

---

[22] "It has been said that dragon-fire could melt and consume the Rings of Power, but there is not now any dragon left on earth in which the old fire is hot enough; nor was there ever any dragon, not even Ancalagon the Black, who could have harmed the One Ring, the Ruling Ring, for that was made by Sauron himself." (*LotR* 70)

[23] In his last battle against the Valar, Morgoth "loosed upon his foes the last desperate assault that he had prepared, and out of the pits of Angband there issued the winged dragons, that had not before been seen; and so sudden and ruinous was the onset of that dreadful fleet that the host of the Valar was driven back, for the coming of the dragons was with great thunder, and lightning, and a tempest of fire" (*S* 302). As already mentioned, this battle calls to mind the Book of Revelations, chapter 12.

[24] In the 21st century of the Third Age Fram of Rohan killed the dragon Scatha (*LotR* III 246); Dáin I., King of the dwarfs, and his second son Frór were "slain by a great cold-drake" in the entrance of his palace in Ered Mithrin in the year 2589 of the same Age (*LotR* III 353).

[25] "Smaug the Golden" was the "greatest of the dragons of his day" (*LotR* III 353). So there must have been more dragons, at least in the time of the expulsion of the dwarves from Erebor, 250 years before the Ring War. Tolkien also thought about the possibility that dragons could have survived the Third Age: "Dragons. They had not stopped; since they were active in far later times, close to our own. Have I said anything to suggest the final ending of dragons? If so it should be altered." (*L* No. 144, 177). If fire-drakes, cold-drakes and fire-dragons had survived and if there had also been surviving cross breeds, this would explain all forms of myths and legends concerning dragons – this is again an example of Tolkien's ability to explain phenomena of the real world with the fantasy world.

Aegidii Ahenobarbi Julii Agricole de Hammo
Domini de Domito
Aule Draconarie Comitis
Regni Minimi Regis
et Basilei mira facinora
et mirabilis

or in the vulgar tongue

The Rise and Wonderful Adventures
of Farmer Giles, Lord of Tame,
Count of Worminghall
and King of the Little Kingdom

Tolkien wrote this story around 1936 and offered it to Allen & Unwin in 1937; the publishing house rejected it. In 1938 he revised it for a lecture in front of a student union, and the revised version was accepted by the publishers. Because of the beginning war, the following economic lull and the shortage of paper as well as disagreements concerning the illustrations, the story was published only later on in 1949, and one year later in the US. In 1955 it was published in Germany by Reclam (in English). Several reprints and translations followed in Swedish (1961), Polish (1965), Hebrew (1968), Dutch (1971), Italian (1975), French (1975) and Japanese (1975). The first German edition was published bilingually in 1970, a licensed edition followed in 1974 by the publishing company dtv and in 1992 and 1999 new editions were made available; both had a slightly changed title. The publishing house Klett-Cotta published the story in the anthology *Fabelhafte Geschichten* (fabulous stories) in 1975.

### CONTENT, TOPIC AND MOTIFS

As in "The Hoard", a dragon and a treasure are two of the main "ingredients" in this profound and humorous story. Another is the Farmer mentioned in the title, and yet there are many more subtly described protagonists. Tolkien writes this mock-heroic tale as if it were a dubious report taken from a medieval family chronicle; the bombastic subheading and the frequent use of Latin words in the tale alone plainly show this. And in a pseudo-scholarly preface he supports this:

> "Of the history of the Little Kingdom few fragments have survived; but by chance an account of its origin has been preserved: a legend, perhaps, rather than an account; for it is evidently a late compilation, full of marvels, derived not from sober annals, but from the popular lays to which its author frequently refers. For him the events that he records lay already in a distant past; but he seems, nonetheless, to have lived himself in the lands of the Little Kingdom. [...] Since Brutus came to Britain many kings and realms have come and gone. The partition under Locrin, Camber, and Albanac, was only the first of many shifting divisions. What with the love of petty independence on the one hand, and on the other the greed of kings for wider realms, the years were filled with swift alternations of war and peace, of mirth and woe, as historians of the reign of Arthur tell us: a time of unsettled frontiers, when men might rise or fall suddenly, and songwriters had abundant material and eager audiences. Somewhere in those long years, after the days of King Coel maybe, but before Arthur or the Seven Kingdoms of the English, we must place the events here related; and their scene is the valley of the Thames, with an excursion northwest to the walls of Wales." (*FGH* 3 – 4)

This is the place where, supposedly during the 5$^{th}$ century, Farmer Giles, his wife and his trusting, if also cowardly dog Garm live a contented life in a little village until the onset of various adventures begins. Giles defeats a giant by accident and becomes a local hero. He unintentionally defeats the dragon Chrysophylax twice, and together with the dragon defends his and the people's rights against their greedy king, thus in the end he becomes king himself.

This story is one of the best that Tolkien ever wrote. It is not only full of humour and fantastical imagination, but also contains irony and sarcasm. This "fairy-story" in the Tolkienian sense (*OFS*)[26] is at the same time a very successful classical fantasy story (e.g. following Weinreich's definition 32 - 38), a political parable, a satire and a socially edifying text[27] – and, last but not least, a linguistic pun and a highly enjoyable piece of literature.

In this story Tolkien uses many popular mythological, legendary and literary topics.

First, the "hero": he is, like in many (folk) tales and sagas a "naïve fool", but stands out due to a great portion of native cunning (just think of Gulliver). Good-natured, traditional and rather cowardly, he grows cleverer during the story, even nearly wise and shows a "laudable discretion" (*FGH* 47) – an absolutely prototypical development in many tales.

Second, the magic weapon is so common in myths, tales and fantasy that it has become a true cliché and is often parodied. Thanks to their magic swords, Arthur, Elric and many others who win numerous fights and entire kingdoms. In connection with dragons, it is especially worth mentioning the swords Gram, the sword of Sigurd (in Richard Wagner's opera version called Notung/Nothung), and Siegfried's sword Balmung.[28]

---

[26] It fulfills every condition Tolkien demands of a fairy-story: "Fantasy, Recovery, Escape and Consolation", *OFS* 138 – 154). The political and social aspects are most important for the latter (see also footnote 30).

[27] It speaks, among other things, about greed, power and exploitation, about cowardice and egoism, about bureaucracy and group pressure, about justice and the moral legitimation of power and finally about a nearly peaceful "bottom-up revolution" – much of this can mean "consolation" in the Tolkienian sense (*OFS* pp. 153-155). Political and social aspects are no novelty in fantastic literature, just think of Swift, Mark Twain and Orwell, or more currently the *Bartimaeus*-trilogy by Jonathan Stroud and the *Harry Potter* novels by J. K. Rowling.

[28] Tolkien does not parody the sword, he puts emphasis on fulfilling his own demands on a fairy story: "There is one proviso: if there is any satire present in the tale, one thing

Third the enemy is, of course, also of great importance. In his lecture on *Beowulf* Tolkien pointed out how important it is to have a mighty and convincing enemy for the hero; indeed, one could almost say that the whole lecture is basically about this message (its name was not chosen without reason: *The Monsters and the Critics*). Only the right enemy lets the "average" hero become a "special" one:

> "The same heroic plot can yield good and bad poems, and good and bad sagas. The recipe for the central situations of such stories, studied in the abstract, is after all as 'simple' and as 'typical' as that of folktales. There are in any case many heroes but very few good dragons. [...] Something more significant than a standard hero, a man faced with a foe more evil than any human enemy of house or realm, is before us, and yet incarnate in time, walking in heroic history [...]" (*BMC* 17)

This is the case in the stories of Beren and of Túrin, of Eärendil and of Gil-galad, of Aragorn and of Frodo: Only by their enemies (which can be monsters, adverse circumstances or even a ring) and their efforts to overcome them do they become truly exceptional heroes. And this is also the case with Giles, who is cheered and applauded because he is seen as a beacon of heroism (and potential employer), when he forces the dragon into the village (*FGH* 49).

Of course, the classical dragon is the ideal enemy and at best only beaten by a deity or someone of similar quality in the myth as in the fairy story (this is also borne out in many new novels):

> "He esteemed dragons, as rare as they are dire, as some do still. He liked them — as a poet, not as a sober zoologist; and he had good reason." (*BMC* 12)

---

must not be made fun of, the magic itself. That must in that story be taken seriously, neither laughed at nor explained away." (*OFS* 114). The farmer, the king, the knights, even the dragon can be humorous, but never ever the magical sword!

"As for the dragon: as far as we know anything about these old poets, we know this: the prince of the heroes of the North [...] was a dragon slayer. And his most renowned deed [...] was the slaying of the prince of legendary worms. Although there is plainly considerable difference between the later Norse and the ancient English form of the story alluded to in *Beowulf,* already there it had these two primary features: the dragon, and the slaying of him as the chief deed of the greatest of heroes [...] A dragon is no idle fancy. Whatever may be his origins, in fact or invention, the dragon in legend is a potent creation of men's imagination, richer in significance than his barrow is in gold." (*BMC* 16)

And Chrysophylax, like Smaug (and created almost at the same time), is a nearly perfect prototype of a dragon: powerful, strong and brave – he kills and drives off a horde of knights – fire-breathing and winged, intelligent and cunning, experienced and clever, deceitful but also a bit cowardly. He is not really "bad", whatever that may be, and his behaviour is more a reaction to the circumstances than anything else. So at the end he becomes an ally against the incompetent bureaucratic representatives of an exploitative regime and allows the hero to preserve his moral integrity, without having to get his hands dirty in the business of civil insurrection.[29] At the end, Chrysophylax is powerful enough to drive out a young dragon from his cave and to give the giant a piece of his mind – it is a happy ending for him, too. Chrysophylax, to conclude, is the perfect enemy in a (comparatively) bloodless, but exciting story.

Other classical topics in myths and legends are, of course, the stupid, incompetent, selfish, greedy and exploitative master/politician and the cowardly, incompetent knights. The contrast between the "simple man" and the aristocracy, between the honest labour in the house and

---

[29] This gives rise to some interesting questions: From what point on can we act against the regime in a justified way? When does the "popular opinion" turn into dangerous injustice on its own behalf? Tolkien gives us a lot to think about in the guise of an innocent story.

on the farm as well as the courtly fuss is pointed out. The decadence of the upper class is typical of many tales and often has a political message. However, like in many other folk tales the system itself is not questioned or exchanged. In this case the more or less enlightened monarchy and its system of aristocracy/knights remains, but the unworthy in power are replaced by (it is to be hoped) better ones. The only things that disappear are the – nicely caricatured – decadent forms of behaviour and the exaggerated bureaucracy.

Two of the characters in the story mirror classical, literary and mythological characters: the parson, who discovers the secret of the sword, is the clever advisor, well-read and familiar with foreign languages and texts. He is more than the wise and magically or scientifically educated advisor, like Nestor or Dumbledore, for as a parson he is at the same time a spiritual advisor; with that he fulfills the same two two functions as Merlin, who was, at least according to the most widespread myth-making, as a druid active in the field of politics and science, as well as religion.

The male form of "Cassandra", the augur of ill, is the blacksmith, "a slow, gloomy man, vulgarly known as Sunny Sam, though his proper name was Fabricius Cunctator" (*FGH* 24). But unlike Cassandra, he is wrong with his warnings of disaster. His Latin surname can be traced back to a popular, pre-Christian Roman general, consul and dictator.[30]

The clever grey mare brings to mind numerous horses that play important roles in myths and tales, from Odin's eight-legged steed

---

[30] Quintus Fabius Maximus Verrucosus (verrusosus: lat., warty), ca. 275 – 203 B.C., general of the Roman Republic, five times consul and twice dictator, fought against Hannibal during the Second Punic War; because of his defensive warfare he was called *Cunctator*, the hesitator. At first, this was an abuse, but after the defeat of Cannae 216 B.C. it became a title of honour. Later on he became the stereotype of the deliberately tough Roman. Fabianism and the Fabian Society are named after him; one of their founders was Edith Nesbit (see also footnote 15). It is quite fitting with the development in the Little Kingdom since the Fabian Society, as a socialist and intellectual movement (and precursor of the Labour Party), wants to turn society in a revolutionary way into the direction of a pure and simple life.

Sleipnir to the many speaking steeds in especially Eastern European and Oriental tales. In these a seemingly old, usually forgotten or neglected mare often turns into a spirited horse for the hero. Although the grey mare does not do exactly this, she becomes braver and has many shrewd ideas.

Garm, the speaking, rather cowardly dog, is almost a parody of a companion and guardian. Named after the giant, four-eyed dog of the Norse goddess of death, Hel, who will die during Ragnarök by killing Tyr, the dog Garm, Giles's dog, is just the exact opposite of a frightening beast and a rather amusing sidekick.

### HUMOUR IN "GOOD" TRADITION

Explaining real phenomena by, in the broadest sense, fantastic, and quite often transcendental ideas is possibly as old as mankind. We can find it in religions and myths – consider, for instance, the Greek stories which try to explain lightning and thunder, volcanos and echoes – as well as in philosophy. But on the literary level, too, there have been early attempts to explain reality by myths or fairy-tales, or (to use Tolkien's count of worlds) phenomena of the primary world by events or conditions in the secondary world. We can state that even the early epic of Gilgamesh belongs to this category of tales.

We now turn to the special area of humorous interpretation or explanation that can be found in *Farmer Giles of Ham*. That Tolkien is here partaking in a long and respectable tradition can be demonstrated by the following examples.

It was already Aristophanes (ca. 448 – ca. 385 B.C.), one of the most important representatives of Greek comedy, who portrayed the mythological explanations of the forces of nature in a parodistic way. In the comedy *Eirene* (421 B.C., "The Peace") a wine-grower flies into the Olymp on a dung beetle to ask Zeus about the war, and he learns that thunder is caused by Zeus's breaking wind.

The Brothers Grimm sometimes also tried to explain reality in a humorous way; some of their tales have an air of parody and explain unfamiliar phenomena. In modern fantasy there is a broad range of humorous explanations of our world, and it is often hard to differentiate between an explanation of commonly accepted phenomena and descriptions "invented" by the authors themselves. Edith Nesbit and Arthur Conan Doyle have been already mentioned, newer authors are, for example, Robert Lynn Asprin and Roger Zelazny. Tolkien himself describes events in our world in *Roverandom* and in the *Father Christmas Letters*, such as the aforementioned lunar eclipses or conspicuously big Northern Lights: the polar bear Karhu, one of Father Christmas's helpers, sets all Northern Lights for the next two years off. Thus, a gigantic firework erupts, the moon splits into four parts, and the Man in the Moon falls down into the kitchen garden of Father Christmas (*FC* 1926). Tolkien provides an especially odd description of the invention of golf. In 1147, Shire reckoning (in 2747 of the Second Age), a group of orcs under their leader Golfimbul attacked the Shire and were defeated by the hobbits at the Battle of the Green Fields. The hobbit-troops were led by

> "[...] Old Took's great-granduncle Bullroarer, who was so huge (for a hobbit) that he could ride a horse. He charged the ranks of the goblins of Mount Gram in the Battle of the Green Fields, and knocked their king Golfimbul's head clean off with a wooden club. It sailed a hundred yards through the air and went down a rabbit hole, and in this way the battle was won and the game of Golf invented at the same moment." (*H* 17)

In *Farmer Giles of Ham* we also find such a humorous explanation, where the fantastic secondary world is connected to our primary world. In this case Tolkien's professional field is concerned: philology. In the preface he explains: "An excuse for presenting a translation of this curious tale [...] may be found in the glimpse that it affords of life in a dark period of the history of Britain, not to mention the light that it throws on the origin of some difficult place-names" (*FGH* 3). And towards the end of the story he writes:

> Now those who live still in the lands of the Little Kingdom will observe in this history the true explanation of the names that some of its towns and villages bear in our time. For the learned in such matters inform us that Ham, being made the chief town of the new realm, by a natural confusion between the Lord of Ham and the Lord of Tame, became known by the latter name, which it retains to this day; for Thame with an h is a folly without warrant. Whereas in memory of the dragon, upon whom their fame and fortune were founded, the Draconarii built themselves a great house, four miles north-west of Tame, upon the spot where Giles and Chrysophylax first made acquaintance. That place became known throughout the kingdom as Aula Draconaria, or in the vulgar Worminghall, after the king's name and his standard.
> 
> The face of the land has changed since that time, and kingdoms have come and gone; woods have fallen, and rivers have shifted, and only the hills remain, and they are worn down by the rain and the wind. But still that name endures; though men now call it Wunnle (or so I am told); for villages have fallen from their pride. But in the days of which this tale speaks Worminghall it was. (*FGH* 56)

Tolkien acknowledges in the preface that the story is also worth reading for those who have no special interest in his games with with language: "Some may find the character and adventures of its hero attractive in themselves." (*FGH* 3).

Tolkien's explanations of lunar eclipses, names of rivers and the game of golf are so wonderfully absurd that they can indeed compete with the things produced on this subject by other great authors in the last years. The following authors are notable for this (and their works recommended for reading): Douglas Adams with *The Hitchhiker's Guide to the Galaxy* and its fellow volumes, Eoin Colfer with his five *Artemis Fowl* novels and Joanne K. Rowling (although her funniest explanations of the world are not in her *Harry Potter* novels, but in the pseudo-school book *Quidditch Through the Ages*). These three authors demonstrate that Tolkien and his humour in *Farmer Giles* belongs to a good, long and continuing tradition.

INFLUENCE ON MODERN DRAGON STORIES

Tolkien's Chrysophylax is a prototype, and Tolkien's mastery as an author is of such import that *Farmer Giles* had a strong influence on subsequent dragon stories (the numerous homages or persiflages are not meant here).

While Nesbit described rather funny and atypical dragons in the aforementioned stories, Tolkien was the first who awarded a typical, dangerous dragon positive aspects (this was not the case in *The Hobbit!*) and described a kind of "Gentlemen's Agreement" or "peaceful coexistence" between dragon and human.

Since then numerous works have been published in which dragons are portrayed as powerful, positive, and wise, and this not only in foreign worlds where dragons have another descent, such as the *Dragonriders of Pern* cycle by Anne McCaffrey. Some of the highlights of dragon literature are the dragon books by Barbara Hambly, which deal with the story of the black dragon Morkeleb, and the *Earthsea* novels by Ursula K. Le Guin.

Following the tradition of *Farmer Giles of Ham* are Roger Zelazny, who inverts the circumstances in "The Monster and the Maiden", and Isaac Asimov with the wonderful parody "Prince Delightful and the Flameless Dragon". Tolkien's influence with Chrysophylax and Smaug on dragon and fantasy literature cannot be measured highly enough.

## CONCLUDING REMARKS

*Farmer Giles of Ham* is the prototype of a dragon story. Tolkien describes a thoroughly "classical" dragon and a thoroughly classical dragon slayer story which nevertheless has a parodistic spin. This story contains everything necessary for such a tale, and Tolkien uses typical literary and mythological topoi which also make him an outstanding role model for modern authors like, for instance, Rowling.

In more than one way, this story is typical for Tolkien: it shows his humour, which is also evident in *The Hobbit* and his other works, and with which he belongs in a good tradition, as well as the fun he has playing with history and language and his passion for explaining phenomenona of the real world by means of literary, invented events in a secondary world.

Thus, this story, like others of his so often underestimated "smaller works", shows Tolkien's humorous and highly entertaining side, as the master of the small form.

FRIEDHELM SCHNEIDEWIND studied Biology and, for a few terms, Computer Science. He is currently working as a teacher and adviser for a variety of topics, mainly DTP/ media presentation/ multimedia and public relations. He is a, journalist, publisher and musician. Furthermore, he is the author of several books and encyclopaedias. (www.friedhelm-schneidewind.de)

## Works Cited

*The Bible*, King James Version [http://www.gutenberg.org/etext/10 and also http://www. bibleserver.com. cited 9.2.2008].

Asimov, Isaac. "Prince Delightful and the Flameless Dragon" (1991). *Magic: The Final Fantasy Collection*. London: HarperCollinsPublishers, 1996.

Gier, Kerstin. "Jeremy Ohneland und der Drache". *Das Vermächtnis des Rings*. Stefan Bauer (Hg.). Bergisch Gladbach: Bastei-Lübbe, 2001. 13-68.

Hammond, Wayne G. and Christina Scull. *J.R.R. Tolkien: Artist & Illustrator*. London: HarperCollinsPublishers, 1995.

Nesbit, Edith. *The Last of the Dragons and Some Others*. London: Puffin Books, 1985.

---, *The Seven Dragons and Other Stories*. [no place]: Alan Rodgers Books, 2006.

Schneidewind, Friedhelm. *Lexikon von Himmel und Hölle*. Berlin: Lexikon Imprint Verlag, 2000.

---, "Biologie, Genetik und Evolution in Mittelerde". *Tolkiens Weltbild(er)*. Thomas Formet-Ponse et. al. (Hg). *Hither Shore* 2. Interdisciplinary Journal on Modern Fantasy Literature. Jahrbuch der Deutschen Tolkien Gesellschaft e. V. (DTG). Düsseldorf: Scriptorium Oxoniae, 2006. 41 – 66.

---, *Drachen. Das Schmökerlexikon*. Saarbrücken: Verlag der Villa Fledermaus, 2008.

Tolkien, John Ronald Reuel. "Beowulf: The Monsters and the Critics" (first published 1937). *The Monsters and the Critics and Other Essays*. London: George Allen & Unwin, 1983. 5 – 48 .

---, *The Hobbit or There And Back Again*. (1937) Revised Edition. New York: Ballantine Books, 1982.

---, "On Translating Beowulf" (1941). *The Monsters and the Critics and Other Essays*. London: George Allen & Unwin, 1983. 49 – 71.

---, "On Fairy Stories" (1947). *The Monsters and the Critics and Other Essays*. London: George Allen & Unwin, 1983. 109 – 161.

---, "Farmer Giles of Ham" (1949). *Tales from The Perilous Realm*. London: HarperCollinsPublishers, 2002. 1 – 57.

---, *Die Geschichte von dem Bauern Giles und dem Drachen Chrysophylax*. zweisprachige Ausgabe. Ebenhausen near München: Verlag Langewiesche-Brandt, 1970.

---, *Farmer Giles of Ham – Die Geschichte vom Bauern Giles und dem Drachen*. Bilingual edition. München: Deutscher Taschenbuch Verlag, 1974.

---, "Bauer Giles von Ham". *Fabelhafte Geschichten*. Stuttgart: Klett-Cotta, 1975.

---, *Farmer Giles of Ham – Der Bauer Giles von Ham und der Drache*. Bilingual edition. München: Deutscher Taschenbuch Verlag, 1992.

---, *Farmer Giles of Ham – Bauer Giles von Ham*. Bilingual edition. München: Deutscher Taschenbuch Verlag, 1999.

---, *The Lords of the Rings* (1954/55). London: HarperCollins, 1995.

---, "The Adventures of Tom Bombadil" (1962) . *Tales from The Perilous Realm*. London: HarperCollinsPublishers, 2002. 59 – 118.

---,  *Letters from Father Christmas* (1976). Ed. Baillie Tolkien. London: HarperCollinsPublishers, 1995.

---,  *The Silmarillion* (1977). Ed. Christopher Tolkien, London: HarperCollinsPublishers, 1999.

---,  *The Letters of J. R. R. Tolkien* (1981). Ed. Humphrey Carpenter with the assistance of Christopher Tolkien. London: HarperCollinsPublishers, 1995.

---,  *Roverandom* (1998). Ed. Christina Scull and Wayne G. Hammond. London: HarperCollinsPublishers, 1998.

---,  *The Children of Hurin* (2007). Ed. Christopher Tolkien. London: HarperCollinsPublishers, 2007.

Weinreich, Frank. *Fantasy. Einführung*. Essen: Oldib-Verlag, 2007.

Zelazny, Roger. "The Monster and the Maiden" (1964). *The Monster Book of Monsters*. Ed. Michael O'Shaughnessy. London: Xanadu Publications, 1988: 69 – 70.

# "... Until the Dragon Comes":
## Tolkien's Dragon-Motif as Poetological Concept

Patrick Brückner

### ABSTRACT

Dragons are a species often encountered in Tolkien's works, as anybody familiar with his essay on *Beowulf* can confirm. This paper argues that Tolkien's dragons are far more than a mere fabulous detail to his oeuvre but that they encroach upon "the machinery and the ideas of a poem or tale" and thus create a reality that transcends the one typically called 'fantastic'. The "deep significance" of Tolkien's dragons adds a world-view that refers to an epic historic quality far beyond and different from the fairy tale elements of his texts.

> *I never imagined that the dragon*
> *was of the same order as the horse.*
> (OFS 135)

### REAL DRAGONS ARE RARE...

In his essay on *Beowulf* Tolkien writes: "Real dragons [...] are actually rare" (*BMC* 12). The dragon, however, is a highly popular phenomenon in medieval literature: romances such as *Yvain* (V. 3341-3414), *Tristan* (V. 8897-9982), and *Lanzelet* (V. 7834-7995) evince the motif's dissemination. In addition, there are the two dragons that, according to Tolkien, can be considered 'real': Fáfnir of the Old Norse *Völsunga saga* and the dragon in *Beowulf* (*BMC* 12) feature prominently on a list that could easily be extended. One may therefore wonder why the dragon in *Yvain* and his relatives in *Tristan, Lanzelet,* and other texts are not accorded the same degree of 'reality'. What exactly distinguishes them from the dragon in *Beowulf* and the lindworm slain by Sigurd? In Tolkien's reasoning, only Fáfnir and Beowulf's dragon are "essential both to the machinery and the ideas of a poem or tale" (*BMC* 12). By contrast, dragons found in the *Matière de Bretagne* (and courtly romance) belong, in the words of Hans Robert Jauss, to "a mythology no longer believed [by a contemporary audience]; [they emerge] in the wake of an adaptation of foreign subject matters and motifs by a different social civilisation, as a result of fictionalization" (Jauss 315),[1] and survive only as fairy-tale elements within the texts.

Tolkien, however, pronounces with certainty that a "dragon is no idle fancy" (*BMC* 16). Dragons that merely play the part of a fairy-tale motif may therefore be described as chivalrous 'adventures' (*âventiuren*) with a certain ethical and moral import for those who encounter them (cf. Unzeitig-Herzog 45). While these dragons may have an impact on the "machinery" of a poem as well, they do not generate meaning surpassing the significance of other 'adventures'.[2] Fáfnir, and the *Beowulf*-dragon especially, cannot be identified as *âventiure*-dragons in the sense outlined above – not if one takes Tolkien's statements seriously. First and foremost, 'real' dragons represent the 'ideas' of a text. The question must then be raised why the two specific creatures that Tolkien names also meet his second requirement for 'real' dragons.

In *Beowulf*, Tolkien recognizes "a fusion that has occurred *at a given point* of contact between old and new" (*BMC* 20). For contemporary listeners, this connection evidently generates a surplus beyond fic-

---

[1] Original quote: "einer [zeitgenössisch] nicht mehr geglaubten Mythologie; [sie erscheinen] in der Folge einer Übernahme fremder Stoffe und Motive durch eine andere gesellschaftliche Zivilisation, als Ergebnis einer Fiktionalisierung." All quotes in languages other than English were translated by Judith Klinger.

[2] Based on the word's immediate meaning, *âventiure* can be translated as 'chance', 'destiny' or 'fortune'. In Arthurian romance since Chrétien de Troyes, it connotes that which is "neither contrived nor suffered, but rather confronted and overcome [by the chivalrous hero]. [...] The significance of *âventiure* [within Arthurian romance] corresponds to the miracle in legend [...], [and] to fate within the epic. [...] It approaches the hero from the open realm of unpredictable events [and] represents a process of encountering the world and [...] encountering the self" (Wehrli 275). As an exemplary figure, the hero of the *âventiure* contributes to the development of an idealized conception of the courtly world (cf. Wehrli 274).

tionality (inherent to the modern reader's understanding of literature): "the illusion of surveying a past, pagan but noble and fraught with a deep significance – a past that itself had depth and reached backward into a dark antiquity of sorrow" (*BMC* 27).

How does the dragon contribute to this 'illusion of surveying the past'? Contrary to the prevalent readings of *Beowulf* in his time, Tolkien's essay shifts the dragon[3] to the very centre of interpretation (cf. *BMC* 12pp.). It ultimately falls to the dragon in *Beowulf* to generate historicity (the meaningful past) by sustaining a balance between the hero – who stands out as "something more significant than a standard hero" (*BMC* 17) – and the "heroic history [in] the named lands of the North" (*BMC* 17). An anachronism seems to be the inevitable result. Dragons that emerge within *history* must always strike modern recipients as anachronistic: they are (in the modern reader's view) purely fictitious creatures, and it seems inconceivable to encounter them not in a collection of fairy-tales, but in a history book. Evidently, "heroic history" does not refer to modern historiography and its descriptive method.

History in *Beowulf* – as in the medieval epic in general – is, in fact, conveyed on the level of the narrative. Encountering the dragon is thus not a 'coincidence', but the hero's doom: the very element that makes his story worth telling (cf. *BMC* 32) and thereby renders it historical, in the specifically epic sense.[4] Jauss' remarks on the medieval epic may serve to highlight the implications:[5]

> The connection between historical incident [...] and fantastical events by no means renders the [story's core] less his-

---

[3] Together with Grendel and Grendel's mother.
[4] The primal epic situation: "A narrator conveys to an audience something that has occurred" (Petersen 14).
[5] Even though Tolkien states that "*Beowulf* is not an 'epic'" (*BMC* 31), the "past that itself had depth" he describes here (*BMC* 27) clearly corresponds to Bakhtin's definition of the 'epic-past' (cf. 13pp.).

torical. For 'historical' does not yet, to the [contemporary] audience, [...] imply the modern sense of the historically accurate [...] but refers to [...] an incident that 'wants to be believed', [...] even if, by our standards, legendary and historical elements are inextricably entangled (313).[6]

The dragon establishes an absolute temporal separation between listener and narrator on the one hand, and narrated story on the other (cf. Bakhtin 13); at the same time he sustains the significance of the noble past (cf. *BMC* 27). Unlike his relatives in Arthurian romance, the dragon in *Beowulf* is not the kind of monster whose defeat and death restore order to the world (cf. Giloy-Hirtz 167pp.), thereby contributing to an exemplary, idealized conception of the courtly universe. Instead he represents an *epically* historical world and its significance – not, it must be noted, as a symbol, but as a 'real' dragon.

For the modern individual, this specific type of historiography raises the question where (verifiable) history ends and mythology begins (cf. Lévi-Strauss 38). Yet Tolkien's allegory of the tower, in *Beowulf: The Monster and the Critics*, clearly reveals that he considered this particular question – the question of 'reality' in the modern sense – not only uninspiring but downright counter-productive. With the conclusion of the tower allegory, he develops an alternative that is set against the rejected approach of literary criticism and historical research: "But from the top of that tower the man had been able to look out upon the sea" (*BMC* 8). This unexpected conclusion resists immediate decoding. While the ruin, the tower, and the stones can be easily identified as the

---

[6] Original quote: "Durch die Verbindung von historischem Ereignis [...] und phantastischem Geschehen wird der [Kern des Erzählten] keineswegs weniger historisch. Denn 'historisch' hat für das [zeitgenössische] Publikum [...] noch nicht den modernen Sinn des historisch Getreuen [...] sondern meint [...] eine Begebenheit, 'die geglaubt werden will', [...] auch wenn [sich dabei] für unsere Begriffe Legendäres und Historisches unentwirrbar vermischen."

(analytically dissected) text, composed of older texts and motifs, the meaning of the gaze out across the sea remains opaque (cf. *BMC* 7pp.).

Now Tolkien's own dragons seem to provide assistance (even though that is not their common habit), where the question of their 'real' existence is concerned. Enlightened readers will flatly deny the existence of creatures whose substantial reality cannot be incorporated into their 'real' world: they must therefore be located in the realm of fairy-tales and symbolism. Tom Shippey's reading of Smaug as a symbol for "dragonsickness [which] is perfectly common" (328) – a condition known to modern readers – seems to exemplify this general tendency.[7]

Yet when Tolkien discusses the dragon in *Beowulf*, his only objection is that he is not "dragon enough, plain pure fairy-story dragon. [...] The large symbolism is near the surface, but it does not break through, nor become allegory" (*BMC* 17). 'Good' dragons, in Tolkien's view, do not represent anything but 'historical' depth. A 'real' dragon thus does not exhibit allegorical or symbolic polysemy (let alone a related 'applicability'). For this reason, 'real' dragons may enter our 'real' world – a world that has been measured, weighed, and rationally examined – only as anachronisms. Indeed, the very historians and literary critics whose

---

[7] At first glance, it may seem obvious that 'dragonsickness' can be translated as 'materialism' or 'greed'. However, Tolkien's critical comments on *Nymphidia* as well as his rejection of allegory oppose such a translation process in its entirety. As a symbolic representation of greed, Smaug would cease to be a "real dragon" in Tolkien's definition. Reducing 'dragonsickness' to a known (modern) attitude, such as materialism, removes the core of historical otherness, the significance of the 'noble past', that Tolkien stressed. – In the Master of Lake-town's case, 'dragonsickness' is readily interpretable as the diametrical opposite of the medieval virtue of generosity (Middle High German *milte*). For the medieval nobility, *milte* functioned as an identity-conferring concept which (despite superficial similarities) has nothing in common with modern notions of equitable distribution or social responsibility. [In the medieval context, generous gifts constitute, represent, and confirm significant social ties.] As a consequence, it is the lord's duty to adopt a generous and beneficial attitude towards his following and his subjects. In *The Hobbit*, Bard acts in accordance with this ideal (cf. *H* 284), whereas the Master of Lake-town fails to observe it. Thus he loses his position of power (his retinue is reduced to mere 'companions'; cf. *H* 285), and the collapse of his social identity eventually results in his death.

conclusions Tolkien contests do not hesitate to characterise the dragon in *Beowulf* as anachronistic.

However, when the conception underpinning 'truth' (as reality) is shifted towards the historical 'truth' of the epic (in the sense established above), the perceived anachronism dissolves. Unlike modern history, the epic does not construct 'truth' from dates and facts – that is, from objective rationality as the founding principle of reality, which has become all-dominant since the Age of Enlightenment (and which renders dragons impossible). Epic 'truth', by contrast, emerges from an encompassing, ordered, yet non-rational perception of the world. The resulting structure contains both the epic narrator and the audience as part of the textual world, even as the narrator asserts its existence. Objectivity, however, results from a temporal and spatial *gap* between the narrated events and narrator/audience (cf. Bakhtin 12pp.). This conception of the world dissolves the categorical distinction between the 'historical' and the 'fantastical', allowing the dragon to become real.

Tolkien's perception of dragons is likely to trouble modern readers. While he discusses the literary dragon of the Old English poem in his *Beowulf* essay, the dragon Tolkien invokes in the closing sentence cannot be easily dismissed as mere fiction: "And for those who are native to that tongue and land, it [*Beowulf*] must ever call with a profound appeal – until the dragon comes" (*BMC* 34). For this dragon to 'come' indeed, he must possess reality beyond fiction, a reality outside the text.

How does a 'real' dragon then achieve a reality that exceeds symbolism? Bauer points out that fairy-tales (similar in this respect to Jauss's paradigm of 'epic truth') exhibit no distinction of 'realistic' and 'fantastical' elements. Instead, "distinctions are [projected] onto a single vector, and [...] an inner distance [experienced by readers][8] is implied by

---

[8] 'Inner distance', as Bauer describes it, refers to the reader's experience of a gap between themselves and events that occur in the *fantastic* sphere, which, in fairy-tales, exists on equal footing with the *realistic* realm.

external remoteness. The fairy-tale projects the plot onto a vector that extends from a starting point 'x', located in the sphere of the *realistic*, to an endpoint 'y', located in the sphere of the *fantastic*" (15).[9] However, even the *fantastic* sphere must be anchored in the known world to a certain degree, so that readers may find their bearings within this universe (cf. Bauer 15).

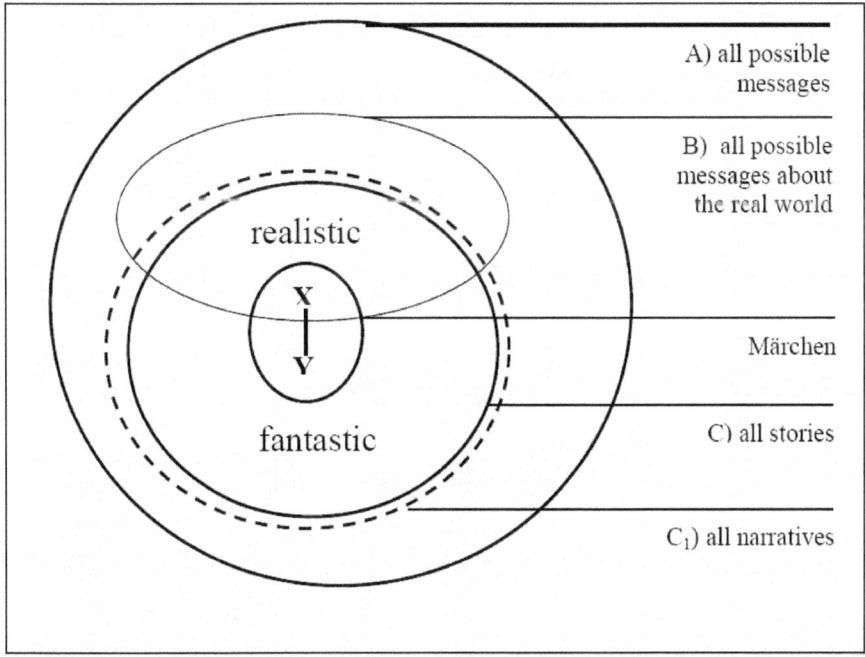

Fig. 1: Bauer's model depicting the narrative structure of fairy-tales (cf. 15)

In the present context, the exact point where the vector crosses over from the sphere of the *realistic* to that of the *fantastic* is of particular

---

[9] Original quote: "differenziertes auf eine einzige Linie [projiziert] und [...] innere Ferne durch äußere Entfernung andeutet. Das Märchen projiziert die Handlung auf eine Linie, die von einem Ausgangspunkt 'x', welcher im Bereich *realistic* liegt, zu einem Endpunkt 'y' reicht, welcher im Bereich *fantastic* liegt."

interest (cf. Bauer 15).[10] Tolkien's remarks about the 'truth' of a (good) fairy-story must come to mind: "Inside it, what he [the narrator] relates is 'true': it accords with the laws of that world" (*OFS* 132). In the following, I will demonstrate that 'real' dragons – and Tolkien's dragons are unquestionably 'real' – serve to *shift the point* that marks entry into the *fantastic* sphere towards the *realistic* realm, so that they themselves gain 'truth', as it were. This specific mechanism, both within the texts and on the level of reception, will be discussed with regard to the different dragons in Tolkien's works.

## THE DRAGON AT THE HEART OF THE STORY: SMAUG

Smaug presents himself as the most obvious launching point for our investigation. More than any other drake in Tolkien's works, he embodies the concept of the 'real' dragon. Since he functions as both the object and the ultimate destination of the Quest, which renders him entirely indispensable for the plot of *The Hobbit*, Smaug is also the most well-known among Tolkien's dragons.

Smaug lives on the far side of a world where no one seems to consider it peculiar when wandering wizards embroil harmless hole-dwellers in a wild adventure. Of course, modern readers will squarely place protagonists such as dwarves and hobbits in the field Bauer labels *fantastic*. It is then all the more interesting to note that Tolkien apparently defined the point of transition from *realistic* to *fantastic* himself by charting *the Edge of the Wild* on the map for *The Hobbit* (Fig. 2, cf. *H* 286; cf. Hammond and Scull 94; cf. Bauer 15).

---

[10] Within this analytic model, 'realistic' and 'fantastic' represent categories that are meaningful only for modern readers. For the audience of pre-modern epics this particular classification system did not exist.

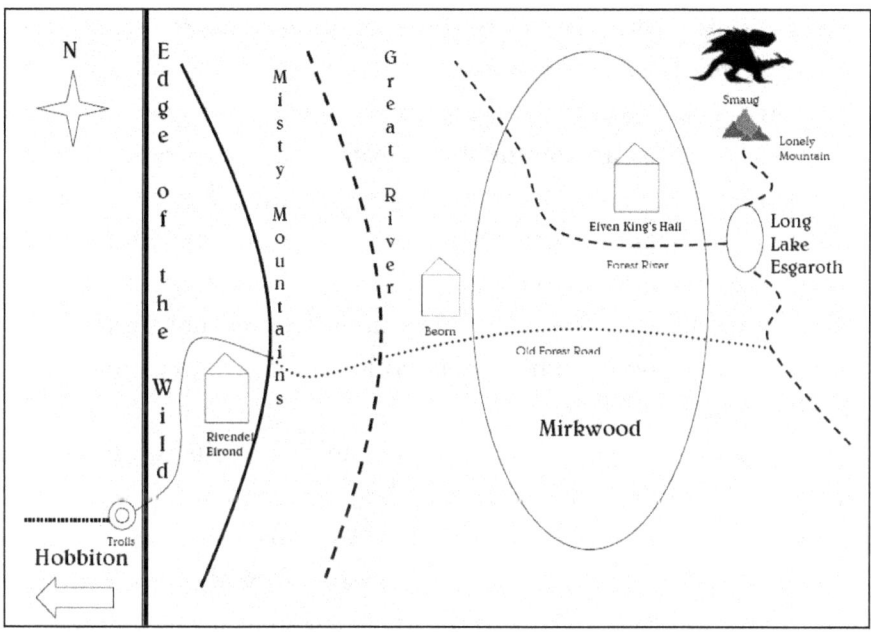

Fig. 2: Outlines of the Wilderland map, based on Tolkien's drawing (cf. *H* 286)

The *Edge of the Wild*, drawn closely to Bilbo's and the dwarves' point of departure, challenges interpretation. First of all, this demarcation apparently does not indicate the outer margin of the wilderness, the boundary of the perilous realm of adventure. Twice, Gandalf points out that Elrond's house is the "Last Homely House west of the [Misty] Mountains" (*H* 54) and explains: "You are come to the very edge of the Wild [...]. Hidden somewhere ahead of us is the fair valley of Rivendell" (*H* 54). The text thus locates the *Edge of the Wild* in a different area than Tolkien's map does (which places Rivendell well beyond the drawn line). While one might assume that the line on the map contains all 'fairy-tale elements' within the text, it is easy to disprove this notion: the troll-cave is, after all, clearly situated on the left side of the line (cf. Bauer 17).

Now readers may well suppose that the hobbits' way of life and the business transactions of dwarves can, just like the trolls' crude violence, be found within their own world. In this reading, the space left of the *Edge of the Wild* corresponds to the *realistic* realm – and that is indeed how Bauer consistently interprets the line on the map. Gandalf's statement "dragons are comfortably far-off (and therefore legendary)" (*H* 31) seems to support Bauer's proposal to locate Smaug at the extremity of the *fantastic* realm, the endpoint 'y'. Conversely, the starting point of the Quest corresponds to 'x' on Bauer's vector, the most *realistic* area in the text (cf. Bauer 17). Yet neither wizards, nor dwarves, nor trolls, nor even hobbits inhabit the world which is known and interpreted by readers.

Upon closer examination, Bauer's reading exhibits two flaws that pertain to the textual level and to the level of reception. To start with the former: for Gandalf, as for the dwarves, Smaug is entirely real to begin with. Indeed Smaug is an integral part of the dwarves' historical knowledge – ultimately, of their history. Their song at the 'Unexpected Party' demonstrates just that fact. The lines "The Dragon's ire more fierce than fire / Laid low their towers and houses frail" (*H* 25) describe why the "Kingdom under the Mountain" was lost (cf. *H* 32), an event that becomes a focus for the narration of a previous history, but which also defines the dwarves' political present (their life in exile) as well as their political vision of the future (the return of the "King under the Mountain").[11] That the dwarves' ancient history is firmly embedded in the textual world becomes evident in Lake-town. When the dwarves arrive, memories of the story about the King under the Mountain are rekindled among the townspeople (cf. *H* 183pp.).[12]

---

[11] At the same time, additional connections to historical events in the larger realm of Middle-earth are established: the necromancer's expulsion from southern Mirkwood, or the renewed colonization of Moria, for instance; cf. *H* 31pp.

[12] The song "The King beneath the mountains / The King of carven stone / The lord of silver fountains / Shall come into his own!" (*H* 190), sung by the townspeople upon the dwarves' arrival in Lake-town, illustrates the textually staged conjunction of the historical context with the *fantastic* (in Bauer's terminology). History is conveyed in the epic mode, as the following description demonstrates: the fact "that it was Thror's grandson not Thror himself that had come back did not bother [the townspeople] at all" (*H* 190).

Indeed, Smaug himself contributes to the textual generation of an epic reality, for his awakening calls Bard onto the scene. Although the defence of Lake-town may be a community affair, as Shippey argues, Bard is anything but a "twentieth-century infantry officer" (40). No infantry officer owns a weapon like Bard's treasured arrow, which he uses to kill Smaug. The bowman's black arrow is, in fact, an epic heirloom of the royal line (cf. *H* 236),[13] and Bard himself is identified as heir to the throne of Dale (cf. *H* 249). He alone is capable of distinguishing the "marauding fire of the Dragon" from the fires of a forge (cf. *H* 232) and gains heroic stature as dragon-slayer. In effect, Smaug transforms Bard's rank from Lake-town archer to that of King of Dale. John Rateliff locates Bard's roots in epic tradition: "The primary external influence for Bard's emergence, aside from sheer narrative necessity, probably lies not in fairy-tales but (as is so often the case in the Smaug chapters) in *Beowulf*" (*HH II* 557). It is no coincidence either that the dragon confers a status beyond that of a 'fairy-tale hero' on Bard: after all, the "dragon-fighter is *the* prototype of the epic hero" (Haug 315).[14]

On the textual level, Smaug therefore marks the point at which ancient history runs into the present state of affairs and generates future history. Endowed with dragon-gold, Bard regains influence (cf. *H* 273) and ultimately becomes King of Dale (cf. *H* 284). Similarly, the King under the Mountain is restored to his throne. (While it is Dain, not Thorin, who finally takes the crown, the king's individual identity is

---

[13] History, in this case, does not depend on historical dates or individuals; it is based instead on an epic tradition, centred on fate and prevision.

That specific weapons may acquire a historical dimension independent of their bearers is equally apparent in the cases of Orcrist and Glamdring, the swords carried by Thorin and Gandalf (cf. *H* 59). A weapon of this sort attests to the bearer's qualities and locates him in a historical context. Once Orcrist has been discovered in Thorin's possession, the orcs' initially unspecific hostility gains a new dimension: historical connections, established across the famous sword, expose an ancient enmity at the root of the conflict (cf. *H* 70).

[14] Original quote: "Der Drachenkämpfer ist der Prototyp des epischen Helden schlechthin."

irrelevant in this context. Only the fact *that* a dwarf ascends the throne truly matters; cf. *H* 273).[15]

The only protagonist who appears to be entirely ignorant of dragons (and who therefore seems most familiar to readers) is Bilbo. Yet the text supports this familiarity only at first glance. Readers may very well sympathize with Bilbo's chagrin when his home is overrun by guests who threaten to destroy their host's furnishings at will (cf. *H* 23). However, while it may startle the hobbit that the intrusive company consists of thirteen dwarves and a wizard, it is entirely inconceivable for modern readers to entertain guests of this sort. The dwarves' song – performed after their initial song of havoc and demolition – then plunges Bilbo into a vision of dragons. This vision clearly demonstrates that Bilbo does not doubt the factual existence of dragons. And how could it be otherwise? After all, dwarves and wizards surprise Bilbo only by the manner of their arrival, not by their very existence. (It strikes the dwarves as rather *fantastical*, however, that Bilbo of all people is supposed to become their fourteenth companion.) Evidently, Bilbo is not "so unlearned in dragon-lore" (*H* 212) as he initially seems.

The impression of Bilbo's ignorance (and his apparent familiarity for readers) can be traced to a single concrete cause: Smaug's history – as well as the dwarves' and Bard's history – does not seem to be Bilbo's (or the reader's) history. It is no coincidence, however, that Gandalf elects Bilbo – who is, after all, related to "Bullroarer Took" (*H* 28) – for the part of the company's "burglar" (*H* 28). The battle of Green Fields – which is mentioned in the course of the 'Unexpected Party' and founds the fame of Bullroarer as a great warrior (cf. *H* 27) – creates an, albeit tenuous, link to the dwarves' epic history. It is this thread that Bilbo picks up when the 'Took side' prevails over his initial reluctance (cf. *H*

---

[15] Kinship and dynastic reasoning legitimate a 'King under the Mountain' as the embodiment of the 'same unchanging essence'. The king's individual identity is thus not independently constituted but *results* from his kingship; he possesses all the qualities of a king *because* he is king.

28). The journey towards the Lonely Mountain leads Bilbo ever more deeply into a historical world that increasingly becomes his own. Smaug, at the end of the road, marks the point where Bilbo is irrevocably anchored in this world. At the story's conclusion, Bilbo has become an 'elf-friend' and the friend of dwarves and wizards (cf. *H* 282).

Considering all the evidence, the *Edge of the Wild* must be interpreted as the exact line that separates fictional from historical narrative within the text – a conclusion that reverses Bauer's proposed reading. Bag-End and Bilbo the hobbit (as the reader first encounters him), Gandalf (who differs greatly from Gandalf in *The Lord of the Rings*) as well as the dwarves and the trolls[16] would all remain fairy-tale characters without the presence of the dragon.

The elves, on the other hand, emerge as adepts and carriers of history,[17] evidenced by Elrond's superior knowledge of sword-inscriptions and dwarven maps: his insight clearly surpasses that of the dwarves (cf. *H* 58pp.). Consistent with this characterisation, the elves are located on the far side of the dividing line. Smaug, the creature that ensures the accumulation of epic history and present events in the text, must then be located at the farthest point of the 'wilderness' – within the *realistic* sphere, that is.

As I have indicated above, the *Edge of the Wild* is immediately relevant on the level of reception as well. Modern readers are likely to assign Smaug to the realm of the *fantastic*, yet the same classification

---

[16] The trolls, who provide Bilbo with a first chance to prove his abilities as a 'burglar' at the beginning of the Quest, are not embedded in an epic context. William's speaking purse (cf. *H* 44) can be identified as an essential fairy-tale motive (reminiscent of folktale-giants, the trolls are finally turned to stone; cf. Simek 125). Bilbo's later theft of a cup from Smaug's hoard, on the other hand, can be easily related to the epic events in *Beowulf* (addressed in more detail below).

[17] Consequently, a connection between elven immortality (in *The Hobbit*, Elrond is identified as "[o]ne of those people whose fathers came into the strange stories before the beginning of History"; *H* 58) and the longevity of dragons (they live "practically for ever, unless they are killed"; *H* 32) seems plausible. The fact that elves and dragons exist in the story's present and, at the same time, in its epic past, lends them a historical depth beyond the scope of fairy-tales.

would necessarily apply to dwarves and hobbits. Bilbo, among all the protagonists, seems most familiar to readers because dragons play as marginal a part (if any) in his reality as they do in the reader's. However, Bilbo's demonstrable knowledge of dragons may suggest that readers, too, are expected to possess some knowledge of these creatures. With regard to *Beowulf*, Tolkien explains:

> Indeed this must be admitted to be practically certain: it was the existence of such connected legends – connected in the mind, not necessarily dealt with in chronicle fashion or in long semi-historical poems – that permitted the peculiar use of them in *Beowulf*. This poem cannot be criticized or comprehended, if its original audience is imagined in like case to ourselves, possessing only *Beowulf* in splendid isolation (*BMC* 31).

Readers who do not encounter *The Hobbit* in 'splendid isolation' will hardly overlook the parallel between the awakening of the dragon in *Beowulf* and that of Smaug. Indeed, the evident similarity has been described by various scholars (cf. Simek 137, Steele 139): both dragons rouse after a precious cup has been purloined from their hoard (cf. *Beowulf* V. 2280-2281; *H* 208). Yet Simek also points out that equating Smaug with the *Beowulf*-dragon does not do justice to the former (cf. 137). Comparison with the dragon in *Beowulf* indeed shows that Tolkien has *improved* Smaug in accordance with his own specifications for 'real' dragons. For instance, Smaug cannot be viewed as a spawn of hell, and it is equally impossible to situate him within a specifically Christian world-view (cf. *Beowulf* V. 2330-2333): Smaug acts out of his very own malice (as a result, he cannot be interpreted in terms of Christian allegory).

This impression largely relies on the incorporation of a second kinship: that between Smaug and Fáfnir, the dragon of the *Völsunga saga* and the *Poetic Edda*. When Smaug asks Bilbo who he is, the hobbit responds with skilful evasions, and the narrator comments: "This of course is the way to talk to dragons" (*H* 213) – an unmistakable reference to Sigurd. In response to the same question from Fáfnir, Sigurd replies:

> A wanderer named
> for a noble beast,
> the son of no mother,
> I had no father
> as other men do;
> Always I go alone
> (*Poems of the Elder Edda* 152).

Smaug's sinister predictions – concerning the dwarves' behaviour, should they ever regain the dragon-gold, and Bilbo's expectably bad end (cf. *H* 214pp.) – correspond to Fáfnir's warning when he asks Sigurd to beware of Regin and his hoard (cf. *Heldenlieder* 105pp.). Among other similarities, the fact that the dragon's soft underside is his most vulnerable spot (cf. *H* 215pp.; *Heldenlieder* 105) stands out.

In this context, it is important to note that the *same source* of knowledge regarding dragons and how to deal with them is (potentially) available to Bilbo, the narrator, and the reader.[18] (It is surely no coincidence that the narrator directly addresses the reader when he expounds the proper manner of conversing with a dragon.) Since the relevant knowledge about dragons in the world of *The Hobbit* stems from the same sources as it does in the reader's world, Smaug can be identified as the agent who draws the two worlds into close conjunction.

Sigurd from the *Poetic Edda* belongs to the same tradition as Siegfried in the Middle High German *Nibelungenlied*, which Max Wehrli

---

[18] Smaug in *The Hobbit* (and, as I will argue below, Tolkien's dragons in genereal) is indeed less *fantastic* than, for instance, Bilbo: witness the fact that the narrator has to explain who or what hobbits are (cf. *H* 14), while taking the reader's knowledge about dragons for granted.

describes in the following terms: "it reflects [...] the downfall of King Gundahari's Burgundian realm in the war against the Huns, mercenaries paid by the Roman Empire" (396).[19] Yet, in the German epic, the explicitly identified cause for this downfall is the hoard of the dragon that Siegfried slew: history and myth are inextricably entwined. The dragon cannot be extricated from this tangle: he becomes 'real' in the epic-historical sense (that is, he exists within the awareness of a well-versed audience), so that his presence extends into our world.

Vis-à-vis this configuration, there is Bilbo the hobbit whose connection with the reader's world is constructed across the dragon – albeit in the context of an alternative historical reality. The dragon, as it were, opens "a door on Other Time, and if we pass through [...], we stand outside our own time" (*OFS* 129).[20] Of course this particular construction of Time has nothing in common with the constructions employed by the modern discipline of history. *The Hobbit* can therefore be read in analogy to Tolkien's description of *Beowulf* as a "historical poem about the [...] past, or an attempt at one – literal historical fidelity founded on modern research was, of course, not attempted. It is a poem by a learned man writing of old times, who looking back on the heroism and sorrow feels in them something permanent" (*BMC* 26).

This reading requires a reversal of Bauer's interpretive scheme, however. If the *realistic* sphere is located left of the *Edge of the Wild* (as

---

[19] Original quote: "so spiegelt sich darin [...] der Untergang des burgundischen Reichs des Königs Gundahari im Kampf gegen die im römischen Sold stehenden Hunnen."

[20] The company's prolonged sitting "on the Doorstep" (*H* 194) shows that the time of Bilbo and the dwarves diverges from the temporal sphere in which Smaug may be found. (The reader's time differs yet again from the dwarves' time.) Yet the sunbeam that reveals the secret entrance's keyhole (cf. *H* 202) is not a manifestation of mere chance. Even before the proper beginning of the Quest, Bilbo suggests that 'sitting on the doorstep' will eventually provide access to Smaug's lair (*H* 35). Obviously, the secret entrance does not open at random: in order to gain entry, not only a historical connection (as evidenced by the map and key in Thorin's possession; cf. *H* 29pp.) but an individual 'doom' is required. For good reason, Gandalf insists "Just let any one say I chose the wrong man or the wrong house, and you can stop at thirteen and have all the bad luck you like" (*H* 29), when the dwarves express their (entirely justified) doubts about Bilbo's abilities.

Bauer suggests), *The Hobbit* would have to be classified as a story full of fairy-tale characters (such as dwarves, wizards, monsters, and dragons), a story that exemplifies what a world governed by "naïve moral standards" could be like (cf. Rötzer 84). Yet, if *The Hobbit* were populated only by fairy-tale characters, Smaug would be reduced to the final great danger in a series of other perils. Rötzer describes the fairy-tale as (phenomenologically) "sufficient unto itself, exhibiting no references beyond itself" (87): "The [fairy-tale] heroes do not project the future, [they] scarcely remember from the past" (80).[21] If Tolkien's protagonists were indeed fairy-tale characters (in Rötzer's sense of the word), they could not possess a "deep significance" either.

Once Bauer's paradigm is reversed and the dragon located in the *realistic* realm, we are looking at the story of a hero embedded in epically historical contexts that define his actions. *The Hobbit* may then be understood as a text that refers to older texts and traditions, populated by heroes – and dragons – that possess historical significance. The relevant epic-historical context that grounds *The Hobbit* becomes most tangible for readers in the presence of Smaug,[22] the dragon with whose epic

---

[21] Original quotes: "sich [phänomenologisch] selbst genügendes, das keinerlei Verweischarakter hat, außer auf sich selbst." "Die Helden [des Märchens] entwerfen nicht die Zukunft, erinnern kaum aus der Vergangenheit."

[22] One may indeed wonder if the dwarves in *The Hobbit* fulfil the same textual function as Smaug, considering that their descent, at least in name, can be traced back to the *Völuspá* (cf. Simek 59). Yet Tolkien's following statement seems to oppose the notion that the dwarves, too, point to epic history: "These dwarves are not quite the dwarfs of better known lore. They have been given Scandinavian names [...], but that is an editorial concession" (*L* 31). On the other hand, the 'Kingdom under the Mountain', to which the dwarves are bound, is inarguably an epically historical realm. The apparent contradiction can be resolved by assuming that the dwarves serve to make *different temporal layers* apparent in the text. (On the concept of the *chronotope*, cf. Gurjewitsch 140). The dwarves from the 'legendary, mythical era' of the 'Kingdom under the Mountain' are transformed into a time which, while still belonging to the past, is not absolutely separated from the reader's time by epical distance. The dwarves are, in this sense, doubled (cf. Gurjewitsch 140). This reading gains support from the notable differences in dwarvish behaviour at different points of the story. Thorin and his speech at the 'Unexpected Party' are characterised by terms such as "plans, ways, means, policy" (*H* 26). A remarkably different Thorin appears at the Battle of Five Armies, where he joins the fray with the battle-cry "To me! To me! Elves and Men! To me! Oh my kinsfolk!" (*H* 263). Evidently, the dwarves at Bag-End are (like Bilbo) located on the 'margins' of

analogues the reader is (or may be) familiar. The dragon unlocks dimensions of meaning that point to a historical narrative beyond fairy-tales. It therefore seems just as reasonable to assign everything on the right side of the *Edge of the Wild* to the *realistic* sphere: a sphere that differs from our contemporary understanding of realism and which begins with the dragon.

## *ROVERANDOM* – THE DRAGON WITHIN 'FAËRIAN DRAMA'

To what an extent can this interpretive model be applied to other dragons in Tolkien's works? Since detailed analysis of the various dragons would exceed the scope of this essay, *Roverandom* may serve as a particularly illuminating example. A wandering wizard plunges the hero of *Roverandom*, just like Bilbo, into adventures he had never dreamed of. Second, the dragon that plays a significant part in this text is not resembling Smaug.[23]

Structurally, the plot of *Roverandom* can be divided into three parts: the moon episode, the episode in the underwater realm, and the episodes on earth that function as a frame for the main narrative.

---

263). Evidently, the dwarves at Bag-End are (like Bilbo) located on the 'margins' of the epically historical realm and have lost contact with it. The text provides ample evidence for this loss: the dwarves are no longer able to detect 'moon-letters' (cf. *H* 60), and – even more strikingly – no dwarf is capable of calculating Durin's Day (cf. *H* 60.). These characteristics mark a clear difference between the dwarves and Smaug whose existence belongs to a single temporal vector, that of epic-historical time.

[23] At least comparison of Tolkien's illustrations for both texts suggests a certain similarity (cf. Hammond and Scull 81, 94).

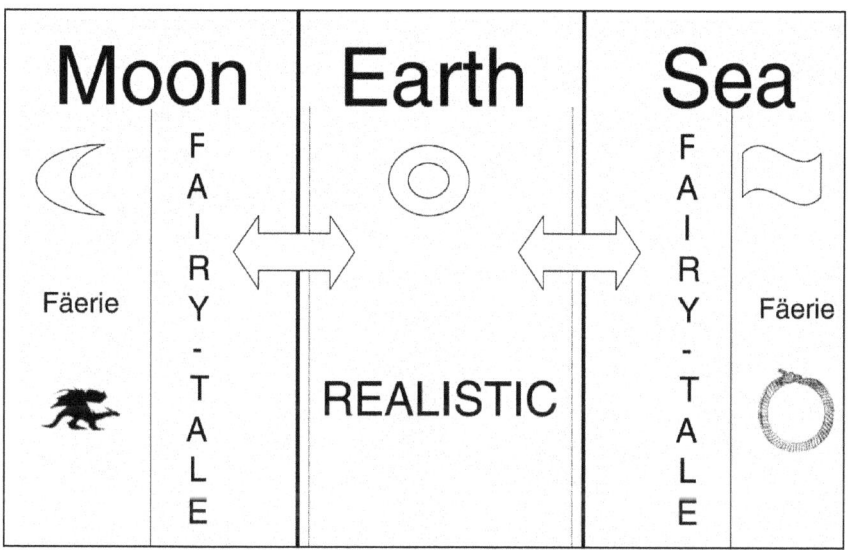

Fig. 3: Basic structure of Roverandom

A reading based on Bauer's paradigm would identify earth as the realm most closely connected to the *realistic* sphere. Events that occur on earth generally match the modern reader's reality and the concomitant order of meaning. Small dogs are just as familiar as their habit of playing with balls (cf. *R* 3); the shopping trip, overall, takes place exactly as readers will expect from their own experience (*R* 5pp.). However, the existence of another world, contiguous to the familiar world, soon becomes apparent: this second world is not organized by the familiar ('enlightened' or rational) order of knowledge. (As mentioned with regard to *The Hobbit*, wandering wizards do not belong to a post-Enlightenment reality, and one rather hopes that the shrimps' complaint does not sound from the reader's shopping basket.)

While the dragon in *Roverandom* must stay at the centre of our investigation, the opening scenes on earth deserve at least brief consideration, in order to characterise the setting. Rover the dog is turned into a toy because he misbehaves. While growling and making demands without so much as a 'please' are inappropriate not only in the company of wizards, in defence of Rover it must be noted that the wizard Artaxerxes is hardly more polite than the little dog (cf. *R* 5). Nevertheless Rover has to face the more dire consequences, for he is magically transformed into a toy. This transformation initiates the plot which is consistently laced with fairy-tale motifs: only after midnight can the toy dog begin to move (cf. *R* 5, 92), the moon-flowers that bear names such as "the whitebells, the fairbells, the silverbells, the tinklebells [...], the ringarose [...], the creamhorns" (*R* 28) rather seem to have escaped from a Disney-picture. The moon itself is peopled by the "moonums" (moon-gnomes), among other creatures, "that ride about on rabbits, and make pancakes out of snowflakes, and grow little golden apple-trees no bigger than buttercups in their neat orchards" (*R* 49), while Artaxerxes travels the sea in "a gigantic shell shaped like a cockle and drawn by seven sharks" (*R* 75).

At this point, a verdict Tolkien articulates in *On Fairy-Stories* must come to mind. Tolkien takes exception to the "prettiness" of Drayton's *Nymphidia* – "The knight Pigwiggen rides on a frisky earwing, and sends his love [...] a bracelet of emmets' eyes, making an assignation in a cowslip-flower" (*OFS* 112) – and ultimately dismisses the poem as "one of the worst [fairy-stories] ever written" (*OFS* 111). This explicit rejection suggests that, while he was working on *Roverandom*, Tolkien either did not take his own concept of a successful fairy-story quite as seriously as he did in later years, or that he had not yet developed the concept to the degree of consistency exhibited in the essay. The fact that *Roverandom* belongs to Tolkien's early works would seem to support such a conclusion – if it wasn't for the dragon.

The moon-dragon in *Roverandom* lives on "the shadowy edge of the dark side", an area "where all sorts of half-forgotten things linger, and paths and memories get confused" (*R* 31). At the same time, this area is the final destination for the dreams made by the Man-in-the-Moon in his tower (cf. *R* 30). The coexistence of dreams and dragons at this particular site is significant. A conceptual reason for this connection can be gleaned from Tolkien's explanations regarding 'Faërian Drama': "Now 'Faërian Drama' [...] can produce Fantasy with [...] realism and immediacy [...]. As a result their usual effect (upon a man) is to go beyond Secondary Belief. If you are present at a Faërian drama you yourself are [...] bodily inside its Secondary World. The experience may be very similar to Dreaming" (*OFS* 142). The dragon evokes the same kind of experience, for, as Tolkien notes, he "had the trade-mark *Of Faërie* written plain upon him. In whatever world he had his being it was an Other-world. Fantasy, the making or glimpsing of Other-worlds, was the heart of the desire of Faërie" (*OFS* 135).

In keeping with these observations, things on the dark side of the moon evidently belong to a reality that differs from the white-side reality. They are, or can become, true, as the conversation between Rover and the Man-in-the-Moon illustrates: "'Do dreams come true?' he asked. 'Some of mine do,' said the old man" (*R* 46). The end of the story demonstrates that both worlds can merge into one at a certain point, for little boy Two is capable of telling Rover's story (cf. *R* 88). Rover's 'real' experiences and the boy's dream coincide: rather than being assigned to separate categories of 'reality', dream and narrated events are identical.

It is thus no coincidence that the Great White Dragon occupies the boundary of the moon's dark side (cf. *R* 31pp.), for the moon-dragon is a familiar creature with a distinct connection to the reader's world: he derives from Arthurian epic. His fabled battle with the Red Dragon[24] is furthermore presented as a factual event – beyond the spe-

---

[24] When King Vortigern has a fortress built in defence against the Saxons, the stones brought to the site during the day always vanish at night. Merlin, called to the site, manages to divine the cause of this mystifying disappearance: a pair of dragons, one red, the other white, live beneath the soil. When Vortigern's men excavate the site, the dragons engage in a fight from which the red dragon emerges victorious. Asked about the significance of these events, Merlin interprets the dragons' fight as a prophecy foretelling Vortigern's victory over the Saxons (cf. *Antikensagas* 96pp.).

cifically epic amount of 'truth' (cf. *Antikensagas* 108) – for, according to *Roverandom*, this battle can be found "in all the more up-to-date history books" (*R* 33). In fact, Walther Martin, in his afterword to the German translation of Malory's *Morte Darthur*, answers the question of King Arthur's actual existence with a "we do not know for sure" (*König Artus* 1018).[25] The king, a potentially historical figure in the modern sense,[26] provides a chance for the dragon to become equally historical. (Needless to say, such a question does not arise for the pre-modern audience of epics.)

In *Roverandom*, the dragon's existence unquestionably extends into the reader's 'real' world: the man who was scared off by the dragon and left a bottle on top of Snowdon is not an epic character but – a tourist (cf. *R* 33, 102). (However, the dragon must have moved on in the meantime, for Snowdon made an altogether tidy impression not long ago.) Equally, locations mentioned in *Roverandom* overlap with those of Arthurian legend and with commonplace geography. Even though Caerdragon, the site of the dragons' battle in *Roverandom*, exists only in Tolkien's text (cf. *R* 33),[27] the "Three Islands" (i.e. England, Scotland, and Wales) as well as Snowdon (the highest mountain in Wales; cf. *R* 43) can be easily located within both pre-modern and modern geography. Legendary and historical elements are inextricably entangled in this episode. The dragon grounds these elements in reality and thereby renders it impossible to interpret them as mere fairy-tale motifs.

---

[25] Original quote: "Wir wissen es nicht genau."
[26] That the historical existence of King Arthur may seem plausible to modern recipients is evidenced by various television programmes in pursuit of historical proof.
[27] The dragons' legendary fight took place in Dinas Emrys or Nant Gwynant in Snowdonia (cf. *R* 102; Voß 362).

The "accord of the fairy-tale's narrative core with that of the historical-heroic legend or that of myth" (Rötzer 19)[28] is thus brought to the narrative surface by the dragon. The result may be described as a transition into Faërie. While fairy-tales are characterised by the lack of specific coordinates in time and space, thereby allowing for a universal experience and its 'applicability', the epic locates both the marvellous and the familiar in a historical context, defined by a specific time and place (cf. Rötzer 7pp.) – a configuration that defies universal applicability. Faërie, as Tolkien defines it, dissolves the discrepancy between history and story. While it is marked by "distance and a great abyss of time, not measurable even by *twe tusend Johr*" (*OFS* 128), it exists in a historical context whose temporal and spatial coordinates, however, remain indeterminate. Contact between the (epic) dragon and fairy-tale motifs (which possess universal applicability) transports the latter, and thus the entire text, into the sphere of Faërie. Because of this shift, the text resists the common approach to fairy-tales – which, in modern literary criticism and historical research, focuses on didactic, psychological or anthropological aspects (cf. Brackert 7).

The moon-dragon in *Roverandom* provides a quintessential illustration of the principle described above. He links the fairy-tale elements on the white side of the moon to a context beyond the scope of fairy-tales. It is therefore noteworthy that all white dragons "originally come from the moon", namely from the dark side (cf. *R* 33). Since this region is also the destination of dreams, dragons evidently originate within "Fantasy", in Tolkien's definition (cf. *OFS* 138pp.). However, the White Dragon does not emerge from the dreams created by the Man-in-the-Moon. That he is well-nigh the Man's equal (cf. *R* 33) indicates that, beyond belonging to Faërie, the dragon possesses independent epic reality. The White Dragon of *Roverandom* occupies a site on earth (a flat

---

[28] Original quote: "Übereinstimmung des Erzählkerns im Märchen mit dem der historischen oder Heldensage bzw. des Mythos".

earth in this text; cf. *R* 73pp.) as well as a site within the epically historical world and, ultimately, within the reader's world, thus blurring the boundary that divides *fantastic* from *real* and rendering it permeable.

Little boy Two dreams of events related in *Roverandom* while Rover experiences them: there is no other reasonable explanation for the boy's concluding knowledge of the story. Equally, the fact that the Man-in-the-Moon "seems busier than I [moon-Rover] have seen him for a long time, since you [Roverandom] arrived" (*R* 29) suggests a direct link between Roverandom's experiences, the dreams made by the Man-in-the-Moon, and the boy's dreams.

At this point, reconsidering the entry into Faërie may prove useful. As demonstrated above, a transition from fairy-tale realm to epic-historical sphere takes place on the boundary between the white and the dark side of the moon – a boundary represented by the dragon. Attentive readers cannot overlook the fact that *Roverandom* describes another access to the dark side: "the moon rose up out of the sea, and laid the silver path across the waters that is the way to places at the edge of the world and beyond, for those that can walk on it" (*R* 8). This description brings to mind the specific constellation that reveals the secret entrance to Smaug's lair: "The little moon was dipping to the horizon. [...] Then suddenly [...] a red ray of the sun escaped like a finger through a rent in the cloud. A gleam of light came straight through the opening into the bay and fell on the smooth rock-face" (*H* 202). While Bilbo and the dwarves gain access to the tunnel as a result, the narrator in *Roverandom* emphasises that not everyone may tread the path he describes. This remark points out the most salient difference between *Roverandom* and *The Hobbit*.

While *The Hobbit* moves epic themes and contexts to the centre of the plot, they remain marginal in *Roverandom*. However, this does not diminish the epic quality of the White Dragon. Instead, the dragon lends a certain historical depth to the toy dog Roverandom and his world, which would otherwise remain completely within the sphere of fairy-tales. At the same time, the dragon separates a fairy-tale plot from the epically historical realm. Rover may reach the moon (albeit only the white side) and enter the fairy-tale regions of the underwater realm (cf. *R* 58pp.), but remains excluded from epic events. Whereas Smaug's awakening sets an epic course of events in motion (for which he is indeed indispensable), the two Rovers are merely driven off as a result of their encounter with the moon-dragon (cf. *R* 34pp.).

It seems that accessing the dark side of the moon by means of the silver moonbeams alone does not allow for an entry into the epic-historical sphere. Rover, the toy dog, lives in the immediate vicinity of the epic dragon (and the Sea-serpent), yet their world ultimately remains inaccessible to him. The moon-dragon drives him away; his adventure with the Sea-serpent almost causes the destruction of the entire submarine world (cf. *R* 79). The division emerges most clearly from the description of the dogs' journey with Uin the whale, in the course of which they "passed the Shadowy Seas and reached the great Bay of Fairyland [...] beyond the Magic Isles; and saw far off in the last West the Mountains of Elvenhome and the light of Faery upon the waves." As Uin says afterwards: "No one from the Outer Lands is supposed ever to come here; and few ever do now." (*R* 73pp.).

The moonbeams belong to the Man-in-the-Moon's domain (hence his recurring admonition "Don't worry the moonbeams"; *R* 26), and the dreams that one may reach across them may become as true as the history of the battle between the Red and the White Dragon. Apparently, these rays can unlock a door into the epically historical realm if 'doom' predicts such a pathway, as it does in the case of Bilbo, Thorin and the other dwarves. (Yet the dragon always lies in wait on the other side.) For toy dogs, on the other hand, they may unclose a path into the fairy-tale realm. That the White Dragon "was only half-afraid of the Man [-in-the-Moon] (and scarcely that when he was angry)" (*R* 33) once again points to his epic dimension. Because of it, the dragon is capable of bursting forth (from and within the text) at any given moment, to erase every reference to a fairy-tale world. And this, too, is the reason why the dragon leads a life of his own, beyond individual experience or history.

On the whole, the story of Roverandom can be read as an alternative explanation for the whereabouts of a little dog – a fairy-tale explanation, that is. Yet the dragon connects this story to a historical world in the epical sense: he bursts into the fairy-tale plot as a 'real' dragon – not an allegory – to establish historicity and 'truth'.

The dragon in *Roverandom* can thus be read as a means and a mainstay for the historical grounding of the entire story. This connection hinges on a system of meaning that differs profoundly from the empirical-descriptive order of knowledge which governs modernity. At the same time, an individual interpretation of the world – in this case, an interpretation concerning the fate of a missing dog – gains relevance beyond the *fantastic* element. Rather than relying on allegory (or immediate applicability), the story's relevance stems from epic-historical contexts and connections.[29]

Unlike the above-mentioned *Nymphidia*, *Roverandom* does not draw on fairy-tale elements to tell a story that could equally occur in the measurable empirical world. *Nymphidia* deals with betrayal and jealousy – and that is indeed Tolkien's chief criticism (*OFS* 112: "a dull story of intrigue and sly go-betweens"). By contrast, fairy-tale aspects in *Roverandom* are not employed to portray events that could, without difficulty, take place on the *realistic* level. Instead, Rover's story charts an alternative world in which the dragon creates a link with the epically

---

[29] Although the dogs in *Roverandom* cannot enter the epic sphere, the dispute of seniority among the three Rovers could be interpreted as an attempt to gain entry (cf. *R* 24, 65). Similarly, the story of the sea-rover and his "strange fate" in particular seem to illustrate such a claim, symbolised not least by his first master's dragon-ship and its wreck in a naval battle (cf. *R* 65pp.).

historical realm and thereby ensures its connection to the reader's world in a manner that exceeds allegory and generates historical significance.[30]

## "I DESIRED DRAGONS"

How does one approach Tolkien's dragons? What exactly are they? Fictitious creatures or creatures from the *realistic* realm, as Bauer labels it? What is their precise relation to the allegory of the tower in Tolkien's essay on *Beowulf*? In order to answer these questions, it must be pointed out first that the terms 'fairy-story', 'fairy-tale' (*Märchen*), 'myth', 'epic' and 'truth' are, in Tolkien's academic texts, just as inextricably entwined as historical and fairy-tale elements are within the epic. This entanglement evidently results from a basic condition opposed to our dichotomic mode of thinking. As Sigrid Löffler writes, Tolkien's stories are "at the same time true and invented. [For the reader they are just as] true and as invented as Malory's 'Morte d'Arthur'" (9).[31] The concept that something may be true (i.e. real) and at the same time imaginary is indeed at odds with the mode of thought that has become hegemonic since the Enlightenment.

Indisputably, "it is [...] absolutely impossible to conceive of meaning without order" (Lévi-Strauss 12). Within the post-Enlightenment orders of meaning, truth (i.e. 'objective' knowledge) is constituted by means of empirical research and measurability, based on an assumed objectivity. Lévi-Strauss states that "in our own societies, history has replaced mythology and fulfils the same function" (42). This observation explains why the *fantastic* realm – more specifically, the sphere Tolkien calls Faërie (cf. *OFS* 11pp.), where dragons dwell – cannot meet the reader's demand for objectivity, truth and newly established knowl-

---

[30] Detailed analysis of the episodes in the sea and of the significance of the Sea-serpent (another dragon) would lead to similar conclusions.

[31] Original quote: "wahr und erfunden zugleich. [Sie sind für den Leser ebenso] wahr und so erfunden wie Malorys «Morte d'Arthur»."

edge. The *fantastic* can obtain a place and become meaningful within the system of empirical perception only insofar as it can be 'translated' – "not [into] a different language like French or German, but [into] different words on a different level" (Lévi-Strauss 12), into a *different meaning*, that is. *Nymphidia*, for instance, provides a different mode of addressing adultery and jealousy as they occur within the *realistic* world. The poem thus exemplifies "the confrontation of the (universally familiar) reality with a different version of the same reality" (Luhmann 383).[32] In accordance with this principle, *Nymphidia* gains relevance within the reader's world.

Clearly, this does not match Tolkien's conception of a successful fairy-story, and his rejection of allegorical readings in general requires no further comment. In his examination of myth, Lévi-Strauss distinguishes between "scientific thought and [...] the logic of the concrete" (13).[33] The order of knowledge that constitutes the world of myth evidently cannot be grasped by empirical means. Moreover, as Lévi-Strauss insists, "the opposition – the simple opposition between mythology and history which we are accustomed to make – is not at all a clear-cut one" (40). History may thus be conveyed in a mode unfamiliar to modern readers and will be recognized only if an order of perception is brought to bear that differs in essence from the scientific paradigm of Modernity. It is this approach that Tolkien adopts in his *Beowulf* essay as well.

Accordingly, the geography of *Beowulf* does not match modern cartography, although the epic's space was once located in the world that has been charted since that time (a time when the world was still flat). In the realms of *Beowulf* (as in those of the *Völsunga saga* or Arthu-

---

[32] Original quote: "die Konfrontierung der (jedermann geläufigen) Realität mit einer anderen Version derselben Realität".

[33] In Owen Barfield's terms, such a 'logic of the concrete' involves "participation [which] as an actual *experience*, is only to be won for [a modern islanded consciousness] by special exertion. It is a matter, not of theorizing, but of 'imagination' in the genial or creative sense of the world" (89).

rian legend), there is room for the dragon – a space that has been lost amidst the countries of modern maps. The order of knowledge that constitutes this world differs fundamentally from its post-Enlightenment counterpart, yet this world is governed by discourses, laws and probabilities that possess a coherence of their own. They are, in fact, just as coherent as the laws that construct the modern reader's perception of the world.

Within this world, it is far more probable that a little dog has to confront wizards and dragons on the moon and in the sea than that he has simply run away (as Rover's original owner, the boy's grandmother, assumes; cf. *R* 88). The assumption that the dragon whom the dog encounters once walked our familiar earth when it was still flat is, within history, just as plausible as an interpretation that identifies little boy Two with Tolkien's son Michael (cf. Hammond and Scull in *R* 93). Ultimately, everything depends on the order of knowledge one applies to the text.

If the dragon is "no idle fancy", a confrontation of the universally familiar reality with a *radically different* reality ensues – for modern readers, that is, not for an audience immersed in epic-historical storytelling and a different order of knowledge. For the latter world-view, dragons are 'more true' than little dogs that get lost or hosts of a tea-party with entirely too disruptive guests. The dragon, once native to the world that has become our own, can create a connection between this world and ours.

Tolkien is in agreement with Lévi-Strauss where the necessity for different rules in, and different modes of access to, the other world is concerned: "The significance of a myth is not easily to be pinned on paper by analytical reasoning. It is at its best when it is presented by a poet who feels rather than makes explicit what his theme portends; who presents it incarnate in the world of history and geography, as [the *Beowulf* poet] has done" (*BMC* 15; cf. Lévi-Strauss 11pp.). This statement points beyond the mere 'internal coherence' of the depicted world, achieved by the application of a different logic. Epic 'truth', which reaches beyond such a coherent construction, results from (the contemporary listeners') collective memory of something specifically familiar, distinguishing it from the fairy-tale with its (almost entirely) self-sufficient system of meaning (cf. Jauss 314). The specific order of knowledge that generates truth in the world of myth, of the epic, and of Faërie is not founded on empirical science: it is, as Tolkien explains it, a poetological concept.

The truth constituted in this manner differs from the constructions of modern sciences, yet the truth generated by poetic speech (or writing) is no less 'real'. Ultimately, the queries framed by two discrepant orders of knowledge define the transmitted historical 'truth'. Whereas modern sciences examine the when, why, and wherefore and study the connections between the real, *relative* past and the present, epic transmission centres on the question: how did these events unfold in the past? The past in question is an *absolute* past that can no longer be experienced directly (cf. Bakthin 19); instead it is perceived as an "illusion of surveying a past" (*BMC* 27). "[R]eal dragons, *essential both to the machinery and the ideas* of a poem or tale" (*BMC* 12; emphasis added), are among its constituents. (They contribute answers to the question *how* epic history came to pass.) This may indeed be the reason why Tolkien states: "I desired dragons with a profound desire" (*OFS* 135). The 'real' dragon is a motif that generates an alternative reality by suspending ours, thus establishing a radically different possible world.

The 'real' dragon guards the boundary between our perception of the world and the mythical or epic-historical reality and opens up a passage into that world, beyond historical research or anthropology[34] – for

---

[34] In *Farmer Giles of Ham*, the story of the sword Tailbiter is revealed only when the 'real' dragon Chrysophylax 'comes' (cf. *FGH* 54). Simultaneously, the story discloses the 'true' historical context for the initially strange tradition of having a Christmas cake shaped like a dragon's tail (cf. *FGH* 32). The same mechanism stands out in *The Lord of*

when the dragon comes, the rules of modern experience are no longer valid. Similarly, the tower in Tolkien's essay on *Beowulf* represents a structure that does not generate meaning from empirically verifiable facts as modern science does (an approach that destroys the tower and banishes the dragon). Instead, meaning emerges from poetic expression and reception, rendering the story "largely significant – as a whole, accepted unanalysed" (*BMC* 15).

The dragon thus opens the door to a world located in ours, yet not identical with it – the world of the epic-historical past, "a past that itself had depth and reached backward into a dark antiquity of sorrow" (*BMC* 27). We can look for it from the top of the tower or reach it by travelling on the moonbeams' silver path. Yet when "the dragon comes" (*BMC* 34), we are unquestionably there.[35]

A dragon is a *drake* is a *wyrm*.

PATRICK BRÜCKNER is a student of German Medieval Literature, Women's Studies and Sociology at the University of Potsdam. He is working on aspects of gender in the works of J.R.R. Tolkien. He held joint seminars with Judith Klinger on 'Tolkien and the Middle Ages' at the University of Potsdam. His publications include: "*Zur Konstruktion 'richtiger' Weiblichkeit in J.R.R. Tolkiens Lord of the Rings*" (Masquerade and Essence, Death and Desire. The construction of 'correct' femininity in J.R.R. Tolkien's The Lord of the Rings) in *Hither Shore 2* (Yearbook of the German Tolkien Society) and "*Tolkien on Love*" in *Tolkien and Modernity*.

## Works Cited

Bakhtin, Mikhail M. "Epic and Novel." *The Dialogic Imagination. Four Essays by M. M. Bakhtin.* Ed. Michael Holquist. Austin: University of Texas Press 1981. 3-40.

Barfield, Owen. *Saving the Appearances. A Study in Idolatry.* Middletown, Connecticut: Wesleyan University Press, 1988.

---

[35] *the Rings* where the dragon of Gandalf's fireworks (*LotR* 27) can be read as a sign for the transition from a 'private' world to epic-historical conditions.

I am most grateful to Judith Klinger for her translation and support and Sandra Schramm for her support.

Bauer, Hanspeter. *Die Verfahren der Textbildung in J. R. R. Tolkiens 'The Hobbit'*. Bern, Frankfurt & New York: Peter Lang, 1983.

*Beowulf. Das Angelsächsische Heldenepos*. Ed. Hans-Jürgen Hube. Prosaübersetzung, Originaltext, versgetreue Stabreimfassung. Wiesbaden: Matrixverlag, 2005.

Brackert, Helmut. *Und wenn sie nicht gestorben sind ... Perspektiven auf das Märchen*. Frankfurt: Suhrkamp, 1982.

Carpenter, Humphrey. Ed. *The Letters of J. R. R. Tolkien*. Paperback ed. New York & Boston: Houghton Mifflin, 2000.

Chrestien de Troyes. *Yvain*. Hg. und Übersetzung Ilse Nolting-Hauff. Altfranzösisch/Deutsch. München: Wilhelm Fink Verlag, 1983.

Giloy-Hirtz, Petra. "Begegnung mit dem Ungeheuer." *An den Grenzen höfischer Kultur. Anfechtungen der Lebensordnung in der deutschen Erzähldichtung des hohen Mittelalters*. Ed. Gert Kaiser. München: Wilhelm Fink Verlag, 1991. 167-210.

Gottfried von Straßburg. *Tristan*. Hg. und Übersetzung Rüdiger Krohn. Mittelhochdeutsch/Neuhochdeutsch. 2 vols. Stuttgart: RUB, 1981.

Gurjewitsch, Aaron J. "Das »Chronotopos« des »Nibelungenlieds«". *Stumme Zeugen des Mittelalters*. Ed. Aaron J. Gurjewitsch. Frankfurt: Fischer Taschenbuch, 2000. 129-149.

Hammond, Wayne G. and Christina Scull. *J. R. R. Tolkien: Artist & Illustrator*. London, HarperCollins, 1998.

Haug, Walter. "Von der Schwierigkeit heimzukehren. Die Walthersage in ihrem motivgeschichtlichen und literaturantropologischen Kontext." *Die Wahrheit der Fiktion. Studien zur weltlichen und geistlichen Literatur des Mittelalters und der frühen Neuzeit*. Ed. Walter Haug. Tübingen: Max Niemeyer Verlag, 2003. 315-329.

*Isländische Antikensagas*. Vol. 1. Übersetzt von Stefanie Würth. München: Diederichs, 1996.

Jauss, Hans Robert. "Epos und Roman – Eine vergleichende Betrachtung an Texten des XII[.] Jahrhunderts." *Alterität und Modernität der mittelalterlichen Literatur. Gesammelte Aufsätze 1956-1976*. München: Wilhelm Fink Verlag, 1977. 310-327.

Lévi-Strauss, Claude. *Myth and Meaning. Talks were broadcast on the CBC Radio series, Ideas in December 1977*. New York: Schocken Books, 1979.

Löffler, Siegrid. "'Ein Drache ist kein eitler Wahn'." *Literaturen* 3 (2002): 4-10.

Luhmann, Niklas. "Das Kunstwerk und die Selbstreproduktion der Kunst." *Texte zur Literaturtheorie der Gegenwart*. Ed. Dorothee Kimmich et al. Stuttgart: RUB, 1996. 379-392.

Malory, Thomas. *Die Geschichte von König Artus und den Rittern seiner Tafelrunde*. 3 vols. Ed. Helmut Findeisen. Leipzig: Insel-Verlag, 1977.

Petersen, Jürgen H. *Erzählsysteme. Eine Poetik epischer Texte*. Stuttgart: Metzler, 1993.

*Poems of the Elder Edda.* Translated by Patricia Terry. Philadelphia: University of Pennsylvania Press, 1991.

Rötzer, Hans Gert. *Märchen.* Bamberg: Buchners Verlag, 1982.

Scull, Christina. "Dragons from Andrew Lang's Retelling of Sigurd to Tolkien's Chrysophylax." *Leaves from the Tree. J. R. R. Tolkien's Shorter Fiction. The 4$^{th}$ Tolkien Society Workshop.* Ed. Tom Shippey et al. London: The Tolkien Society, 1991. 49-62.

Shippey, Tom. *J. R. R. Tolkien. Author of the Century.* Paperback ed. London: HarperCollins, 2001.

Simek, Rudolf. *Mittelerde. Tolkien und die germanische Mythologie.* München: C. H. Beck, 2005.

Steele, Felicia Jean. "Dreaming of Dragons: Tolkien's Impact on Heaney's *Beowulf.*" *Mythlore* Volume 25, Number 1/2 (Fall/Winter 2006): 137-146.

Tolkien, John Ronald Reuel. "Beowulf: The Monster and the Critics". *The Monsters and the Critics and Other Essays.* Ed. Christopher Tolkien. London: HarperCollins, 2006. 5-48.

---, *Farmer Giles of Ham / Bauer Giles von Ham.* Zweisprachig. München: DTV, 1999.

---, "On Fairy-Stories." *The Monsters and the Critics and Other Essays.* Ed. Christopher Tolkien. London: HarperCollins, 2006. 109-161.

---, *The History of the Hobbit* (vol. 2). *Return to Bag-End.* Ed. John D. Rateliff. London: HarperCollinsPublishers, 2007.

---, *Roverandom.* Ed. Christina Scull and Wayne G. Hammond. Paperback ed. London: HarperCollins, 2002.

---, *The Hobbit, or, There and back again.* Paperback ed. London & Sydney: Allen & Unwin 1983.

---, *The Lord of the Rings.* One volume paperback ed. London: HarperCollinsPublishers, 1995.

Unzeitig-Herzog, Monika. "Vom Sieg über den Drachen: alte und neue Helden." *Chevaliers errants, demoiselles et l'Autre: höfische und nachhöfische Literatur im europäischen Mittelalter. Festschrift für Xenja von Ertzdorff zum 65. Geburtstag.* Ed. Trude Ehlert. Göppingen: Kümmerle Verlag, 1998. 41-61.

Ulrich von Zatzikhoven: *Lanzelet.* Ed. Karl A. Hahn. Berlin: De Gruyter, 1965.

Voß, Karl. *England und Wales. Reiseführer für Literaturfreunde.* Frankfurt: Ullstein, 1989.

Wehrli, Max. *Geschichte der deutschen Literatur im Mittelalter. Von den Anfängen bis zum 16. Jahrhundert.* Stuttgart: RUB, 1997.

# Theology and Fairy-Stories: A Theological Reading of Tolkien's Shorter Works?

THOMAS FORNET-PONSE[1]

ABSTRACT

This article will examine the possibility of a theological reading of Tolkien's shorter works by theologically analyzing his essay "On Fairy-stories" concerning the aspects of his theory of sub-creation, the functions of fantasy (Recovery, Escape and Consolation) and the connection between fantasy and *evangelium*. Thus, it will be shown that Tolkien depicts the creative activity of Man as analogous to God's creating activity and as necessary for accomplishing his own likeness to god. Although Tolkien does not deny the Fall, it does not abrogate the right to be creatively active. Arising out of Man's creative activity, successful fantasy can be – by its functions Recovery, Escape and Consolation and the eucatastrophe contained in it – a gleam of *evangelium*.

The second part of the paper deals with four shorter works and the way in which these elements are present in them: *Roverandom*, *Leaf by Niggle*, *Farmer Giles of Ham*, and *Smith of Wootton Major*. Whereas *Roverandom* shows clearly how Tolkien worked as a sub-creator and how his depiction of Faërie and fairy-stories changed, *Leaf by Niggle* and *Smith of Wootton Major* cannot be regarded as classical fairy-stories either, since they illustrate narratively the central characteristics for a fairy-story which are demanded by Tolkien. Only *Farmer Giles of Ham* seems to represent the main characteristics as a story and not a narrative illustration of a concept. But each of the four analyzed works support Tolkien's theory of sub-creation and fantasy in its own way.

INTRODUCTION

A theological reading of Tolkien's shorter works? Whereas this might suggest itself in the case of *Leaf by Niggle* and seems helpful with *Smith of Wootton Major*, it does not appear so with works like *Farmer Giles of*

---

[1] I want to thank Heidi Steimel for carefully proof-reading this article.

*Ham* or *Roverandom*. The parody of a medieval text or the travel-story of an enchanted dog do not seem to have any theological meaning.

However, a specifically theological as well as a specifically Tolkienian foundation of a theological reading of the shorter works exists. The genuine theological one for which I wish to argue is based on some convictions of intercultural philosophy; theology has "to widen its field of theological rationality, or – better said – to not restrict this field on the areas ruled by logical categories or analytical concepts" (Fornet-Betancourt 194; my translation). Therefore, the limits of a rational theological discourse do not necessarily have to correspond with the limits of a strict categorial knowledge which is logically-conceptually and analytically orientated. Encountering poetry and literature, theology learns to esteem folksongs, legends, oral traditions and so on especially for their hermeneutical and cognitial relevance. Similarly to this, in his fundamental reflections on salvation history and salvation in the history of theology the renowned liberation theologian Ignacio Ellacuría SJ demands: "Faith and theology must take the world of today in all seriousness" (Ellacuría 7). Eventually, theology has to orientate itself towards the situations and needs of real life. "Now if the growth of the *saeculum* (the temporalized world) and the decline of the sacral-religious realm are facts, it is obvious that only a secularized faith and theology have, or can have, complete meaning for an increasingly secularized world" (Ellacuría 7). Therefore, in my opinion, it is necessary for a theologian to reflect especially on the elements of a secularized culture – for example fantasy as a very influential current in popular culture..

Epistemologically expressed, human culture and human art are *loci theologici* – no doubt *alieni* (recurring to Cano's typology), but nevertheless *loci theologici*. For the initial sentence of Vatican II pastoral constitution *Gaudium et spes* is still valid:

> The joys and the hopes, the griefs and the anxieties of the men of this age, especially those who are poor or in any way

afflicted, these are the joys and hopes, the griefs and anxieties of the followers of Christ. Indeed, nothing genuinely human fails to raise an echo in their hearts. (GS 1)

That does not limit a theological examination of works of art and culture only to those with obvious theological or religious connotations, but also includes those seemingly secular.

The specific Tolkienian grounds are expressed in "Mythopoeia" and "On Fairy-stories". The possible basis for a theological reading even of those fairy-stories which do not explicitly contain religion or religious elements consists in Tolkien's concept of sub-creation and the functions of fairy stories because in successful fairy-stories there may be a "far-off gleam or echo of *evangelium*" (*FS* 71).

Before turning to the shorter works mentioned above and depicting some of the elements that may be of interest for theology, I will discuss the theological implications of Tolkien's concept of sub-creation.

## SUB-CREATION AND FANTASY
### TOLKIEN'S THEORY OF SUB-CREATION[2]

At first it is important to mention some conditions of the Primary World Tolkien believed in and which are necessary for his concept of sub-creation (but which had also an impact on his Legendarium). First, there exists an (almighty) God who created all things. Second, this God created free beings as his image in his likeness. Third, Man fell and his ontological status was substantially changed with this fall.

---

[2] Cf. in general Birzer 37-44; Ferré 92-96; Flieger 40-48 and Agøy for a comparison of Tolkien's and Grundtvig's position. He bases his explanations on the conviction that Tolkien's theory of sub-creation is rooted in a deeply felt personal theological dilemma and concludes: "In short, all the central elements in Tolkien's sub-creation theory can be found in Grundtvig and are expressed in very similar terms." (34)

Man's actual status in comparison to his original one is discussed by Tolkien especially in his poem "Mythopoeia":

> The heart of man is not compound of lies,
> but draws some wisdom from the only Wise,
> and still recalls him. Though now long estranged,
> man is not wholly lost nor wholly changed.
> Dis-graced he may be, yet is not dethroned,
> and keeps the rags of lordship once he owned,
> his world-dominion by creative act:
> (*My* 87)

In these lines, Tolkien refers to Man as God's image. According to Tolkien, this quality consists mainly in Man's creative capacity. This is the means by which Man accomplishes the command of Gen 1:28 to subdue the earth and have dominion over fishes, fowl and every living thing. It includes all areas of Man's artistic activity, whereby Tolkien is mainly concerned with the literary one. Even the fall has not led to the loss of Man's exposed status in creation, his godlikeness and his capacity ("not dethroned"[3]). "In acting as a prism and this refracting light and word, 'Man, sub-creator' fulfills God's purpose by making a fantasy world that will of necessity reflect the phenomena of our world. Sub-creation, then, is not idle play or random imitation of God; it is part of His intent" (Flieger 47). Furthermore, Tolkien refutes a total corruption of Man's nature as an effect of the Fall and underlines Man's still present fundamental orientation or remembrance respective to God and his wisdom. He may be long estranged from God, but that does not mean

---

[3] Flieger refers to Tolkien's lecture on Beowulf in which Tolkien talks of "man fallen and not yet saved, disgraced but not dethroned" (*BMC* 23) and states a connection of essay and poem. "There, it was used to characterize pagan yet noble man doomed to find his only glory in the losing battle against the monsters. Here it refers to "man, sub-creator," man the maker rather than man the fighter; fallen, yes, but not dethroned, still the child of God and capable, like his creator, of creating" (43).

that he is wholly lost or corrupted.⁴ Therefore, Tolkien can be convinced that even in Paradise Man will be creative:

> Be sure they still will make, not being dead,
> and poets shall have flames upon their head,
> and harps whereon their faultless fingers fall:
> there each shall choose for ever from the All.
> (*My* 90, cf. *OFS* 73).

By equating Man's godlikeness with his creative capacity, Tolkien goes beyond the traditional theological mainstream. Generally, the fathers of the church regarded the soul of Man as the main characteristic of the godlikeness. According to the scholastic theologians, the natural godlikeness consists in rationality and the supernatural in the grace of justification. Even today, the creative capacity of Man is seldom treated in connection with his godlikeness. Johann Auer is an exception; he

---

[4] The lies of which "the heart of man is not compound"" are primarily myths and mythical expressions which seem to contradict the scientifical approach of the same phenomenons. Tolkien does not understand them as lies because of his optimistic anthropology and his conception of human art as sub-creation, which is analogous to God's creation, and also serves as memory of the divine wisdom, whereby a certain truth is inherent in them. "For Tolkien, however, even pagan myths attempted to express God's greater truths. True myth has the power to revive us, to serve as an *anamnesis*, or way of bringing to conscious experience ancient experiences with transcendence" (Birzer xxiii).

Furthermore, Tolkien refuses the challenge that myths are "wish-fulfilment dreams" (*My* 87) to deceive frightened hearts. Wishes, dreams and the distinction between beautiful and ugly (good and evil respectively) are necessary, they arise out of the experience that evil is. Man's creative capacity is opposed to this. "Blessed are the legend-makers with their rhyme / of things not found within recorded time. / It is not they that have forgot the Night, / or bid us flee to organized delight, / [...] They have seen Death and ultimate defeat, / and yet they would not in despair retreat, / but oft to victory have turned the lyre / and kindled hearts with legendary fire, / illuminating Now and dark Hath-been / with light of suns as yet by no man seen." (*My* 88f).

This is the kind of world Tolkien wants to live in and not one of "progressive apes, / erect and sapient" (*My* 89) which progress tends to lead to a dark abyss, not a world with no part for a little maker with his maker's art. "I bow not yet before the Iron Crown, / nor cast my own small golden sceptre down." (*My* 89) Tolkien refuses vehemently any self-abolition of Man by technique or scientific progress which forgets Man's transcendence. The Iron Crown is a reference to Melkor/Morgoth who wants to replace Eru and subject all free beings in Arda.

discusses Man's creative art in context of his reflections on cultural anthropology. Man is not autonomous but all his deeds as *geschöpfliches Schöpfertum* ("created creativity") have to serve higher, ultimate realities, "serving God and his creation, deeply Man, who is God's image and finally destined to the 'participation on God's glory" (365).

Stressing this transcendence, Tolkien mentions another important aspect at the beginning of his essay "On Fairy-stories". He refuses the term *supernatural beings* for *fairies*.

> For it is man who is, in contrast to fairies, supernatural (and often of diminutive stature); whereas they are natural, far more natural than he. Such is their doom. The road to fairyland is not the road to Heaven; nor even to Hell, I believe, though some have held that it may lead thither indirectly by the Devil's tithe. (*FS* 5)

Consequently, Tolkien defines the nature of Man in contrast to fairies by way of of their different eschatological destination. Whereas Man is inclined to a supernatural doom, the fairies are not. Because neither Heaven nor Hell is their doom, obviously they are completely bound to earth.[5] While both share the possibility of acting as a sub-creator, Elves are able to do so to a greater degree or with more success than men. In view of his *legendarium*, Tolkien writes to Milton Waldman concerning the elven magic: "Their 'magic' is Art, delivered from many of its human limitations: more effortless, more quick, more complete (product, and vision in unflawed correspondence). And its object is Art not Power, sub-creation not domination and tyrannous re-forming of Creation" (*L* 146).

---

[5] This reflects Tolkien's conception of the Elves bound to Arda and being subject to the Music of the Ainur. This is discussed in *Athrabeth Finrod ah Andreth* where Finrod utters the hope that by Man and Arda Remade Elves may be delivered from this final death (cf. *MR* 319).

Whereas in "Mythopoeia" the term "sub-creator" is mentioned only once and barely further explained, in "On Fairy-stories" Tolkien describes in more detail how sub-creation happens:

> When we can take green from grass, blue from heaven, and red from blood, we have already an enchanter's power – upon one plane; and the desire to wield that power in the world external to our minds awakes. It does not follow that we shall use that power well upon any plane. We may put a deadly green upon a man's face and produce a horror; we may make the rare and terrible blue moon to shine; or we may cause woods to spring with silver leaves and rams to wear fleeces of gold, and put hot fire into the belly of the cold worm. But in such 'fantasy', as it is called, new form is made; Faërie begins; Man becomes a sub-creator. (*FS* 23)

Consequently, in sub-creation the artist creates something not present in the primary world. But he uses categories known from the primary world (e.g. green, blue, red). The new results from a novel type of combination; it is not the ingredients that are new, but the composition. Man's artistic creative activity is a gift and a task given by God which Man performs with the things created by Him. Flieger mentions an important difference between this passage of "On Fairy-stories" and the corresponding lines of "Mythopoeia" ("Man, Sub-creator, the refracted Light / Through whom is splintered from a single White / to many hues, and endlessly combined / in living shapes that move from mind to mind." [87]). She points out: "The sub-creative process is now the splintering or dividing and recombining of light to create the 'living shapes that move from mind to mind,' whereas in the prose passage it was simply the combining of words, the incantatory use of adjectives in a mythical grammar" (43). But in both texts, it is a re-combination of something given. Therefore: "The heart of man is not compound of lies, / but draws some wisdom from the only Wise, / and still recalls him" (*My* 87). This explains why in "On Fairy-stories" and "Mythopoeia"

Tolkien does not distinguish sharply between *make* and *create* although he stresses ceaselessly that Melkor/Morgoth has lost his creative capacity and cannot create something of his own but only corrupt.⁶ Furthermore, this shows that the term *sub-creation* should not be used only by men who believe in a creating God. Rather, it is demanded by the dependence on the real world (cf. Weinreich 50). For example, the Gods of (higher and lower) mythologies doubtless are human constructs, but they need a reference to the real world. When Man relates them to natural phenomena which are derived from sun, moon and clouds, "their personality they get direct from him; the shadow or flicker of divinity that is upon them they receive through him from the invisible world, the Supernatural." (*FS* 24)⁷ By creatively re-combining the given material, an essential power of Faërie consists in making immediately effective the visions of *fantasy*. By no means are they purely beautiful or wholesome, because the fantasies of fallen Man are not purely beautiful and wholesome and "he has stained the elves who have this power [...] with his own stain" (*FS* 23).

*Fantasy* is to be understood in close connection to sub-creation. "Successful Fantasy is the conscious sub-creation of a Secondary World by man, whose birthright it is to make in imitation of his Maker" (Flieger 25). The success of a sub-creation is measured by the belief the audience credits the story with. Tolkien refuses Coleridge's depiction of a *willing suspension of disbelief* and states that a successful sub-creation

---

⁶ Cf. Fornet-Ponse "Tolkiens Verständnis des Bösen". 208-210.

⁷ In this respect, a fundamental difference between higher and lower mythologies does not exist. In both of them Man's orientation to God, which is present even after the Fall, is expressed, because at times something Higher can be seen: "Divinity, the right to power (as distinct from its possession), the due of worship; in fact 'religion'" (FS 26). Mythology and religion are – though they have to be distinguished – closely related to one another.

"In his essay 'On Fairy Stories', Tolkien makes a distinction between primary belief, which is what believers in a gospel give to that gospel, and secondary belief, which we give to fiction. As Tolkien himself was well aware, the kind of belief that the pre-Christian world gave to original myth was somewhere in between primary and secondary belief; in fact, for convenience we will call it intermediate belief" (Purtill 4).

can be *entered* and the accounts and tales from it are – according to its laws – *true*. Belief in a story is not necessarily limited by the impossibility of this story in the primary world. "You therefore believe it, while you are, as it were, inside. The moment disbelief arises, the spell is broken; the magic, or rather art, has failed" (*FS* 37).[8] The disbelief may be suspended, but then it remains only a substitute for a genuine experience. The belief in a story has nothing to do with its possible realization in the primary world. "Fairy-stories were plainly not primarily concerned with possibility, but with desirability" (*FS* 40pp.). Tolkien explains this point in a draft letter to Peter Hastings reacting to the question whether he had gone too far in metaphysical matters. Tolkien answers by stating that his whole mythology is concerned with the relation of Creation and sub-creation. Things may be wrong from the external point of view.

> But they cannot be wrong inside this imaginary world, since that is how it is made.
> We differ entirely about the nature of the relation of sub-creation to Creation. I should have said that liberation 'from the channels the creator is known to have used already' is the fundamental function of 'sub-creation', a tribute to the infinity of His potential variety, one of the ways in which indeed it is exhibited, as indeed I said in the Essay. I am not a metaphysician; but I should have thought it a curious metaphysic – there is not one but many, indeed potentially innumerable ones – that declared the channels known (in such a finite corner as we have any inkling of) to

---

[8] "To create secondary belief in the reader of a modern tale of marvels, there must be no break in the mood, no laughing at the magic, no metaphorical nudging of the reader in the ribs. This seriousness about the work must be in the writer before it can be in the reader, and it is one reason why Tolkien speaks of his stories as if they were discovered rather than invented, one reason why in lecturing to a university audience on fairy stories he deliberately speaks as if it were an open question whether the Elves and the realm of Faerie exist in reality" (Purtill 20).

have been used, are the only possible ones, or efficacious, or possibly acceptable to and by Him! (*L* 188pp.)

Consequently, the recombination in sub-creative art of things and issues known from the primary world is an expression of God's infinity.[9] God gave Man imagination especially with its quality to transcend the known material and to cope with it creatively.[10]

The operative link between imagination and sub-creation is the art which Tolkien provisionally calls *Fantasy*. "Fantasy (in this sense) is, I think, not a lower but a higher form of Art, indeed the most nearly pure form, and so (when achieved) the most potent" (*FS* 48). To make credible a secondary world with a green sun probably requires labour and thought and certainly demands "a special skill, a kind of elvish craft" (*FS* 48). In human art Fantasy is achieved best in literature, because the visual presentation of the imagined in painting is technically too easy.[11]

In order to prove the legitimacy of Fantasy, the sub-creational art, in "On Fairy-stories" Tolkien quotes a passage from "Mythopoeia", in which he stresses the analogy between divine creation and human artistic sub-creation as expression of Man's status as God's image:

> not his to worship the great Artefact,
> man, sub-creator, the refracted light,
> through whom is splintered from a single White
> to many hues, and endlessly combined
> in living shapes that move from mind to mind.

---

[9] "Fantasy is made out of the Primary World, but a good craftsman loves his material, and has a knowledge and feeling for clay, stone and wood which only the art of making can give" (*FS* 59).

[10] "Faëry might be said indeed to represent Imagination (without definition because taking in all the definitions of this world): aesthetic: exploratory and receptive; and artistic; intentive, dynamic, (sub)creative" (*SWM* 101).

[11] "For Tolkien, story is the most effective carrier of truth because it works with images rather than concepts, with forms rather than abstract ideas, and with action rather than argument" (Flieger 10).

> Though all the crannies of the world we filled
> with elves and goblins, though we dared to build
> gods and their houses out of dark and light,
> and sow the seed of dragons, 'twas our right
> (used or misused). The right has not decayed.
> We make still by the law in which we're made.
> (*My* 87, cf. *OFS* 55)

By stressing this analogy, Tolkien claims the reasonability of Fantasy: "Fantasy is a natural human activity. It certainly does not destroy or even insult Reason; and it does not either blunt the appetite for, nor obscure the perception of, scientific verity" (*FS* 55). On the contrary, inner logic is necessary for a credible secondary world – a world which does not follow its own laws cannot be a successful sub-creation because it cannot be accepted as true. Even if Man's right and obligation (given by God) can be used in a wrongful way, they are not decayed. The light of divine wisdom is splintered to many hues by Man and recombined "in living shapes that move from mind to mind." Likewise referring to Man as God's image, Tolkien defends his right to use his fantasy though it can be misused: "Fantasy remains a human right: we make in our measure and in our derivative mode, because we are made: and not only made, but made in the image and likeness of a maker" (*FS* 56). Therefore, probably every human artist wants to create something real: "Probably every writer making a secondary world, a fantasy, every sub-creator, wishes in some measure to be a real maker, or hopes that he is drawing on reality: hopes that the peculiar quality of this secondary world (if not all the details) are derived from Reality, or are flowing into it" (*FS* 70pp). Without any participation in reality, the inner consistency of reality cannot be achieved. In Tolkien's *legendarium*, this aspect of sub-creation is shown most distinctly by the Ainur, as he writes in a draft letter to Rhona Beare: "The Ainur took part in the making of the world as 'sub-creators': in various degrees, after this fashion. They interpreted according to their powers, and completed in detail, the Design propounded to them by the One" (*L* 284). Even they do not create arbitrarily but are following the propounded theme and thereby realizing creation. But they cannot call it into being, only by the word of the One did their tale become history – as is shown clearly in the origin of the dwarves. But Tolkien claims that God does not give any sub-creative powers to created beings without guaranteeing to grant the reality of creation to their sub-creation: "So in this myth, it is 'feigned' (legitimately whether that is a feature of the real world or not) that He gave special 'sub-creative' powers to certain of His highest created beings: that is a guarantee that what they devised and made should be given the reality of Creation" (*L* 195). Although he does not explicitly claim that this is a feature of the Primary World, the line of argument as in "Mythopoeia" and "On Fairy Stories" seems to support the assumption that human artistic sub-creation can be understood as cooperation with God in the work of creation (cf. *GS* 39). This is further backed up by a hint concerning *Leaf by Niggle*: "I tried to show allegorically how that [sub-creation] might come to be taken up into Creation in some plane in my 'purgatorial' story *Leaf by Niggle* (Dublin Review 1945)" (*L* 195).

> Because of the participation of a successful sub-creation in reality, the peculiar qualitiy of the joy evoked by the *eucatastrophe* (the "sudden joyous 'turn'" *OFS* 68), "can thus be explained as a sudden glimpse of the underlying reality or truth" (*FS* 71). While it is primarily related to the secondary world, in the eucatastrophe something greater appears, "it may be a far-off gleam or echo of *evangelium* in the real world" (*FS* 71).[12]

---

[12] In view of myths and Tolkien's defence of myths in *On Fairy-Stories*, respectively, Birzer states: "Indeed, for Tolkien, myths expressed far greater truths than did historical facts or events. Sanctified myths, inspired by grace, served as an *anamnesis*, or a way for a people to recall encounters with transcendence that had helped to order their souls and their society. Myth, inherited or created, could also offer a "sudden glimpse of Truth,"

## FUNCTIONS OF FANTASY

Based on Tolkien's remarks concerning successful Fantasy as "a far-off gleam or echo of *evangelium* in the real world" (*FS* 71), we can turn to the three functions of Fantasy he discusses in his essay: Recovery, Escape and Consolation.

> Fairy stories offer their readers four things that the human spirit needs: Fantasy, Recovery, Escape, and Consolation. Of these, the primary element is Fantasy, for the other three derive from it. Fantasy is both a mode of thinking and the created result of that thinking. Recovery, Escape, and Consolation are experiential terms describing varieties of response to Fantasy. (Flieger 24)

Recovery means the regaining of a clear vision. "I do not say 'seeing things as they are' and involve myself with the philosophers, though I might venture to say 'seeing things as we are (or were) meant to see them' – as things apart from ourselves" (*FS* 57pp).[13] He compares this to the cleaning of windows that is necessary to free things from the blur of familiarity, triteness or possessiveness; one may learn to marvel at things again.[14] This is made possible by the willingness to be enchanted by the narrative power. Fantasy in the sense of Chesterton's *Mooreffoc* also allows a re-gaining of a clear view – England might be perceived as a totally different land. "But it cannot do more than that: act as a time-telescope focused on one spot. Creative fantasy, because it is mainly trying to do something else (make something new), may open your

---

[13] that is, a brief view of heaven. At the very least, sanctified myth revealed the life humans were meant to have prior to the Fall" (Birzer 24).

Birzer interprets this passage as concerning the Eucharist and transsubstantiation (cf. 39).

[14] "Indeed, as high art forms, fairy stories and fantasy offer much to human existence. First, fairy stories illuminate the vast inheritance our ancestors have bequeathed to us. Second, fairy stories give us a new sense of wonder about things we have taken for granted or which have become commonplace" (Birzer 38).

hoard and let all the locked things fly away like cage-birds" (*FS* 59). In principle, this is made clear by fantastic elements in verse or prosa, but nowhere as clear as in a fairy-story. "By the forging of Gram cold iron was revealed; by the making of Pegasus horses were ennobled; in the Trees of the Sun and Moon root and stock, flower and fruit are manifested in glory" (*FS* 59). Fairy-stories are mainly concerned with fundamental or simple things – untouched by fantasy – (such as iron or horses), but these simplicities are seen more clearly by their fantastic setting. A story-maker who is 'free with' Nature is not her slave but can be her lover. "It was in fairy-stories that I first divined the potency of words, and the wonder of the things, such as stone, and wood, and iron; tree and grass; house and fire; bread and wine" (*FS* 60).

The two other functions of a fairy-story, Escape and Consolation, are closely connected. The connection of Recovery with Escape is treated by Tolkien in his essay on *Smith of Wootton Major*.

> Faëry represents at its weakest a breaking out (at least in mind) from the iron ring of the familiar, still more from the adamantine ring of belief that it is known, possessed, controlled, and so (ultimately) all that is worth being considered – a constant awareness of a world beyond these rings. (*SWM* 101)

If Faëry is more potent, it represents an unpossessive love and respect to all things as *other*. This love produces truth and delight and leads to respect things in this light, to regard them as delightful, beautiful, wonderful, even glorious.

Regarding Escape (and the blame of *escapism*), Tolkien's distinction of the two fundamentally different ways of escape is highly relevant because the critics of escape "are confusing, not always by sincere error, the Escape of the Prisoner with the Flight of the Deserter" (*FS* 61). Whereas the deserter wants to run away from reality, the possibility of escape by the means of a fairy-story is rather resistance than flight. The *breaking out* of the familiar mentioned above is the active escape of a prisoner with its inherent protest against the familiar. Thus not mentioning any mass-produced electric street-lamps may express their rejection. Because the escapist does not simply regard things as indispensable, his opponents have no guarantee that he will not "rouse men to pull down the street-lamps. Escapism has another and even wickeder face: Reaction" (*FS* 62). Furthermore, Tolkien objects to ideas like the opinion that factories or cars are more real (or *alive*) than centaurs or dragons:

> For my part, I cannot convince myself that the roof of Bletchley station is more 'real' than the clouds. And as an artefact I find it less inspiring than the legendary dome of heaven. The bridge to platform 4 is to me less interesting than Bifröst guarded by Heimdall with the Gjallarhorn. (*FS* 63)

Fairy-stories have in common with romances and other stories out of or about the past the *escapist* aspect of critique of modern life and its rawness and ugliness. The connection between beauty and goodness is lessened: Whereas in Faëry a place with a good purpose cannot be sickeningly ugly, it is not so in the present.

Very important and hinting at the aspect of consolation is the more profound escape from hunger, thirst, poverty which are much more terrible than the noise, stench, etc. of the modern world. "And even when men are not facing hard things such as these, there are ancient limitations from which fairy-stories offer a sort of escape, and old ambitions and desires (touching the very roots of fantasy) to which they offer a kind of satisfaction and consolation" (*FS* 66). An expression of these is the desire to converse with other living beings.

Nevertheless, the oldest and deepest desire is "the Great Escape: the Escape from Death" (*FS* 68) – fairy-stories provide many examples and possibilities of this.

Consequently, Tolkien understands the possibilities of escape made possible by fairy-stories primarily as "a possibility of fulfillment of desires and satisfactions, which the primary world cannot offer" (Weinreich 54, my translation).[15]

Besides this consolation by the imaginary fulfillment of ancient desires the consolation of a fairy-story has yet another dimension. "Far more important is the Consolation of the Happy Ending" (*FS* 68). While tragedy is the true and highest function of drama, the opposite is true with regard to fairy-stories. In the absence of a word for this state Tolkien invented the term *eucatastrophe*. "The *eucatastrophic* tale is the true form of fairy-tale, and its highest function" (*FS* 68).[16]

> The consolation of fairy-stories, the joy of the happy ending: or more correctly of the good catastrophe, the sudden joyous 'turn' (for there is no true end to any fairy-tale): this joy, which is one of the things which fairy-stories can produce supremely well, is not essentially 'escapist', nor 'fugitive'. In its fairy-tale – or otherworld – setting, it is a sudden and miraculous grace: never to be counted on to recur. (*FS* 69)

Thereby, the existence of suffering and pain is not denied; on the contrary their possibility is the condition of the joy at the redemption of this suffering. The universal final defeat is denied, whereby this consolation "in so far is *evangelium*, giving a fleeting glimpse of Joy, Joy beyond the walls of the world, poignant as grief" (*FS* 69). As mentioned above, this joy may be a gleam of evangelium in the real World.

---

[15] "And though in Tolkien's view the Christian gospel does satisfy certain intense longings in the human personality, it should not be accepted *because* it satisfies those longings: rather, it can really satisfy those longings only because it is true" (Purtill 20).

[16] Tolkien's use of 'fairy-tale' in this passage is exceptional.

## FAIRY-STORY AND EVANGELIUM

On this basis, Tolkien mentions his long felt conviction that God redeems his "corrupt making-creatures, men" (*FS* 72) according to their nature. "The Gospels contain a fairy-story, or a story of a larger kind which embraces all the essence of fairy-stories" (*FS* 72). Among the many marvels they contain is "the greatest and most complete conceivable eucatastrophe" (*FS* 72): the birth and resurrection of Christ. The difference of this story to all others is that it has entered history and the primary world.

> The desire and aspiration of sub-creation has been raised to the fulfilment of Creation. The Birth of Christ is the eucatastrophe of Man's history. The Resurrection is the eucatastrophe of the story of the Incarnation. This story begins and ends in joy. It has pre-eminently the 'inner consistency of reality'. (*FS* 72)

The supremely convincing success of this story is due to it being Primary Art, Creation. Tolkien compares the joy about the historicity of an especially beautiful fairy-story with the joy caused by a eucatastrophe because both hint at the Great Eucatastrophe.

> The Christian joy, the *Gloria*, is of the same kind; but it is pre-eminently (infinitely, if our capacity were not finite) high and joyous. Because this story is supreme; and it is true. Art has been verified. God is the Lord, of angels, and of men – and of Elves. Legend and History have met and fused. (*FS* 73)

"On Fairy-stories" and "Mythopoeia" both end with an expression of eschatological hope. In Paradise, the likeness of the True will be renewed, "looking on the Blessed Land 'twill see / that all is as it is, and yet made free: / Salvation changes not, nor yet destroys, / garden nor gardener, children nor their toys." (*My* 90) Evil is not seen because evil lies in crooked eyes and malicious choice and not in God's picture or the source.

Likewise, Tolkien says in "On Fairy-stories": "Redeemed Man is still man. Story, fantasy, still go on, and should go on. The Evangelium has not abrogated legends; it has hallowed them, especially the 'happy ending'" (*FS* 73). There is still work, suffering, hope and death, but people of Christian faith may perceive that all has a purpose. "All tales may come true; and yet, at the last, redeemed, they may be as like and as unlike the forms that we give them as Man, finally redeemed, will be like and unlike the fallen that we know" (*FS* 73).

## SUMMARY

Consequently, in "Mythopoeia" and "On Fairy-stories" Tolkien depicts the artistic and, above all, the literary activity of Man as sub-creation, analogous to God's creating activity. Sub-creation is highly relevant for Fantasy. Creativity is a capacity given by God to Man and necessary for Man to accomplish his godlikeness. Without denying the grave change of Man's actual nature this capacity continues after the Fall. Furthermore, the right to be creatively active was not abrogated. Via this capacity Man can draw nearer to the complete reality of the world, he can struggle with Evil and hope for redemption, which is not understood as limitation but as completion of Man's creative activity. Without explicitly treating religious subjects, successful fantasy can provide – especially through its functions Recovery, Escape and Consolation and the eucatastrophe contained in it – a gleam of *evangelium*.

All this is in accordance to a demand Tolkien expressed in a letter to Milton Waldman: "Myth and fairy-story must, as all art, reflect and contain in solution elements of moral and religious truth (or error), but not explicit, not in the known form of the primary 'real' world" (*L* 131).[17]

## THE SHORTER WORKS – FAIRY-STORIES?
## WHAT IS A FAIRY-STORY?

After this detailed analysis of Tolkien's theory of sub-creation I will give only a short quotation which explains what constitutes a fairy-story (and thereby fulfills the functions discussed above):

> The definition of a fairy-story – what it is, or what it should be – does not, then, depend on any definition or historical account of elf or fairy, but upon the nature of *Faërie*: the Perilous Realm itself, and the air that blows in that country. [...] Faërie cannot be caught in a net of words; for it is one of its qualities to be indescribable, though not imperceptible. (*FS* 10)

As quoted above, Faërie begins where Fantasy is effective and when Man becomes a sub-creator. Furthermore, Tolkien mentions three faces of fairy-stories[18] referred to by Purtill who states with regard to the three shorter works known by then:

> This passage gives us the essential clue to understanding Tolkien's minor works of fiction. 'Leaf by Niggle' shows us the mystical face of fairy story; *Farmer Giles of Ham* shows us the mirror of Man, pity and scorn masked by laughter

---

[17] Cf. Tolkien's statements in *The Monster and the Critics*: "The significance of a myth is not easily to be pinned on paper by analytical reasoning. It is at its best when it is presented by a poet who feels rather than makes explicit what his theme portends; who presents it incarnate in the world of history and geography, as our poet has done" (*MC* 15). Cf. in more detail Fornet-Ponse, *Tolkien* 52pp.

[18] "The Mystical towards the Supernatural; the Magical towards Nature; and the Mirror of scorn and pity towards Man. The essential face of Faërie is the middle one, the Magical. But the degree in which the others appear (if at all) is variable, and may be decided by the individual story-teller" (*FS* 26).

but still there as in all comedy with any depth. *Smith of Wootton Major* gives us the central, magical face of fairy tale. (Purtill 36pp)

## ROVERANDOM

Written in 1925-27, this is the earliest of the analyzed works. Hammond and Scull already mentioned a discrepancy between "On Fairy-stories" and *Roverandom*, for Tolkien criticizes "flower-and-butterfly minuteness" (*FS* 6) in his essay, but in *Roverandom* there are "whimsical ideas such as moon-gnomes riding on rabbits and making pancakes out of snowflakes, and sea-faries who drive in shell carriages harnessed to tiny fishes" (*R* xxi). Scull and Hammond refer to a draft letter of 1959 in which Tolkien admits that in the 20s and 30s he was convinced that fairy-stories are literature for children – which he refuses strictly in "On Fairy-stories". Finally, there are interesting connections between *Roverandom* and his *Legendarium*, e.g. the depiction of Elvenhome and Valinor at this time and the forbidden entrance to it for living beings of the Outer Lands.

Regarding other characteristics of fairy-stories, *Roverandom* is a striking example of Tolkien's sub-creational work, of his use and recombination of the known material of the primary world: the Man in the moon, Rover and Roverandom flying across the area, the sea-fairies, the whale – all shows a creative and playful dealing with the materials of the primary world, producing something new in their combination.

Even eucatastrophe is present, for as Roverandom nearly loses the hope to get his original size back due to Artaxerxes believing that he has no more magic left, the hint of Artaxerxes's wife causes a sudden joyous turn (cf. *R* 85); furthermore, when it is known that Roverandom's original owner is the grandmother of *Little Boy Two* (cf. *R* 88). Out of the three functions of Fantasy the first two are existent already by virtue of the fantastic setting of the story – which consolation it causes depends on the one hand on the effect of the eucatastrophe and on the other hand on the situation of its origin – since *Roverandom* was written as consolation for Michael Tolkien who had lost his toy dog.

Consequently, *Roverandom* in comparison to *Smith* shows clearly how Tolkien worked as a sub-creator and how his depiction of Faëry and fairy-stories changed – for *Roverandom* is unequivocally a story for children, while he stresses in "On Fairy-stories": "The value of fairy-stories is thus not, in my opinion, to be found by considering children in particular" (*FS* 36).

### LEAF BY NIGGLE

Although in this work one can find religious and theological connotations without any problems and it is therefore not necessary to point out the legitimacy of a theological analysis – Tolkien's own characterization of this story as a "purgatorial story" (*L* 195) supports (and demands) it – its strong allegorical character does not support a characterization as a fairy-story.[19] If we include this work nevertheless, it is because the concept of sub-creation and its possible integration into Creation is realized very clearly in the narrative. This explains Ellison's statement that it is "a fictional and poetic counterpart of the essay, a fable or fantasy woven around the theme of 'sub-creation'" (23).

Within the scope of this article, it is not necessary to deal with the autobiographical aspect of this work extricated by Shippey and other scholars (cf. Shippey, *Author of the Century* 266pp). More important is the depiction of Niggle's picture:

---

[19] Shippey (*Author* 266pp) analyzes it as an "autobiographical allegory". Purtill mentions three different possibilities of allegorical applicability: the moral, the aesthetic and the religious (cf. Purtill 24pp). "The very fact that it can be given a religious interpretation at all makes it unique among Tolkien's work; there is no plausible religious interpretation of, for example, 'Smith of Wootton Major' or *The Hobbit*" (Purtill 35).

> There was one picture in particular which bothered him. It had begun with a leaf caught in the wind, and it became a tree; and the tree grew, sending out innumerable branches, and thrusting out the most fantastic roots. Strange birds came and settled on the twigs and had to be attended to. Then all round the Tree, and behind it, through the gaps in the leaves and boughs, a country began to open out; and there were glimpses of a forest marching over the land, and of mountains tipped with snow. (*LN* 94)

Besides the clear, already analyzed parallels of Niggle's picture with Tolkien's *legendarium* this depiction shows clearly how a highly sophisticated (literary) sub-creation exceeds what was intended in the beginning and gets a life of its own.

Although Niggle knows that he has to begin a journey and wants to finish the picture, for different reasons he is not able to do it before his journey. After his treatment he enters his picture and with the aid of his neighbour Parish is able to complete it. Because the landscape *Niggle's Parish* is appropriate even for other human beings as an introduction to the mountains, the sub-creation is integrated in the Creation and fulfills a good purpose (cf. *LN* 118).

In *Leaf by Niggle*, the functions of Fantasy are illustrated by the stark contrast of this world, in which Niggle is soon forgotten because he did not produce anything useful for society (cf. *LN* 116pp), to the world in which his sub-creation is given being and assumes a positive function.[20] Chance regards Niggle's knowledge that some of the most beautiful leaves could only originate in cooperation with Parish as a part of the recovery of the clear vision. On the other hand Parish is finally able to understand his neighbour. Both can escape from the sufferings of this world depicted distinctly in the story, "to receive Consolation in the

---

[20] "Tolkien here illustrates the virtues of Faërie's secondary world in this 'world' called Niggle, the virtues of Escape, Recovery, and Consolation" (Chance 97).

secondary world" (Chance 98). *Leaf by Niggle* is able to console in different ways: on the one hand, it can console a sub-creator who is afraid of being completely forgotten after his death and his work being regarded as worth naught. Otherwise – read as *purgatorial story* – it can reduce the fear of death by depicting death and purgatory as necessary states to final redemption (cf. Fornet-Ponse, *Theologie*).

Furthermore, *Leaf by Niggle* contains a eucatastrophe: "'Leaf by Niggle' is a 'eucatastrophic' story in Tolkien's terminology. The final sentence, 'They both laughed. Laughed – the Mountains rang with it!', is a flash of pure joy" (Ellison 30). According to Shippey, this successful end depends on the cooperation of Niggle and Parish who are often regarded as two sides of one personality (sometimes even Tolkien himself; cf. Ellison, Chance). This cooperation leads so far "that 'Niggle's Picture' and 'Parish's Garden' combine, to become 'Niggle's Parish'" (Shippey, *Author* 274). But this positive end exists only in the world which Niggle enters after his purgatorial sojourn since the real world forgets him – from its point of view his story is a tragedy. "The *other* real world, the world after death, turns to 'eucatastrophe'" (Shippey, *Author of the Century* 276).

Although *Leaf by Niggle* cannot be regarded as a classical fairy-story, it illustrates narratively the central characteristics for a fairy-story which are demanded by Tolkien in "On Fairy-stories". Therefore, it can have the functions of Recovery, Escape and Consolation only through mediation.

## FARMER GILES OF HAM

In contrast to *Leaf by Niggle*, *Farmer Giles of Ham* cannot be regarded as a narrative explanation of his theory of sub-creation and in contrast to *Roverandom*, it does not nearly contain such a playful and vast dealing with traditions and elements of the primary world. Furthermore, *Farmer Giles of Ham* is localized in our world by the names, dates and other elements and the preface is also an argument for a parody as which Chance regards it (Chance 125-133). Whereas Shippey proposed an allegorical reading in *The Road to Middle-earth* (Shippey *Road to Middle-earth* 89pp), he criticizes this view in *Author of a Century*. "I freely concede, however, that this is probably *furor allegoricus,* or allegorist's mania: *Farmer Giles of Ham* makes too much sense as a narrative in its own right to need an allegorical reading, and is furthermore entirely light-hearted" (Shippey *Author of the Century* 289). In referring to the only successful person apart from Giles (the parson with his learning), Shippey refers to the significance of legends forgotten in a society – similar to the people of Laketown in *The Hobbit*. That hints at a necessary recovery of a clear view and at the possibility of escape from the profane modern world in which legends play a less and less significant role.

> Nevertheless, the existence of a dragon, a giant, a famous sword, etc. pleads for a characterization as fairy-story in Tolkien's sense. The success of the story argues for a credible sub-creation – e.g. the existence of the dragon does not lead to disbelief but is an integral part of the story and proves the repression of the old legends at court exemplified by the Mock Dragon's Tail degenerated to a confection "of cake and almond-paste, with cunning scales of hard icing-sugar" (*FGH* 15).

Even some small eucatastrophies may be found – after Chrysophylax's attack on the knights, when only Giles resists and triumphs with the aid of Caudimordax; but also finally at the King's atttempt to claim the dragon's treasure for himself:

> 'Lightning of Heaven! Seize him and bind him!' cried the King, justly enraged beyond bearing. 'What do you hang back for? Seize him or slay him!'
> The men-at-arms strode forward.

> 'Help! Help! Help!' cried Garm.
> Just at that moment the dragon got up from the bridge.
> (*FGH* 53)

With regard to the question of the existence of the different functions of sucessful fantasy, it is possible to find them too. Shippey mentions in particular the function of recovery:

> The story of *Farmer Giles* is therefore largely the triumph of native over foreign (for in Giles's court 'the vulgar tongue came into fashion, and none of his speeches were in the Book-latin'), as simultaneously of worth over fashion and of heroic song and popular lay over pompous pernickety rationalistic scholarship. (*Road to Middle-earth* 89, cf. *Author of the Century* 291)

This implies the possible escape in this simple world and thereby can offer consolation. Assuming that the defense of the simple, unlearned and the old legends may be a gleam of *evangelium*, it could consist in the defense of popular piety, of the *sensus fidelium*, of the belief against the attacks of rationalism, of the old theology against the new ones – one is reminded of of Tolkien's contemporariness with the Roman Catholic Church's opposition to the so-called "modernism" – etc.

## SMITH OF WOOTTON MAJOR

Characterizing *Smith* as a fairy-story meets with similar difficulties as is the case in *Leaf by Niggle* – especially if one follows Martin Simonson's depiction of it as a "re-enactment of *On Fairy-Stories*" (cf. Simonson in the present volume). Furthermore, it is regarded by Shippey and Ilgner – in contrast to Flieger and Doughan – as an autobiographical allegory (cf. Shippey *Author of fthe Century* 296; Ilgner 290). Tolkien himself refuses an allegorical interpretation for the most part but admits that the Great Hall could be understood as allegory of the village church, the

Master Cook as representing the parson, etc. – wherein Tolkien's refusal of some changes of the Second Vatican Council is shown or his prejudices against the protestant churches surface (*SWM* 100). But he insists on the statement that religion is not the primary subject of the story.

Regarding the genesis of the *Smith* and Tolkien's essay, the attention is focused mainly on the question about essence and effects of Faëry. Thereby, it fulfills the above quoted definition of a fairy-story in depending more on Faëry than on fairies. He stresses unmistakably in which sense *Smith* should be understood as a fairy-story:

> It is a 'Fairy Story', of the kind in which beings that may be called 'fairies' or 'elves' play a part and are associates in action with human people, and are regarded as having a 'real' existence, that is one in their own right and independent of human imagination and invention. (*SWM* 84)

Following this, Tolkien discusses the relationship of Faëry and the real world. In *Smith* a transition between both worlds is possible without any problems. But although they are connected to each other they occupy a different time and a different space – which explains the different spans passed in each realm.

The story plays at a time at which the vulgarization of the village – paradigmatically shown by Nokes – is progressed quite far and is manifested in the way of celebration. Now the feasts are solely about eating and drinking, whereas songs, legends and dancing do not play an important part any more. Also the legends about Faëry are less regarded. The King of Faëry's coming to Wootton Major as countereffect to this trend shows that Faëry is concerned with Mankind. But since it is independent of the world of Men it has to be a relationship founded on love: "the Elven Folk, the chief and ruling inhabitants of Faëry, have an ultimate kinship with Men and have a permanent love for them in general" (*SWM* 93). Tolkien further characterizes this love as a relationship to all living and non-living things, which includes love and respect and removes or modifies the spirit of possessiveness and domination (cf. *SWM* 94, 101). In this regard men could learn much from the elves which is very obvious in the story of Rider and Smith.

The contact with Faëry is of great advantage for men – which is shown in the art of the Smith and his delight at work. Furthermore, it is about the restoration of a culture of celebration which transcends the mere satisfaction of material needs and refers to something else in songs, legends, music and dance.

The functions of a successful Faëry (story) mentioned by Tolkien are realized and illustrated in this story: Rider and Smith escape from their world by the visits of Faëry which are possible only for them. They return refreshed and have a different view of things than before.[21]

From this point of view Tolkien's statement in his essay may be explained: "BUT Faëry is *not* religious. It is fairly evident that it is not Heaven or Paradise" (*SWM* 100). This is in accordance to "On Fairy-stories" since the elves are not concerned with the improvement of the religious devotion of men – but they indeed wish to escape from the iron ring of the familiar, they want to keep alive the knowledge of a world beyond this ring. Furthermore, this is about the love mentioned above.

By representing the imagination and establishing a connection to the consciousness of an unlimited world beyond our domesticated area, to the unpossessive love of all things which are contained in it and to the desire for wonder and miracles, Faëry is "as necessary for the health and complete functioning of the Human as is sunlight for physical life:

---

[21] Smith "seems to have reached in life the balance which characters like Niggle and Parish could only achieve jointly, and then only after death. The star seems, then, to represent something like Tolkien's own impulse towards fantasy, the quality of vision; while Smith represents the ideal response to it, using it as an enrichment of normal life rather than a distraction. In this view the story begins to look like another 'mediation', this time a successful one, between fantasy and reality" (Shippey *Author* 300).

sunlight as distinguished from the soil, say, through it in fact permeates and modifies even that" (*SWM* 101).

Thus combining and narratively demonstrating the three functions of Fantasy but also providing these functions for the reader and with Faëry playing a very important part, *Smith of Wootton Major* can be regarded as a fairy-story although it also is a narrative realisation of Tolkien's concept of fairy-stories. By realising it, *Smith* implicitly supports his remarks in ""On Fairy-stories".

## IS THAT THEOLOGY?

It should have become clear how each of the analyzed shorter works of Tolkien support his theory of sub-creation in their own way by containing or narratively exposing the decisive elements of a fairy-story – with exception of the only work which is older than "On Fairy-stories", *Roverandom*, which is nevertheless an excellent example for the way a sub-creator works.

Following Tolkien's argument that a successful sub-creation may be a far-off gleam of *evangelium*, and following his conviction that a fairy-story should only implicitly contain elements of religious truth or error, these can be looked for precisely in his fairy-stories. The functions of Fantasy or Faëry respectively (Recovery, Escape and Consolation) show the needs of Men and the limits of a (fallen) Creation – while at the same time hinting at the *eschaton* and the supernatural fulfilment of Man. In this way they indeed can be a gleam of the *evangelium* of God's universal will of salvation, and a discussing them is worthwhile from a theological point of view – not to analyze these traces in a speculative-theological sense but rather in a pastoral interest which is in accordance to the last canon of the *Codex Iuris Canonici*: "salus animarum suprema lex debet esse" ("The salvation of souls must always be the supreme law").

THOMAS FORNET-PONSE studied Catholic theology, philosophy, and ancient history in Bonn and Jerusalem. He is currently preparing his theological doctorate and working as a research assistant at the Faculty of Catholic Theology at Bonn University. His research interests focus on philosophical and theological analyses of Tolkien and other (fantasy) authors, ecumenical problems, Jewish-Christian dialogue and 'classical' questions of Fundamental Theology. He is a committee member of the German Tolkien Society (DTG) and is the conceptual coordinator of the Tolkien Seminars as well as *Hither Shore*, the annual journal of the DTG. He has published several articles on theological and philosophical questions in the works of Tolkien, C.S. Lewis and Terry Pratchett.

## Works Cited

Agøy, Nils Ivar. "Quid Hinieldus cum Christo? – New Perspectives on Tolkien's Theological Dilemma and his Sub-Creation Theory". *Proceedings of the J.R.R. Tolkien Centenary Conference*. Patricia Reynolds and Glen H. Goodknight. Milton Keynes and Altadena: Mythopoeic Press, 1995. 31-38.

Auer, Johann. *Die Welt – Gottes Schöpfung*. KKD III. Regensburg: Pustet, 1975.

Birzer, Bradley J. *Tolkien's Sanctifying Myth. Understanding Middle-earth*. Wilmington: ISI Books, 2002.

Carpenter, Humphrey. Ed. with the assistance of Christopher Tolkien. *The Letters of J.R.R. Tolkien*. Boston und New York: Houghton Mifflin, 2000.

Chance, Jane. *Tolkien's Art. A Mythology for England. Revised Edition*. Kentucky: University Press, 2001.

Doughan, David. "In search of the bounce: Tolkien seen through Smith". *Leaves from the Tree*. Tom Shippey et. al. Tolkien Society 1991. 17-22.

Ellacuría, Ignacio. *Freedom made Flesh. The mission of Christ and his Church*. New York: Orbis, 1976.

Ellison, John A. "The 'Why', and the 'How': Reflections on 'Leaf by Niggle'". *Leaves from the Tree*. Tom Shippey et. al. Tolkien Society 1991. 23-32.

Ferré, Vincent. *Tolkien: Sur les rivages de la terre du milieu*. Paris: Christian Bourgois, 2001.

Flieger, Verlyn. *Splintered Light. Logos and Language in Tolkien's World*. Kent: Kent State University Press, 2002.

Fornet-Betancourt, Raúl. *Lateinamerikanische Philosophie zwischen Inkulturation und Interkulturalität*. Frankfurt a.M.: IKO, 1997.

Fornet-Ponse, Thomas. "Tolkiens Verständnis des Bösen". *Inklings* 20 (2002): 189-228.

---. "Tolkien und die Theologie". *Stimmen der Zeit* 223 (2005): 51-62.

---. "Tolkiens Theologie des Todes". *Hither Shore* 2 (2005): 157-186.

Ilgner, Oliver. *Biographische, theologische und literaturpsychologische Analysen zur Person und zum Werk J. R. R. Tolkiens.* Aachen: Shaker, 2004.

Pastoral Constitution on the Church in the modern world *Gaudium et Spes.* 15 July 2007. [http://www.vatican.va/archive/hist_councils /ii_vatican_council/ documents/vat-ii_cons_19651207_gaudium-et-spes_en.html, cited 9.2.2008]

Purtill, Richard L. *J.R.R. Tolkien. Myth, Morality, and Religion.* San Francisco: Ignatius Press, 2003.

Shippey, Tom. *The Road to Middle-earth. How J.R.R. Tolkien created a Mythology.* London: HarperCollins, 1992.

---, *J.R.R. Tolkien – Author of the Century.* London: HarperCollins, 2000.

Tolkien, John Ronald Reuel. "Farmer Giles of Ham". *Tales from the Perilous Realm.* London: HarperCollins, 1998. 1-57.

---, "Leaf by Niggle". *Tree and Leaf.* London: HarperCollins, 2001, 93-118.

---, "Mythopoeia". *Tree and Leaf.* London: HarperCollins, 2001, 85-90.

---, "On Fairy-stories". *Tree and Leaf.* London: HarperCollins, 2001, 1-81.

---, *Roverandom.* London: HarperCollins, 1998.

---, *Smith of Wootton Major. Extended Edition.* Ed. Verlyn Flieger. HarperCollins, 2005.

---, "Beowulf: The Monster and the Critics". *The Monster and the Critics and Other Essays.* Ed. Christopher Tolkien. London: HarperCollins, 1997. 5-48.

---, *Morgoth's Ring. The History of Middle-earth X.* Edited by Christopher Tolkien. London: HarperCollins, 1994.

Weinreich, Frank. *The Lord of the Rings.* Mentor-Lektürehilfen. Stuttgart: Mentor, 2002.

# The "Meaning" of *Leaf by Niggle*

BERTRAND ALLIOT

ABSTRACT[1]

In this article, we try to understand what Tolkien tried to express through *Leaf, by Niggle*. This tale centres on what Tolkien calls "*the laws*". The laws are things that have to be respected for life – or to survival to be possible – in a sense they are almost biological. For this very reason, respecting them is crucial. Unfortunately for Niggle – and Tolkien – and contrary to his neighbour Parish, he is involved in a creative activity that tends to make him forget that he has to respect the laws. This story shows up to which point Tolkien was tormented by the incompatibility between the necessity to satisfy daily needs and his urge to be involved in artistic creation. Throughout his long life and despite this incompatibility, Tolkien tried to adopt an attitude which would allow the reconciliation of these two apparently irreconcilable things. *Leaf, by Niggle* tells this attempt.

The title of my paper, *The "Meaning" of Leaf, by Niggle*, may seem a bit pretentious. Nobody really knows the "meaning" of *Leaf, by Niggle*; there can only ever be interpretations of the text. If Tolkien were among us today he would probably tell us: "you should not talk so much about my stories but you should rather enjoy them for their own sake". In fact, it is because he wrote his stories to stimulate literary pleasure that most of them have to be appreciated for what they are: fascinating tales.

Nonetheless, if Tolkien told us this we might respond as follows: "Sorry, Professor, but *Leaf, by Niggle* is not a mere story and we can speak about it as much as we want since in writing it you wanted to do more than entertain us; your story is an allegory worthy of special attention". Indeed, it won't hurt for once, Tolkien used an allegorical method to write *Leaf by Niggle*, which is, considering his usual creative

---

[1] Acknowledgments: thanks to Nikki Funke and Héléne Beaugy for having proofread this article.

process, very uncommon. For once with Tolkien, the tale is not self-sufficient; we do not have to content ourselves with appreciating a "mere story" (*L* 144), but we can try to go beyond the words to understand a "meaning". In fact, *Leaf, by Niggle* gives us the opportunity to study what Tolkien "meant" whereas usually we have to be content with what his stories may mean through or even despite himself.

We will see that, throughout this little story, Tolkien presents something that worried him during his entire life: the incompatibility between the necessities of life (or the satisfaction of daily needs – in a sense almost biological needs) and artistic creation. This observation particularly affected him because he was deeply involved in the latter but, at the same time, for reasons that we will try to clarify, also quite convinced that priority must be given to the first necessity. *Leaf by Niggle* shows a character just as Tolkien was: tormented by this incompatibility and, no matter what, even clumsily, trying to put up with it. Despite his weakness and failures, thanks to his hopes and deep desires, he will try to find a path in a life for him made more complicated by his determination not to neglect two things driven by contradictory forces.

## THE "LAWS" AND THE WORLD SPLIT DOWN THE MIDDLE

First of all, *Leaf, by Niggle* shows the concerns the author had about what he calls the "laws". We learn at the beginning of the story that Niggle "might get a visit from an inspector" (*TL* 77) and that the latter might notice that his garden is "rather neglected" (*TL* 77). As we all know, an inspector is tasked with enforcing the law and we can already deduce that in Niggle's "world" not taking care of your garden is forbidden; it is against the law. Later, when, as expected, an inspector has arrived, we learn more about these laws. The inspector reproaches Niggle during the storm, while the Emergency Services are trying to deal with crises in the rest of the neighbourhood, for not having helped his neighbour to "make temporary repairs and prevent the damage from getting more costly to mend than necessary" (*TL* 81). The inspector even tells Niggle that he should have used the only materials available: canvas, wood and waterproof paint from his picture! Niggle seems terrified by the idea of using his picture to repair a roof but the inspector is very clear about the fact that "houses come first." As he puts it, "that is the law" (*TL* 82).

Niggle's interaction with the inspector shows us what these laws are: very basic rules to be respected under any circumstances, things that come first in order of priority. Why? Simply because not respecting them could jeopardise life itself. You first have to have a house and food; only then can you think about taking up a hobby like painting or playing football. Denis Diderot used to say, "first survive, then philosophise". This, in fact, could be the motto of Niggle's world. The laws which the inspectors have to enforce on Niggle and his fellow citizens are an allegory of what in life we cannot escape from, what was imposed on us from the very beginning of human life on earth and what we have to accept so as not to compromise our own existence in the world. In real life these laws don't need to be written down anywhere or be enforced by anyone. Still, it would be appropriate to respect them.

Two types of men make their appearance in this story, each with a very different attitude towards the laws. The first type is personified by Niggle, the second by Parish. Niggle seems to find it very difficult to comply with the laws: he is obsessed by his painting, that is to say by a creative activity, and this seems to distance him from reality and from the necessity of observing his legal duties. Parish, on the other hand, has no difficulties in adhering to the laws and we could even argue that the laws are the only things that he is aware of. Parish does not understand the first thing about Niggle's picture but notices immediately that Niggle's garden is overrun with weeds, as is evident in the following passage:

> When Parish looked at Niggle's garden (which was often) he saw mostly weeds ; and when he looked at Niggle's pic-

> tures (which was seldom) he saw only green and grey patches and black lines, which seemed to him nonsensical. He did not mind mentioning the weeds (a neighbourly duty), but he refrained from giving any opinion of the pictures. (*TL* 79)

Readers of *Leaf by Niggle* are given the impression that although Niggle and Parish are neighbours, they do not live on the same planet. One lives in a world where pointing out the presence of weeds is a "neighbourly duty", while the other is obsessed by his paintings. They are strangers to each other and don't see the world in the same way. Although they treat each other with respect, we still feel that they don't like each other very much.

However, to be fair, we have to mention that Niggle sometimes goes to visit Parish's planet. In fact, the story often shows Niggle trying as best he can to adhere to the laws. For instance, he abandons his picture and rides in the rain to fetch the doctor and the builder for Parish. However, importantly, he doesn't do so spontaneously but rather because he cannot escape from doing it. In a sense, the necessity of having to respect the laws catches up with him. As one of the voices says when the time comes for Niggle to be judged, "He did answer a good many Calls" (*TL* 85), mainly because he feels "things ordered by the laws" cannot be neglected. On the other hand, though, although he tries to respect the laws, he cannot help but consider them as "interruptions". This is the reason why he tries to comply with them as quickly as possible (to go back to what he likes doing most). In his haste, Niggle doesn't really fulfil his tasks to the best of his abilities. Rather, we could say that most of the time he contents himself with a "skeleton service" and this is why his case has to be considered carefully by the voices in charge of judging him. Niggle eventually does "pass the exam" but only meets minimum requirements.

It is a pity that Tolkien does not depict how Parish is judged, but we can easily imagine that he would have passed his "test" more easily than Niggle did. Considering the respect that Parish has for the laws, we can assume that he would not consider the laws as "interruptions" to the things that he would rather do, but simply as things that have to be done. In complying with the laws, he is at peace with himself. In fact, Parish seems to have quite a relaxed attitude towards life, taking things in his stride.

The particular importance Tolkien attributes to the laws in *Leaf by Niggle* certainly reflects a phenomenon that he seems to have been grappling with for a significant part of his life. This phenomenon can be summarised as the assumption that in everyday life the world is split in two as far as people's attitude towards the laws is concerned. In his writings, we very often find representatives of both worlds. In *The Lord of the Rings*, for instance, the Hobbits are no doubt, like Parish, very aware of the laws. They are very sensible and have both feet firmly planted on the ground. On the other hand, the Elves are "out of the world"; they are engrossed by poetry and beauty, just as Niggle is engrossed by his picture. The Elves have to force themselves when it is time for them to participate in saving Middle-earth; similarly, it takes quite some time for Niggle to finally respond to Parish's demands. But even in the small Hobbit society there are varying levels of awareness of the laws. We can imagine that what Tolkien calls a "genuine Hobbit" (*L* 105) is the type of Hobbit who has an immediate respect for the laws. Other Hobbits, like Bilbo, are more "sophisticated" in that they are haunted by the temptation to withdraw from the world and to leave their immediate surroundings for an imaginary "elsewhere". There would certainly be many other examples showing that Middle-earth's characters tend to be naturally divided into these two different camps.

It would appear that Tolkien, in terms of how he perceives the laws, falls in the Elves or Niggle rather than Hobbit or Parish camp (in

*Leaf by Niggle*, Niggle is Tolkien himself²). Still, although he is perfectly aware of "belonging" to the side that attributes less importance to the laws, he nonetheless highlights the qualities of individuals "from the other side". Amongst all the races inhabiting Middle-earth, he has a clear preference for the Hobbits and amongst the Hobbits for the most law-abiding of creatures, namely Samwise Gamgee.³ In his letters, Tolkien also shows great respect for what he calls the "dull stodges": "young men and women of sub-public school class and home backgrounds book-less and cultureless" (*L* 303-304) and of course for the common people he met in the trenches of World War I. By contrast, he distrusts those of "higher intelligence". He thinks that simple people, like Parish, are somehow superior or better than himself or others like him. Also, it is evident that during his life Tolkien tried to let himself be inspired by these simple people, forcing himself to pay more careful attention to the laws. In his letters, he often mentions the effort he is making in trying to respect them and that his work is neither essential nor really important, that he and his correspondents should not speak

---

[2] In his letters, Tolkien clearly compares his own situation to Niggle's. *L* 199, p.257, he says that *Leaf by Niggle* "arose from [his] own pre-occupation with *The Lord of the Rings*, the knowledge that it would be finished in great detail or not at all, and the fear (near certainty) that it would be 'not at all'." *L* 241, p. Page 321, he tries to explain why Leaf by Niggle was written. Among other explanations he says "(...) of course, I was anxious about my own internal Tree, *The Lord of the Rings*. It was growing out of hand, and revealing endless new vistas – and I wanted to finish it, but the world was threatening." It is also true that in the same letter he tries to minimise the allegorical aspects of the story but I still think that Niggle represents Tolkien himself. He minimises this aspect because, for him, as we have already said, stories have to be appreciated as mere stories; that is to say that even if there is an allegory, the latter has no importance: the story must continue to exist without it. Tolkien encourages his interlocutors to not pay attention to this king of thinks but rather to read any story with a 'basic' manner. We think he states this clearly in the letter to his aunt, *L* 241, p. 322: "But none of that really illuminates 'Leaf by Niggle' much, does it? If it has any virtues, they remain as such, whether you know all this or not."

[3] I think a preference for Hobbits is visible throughout his letters. See for exemple *L* 109, p.121 ("hobbits (whom I love)...") or *L* 246, p. 329 ("all Hobbits at times affect me the same way, though I remain fond of them."). I try to analyse his preference for Hobbits as a love for the "simple" in a previous article "Tolkien: a simplicity between the truly earthy and the absolutely modern", published in *Tolkien and Modernity*, Vol. 1.

too much or too seriously about it. Tolkien knew that he tended to stay shut up indoors with his only company being his "tree". To compensate for his lack of consideration for the real world he made it his duty to respond to the "calls" and to focus on the laws as much he possibly could.[4]

Why, according to Tolkien, was making so great an effort so important? Because, otherwise, we might be swept aside by life's dynamics or by the wind of history. To live, we need to eat first. Of course, we do not forget to eat because our bodies remind us to feed ourselves, but there are many other basic needs which we are not reminded of. Life within the world provides a new challenge every day, which is why we have to face reality. To remain, like Niggle, in a "tall shed" is dangerous or is a sign of obliviousness that could be fatal.

Niggle's carefree life is fragile and is only possible because others are now in charge of what Niggle previously discarded with thoughtlessness. Tolkien says Niggle "was thinking all the time about his big canvas, in the tall shed that had been built for it out in his garden (on a plot where once he had grown potatoes)" (*TL* 76). The mention of the potatoes being replaced by the tall shed is of crucial importance, because it means that there is an incompatibility between being engaged in a creative activity and responding appropriately to life's daily needs. The more time we spend painting or singing or even studying, for example, the less time we have to grow potatoes. However, what is certain is that we cannot escape from the fact that we need potatoes to survive and this is why growing potatoes should take priority. Niggle, after his course of

---

[4] In the foreword to the first and second editions (1954 and 1966) of *The Lord of the Rings*, Tolkien insists that writing *The Lord of the Rings* took a long time because he had no spare time during the period and because he did not neglect his numerous obligations. It is as though he feels the need to justify himself for having written a big book, feeling guilty for having done so. In fact, to forestall any critics, he explains how the writing of his book did not prevent him from respecting the laws and from paying attention to things that really matter. These words are meant for some hypothetical judges in case he would have to answer for his acts.

treatment in the Workhouse, realises that Parish has been a good neighbour because he "let [him] have excellent potatoes very cheap, which saved [him] a lot of time" (*TL* 87). Niggle can devote himself to his canvas thanks to Parish's kindness, thanks to the man who does not understand anything about painting, but who is level-headed enough to deal with supplying food. In a letter to Sir Stanley Unwin, Tolkien again refers to the apparent incompatibility between art and what we could call "necessity" by saying that creative desire "seems to have no biological function, and to be apart from the satisfactions of plain ordinary biological life, with which, in our world, it is indeed usually at strife" (*L* 145).

## THE LIGHT AND CONSISTENT WORLDS

This conflict or antagonism appears everywhere in Tolkien's work. It often materialises in the form of a recurring superimposition: that of the "light" world on the "consistent" world. The light world is a world where nothing really matters, where there are no consequences to one's actions, where Niggle and his canvas move for example. The consistent world, on the other hand, is where things matter. This is the world of Parish and his potatoes. In *The Lord of the Rings*, Tom Bombadil lives in the light world, while the others live in the consistent world. The moon from "The Man in the Moon" also represents the light world, whereas the earth is the consistent world. Finally, then, what is very important for Tolkien is that adventures take place in a "light world" and differ considerably from "real life" or history that are set in the "consistent world".

In *The Hobbit*, Gandalf sends Bilbo on an "adventure"; this means that the hero will not suffer any negative consequences as a result of his actions.⁵ *The Lord of the Rings* begins in the same setting and the reader might think that Bilbo is about to experience another adventure. However, Frodo, the new Bilbo, is soon drawn onto a new path, that of real life. This means that his adventure has the potential to become serious and to potentially turn tragic. Here then we have the difference between adventures and history or real life. On the stairs of Cirith Ungol Sam tells Frodo the following:

> I used to think that [adventures] were things the wonderful folk of the stories went out and looked for, because they wanted them, because they were exciting and life was a bit dull, a kind of a sport, as you might say. But that's not the way of it with the tales that really mattered, or the ones that stay in the mind. (*TT* 321)

Here, we find a kind of disillusionment: the character realises that life is not a game, that it is made of "tales that really mattered", therefore of things that are not tales. As Sam is experiencing Middle-earth he progressively feels the consistency of it, and the laws (and his growing awareness of the fragility of life) are weighing more and more on his shoulders.

In *The Lord of the Rings*, Bombadil is the only character who lives in a world where nothing really matters. Firstly, he is brought into the narrative because Tolkien wanted "an adventure on the way" (*L* 192): at this stage of the story, Tolkien still thought that his new book would be intended for children, in other words, he wanted his characters to meet a new challenge that they could overcome before the next one, of course every time succeeding in being safe and sound, reaching the end victori-

---

5   Tolkien insists a lot in his letter (p.145, 215, 298, 346) on the fact that *The Hobbit* was destined to children. The tone and style change between *The Hobbit* and *The Lord of the Rings*. The first is not "serious", it is just an adventure made to entertain us. Tolkien says the Hobbit "can be seen to begin in what might be called a more 'whimsy' mode, and in places even more facetious" (L 298). In this context, nothing bad can really happen to the protagonists.

ous. Bombadil is a remnant of the country of adventures, which is why the Ring fails to affect him[6]. This is also the reason why so many people find the character to be out of touch with the rest of the story. Secondly, Bombadil is, according to Tolkien, a "particular embodying of pure natural science" (*L* 179) which means that he "studies" natural things for no other purpose than studying itself. Like Niggle with his canvas, Bombadil is engrossed in something that is of no practical use and is therefore, by implication, locked in a type of "tall shed" of his own. Tolkien, however, does make it clear that Bombadil lives in a more consistent world: "ultimately only the victory of the West will allow Bombadil to continue, or *even to survive*. Nothing would be left for him in the world of Sauron" (*L* 179; italics added). Bombadil lives within the light world that lies within the consistent world. Tolkien's words on Bombadil highlight the fact that it would be impossible to live in a light world with an existence of its own, that would be self-sufficient with its own rules. The only rules that count are those of the consistent world that also includes the light world. There, one cannot allow oneself to be careless, the laws have to be respected and the calls have to be answered. Tolkien was most likely also tempted to stay peacefully in the shed and, like Niggle, probably also secretly dreamt of having a "public pension" that would allow him to spend more time in it. However Tolkien knew his dream to be dangerous because it would make the occasions on which he was called into the real world rarer and would result in a progressive loss of his sense of the consistent world.

---

[6] Moreover, a Ring such as Sauron's, with all its characteristics, could not fit in *The Hobbit* or in Bombadil's kingdom: this item is too fraught with consequences to be part of such a light world. Here, the Ring is inevitably harmless because it has to fit in with the atmosphere it is in. There is just no way a Ring such as Sauron's can exist in Bombadil's country. In the same way, it is impossible to find a piece of scorching coal in water because in entering into water the incandescence automatically vanishes. Then, there is no problem with taking it with the hands and playing with it. In penetrating water embers change nature; it is the same thing for the *Ring*.

Therefore, Tolkien's characters are irresistibly drawn towards the side of the consistent world: the Man in the Moon falls down to the earth, the light environment in which first Bombadil and Bilbo move (in *The Hobbit* and at the beginning of *The Lord of the Rings*) becomes progressively more consistent and "serious", adventures become history and real life, and so on. To use an image, the reader is placed with the Hobbits in a hot-air balloon that is irresistibly going down to the ground. Leaving the basket and treading land underfoot, the passengers feel themselves suddenly vulnerable because the environment has changed. This movement with which the characters are carried away, from the light to the heavy, from the air to the earth, reflects the fact that the author cannot forget the seriousness of life, this seriousness that always ends up catching up with him. He can no more free himself from the heaviness of the laws than he can escape gravity. In *The Lord of the Rings*, a poem heralds the change of tone and style and warns the reader that *terra firma* has been reached. The poem is first said by Bilbo and later by Frodo. It is almost exactly the same poem: only one word changes, a word that changes everything:

*By Bilbo*
The Road goes ever on and on
Down from the door where it began,
Now far ahead the Road has gone,
And I must follow, if I can,
Pursuing it with *eager* feet
Until it joins some larger way
Where many paths and errands meet.
And whither then? I cannot say.
(*LotR* 44; my emphasis)

> *By Frodo*
> The Road goes ever on and on
> Down from the door where it began,
> Now far ahead the Road has gone,
> And I must follow, if I can,
> Pursuing it with *weary* feet
> Until it joins some larger way
> Where many paths and errands meet.
> And whither then? I cannot say.
> (*LotR* 82; my emphasis)

Once 'on the ground', the atmosphere is tense because it is now filled with rules and laws that weigh on every individual, putting his or her life within impassable limits. It is precisely the presence of these limits framing life that imposes a particular discipline, that decides that not everything is possible, and that finally force the protagonist to walk hesitantly with *weary feet*. The feet are no longer *eager* because from now on, each additional step will leave on the ground a footprint, each act shall have a consequence.

By stating that the obligations and duties of every day life are in conflict with one's creative desire, Tolkien probably realised what each of us should easily be able to notice: the less one busies oneself with practical things, the less one is aware of what is important or crucial. By contrast, the more one occupies oneself with the nitty-gritty of "real" life, the more one is "in water", to borrow a Tolkienian expression[7]; in other words, the more one is able to face reality and to survive.

Tolkien's experience of the war probably convinced him of this and of the fact that simple people, those who naturally respond to the calls and respect the laws, are better equipped to take up the challenges we face in everyday life. Before the war, Tolkien was part of the TCBS (Tea Club and Barrovian Society): a club of four cultured and ambitious

---

[7] See *L* 52, p.64 "I imagine the fish out of water is the only fish to have an inkling of water."

young men. According to one of them, G.B. Smith, the TCBSians wanted the members of the club "to leave the world a better place than when they found it, 'to re-establish sanity, cleanliness, and the love of real and true beauty'" (Garth 253). Tolkien himself in his early years thought the TCBSians were destined to kindle a "new light in the world at large" (*L* 10).

And how did the TCBSians think they would do that? With words: they wanted to change the world by means of poetry and art. But after his experiences in the trenches we can imagine how pretentious this appeared to Tolkien. In the trenches, those that really make a difference were not the individuals who had the pretension to change the world by writing verses but the tommy, "the plain soldier from the agricultural counties" (*L* 54). Tolkien wanted to change the world and he realised that, according to his own words, he was in the battle "inefficient and unmilitary" (*L* 54). He wanted to change the world but he couldn't efficiently participate in saving it. Therefore, he probably progressively realised the lightness of the TCBS's words and project, a project easy to formulate in the mind but reduced to nothing in the acid water of reality.

In a sense, he admired the *tommies* because they do not think too much, and instead face their challenges head on. Someone more "sophisticated", such as Niggle, Tolkien, or you and me, is too much "out of water" and out of reality. This means that if someone sophisticated sees danger coming, he/she will be thinking so much about the nature of this danger that he/she will not be able to respond to it effectively. A very intelligent individual will attentively study the situation and will soon be completely paralysed by the complexity of the problem. Intelligence or sophistication are not in keeping with courage: Rousseau already noticed that during antiquity, the less sophisticated people, those who had not been "corrupted" by *arts and sciences*, were far more courageous than the Greeks or the Romans.

## REDUCING THE CONTRADICTION

Now that we know why Tolkien thought being out of real life was rather perilous and why he trusted those who were simpler than himself or Niggle it is time to try and understand how he dealt with this apparent contradiction. We have already revealed a part of the answer. Tolkien, like Niggle, tried as much he could to respond to the calls and to respect the laws without considering them as interruptions. He also never took his creative work seriously. The voices echo that: "there are no notes in the Records of his pretending, even to himself, that [his painting activity] excused his neglect of things ordered by the laws" (*TL* 85). Tolkien thought that one should be able to make sacrifices, to give priority to the tangible rather than the abstract. The voices show leniency towards Niggle notably because he has been capable of a "genuine sacrifice"; in order to help Parish he does a "wet bicycle ride" and in so doing he "was throwing away his last chance with his picture" (*TL* 86). And what at last saves Niggle is his sudden and almost unexpected acknowledgement: Parish "was a very good neighbour, and let me have excellent potatoes very cheap, which saved me a lot of time," Niggle says. In response, the First Voice answers, "Did he? … I am glad to hear it" (*TL* 87). This is exactly the kind of acknowledgement that shows the reader that the Voice is no longer sceptical about letting Niggle off. Tolkien was deeply convinced of the absolute necessity of swearing allegiance to what I, in a previous paper, have called the "simple" (Alliot).

Tolkien, despite his admiration for all things simple, did not try to become a simple man. He did not discard his creative activity because he knew that this would be impossible; the fact that he was attracted to the aesthetic was something he had to accept. "He was a painter by nature" says the Second Voice (*TL* 85), which is very true of Niggle, because in painting he simply responds to nature, thereby respecting a kind of law. To paint is not a "glamorous pose" for Niggle, but should rather be seen as a natural act. Even the voices are compelled to consider that in his favour. Another important point to consider here is that Niggle "took a great deal of pains with leaves, just for their own sake" (*TL* 85). This means that Niggle is not engrossed in a big, grandiose, complicated project and this is probably the reason why he stays humble when it comes to his work and why he is capable of fulfilling his other duties. He is not pretentious, he does not reason too much and he respects what his heart commands him to do. He focuses neither on the tree nor on the entire landscape but only on the leaves. In painting them he is only catching something that is already in the air: "It had begun with a leaf caught in the wind, and it became a tree; and the tree grew, sending out innumerable branches, and thrusting out the most fantastic roots" (*TL* 76). Everything passes through him and finally creates a painting of a greater scope that is the result of a surge, of a movement that has never stopped since the beginning of the world and that has been breathed into life by the creator himself. Tolkien's entire subcreative process is represented here. Tolkien once had an ambitious project: he planned to build a body of legend "high and purged of gross [...] ranging from the large and cosmogonic to the level of romantic fairy" (*L* 144) but he told Milton Waldman it was "absurd" and added:

> The mere stories were the thing. They arose in my mind as 'given' things, and as they came, separately, so too the links grew. An absorbing, though continually interrupted labour (...): yet always I had the sense of recording what was already 'there', somewhere: not of 'inventing'" (*L* 145)

Tolkien discarded his initial complicated project to focus on the *mere stories* that are the equivalent of Niggle's leaves. This attitude reveals the subcreator's humility. The subcreator contents himself with being carried away by something that has surpassed him, something he does not need to invent but that is already there. In order to be revealed, this "something" needs to pass through somebody. Then, the subcreator has to pay attention and trust his own deep feelings: if he is attracted to fascinating stories, then he has to "follow" them and will see where they take him. The result is of course often unexpected and wonderful: *The Lord of the Rings* is the tree that emerged thanks to the confidence that Tolkien put in leaves. One can easily see that this humble attitude towards creation could prevent the widening of the gap that usually separates the creator from the world he or she is living in. The subcreator is not asked to withdraw himself from reality in inventing something that does not really exist. He or she is not engaged in a sophisticated process that could finally result in his or her isolation from real life. This attitude that characterises the creative process remains compatible with the necessary attitude that everybody has to remain plainly aware of the laws. There seems to be something like a link between having the good sense to be aware of life's challenges, while at the same time being attracted by fascinating stories. Both attitudes are a product of the same "habit of thinking".

## THE 'BACK COUNTRY'

Finally, it becomes necessary to examine what it is that occupies Niggle's mind while he is working in his tall shed. Of course, he absolutely wants to finish his painting and he needs to spend time on doing that, but we also feel that this is the kind of work that cannot be finished, that is always in progress. Niggle always seems dissatisfied and spends a lot of time trying to improve his leaves. Unfortunately, he is only able to imagine the perfect leaf that he would like to paint, for example when he is riding in the rain: "now he was out of the shed, he saw exactly the way in which to treat that shining spray which framed the distant vision of the mountain" (*TL* 80). Niggle is seeking something that cannot be captured.

To better understand what Niggle's dilemma is all about, I would like to take a quick detour to look at the work of the French poet Yves Bonnefoy. In one of his loveliest prose texts, Bonnefoy tells us that his entire life he has been drawn to what he calls *l'Arrière-Pays*. *L'Arrière Pays*, also the title of this text, can be translated as *hinterland* or *back country*. During his boyhood, he mostly felt this longing when he returned to visit his parents' home in the country each summer. Experiencing the call of the back country can be compared to looking at a precise location in the distance and having the sensation that the latter is the "vrai lieu" ("real place", my translation; Bonnefoy 16) to beas the poet would put it. The "real place" is a place where we would be able to live in contentment and fulfilment, whereas our situation as after-the-fall creatures makes us dissatisfied by nature. The back country can be interpreted as the place of the absolute, a place, in a non-modern context, that would be filled with some essence of God and with which one could fill oneself. One could compare it to a dwelling place, a brief survey of paradise. Bonnefoy gives the reader an idea of what the back country looks like by likening it to a place that is bathed in light - a tree on the other side of a valley, for example.[8] Twilight and dawn seem to be particularly good times to recognise or see such a place.

Being drawn to the back country is something that many modern human beings have experienced; it is certainly the revelation of what Bonnefoy has often called *being* ("l'être") in a world that has been deserted by being.[9]

---

[8] See p.106. Bonnefoy also says that the Massif Central of his boyhood or Toscanie, that he visited many years later, also resemble the "arrière-pays" even if these two different places cannot really provide the fullness that the back country could possibly offer.

[9] *Being* ("*l'être*") is a word that only appears marginaly in *l'Arrière-pays* but this word is essential in Bonnefoy's poetry and thought and that is why I link it to his experience of the back country. It is quite delicate to understand what being is. In order to clarify its meaning, I am referring to a lecture that Bonnefoy gave at the Bibliothèque Nationale de France in 2001 where he spoke about being. I think that would allow us to better understand l'Arrière-pays and ultimately, Leaf by Niggle. The title of the conference was *Passants et passantes d'un Paris qui change*, 26th November 2001. Available as a enregistrement sonore at the Bibiothèque Nationale de France.

For the medieval thinking, Bonnefoy states, God offered some of his "being"[10] to all living creatures and even to all inert things. Being could be what God, as the pefect being, spread around himself: it was a kind of warmth that one could feel if one would approach him. Therefore, for man at that time, all things and creatures were filled with such a warmth; they were filled with "being" that came directly from God. God was everywhere in the natural world, signs of his presence showed through numerous symbols and signs. The cosmos was a book full of these signs testifying His presence. The individual knew the "pourquoi du monde" (the "why of the world"). Man felt being in him and around him and if he lived in a miserable conditions he, at least, had a compensation: "ontologic security" (the certainty to be accompanied by being, to be part of something bigger). In addition, Bonnefoy explains, everyone's lives were meaningful because their function in society had been determined by the supreme being. Therefore for people of that time, everything made sense and formed part of an order, an order that the artist tried to duplicate on his canvas: the paintings show a cosmos organised by God. But, Bonnefoy continues,from the 17$^{th}$ century onwards the scientific reading of the univers had come to progressively disqualify the inherited vision of the elders. For the modern and enlighted man the world is not a display of being: God withdrew from the world. No signs or symbols remained in the cosmos which no longer was an ordered one. Therefore, for humanity, from the advent of modern science onwards being progressively left the world and the latter became meaningless: only remained the matter. Modern humans, because they got rid of God, ended up living in a barren environment, and found themselves lost and desperate in a silent and dry world. They discovered the world's and life's absurdity: they lost the "ontologic security" and loosing that is probably what charaterises modern condition.

---

[10] In this paragraph all the words or expressions in quotation marks are used by Bonnefoy in his lecture.

Sometimes, though, in the middle of this lunar landscape, this meaningless world, modern man, thanks to a type of miraculous intervention, seems to be able to see or to slowly approach something like the former "being". Bonnefoy, in his lecture but also, for instance, in a preface of a new edition of a book of Gaëtan Picon[11] (and Gaëtan Picon himself) try to explain that the modern artist, almost subconsciously, is finally in the search of the lost being. The modern artist experiences something mysterious: sometimes, somewhere in the distance, being seems to appear again (in the form, for example, of an apparent "real place"), although it is only sporadically visible. The modern artist, instead of depicting an order as ancient artists did, will simply try to take advantage of such a moment and will try to capture this thing that resembles "being", or the location of the fullness, when he comes face to face with it. Painting a landscape, with which, Gaëtan Picon states, the modern painting begins,[12] is the fruit of such an attempt: a landscape is not a depiction of an order but rather a depiction of the 'visible' as it is at a precise moment, as it is "here and now"[13]. In the same way, the Impressionists tried to capture an "impression", an impression the artist was given and thanks to which he had the feeling of telling or depicting something of a truth .

My interpretation is that Bonnefoy lived the same fundamental and characteristic experience when referring to the back country. He also realised, however, that the back country (the country of being) always remains in the distance and that one is only able to see it for a short period of time: for instance, a change in the light could make it disappear. Also, the more he was approaching what he thought to be the

---

[11] Picon: 1863, naissance de la peinture moderne

[12] Gaëtan Picon (119) says: "L'histoire thématique de la peinture moderne commence avec le paysage, quand il est traité lui-même et directement. La tradition classique n'admet le paysage qu'intégré à une composition: comme décor d'une scène, et comme idéalisation".

[13] This expression, "ici et maintenant", is used by Gaëtan Picon, (101).

back country, the more the latter was disappearing. Thus, he was taken in by an everlasting movement that was dragging him towards the horizon. The explicit lesson of *l'Arrière-pays* ultimately is that the back country is an illusion, that it is a point that does not exist and that cannot be reached[14]. In other words, we are condemned to see it only from a distance, we cannot enter the setting without at the same time losing what we are looking for. We will remain disunited, for ever removed from the 'full dwelling place'. Therefore, we can deduce from our interpretation of Bonnefoy and Picon, that the modern artist tries capture this elusive Truth before it has vanished entirely and also tries to hold on to it.

I believe that Niggle, in trying constantly to improve his leaves, as well as Tolkien, who – in his own eyes – tried without fail to improve his stories, are in a way in search of this Truth. They remain dissatisfied because it is quite impossible to reach it, even for the best subcreator. The artist's work will forever stay imperfect because the perfection of the Truth cannot be matched. Truth or being are in the distance and the leaves or the stories might be headed in its direction but are unable to reach it. They are drawn, along with the author, to the back country and the horizon. Tolkien sums all that up in these few words written to his son in 1945:

> "A story must be told or there'll be no story, yet it is the untold stories that are most moving. I think you are moved by Celebrimbor because it conveys a sudden sense of endless untold stories: mountains seen far away, never to be climbed, distant trees (like Niggle's) never to be approached – or if so only to become 'near trees' (unless in Paradise or Niggle's Parish)" (*L* 111).

---

[14] Bonnefoy acknowleges quite rapidly in his text that he has always known that the back country does not exist: "Et je dirai d'abord que si l'arrière-pays m'est resté inaccessible – et même, je le sais bien, je l'ai toujours su, n'existe pas – [...]" (33).

Tolkien and Niggle are in search of this place and try to reach it through their art. They are drawn to that which is shying away. Now, we can better understand what differentiates the people in the two different camps. People such as Niggle and Tolkien from the first camp are those who are much more sensitive to the call of the back country, who are more capable of catching a glimpse of it in the distance and above all who have the time to try and meet it at. On the contrary, others such as Parish are not at all haunted by the back country, they are not attracted by something moving away, but, rather, by something that is approaching them or that is already there and not likely to disappear.

But what makes an individual more sensitive than others to the call of the back country? First, as we have seen, it depends on up to which point one is kept "busy" with satisfying the demands of one's plain ordinary biological life. The more time you spend satisfying your metabolism the less you are sensitive to the other dimensions of life. It is precisely why Niggle/Tolkien dreamed of getting a "public pension". A public pension allows the person who receives it to get rid of the necessity of "earning a living", in other words of working to get the money that he or she needs to live and therefore to satisfy his or her body. With a public pension one has a tendency to become carefree because one no longer worries about the necessities of life. Then, with such assistance, Niggle or Tolkien could, without any obstacle, devote themselves entirely to their art, they could freely search for this unobtainable Truth after which they are running and that makes them dream. But, as we know now, they would also progressively lose their sense of reality, they would live in a world that does not exist and they would, as mortals, waste the little time they have been given for something lost already. Secondly, this distancing depends on up to which point one has been educated. Education allows an individual to distance himself or herself from the world he or she is living in. It allows anybody to remove the hold of reality and to perceive new things amongst which are the beauty of nature and the call of the back country. The distance also allows humans to better understand the world and to explain phenomena (but only thanks to mental representation, therefore, they still remain distant from the world); in a manner of speaking, they become more "intelligent". Unfortunately the distance makes humans less adapted to life on earth because they tend to get lost in conjecture and details rather than taking things as simply as they are and as they feel them; they become more sophisticated. This is why, when Tolkien mentioned in 1969 the "dull stodges" and "those of higher intelligence", he said the second were "corrupted and disintegrated by school, and the climate of our present days" (*L* 403-404).

Tolkien, with the ability of one who was educated and partly freed from necessities, realised that the particular location where being lies cannot be approached, and if so "distant trees become only 'near trees'". Bonnefoy and he both noticed the same thing. This search will always turn out to be fruitless and this is why it is all the more important not to stay in the tall shed but to respond to the calls and to respect the laws that are "already here". Trying to reach the back country is vanity and should be resisted. From the moment the Númenóreans decided to sail west towards the "Blessed Realm" they turned from "beneficence (…) to pride, desire of power and wealth" (*L* 205). In 1964 Tolkien says "One loyal to the Valar, content with the bliss and prosperity within the limits prescribed" (*L* 347).

The impossibility of reaching the "Undying Land" (*L* 194) is also the theme of the poem "The Last Ship" published in *The Adventures of Tom Bombadil*. A girl named Fíriel sees an elf-boat going by and the elves invite her to join them ; they are going to "Elvenhome, where the white tree is growing". "Do you hear the call, Earth-maiden?" the elves say; this call Niggle, Tolkien and Bonnefoy also received. But when Fíriel dares to take one step to come on board, "deep in clay her feet sank" and "slowly the elven-ship went by". "I cannot come […] I was born Earth's daughter!", cries Firiel. Inhabitants of the earth can see the boat going to the Blessed Realm but they cannot reach the ship. It is only possible to see it moving away from the river-bank, as only in the distance is it possible to see the back country. Here arises one of the biggest frustrations that can possibly be felt by modern man: being able to see heaven but being unable to be in it.

The lesson of *Leaf, by Niggle* is that the back country is not to be found here and while we are on earth we have to stay "within the limits prescribed". If we are meant to find it, it can only be after death: in paradise or Niggle's Parish. It is after his journey and his judgement and not before that Niggle is able to enter the landscape and move among his leaves "as he had imagined them rather than as he had made them" (*TL* 88-89).

> As he walked away, he discovered an odd thing: the forest, of course, was a distant Forest, yet he could approach it, even enter it, without its losing that particular charm. He had never before been able to walk into the distance without turning it into mere surroundings. (*TL* 89)

Niggle has finally reached his place, but he has left for good the consistent world. Now he will be able to finish his painting that is also a garden, with the help of Parish of course. Then he will go to where it had always been forbidden or impossible for him to go when he was still on earth: beyond the mountains.

> "Beyond that I cannot guess what became of him. Even little Niggle in his old home could glimpse the Mountains far away, and they got into the borders of his picture ; but what they are really like, and what lies beyond them only those can say who have climbed them" (TL 93)

says the tale at the end. However, we know that Tolkien was also hoping to find a resting place, the celestial dwelling place, a place, he told his son, "called 'heaven' where the good here unfinished is completed, and where the stories unwritten, and the hopes unfulfilled are continued" (*L* 55). This Tolkien's deep desire is the same as Bilbo's at the beginning of *The Lord of the Rings* and gives an extraordinary strength to this heartfelt cry: "I want to see mountains again, (…) – mountains; and then find somewhere where I can rest." (I, 41).

## CONCLUSION

The message conveyed by Tolkien through *Leaf, by Niggle* is no doubt very relevant to the present situation. In fact, on a large scale, humans tend to be more and more sophisticated. Firstly, today, humans "know" probably more than they have ever known. Thanks to science and schooling, knowledge has spread. But, for all that, it doesn't mean that we are better equipped for facing reality. In the Fifties in the Netherlands, it was perfectly well known that the country would be the victim of terrible flooding because of the fragility of the sea walls and of the fact that many people lived under the sea level. The Dutch "knew" it thanks to their thinking abilities and intelligence. Unfortunately, "to know" something is often useless, only to "live" something is really useful: the heralded catastrophe happened, thousands of peoples died and finally the authorities decided to improve their protections against the sea. There would be many other examples showing that the sphere of intelligence and reason does not intersect with the sphere of real life. Sometimes, one can have the impression that both are side by side unable to act on each other. Secondly, humans have been able to make their lifes more comfortable . Rather than growing potatoes, we go to the supermarket to get food: it's much faster and really less tiring. With the saved time and efforts, we study, have some spare-time activities, play sport, go to cinema, write books or papers… ultimately, we live far from the earth, shut up indoors in a secondary reality. But, the problem is we might find ourselves in the situation of the inhabitants of Antioch in the year 256. That year, Chantal Delsol tells[15] on one occasion everyone was at the theatre and no one saw the archers from the Persian army deploying under the terraces. No longer reminded of reality and concrete things by the necessity to satisfy their biological needs and also without the earth's teaching, inhabitants of the city forgot the essential: that their city could be attacked and must be defended. This is the biggest danger which carefree man is confronted with and which, I think, Tolkien had always in mind: to forget tangible realities.

At last, we can also evoke how this story is marked by Christian morals[16]. At first glance, Christian faith might not seem to value the earthly life because it never stopped saying that the "genuine life" would be after death in the celestial dwelling place. The terrestrial sojourn is imperfect and is nothing compared to what humanity has been promised later. But something essential came and changed the deal: God himself became a human through His son. Jesus came down on earth, he came to Firiel's river bank and he too trod the clay. While he could have stayed in the perfect, he decided to descend to the imperfect. The message of the incarnation was made for the humans tending to gaze too much beyond the mountains, to remind them that the time had not come. More important and urgent things are waiting for them during their terrestrial sojourn, things not to be neglected.

---

[15] In *le souci contemporain*, 273. This book has been translated in english under the title *Icarus Fallen*.

[16] We have to remember that the story was delivered to the *Dublin Review* after the editor of the latter asked Tolkien in 1944 "for a story which would help his magazine to be a 'effective expression of Catholic humanity'" (Shippey 266).

BERTRAND ALLIOT works as a teaching and research assistant at the Hannah Arendt Institute of the University Paris-Est. He is also a doctoral candidate specialising in Political Science whose thesis focuses on nature and environment. He has already published an article on Tolkien in Tolkien and Modernity, published in 2006 by Walking Tree Publishers.

## Works Cited

Alliot, Bertrand. Tolkien: a simplicity between the truly earthy and the absolutely modern. *Tolkien and Modernity*, Vol. 1 (ed. Frank Weinreich and Th Honegger). Zurich, Bern: Walking Tree Publishers 2006.

Bonnefoy, Yves. *L'Arrière Pays* (first edition 1972). Paris: Poésie/Gallimard, 1992.

Delsol, Chantal. *Le souci contemporain.* Paris: La Table Ronde, la peteite vermillon 2004

---, Icarus Fallen, The Search for Meaning in an Uncertain World. Wilmington: ISI Books, 2003

Garth, John. *Tolkien and the Great War: the Treshhold of Middle Earth.* Boston New-York: Houghton Mifflin, 2003.

Picon, Gaëtan. *1863, naissance de la peinture moderne,* Paris: Gallimard 1988.

Shippey, Tom. *J.R.R. Tolkien Author of the Century.* Boston, New-York: Houghton Mifflin, 2000.

Tolkien, John Ronald Reuel. *The Fellowship of the Ring.* Boston, New York: Houghton Mifflin, 1993.

---, *The Two Towers.* 2nd ed. Boston: Houghton Mifflin, 1993.

---, *Tree and Leaf.* London: George Allen & Unwin, 1975

---, *The Letters of J.R.R. Tolkien* (edited by Humphrey Carpenter, with the assistance of Christopher Tolkien). London: George Allen & Unwin, 1981.

---, *The Hobbit.* London: George Allen & Unwin, 1987.

---, *The Adventures of Tom Bombadil,* (first edition 1962). London: Harper-Collins, 1995.

# The Autobiographical Tolkien

HEIDI STEIMEL

ABSTRACT

Despite Tolkien's emphatic statements that he did not write allegory, even detested it, and his denial of the reader's need to know anything about the author in order to understand and enjoy his works, he wrote two stories which contain various allegorical aspects, namely *Leaf by Niggle* and *Smith of Wootton Major*. This paper explores what he says about himself as a person, about his relationship to his family and their connection to his work, and about the rift and conflict between the author and the private person. Special emphasis is placed on the differences and contrasts shown in the two books and their significance in the context of the time of their writing. The conclusion ponders the effect they have had on both the author and his readers.

Public interest in the person of J.R.R. Tolkien has run high throughout the years as his books have grown popular, and many who have read one of the biographies written by others have surely wished that he had left his admirers a journal or an autobiography to peruse. It would have been wonderful to find out more about the creator of Middle-earth from the author himself! However, it is highly unlikely that he would ever have contemplated recording his life for the public to read.

Still, we have some information about the person of this fascinating man, the 'Author of the Century' (to use Shippey's phrase), from his own pen. We can read hundreds of the letters he wrote to his family, friends, and fans. We can glean scraps of personal information from his scholarly essays. And we have two tales, *Leaf by Niggle* and *Smith of Wootton Major*, which Shippey calls "autobiographical allegories" (*Author of the Century* 265), that give us a glimpse of the author himself in his characters.

For all who would protest that Tolkien disliked allegory and we should not attempt to read his works as such, I would like to clarify my intentions in his own words: My conclusions "reside in the freedom of the reader", not in "the purposed domination of the author" (*LotR* xi). A number of Tolkien experts and reviewers who have written about these two stories agree that there is an element of allegory in them, though their views differ greatly as to the nature and extent of it.

In one early review of *Smith* that was written during Tolkien's lifetime, soon after the publication of the story in 1967, Roger Lancelyn Green penned the now famous sentence, "To seek for the meaning is to cut open the ball in search of its bounce" (*L* 388). Tolkien liked that metaphor, which speaks against a search for allegorical meaning and is strongly reminiscent of Gandalf's words to Saruman: "He that breaks a thing to find out what it is has left the path of wisdom" (*LotR* 339).

Verlyn Flieger picks up on that comment approvingly, strongly advocating *Smith*'s interpretation on its own terms, as a fairy tale. But even she admits that there are "half-hidden references to the choices of his own life" and "obvious parallels with its author's creative life", concluding: "There is some validity in both the autobiographical and the allegorical elements that are genuinely to be found for those who seek them" (*A Question of Time* 231).

Tom Shippey, on the other hand, rejects Green's metaphor of the bounce and says, "Much of the pleasure I take in the story comes from searching out allegory" (Flieger and Shippey 192). and "An allegorical story is much more like a crossword-puzzle" (*Author of the Century* 297). He then goes on to allegorize details of the story until no white spaces are left – an interesting approach, but one that perhaps goes too far, even for a puzzle-lover like myself!

In *Master of Middle-Earth* Paul Kocher finds that both Niggle and Smith have autobiographical references and goes on to say of the first: "Allowing for artistic differences, the story may well be looked at as an effort on Tolkien's part to find some underlying meaning for all his labors, if not in this life then in the next" (161). Of the second story he says: "Reading "Smith of Wootton Major" as Tolkien's personal farewell to his art is tempting, and has at least as good an argument to support it as reading Shakespeare's *The Tempest* in the same autobiographical light" (201).

In her book *Tolkien's Art,* Jane Chance calls the stories "fictional autobiography" (83), saying that "Tolkien rewrites his own life as a fairy-story" and that "his hopes and fears as a man, an artist, and a Christian surface in these two stories" (84).

In *Tolkien: Man and Myth* Joseph Pearce says that Priscilla Tolkien believed *Leaf by Niggle* was the 'most autobiographical' (174) of all of her father's works. He adds, "'Niggle's Tree' is clearly a euphemism for Tolkien's own subcreation, principally *The Lord of the Rings* but also *The Silmarillion* on which he laboured all his life and which, like Niggle's Tree, would ultimately remain uncompleted at his death" (174).

Since I had read Carpenter's biography of Tolkien before I discovered his minor works, I felt the connection between his characters and his own person upon first reading, even if I did not immediately think about specific details. The better I get to know them, the more I see, and without wishing to overburden the stories with too much psychoanalytical interpretation, I am convinced that more of the author's own person slipped into them than he himself realized.

## THE BACKGROUND

The first story, *Leaf by Niggle*, was very likely written by Tolkien in 1942 and published in 1945. It was unusual in its conception, since there was no lengthy process of planning, writing, and revision. Tolkien later said that he awoke with the tale complete in his mind, and that it changed very little from the first writing to its final form. Did he dream the story? We don't know, but it appears to have sprung directly from his subconscious mind – a very appealing notion for psychological interpretation!

It was written during a time in which he was working on *The Lord of the Rings*. The struggle and uncertainty of that creative process is reflected in it, and it seems that some of the despair of World War II crept into it as well. He struggled to find a purpose in his creative work – 'midlife crisis' we would call it nowadays.

*Smith of Wootton Major* is the last story that Tolkien wrote, and was the last of his works published during his lifetime. By the time he wrote it in the mid 1960s, his major work, *The Lord of the Rings*, had become a success and he had retired from his profession; the outright and frequently annoying fame of his late years had not yet come to him. *The Silmarillion* seemed to have little or no chance of being finished and published, and he apparently no longer had the energy to focus on it seriously enough to complete its narrative. It was time to look back and take stock of his life.

The story was actually a side-product, developing from an introduction to MacDonald's book *The Golden Key*, a project which was eventually abandoned. Tolkien began to explain his idea of Faery with the Great Cake, and the story was developed, expanded and changed until it found its final form. He worked out a list of characters, some of which never actually appearcome into the story, but form a geneological background for the main character, and a timeline. Thanks to Verlyn Flieger's work, we have access to those in the Extended Edition of *Smith*.

### THE PROTAGONISTS

The main character of each story is named in the title, and the seemingly small differences are worth noting. *Leaf by Niggle* names the character together with his only surviving creative work – the artist and his painting. *Smith of Wootton Major* places the hero of his story firmly in the context of his village, his community. After all, the tale is not called "Smith in Faerie", as one might have expected when thinking of "Alice in Wonderland", another Oxford professor's fantastic story.

It is also interesting to compare the original story titles: the first was called "The Tree" (Scull and Hammond, *Companion and Guide: Reader's Guide* 495), a concentration on the artist's complete work; in its final version, it is reduced to one leaf, together with the humble name of the artist. The story of Smith was originally called "The Great Cake" (*SWM* 136), at that point leaving out the main character in favour of the human depiction of Faery which includes the passport star.

Tolkien chose the names of his characters with care; they are quite different from each other, yet both show the autobiographical nature of the character. 'Niggle' is not a commonly found surname; it comes from a verb that describes a character trait. Shippey quotes the definition given by the Oxford English Dictionary: "To work ... in a trifling, fiddling, or ineffective way ... to work or spend time unnecessarily on petty details; to be over-elaborate in minor points." He then comments, "This was certainly a vice of which Tolkien could be accused." (*Author* 267) And indeed, in one of his letters Tolkien says of himself, "I am a natural niggler, alas!" (*L* 313)

'Smith' is one of the most common traditional English surnames, coming from the craft which the character pursues. A smith makes useful items of metal and is a necessary craftsman in his community. Utility is the first purpose of his products (and unlike Tolkien's character here, many smiths considered weapon-making their most important task), yet there is still the possibility of creativity as well, either in the design or the embellishment of a necessary object, or in the making of objects intended for decoration or play. The name 'Smith' tells us nothing about the individual himself, but merely names his occupation.

Niggle has no apparent profession; we are not told how he earns his living. He is a dilettante rather than a professional artist, described as a "painter by nature" (*TL* 106), "not a very successful one" (*TL* 93), who paints pictures that are for the most part "too large and ambitious for his skill." (*TL* 94) He has creative ideas that are unique, and his paintings are beautiful, exquisite, with a distinctive style. Still, he does not paint houses nor produce posters, so his painting is neither useful nor productive.

Tolkien combines aspects of both the craftsman and the dilettante. His writing is not entirely separate from his profession as a philologist, but he was not a professional author. His style is unique, often imitated but never copied, full of breathtaking beauty, and unforgettable for those who have gotten to know it. His creativity is unparalleled.

There is one very literal autobiographical connection between Tolkien and Niggle that most commentators have missed – Tolkien himself was a painter! Hammond and Scull point out:

> Tolkien was also himself an artist, who painted and drew despite many demands upon his time, and who would struggle through several versions of a picture, if needed, to capture his inner vision. He was Niggle-like also in glimpsing, in his mind's eye, far countries, and forests 'marching over the land', and 'mountains tipped with snow', which he put into pictures as well as into words. And he seems to have genuinely believed of himself the criticism he directed at Niggle, that his ambition in art usually exceeded his talent – an arguable point [...]. (*Artist and Illustrator* 9)

So many artists have illustrated Tolkien's books since they were published that we often forget that he drew and painted the first illustrations and dust-jackets for *The Hobbit* and *The Lord of the Rings* himself, as well as many pictures of *Silmarillion* themes.

Smith is a professional, a craftsman by trade. His workmanship is good, and though he had learned the trade from his father, he improved upon it and excelled in it. Most of his products are

> "[...] plain and useful, meant for daily needs [...] strong and lasting, but they also had a grace about them, being shapely in their kinds, good to handle and to look at. But some things, when he had time, he made for delight, and they were beautiful, for he could work iron into wonderful forms that looked as light and delicate as a spray of leaves and blossom, but kept the stern strength of iron [...]" (*SWM* 21)

This can be compared to Tolkien's chosen profession; as a philologist and professor – words were his daily business. Yet they were also his passion: "He had been inside language", C. S. Lewis said. (*Biography* 180) He was both craftsman and artist with words. He spent most of his time concerned with academic matters, the practical aspect of his trade; but his true genius shone when he took the time to write for pleasure. What Tolkien writes about Smith's creativity, involved in both practical daily life and in objects made for pleasure, but both coming from the same craft, seems to indicate that he was able to see a connection between his own professional and creative writing toward the end of his life.[1]

## THE PLACES

Neither story takes place at a specifically defined time, though we can draw some general conclusions from details. Niggle lives in a time mod-

---

[1] Shippey goes into additional detail with his allegorization of birch and oak in the story as symbols for the two contrasting schemes of philological education. (*Author* 302-3) Those are interesting thoughts, but since they involve information unknown to most readers, I consider them irrelevant for a general interpretation of the story.

ern enough to include bicycles and trains. Smith's time is more medieval and even less possible to pin down.

The characters live in greatly divergent situations. Niggle lives alone, in a house miles away from the town (which is not named). The only neighbours that live close by are Parish and his wife. He has a number of acquaintances from further away who visit him or ask for his help, but it appears that none of them are actually close to him. He is basically isolated, an individual by himself, with no mention of family background.

Smith lives in a village, is integrated and has his function within a closely-knit community. He has not only a wife and children, but is given a family background as well. His grandfather was the Master Cook at the beginning of the story, the person who was instrumental in setting its events in motion. And by the end of the story, Smith has a grandson too – the family line continues.

## THE SECONDARY CHARACTERS

Though Niggle seems to be a solitary main character, his neighbour Parish becomes more and more important in the course of the story. Tolkien wrote that he chose the name Parish because it worked for the Porter's joke (*L* 321), but did not intend it to have any special significance. However, we can assume that the philologist in him did not choose a random word for this important character. 'Parish' is a term used in the church, where it is used for a district or an area of responsibility. It can also denote a civil community, a subdivision for administrative purposes.

I can see no overt religious significance in the character of Parish within this story; his role is secular. He is an administrator in his own small way: interested in making things orderly, such as removing weeds; in achieving results, such as growing potatoes; and in being practical, repairing the roof of his house, for example. He has all the traits that Niggle is missing.

Chance comments, "If "Parish" personifies the practical and economic needs of a geographical area, then "Niggle" personifies the earthly failure to supply those needs." (89) To her, Parish symbolizes the body, Niggle the soul. Like the often conflicting interests of body and soul, the two men are in conflict during earthly life, not recognizing each other's needs, unwillingly providing for them, and finally achieving harmony only after the purgatorial learning process.

Furthermore, Parish is a family man; his wife is mentioned, though she does not enter directly into the story. In life Niggle and Parish neither understand nor appreciate each other and are more critical than sympathetic.

When I first read this story, I was puzzled over Niggle's isolation. Though he was obviously linked with Tolkien, so much of what made up Tolkien's person was missing in Niggle. Then I read what Shippey wrote about Parish, and things fell into place.

> It is attractive to see Niggle and Parish as a 'bifurcation', as two aspects of Tolkien's own personality which he wished he could combine: the one creative, irresponsible, without ties [...] the other [...] earthbound, practical, immediately productive. (*Author of the Century* 274)

Parish annoys Niggle with interruptions concerning daily cares, and the interrupted flow of artistic creativity cannot be resumed at will. In Carpenter's biography we read of the demands of domestic affairs – punctual meals, household repairs, and other daily matters – as well as of academic matters – lectures, meetings, students, and paper correcting – on Tolkien's time. For those reasons much of his creative writing was done during the night hours. In the Foreword to the American paperback edition of *The Lord of the Rings*, he says of this time in his life: "The composition of *The Lord of the Rings* went on at intervals during the years 1936 to 1949, a period in which I had many duties that I did not neglect, and many other interests [...]" (*LotR* viii – ix).

In addition, we find out that Parish has a lame leg and that he and his wife are subject to illnesses. One of the things that I found both significant and sad when reading Tolkien's biography and Hammond and Scull's *Chronology* was how much illness interfered with his life and that of his family. So much time and energy seems to have been wasted because of it! Parish's overly concerned appeal to Niggle for help when his wife is ill seems to echo what Carpenter wrote about the Tolkiens: "He was [...] greatly concerned about her health (as she was about his)" [...] (*Biography* 207).

Smith, on the other hand, is not a divided character, though he is a traveller in both worlds. He has a wife and two children: a son who follows in his footsteps as a craftsman, and a daughter through whom the family line already continues, in his grandson.

He journeys to Faery alone, without his family, which waits for him at home. Do they resent having to share him with that other world? Do they feel excluded from something that is important to him? Do they think he is shirking his duties at home? Tolkien's biographer writes that his wife Edith resented the time he spent with his male friends, who were so important to him (*Biography* 208).

However, though the family cannot share Smith's adventures, they are his attentive, appreciative, and supportive audience when he comes back. He can speak to them freely of things that he does not tell others. They can see the star on his brow and cherish the flower that he brought from Faery as a secret treasure.

In his essay on *Smith*, Tolkien wrote that Nell and Nan "were probably themselves elf-friends and even walkers in Outer Faery" (*SWM* 99). That he should say this, though his communication concerning his creative works took place primarily with his male friends, shows how important it was to him to have his family share in his experience. Interestingly, Carpenter writes that Edith was the first person to whom Tolkien showed these two stories, not a member of the Inklings or another friend (*Biography* 210).

Smith's son Ned can easily be identified with Tolkien's youngest son Christopher. Both followed in their fathers' professional footsteps, but without the same creative spark of genius. In Tolkien's "Suggestions for the ending of the story", he writes several lines about Ned. Could they perhaps be applied to Christopher as well?

> The son is obviously taking up his father['s] work in the world of Men though his intimations of 'Fayery' will never go beyond what he has received at second hand from his father [...]. (*SWM* 81)
>
> Ned was dependent on his father: he could receive 'Faery' only through the love and companionship of the older Smith. (*SWM* 99).

Both sons were able to recognize the greatness of their fathers; Ned tells Smith, "You look like a giant, Dad" (*SWM* 35). Christopher was named by his father as his literary heir and executor, because he was felt to have the necessary appreciation for and knowledge of his father's works. As far as we know, the son did not contribute any new leaves to the Great Tree, but we are all greatly indebted to him for making so many of his father's leaves available to us.

At the time of the writing of this story, the author already had grandchildren, though unlike the fictional Smith family, the Tolkien line continues through the sons, not the daughter.

Flieger points out that there is another autobiographical character in this tale – Rider, Smith's grandfather, the Master Cook at the beginning of the story. Tolkien himself said that he "seems to have set going the events that occupy this tale" (*SWM* 88), and Flieger adds: "He is the major human motive force behind the action" (*A Question of Time* 237). He introduces the Elven king to Wootton Major as the apprentice Alf, then leaves the passport star that will be baked into the cake. The similarity to the role of the author himself may well be more than mere chance. Rider is also a traveller in both worlds, like Tolkien.

## THE STORIES

The stories depict the lives of their characters. At which points do they coincide with the biography of the author? Niggle's story begins with one man, alone: "There was once a little man called Niggle" (*TL* 93). Only one-third of his story takes place during his earthly life; the main focus is on the afterlife. In this, Tolkien's Christian faith (more specifically Catholic, since Purgatory is involved) is shown clearly. The story is deeply religious.

It concentrates on the artist's creative work – the Great Tree. Tolkien often used the allegory of a tree for his works, even for himself, and his own paintings and drawings frequently feature trees. The "Tree of Amalion" seems closely related to Niggle's tree:

> I have among my papers more than one version of a mythical 'tree', which crops up regularly at those times when I feel driven to pattern-designing. They are elaborate and coloured and more suitable for embroidery than printing; and the tree bears besides various shapes of leaves many flowers small and large signifying poems and major legends. (*L* 342)

The tree on the cover of the book *Tree and Leaf* is a version of that tree.

In connection with the tale of Niggle, he himself gives an autobiographical link, writing about a beloved tree which was in danger of being felled: "Also, of course, I was anxious about my own internal Tree, *The Lord of the Rings*. It was growing out of hand, and revealing endless new vistas – and I wanted to finish it, but the world was threatening" (*L* 321).

After the purgatorial learning process, Niggle finds that his tree exists in the reality of the afterlife. He and Parish meet again, and now they not only appreciate each other's abilities, but work together in companionship to continue the sub-creative process. The rift between the artist and the gardener is healed, and practical use is combined with beauty.

Kocher has some very interesting thoughts on this:

> Niggle's astounded perception that his best painting has been done in collaboration with Parish exemplifies a further doctrine of Tolkien's, that no writer can subcreate a secondary world successfully without first having a clear-eyed knowledge of life in our primary world. The only contribution which could possibly have been made to Niggle's painting by this lame, whining neighbor with his endless demands on Niggle's time and energy must consist in these very demands. Without them Niggle would not have been forced daily to grapple so closely with the hard facts of actual existence. Morally, this is his salvation. Artistically, it gives him a strong sense of fact essential to fantasy.
>
> Parish's gift to Niggle, then, was to provide the frustrating dreariness that prickled his imagination to frame ("glimpse") a greener, more spacious world for the refreshment of himself and others. (166)

Tolkien must have longed for that inner oneness; did he despair of achieving it during his lifetime? His main character in *The Lord of the Rings*, Frodo, does not find that healing in his home in the Shire. When he leaves for the Undying Lands, he says to Sam: "Do not be too sad, Sam. You cannot always be torn in two" *(LotR* 382). Though the cause of Frodo's wounds is more drastic, the longing for wholeness is similar.

Niggle looks forward; his gaze concentrates on the future in the Otherworld of the Afterlife. The work that the artist accomplished during life was only a prelude. What he left behind on Earth found destruction for the most part, some cynical criticism, and very little genuine appreciation. Even the one small picture that was kept (which I interpret as a symbol for his one published book at that time, *The Hobbit*) was eventually destroyed. Nothing was left to remind the world that Niggle had ever existed. That must have been a "worst case scenario" for Tolkien when he thought of his life's work! Yet for Niggle, the real work of art comes alive in paradise. Therein lies this story's hope, and its eucatastrophe. It ends in laughter.

Smith's story begins with the village: "There was a village once [...]" (*SWM* 5). Its organisation and special characteristics are described, the feast and the Great Cake are explained, and we get to know the Master Cook, Alf Prentice, and Nokes long before we are introduced to Smith. According to Tolkien's timeline, he is 9 years old when he swallows the Star, and awakens to Faery on his 10$^{th}$ birthday. I wonder, did Tolkien feel that this age had any significance for him? There was certainly an awaking to the enchantment of language during his childhood, though perhaps not pinned down to a particular point of time.

The journeys to Faery are only described, not explained. Verlyn Flieger says that the reader participates in Smith's "enchantment, bewilderment, and acceptance of that which he cannot understand" ("Allegory Versus Bounce" 189) I have not attempted to equate any of his experiences there with Tolkien's own biography. However, it is interesting to realise that this story does not focus on the character's creative work, as Niggle's does, but on his experiences, his journeys to Faery. Had Tolkien's view of what was important in his life changed by that time?

There is no mention of religion in the story, though Tolkien himself said that there was some allegory in the Great Hall (as church) and the Master Cook (as parson). This aspect is rarely noticed by first-time readers.

Most significantly, the story ends not with a "happily ever after", not with death and afterlife, but with loss and bereavement. Though eucatastrophe is present, as it must be in a fairy tale, I find it less tangible here than elsewhere in Tolkien's works. Smith relinquishes the star, the King of Faery leaves Wootton Major, Nokes remains inwardly unchanged despite his weight loss.

Yet life goes on. The next generation has been born – a physical heir; the star has passed on to a new spiritual heir, and the next Smith prepares to take over as professional heir. There is peace, a measure of satisfaction and fulfillment, but in my eyes also a melancholy air of resignation. Smith does not look forward; his gaze lingers on the past, though he finds "consolation in family and friends", "transcending the grief", "sweetening the bitterness of the pain and gently balancing the loss with renewed appreciation for the things of this world" (Flieger, *Question of Time* 229).

Tolkien himself called this "An old man's book, already weighted with the presage of 'bereavement'" (*L* 389). It seems that Middle-earth is no longer as easily accessible to him; he continues to work on the *Silmarillion*, but without a publishing goal and without the energy for the extensive revision that would have been required, it must have lost some of its enchantment for him.

I cannot help but feel that C. S. Lewis' death in 1963, not long before this story was written, added to Tolkien's sense of permanent loss. Lewis was his staunchest encourager when he wrote *The Lord of the Rings*, and though they had less contact in later years, after his death Tolkien wrote: "So far I have felt [...] like an old tree that is losing all its leaves one by one: this feels like an axe-blow to the roots" (*L* 341).

Still, the ending is not entirely without hope: the enchantment of Faery is not dependent upon one individual and cannot be destroyed by those who deny its existence. It is there for those who wish to discover it, and Tolkien must have hoped that many would continue where he had led the way.

## CONCLUSION

What did Tolkien achieve for himself in these stories? Did he find recovery, refreshment, consolation, in them? When we look at the differences between his main characters in the first and second of these autobiographical fairy-tales, we can see a learning process that the author experienced in the course of those twenty years of his own life.

> If he meant, even sub-consciously, the first story to be applicable to his life, it cannot have been merely an analogy to the afterlife. It was too early in his life for him to wish earnestly for death in order to gain what he thought he needed! He felt his deficiencies and wished for a balance, a corrective influence, though he could not yet clearly see how it was to be achieved. And apparently the practical issues of life, the interruptions, the illnesses, the drudgeries brought that to him.
> The whole tale expresses both Tolkien's self-accusation and self-justification, and [...] its solution in Heaven lies in Niggle and Parish, the creative and the practical aspects of Tolkien himself, learning to work together – though what they work on, you notice, is very definitely Niggle's Tree and Country, not Parish's potatoes at all. (Shippey, *Road to Middle-earth* 41)

In the second story we find that his autobiographical character is whole, no longer divided into two separate persons. Though he wanders to Faery and is filled with longing for it, his true home is in real life, in the context of his family, his profession, his village.

Yet this story too is written as part of a learning process which the author experiences.

> It was in the writing of *Smith* that Tolkien came to confront and accept the limits of his own ventures into Faërie... and it was in that story that he came finally to acknowledge in the way he knows best his growing sense that his time was running out. (Flieger, *Question of Time* 236)

What about us, his readers? Why am I, why are we so eager to find out as much as possible about the author whose works we love?

Certainly Tolkien was right when he said that it is not necessary for the understanding of his stories; the enchantment is there, whether we know more about him or not. Neither can a mere knowledge of information about the person and his life explain the fascination.

Getting to know Tolkien in the biographical works of others and in his own autobiographical writing shows me a man who is deeply human in his geniality. It encourages me to emulate him in overcoming my weaknesses and living my life the best I can. It shows me that there is a purpose to the things which I resent because they seem to take me away from what I wish to experience, away from the reality of daily life. I can look forward to personal wholeness because even one as torn as he ultimately found it.

Perhaps most importantly, Tolkien inspires me to become an active sub-creator, though my chosen form of art is very different from his. In that way, I can add my small leaves to his Great Tree and follow his footsteps into Faerie.

HEIDI STEIMEL graduated from Grace University, Omaha, Nebraska, U.S.A. with a degree in sacred music, majoring in piano. Besides serving as a church musician, she plays piano concerts featuring spirituals and gospel music and has been a piano teacher for many years. She also freelances as a translator and interpreter. Her interest in Tolkien's works goes back to her college days. As an amateur textile artist, she has created several works on Tolkien themes, including one that was developed in conjunction with this paper. She lives in Lippstadt, Germany.

## Works Cited

Carpenter, Humphrey. *J.R.R. Tolkien: A Biography*. London: George Allen & Unwin, 1977. London: HarperCollins, 2002.

Carpenter, Humphrey. *The Letters of J.R.R. Tolkien*. London: HarperCollins, 1995.

Chance, Jane. *Tolkien's Art. A Mythology for England. Revised Edition*. Kentucky: University Press, 2001.

Flieger, Verlyn. *A Question of Time*. Kent, Ohio: Kent State University Press, 1997.

Flieger, Verlyn, and Tom Shippey. "Allegory Versus Bounce: Tolkien's *Smith of Wootton Major*." *Journal of the Fantastic in the Arts*, Vol. 12, No. 2: 186 – 200.

Hammond, Wayne G., and Christina Scull. *J.R.R. Tolkien: Artist and Illustrator*. New York: Houghton Mifflin, 1995.

Kocher, Paul H. *Master of Middle-earth*. New York: Ballantine, 1977.

Pearce, Joseph. Tolkien: Man and Myth. London: HarperCollins, 1998.

Scull, Christina, and Wayne G. Hammond. *The J.R.R. Tolkien Companion and Guide*. 2 vols.: *Reader's Guide, Chronology*. London: HarperCollins, 2006.

Shippey, Tom. *The Road to Middle-earth*. London: HarperCollins, 1992.

---, *J.R.R. Tolkien: Author of the Century*. London: HarperCollins, 2000.

Tolkien, John Ronald Reuel. "Leaf by Niggle". *Tree and Leaf*. London: HarperCollins, 2001, 93-118.

---, ed. Verlyn Flieger. *Smith of Wootton Major. Extended Edition*. London: HarperCollins, 2005.

---, *The Lord of the Rings*. New York: Ballantine, 1965.

# Leaf by Tolkien? Allegory and Biography in Tolkien's Literary Theory and Practice

FABIAN GEIER

ABSTRACT[1]

This essay deals with the seeming contradictions between Tolkien's depreciation of biographical and allegorical readings on the one hand and his frequent use of such elements in his writings on the other. The main goal is to show that Tolkien's attitude towards allegory and biography is not ambivalent, as it has often been considered, but indicates a fully consistent position, especially when we regard it in the wider context of Tolkien's theory of literature. In order to make this plausible I attempt to discuss step by step the relevant statements and texts. Special regard is paid to *Leaf by Niggle*, which proves to be the toughest challenge when it comes to reconciling Tolkien's theoretical statements with his literary works. Here a major issue will be to distinguish different notions, like *allegory* and *applicability*, *universal* and *concrete allegories*, or the *occurrence* of biographical elements as opposed to their *representation*. Tolkien's denial of various theoretical approaches does nevertheless stem from one common origin: his overall attitude to consider immediate fascination as prior to theoretical reflection, both in writing and reading. And this position is not arbitrary, but grounded both in the idea of sub-creation as well as in Tolkien's objective aesthetics.

INTERPRETATIONS

If an author deliberately writes an allegory, he usually makes the representations he intends not too difficult to spot. The allegorical readings of *Leaf by Niggle* that I want to give are therefore either not very new or cannot be ascertained beyond any doubt. However, these interpretations are not the core of my talk, but merely the starting-point for investigating Tolkien's attitude towards such interpretations.

---

[1] "I want to thank Heidi Steimel warmly for proofreading this paper."

Let us first have a look at the skeleton-plot[2] of the story: the sequence of everyday life, irreversible departure, sublimation and a final idyll corresponds (as has often been noticed) with the Christian, or more specifically the Catholic idea of afterlife (because Catholicism alone includes Purgatory). Even this interpretation leaves room for doubts, but (at least for those who do grant an author a certain measure of insight into his own texts) we do have Tolkien's own confirmation, who calls *Leaf by Niggle* "my 'purgatorial' story"(*L* 195). Following this interpretation we can try to analyse more specific elements: we could for example attempt to identify the two voices at the ward with God and Jesus, or, in a more abstract fashion, with the dichotomy of law and mercy, between which Christianity always oscillates. And we could as well try to view the laws and customs within the story as representations of social and academic duties. However it is easy to see that the traces of allegory become fainter and fainter the further we go beyond the general pattern and turn to the details. The more specifically we look at it, the more vague the allegory seems to be.

There is, however, aside from the theological aspects, another allegorical dimension to *Leaf by Niggle* that provides us with clear parallels: the story mirrors many aspects of Tolkien's life[3]. Here, too, we do have his own words, when he identifies Niggle's tree with *The Lord of the Rings*, which was then in the making (L 321). But we have also the sheer text as a proof, that describes much of the situation in which Tolkien found himself, as Tom Shippey has shown in detail (Shippey, *Author* 264ff). I do not want to repeat Shippey's findings and thus confine my remarks to three main issues:

---

[2] See *BMC* 14.

[3] Therefore I would doubt a primarily social reading of *Leaf by Niggle*. Of course the demands and ignorance of the community towards *Niggle* have an equivalent in the behaviour of many people in primary reality. However the depiction of Niggle is much too (self-)critical to view him as a unrecognised genius. And Tolkien does not cast any doubt on the legitimacy of the duties Niggle is supposed to perform.

There is a first parallel between Tolkien's and Niggle's *working attitude*. They suffer from the same faults: they "paint leaves better than trees"(*LN* 121), which means they easily end up fiddling with details so that they never reach their overall goal. This is indeed the meaning of the name "Niggle", according to the OED: "to work in a trifling, fiddling or ineffective way... to spend much time unnecessarily on petty details and be over-elaborate in minor points". And this is a name that Tolkien adopts also for himself, calling himself a "natural niggler" (*L* 313). Both the natural niggler and the imaginary Niggle are permanently in a hurry and worry that they will never be able to finish any of their works. Both experience their duties as distractions from their private works (Tolkien mentions this frequently in his letters) and their life is always split between public duties and private passions, often hampering each other. The voices' verdict in the ward is thus as appropriate for Tolkien himself as it would have been for Niggle.

A second parallel can be observed between Niggle's and Tolkien's *hopes and expectations*: since they do not manage to complete their great work, they know that only a few leaves (literally and metaphorically) will survive. And independently from its completion neither Tolkien nor Niggle can hope that their works will ever be appreciated by their contemporaries. They work in a too old-fashioned style, incompatible with prevailing movements in arts and criticism (*LN* 142), so that their works can never be anything but a private pleasure. Of course even Tolkien did not just write for himself alone (*L* 211), but neither he nor Niggle ever considered their works to be important. These works were were privately important to their creators, but (as it then seemed) not of historical importance. Tolkien never saw himself as a literary reformer and it was never part of his motivation to occupy a central position in a future history of literature. His motivation was, like Niggle's, almost entirely intrinsic.

Third (and this has been observed less frequently) there is also a parallel between the aesthetic theory purported in *Leaf by Niggle* and the position Tolkien held in such matters. One central thought is that creative acts are (seemingly) objective: the artist feels like an observer rather than a maker[4]. Works of art seem to create themselves and develop according to an inner logic, which the artist only follows (if he is sensitive enough)[5]. This is why Tolkien describes the content of Niggle's picture as if it, not Niggle, were active: "[The picture] had begun with a leaf caught in the wind, and it became a tree. And the tree grew, sending out innumerable branches, and thrusting out the most fantastic roots. Strange birds came and rested on its twigs and had to be attended to. Then all round the tree, and behind it, through the gaps in the leaves and boughs, a country began to open out" (*LN* 122).

On the biographical side, however, we face the phenomenon that the parallels become vaguer and vaguer the further we go. Not for every person that occurs in *Leaf by Niggle* is there a corresponding aspect in Tolkien's life – not even for the most important protagonist, Parish. We can try to read him and Niggle as a bifurcation or complementary branches of Tolkien's character (cf. Shippey *Author* 274), or, as Bertrand Alliot has suggested in the preceeding paper, read Parish as a representation of the demands of the body as opposed to the demands of the mind. Or we could, as I am personally inclined to think, read him as a representation of Tolkien's wife and the duties surrounding his family. There are even arguments in favour of this: Parish is much closer to Niggle than any other member of society (they live, so to say, "side by side"). Parish is also the most frequent inquirer showing up in Niggle's private rooms. He is (as Edith was) often struck with diseases and he lays considerable stress on gardening, while Niggle prefers a more natu-

---

[4] See *L* 145, *L* 212 (footnote), *L* 231 or *L* 179, when Tolkien writes about his own speculations on the fate of Ent-women: "I hope so. I don't know."

[5] It is an interesting question how this is related to the theory of subcreation. But the two theories are in principle independent.

ral wild growth. This is a difference that Tolkien often associates with the two sexes, especially in his conception of Ents. Furthermore, even though Parish has no feeling for Niggle's works at all, Niggle emphasizes that Parish is of great importance to his creativity. Despite their different outlooks on life, there is a very strong bond between them that lets them gravitate towards each other even after their departure.

A parallel between Edith and Parish is therefore plausible at least to a certain degree, since there is not just one but quite a few properties that suggest such an interpretation (and such a concentration of similarities is indeed the only possible criterion to infer an allegory from the text alone). But even the points I have listed are not clear enough to leave no room for doubt. And indeed there are some minor points that do not fit as well into the suggested pattern, of which the existence of Parish's own wife and his dedication to her ist not the least problematic.

However as for the parallels between Niggle and Tolkien himself such discrepancies do not occur and the number of similar points is considerably greater than in the case of Parish-Edith. It thus seems to be safe to call at least Niggle an allegory of Tolkien. And this would bring us into a position to consider the story *Leaf by Niggle* itself to be one of the few published leaves from Tolkien's works that could have lasted a little while, judging by the state of affairs at the beginning of the 40s.

## AMBIVALENCES

But there is, of course, a problem. Tolkien himself strongly opposed any biographical or allegorical interpretation of his works: "One of my strongest opinions is that investigation of an author's biography (or such other glimpses of his 'personality' as can be gleaned by the curious) is an entirely vain and false approach to his works - and especially to a work of narrative art, of which the object aimed at by the author was to be enjoyed as such: to be read with literary pleasure" (*L* 414).

Nevertheless if we look closer at Tolkien's life and attitudes, we cannot help recognising them in his works. Both in *The Hobbit*, *The Lord of the Rings* and in the wider Legendarium we frequently stumble over elements that can be traced back to concrete events in Tolkien's life, like situations from Tolkien's visit to the Alps in 1912 as the model for Bilbo's journey over the Misty Mountains (*L* 391) or as an inspiration for Hunthor's death in the story of Turin; the glittering caves of Cheddar Gorge were the model for Helm's Deep (*L* 407), the Gaffer was modelled on a man Tolkien met during a vacation, Sam on the officers' servants in WW I, and Tom Bombadil on a Dutch doll of Tolkien's son Michael. Frodo being chased by Farmer Maggot and his dogs after collecting mushrooms on his ground (*LotR* 91pp) mirrors a nearly identical event in Tolkien's youth; *Smith of Wootton Major* is, as Tolkien says, "an old man's book, already weighted with the presage of 'bereavement'" (*L* 389). *The Lost Road* discusses a father-son-relationship, just when Christopher's special interest in his father's works awakes, and the *The Notion Club Papers* catch many of the characteristics of the Inklings. It is therefore obvious that there are many biographical references. So why does Tolkien not allow us to see them?

The situation that occurs with regard to biographical aspects is identical with the situation we face with regard to allegories. Tolkien writes in the preface to *The Lord of the Rings*: "I cordially dislike allegory in all its manifestations, and always have done so, since I grew old enough to detect its presence." (*LotR* xxiv) and he frequently repeats this position in his letters, i.e. when he turns down the association of the five wizards with the five senses, being "wholly foreign to my way of thinking" (*L* 262); or when he opposes the incessant attempts to establish connections between *The Lord of the Rings* and WW II.

But just as in the above case, contradictions seem to arise here as well: as I have mentioned before, Tolkien calls *Leaf by Niggle* a "'purgatorial' story", or he compares the Great Hall in *Smith of Wootton Major* to a village church[6]. He even calls Tom Bombadil an allegory (*L* 192) and in a letter to Joanna de Bortadano he points out that *The Lord of the Rings* was no allegory for atomic power - but for power as such (*L* 246). In a letter to W.H. Auden he even writes: "In a larger sense, it is I suppose impossible to write any 'story' that is not allegorical in proportion as it 'comes to life'" (*L* 212).

In addition to this Tolkien was also very fond of establishing analogies between his work and reality, and comments on historical events often by using metaphors from *The Lord of the Rings*. He says "we are attempting to conquer Sauron with the Ring", calls technicians and reckless people Orcs, calls himself a Hobbit on more than one occasion and would also frequently quote Gandalf as a source of wisdom[7]. And this he does not only in lighthearted moods, but even when his beloved Edith dies in 1971, "leaving [Beren] indeed one-handed, but he has no power to move the inexorable Mandos"[8].

It is apparent why so many critics have described Tolkien's attitude towards allegories as "ambivalent", i.e. Wayne G. Hammond and Christina Scull (Hammond and Scull, *Companion* lxxvii; Hammond and Scull, *Reader's Guide* 41), or Tolkien's old friend Robert Murray (Murray, *Sermon* 18). After all we must admit that even Tolkien's own reflections sound quite paradox. He writes: "But in spite of this, do not let Rayner suspect 'Allegory'", but only a few lines later: "Of course, Allegory and Story converge, meeting somewhere in Truth. So that the only perfectly consistent allegory is a real life; and the only fully intelligible story is an allegory." (*L* 212). A similar discrepancy we see in his letter to Milton Waldman: "I dislike Allegory — the conscious and in-

---

[6] Tolkien manuscripts, quoted according to Hammond/Scull, *Reader's Guide* 40.
[7] I.e. *L* 232, *L* 348pp, *L* 402 and *L* 413.
[8] *L* 417; The story of Beren and Lúthien is indeed a special one. Except in this single case, Tolkien completely avoids projecting himself into his Legendarium. ("I could of course invent [an elvish name for myself]. But I do not really belong inside my invented history; and do not wish to!", *L* 398).

tentional allegory – yet any attempt to explain the purport of myth or fairytale must use allegorical language." (*L* 145)

However ambivalences are often diagnosed prematurely – since a literal contradiction will do as a sufficient reason. The origin of such contradictions is usually presumed to be psychological, either because he was not farsighted enough to grasp the problem at all, or because he avoids reconsidering his own dogmatic premises by ignoring the contradictions in which they result. However I do have the impression that neither of these possibilities apply to Tolkien. Indeed his attitude towards allegory is coherent and clear. This is the thesis I want to defend in this paper.

## DISTINCTIONS

In order to discuss this thesis properly it is necessary to differentiate between and clarify some of the basic concepts. Especially the word "allegory" has undergone a difficult development since its first appearance in ancient rhetoric. This has resulted in a wide variety of meanings that cannot be tamed easily[9]. It refers not only to narrative but also to graphical substitutions, and it is sometimes used for substitution in a general sense and sometimes subtly differentiated against metaphor, simile or symbol. Tolkien himself fortunately uses only two meanings of the term: in a narrow sense an allegory is solely a personification of a universal virtue or sin (see i.e. *L* 320pp or *L* 121), like Boethius's "philosophia" or the protagonists in Bunyan's or C.S. Lewis' "pilgrim" nov-

---

[9] In the Middle Ages the notion of allegoresis was especially important with regard to the interpretation of the Holy Scripture. The approach was largely apologetic though. The goal was to adapt the text to other facts and beliefs (compare Spahn, *Hermeneutik* 24pp). And since quoting of authorities was also the obligatory way of expressing one's own thoughts, it is understandable why medieval scholars allowed a rather large leeway when it came to interpretation. The concept of such a "tradition-generating hermeneutics" ("traditionsstiftende Hermeneutik", ibid.) thus cannot be applied to modern or to Tolkien's uses of the word, in which the question of appropriateness of a reading is much more central.

els. In a wider sense (and more frequently) Tolkien conceives "allegory" as any form of narrative representation of a real thing, be it concrete or abstract. And once he divides this concept into "general, particular, or topical, moral, religious, or political" allegories (*L* 220). These distinctions could be summarized as follows:

**Allegory in the widest sense**
Any type of representation of a real thing within a narrative

| Universal ideas: | Concrete things (= things in space and time): |
|---|---|
| moral, religious, mythical, political or psychological ideas, among them vices and virtues (= *Tolkien's "allegory" in the narrow sense*) | events from one's personal life, or public events (e.g. WWII and its protagonists). |

Fig. 1: Allegory

Besides the different types of allegory there are also *non-allegorical* biographical elements. These include many of the examples given above: the Gaffer, Frodo's mushroom-adventure, the Bombadil doll – all these are taken from Tolkien's experience, but they are no allegories. They *occur* in Tolkien's writings, but they do not *represent* anything. Non-allegorical elements, too, can be divided into at least four categories, of which only the first can be called biographical:

1. *Concrete events* in space and time.
2. *General knowledge* about people and nature – characterology, laws and chances of natural phenomena on which an author draws without having a paradigmatic situation in mind.

3. *Inspirations*, which means elements taken from other sources that have however only provided a first kick-off, after which the narrative develops independently from the source (e.g. C.S. Lewis's voice as a model for Treebeard's "Hrum Hoom", Wyke-Smith's snergs as a root of Tolkien's hobbits, or that little word in Andrew Lang's fairy-tale *Soria Moria Castle*).
4. *Literary material*, like the myth of Atlantis or Kullervo, which Tolkien deliberately tried to recreate and that, as opposed to inspirations, serve as a guiding idea.

Allegory and biography are therefore neither the same nor is one a special case of the other. They do overlap in the case of biographical allegories, but there are both non-allegorical biographical elements and non-biographical allegories.

The *differentia specifica* of allegories is that they are always representations of something beyond the narrative. This assignment is always partly contingent, and therefore this aspect does have to be learned before we can understand an allegory (for this reason allegory has often been chided as "mechanical"). But allegories would be completely non-sensical and arbitrary if there were not also a similarity or analogy (which is: a similarity between relations) in them. Full similarity between representation and extra-narrative idea is however impossible – or there would be no allegory at all, but a non-allegorical element directly taken from and not representing reality. Therefore allegories must have both a contingent aspect and an aspect of similarity (or mimesis), the latter of which allows us to identify and understand an allegory without knowing anything about the authors' intentions.

Biographical allegories and non-allegorical biographical elements do, however, have something in common. Indeed Tolkien despises both allegorical and biographical readings equally. And he despises both of them (as I want to show in the following) for the same reasons. These reasons even make him hold similar views about at least one, if not two, other things:

1. The question of a "message" of *The Lord of the Rings* (or any other if Tolkien's works). Tolkien has given at least half a dozen answers to this: power, death and immortality, linguistic aesthetics, original sin, technology, god etc.. But he also says: "It is not 'about' anything but itself" (*L* 220; cf. *L* 267).
2. The quest for Tolkien's sources (see *L* 379pp, *L* 418), no matter whether they are correct (like the use of the Old-Mercian dialect by the Rohirrim, or use of the dwarrows' names from the Völuspa in the *Hobbit*) or incorrect (like the idea that the word "Rohirrim" is influenced by Hebrew). We will come back to these things at a later point in this study.

## ALLEGORY AND APPLICABILITY

As for the discussion of the notion of allegory, Tolkien puts forward another distinction that is of vital importance for understanding his views: the distinction between allegory and applicability[10]. The passage quoted above continues as follows: "I cordially dislike allegory in all its manifestations, and always have done so, since I grew old enough to detect its presence. I much prefer history, true or feigned, with its varied applicability to the thought and experience of readers. I think that many confuse ,applicability' with ,allegory'; but the one resides in the freedom

---

[10] The distinction between allegory and applicability could perhaps even be related to the distinction between allegory and symbol, which, since Goethe named it in his writings, has been a long-discussed topic in the theory of literature. There are certainly some similarities there in that applicability refers to a more intuitive and complex textual fabric than allegory does. However I have no idea whether this suffices to associate the two distinctions with each other.

of the reader, and the other in the purposed domination of the author" (*LotR* xxiv) .

The difference described here occurs frequently in Tolkien's thinking, though he does not always describe it with the same words. In his letter to Jane Neave, for example, he talks about "myth" as opposed to "allegory" (*L* 320). And C.S. Lewis, too, writes along the same line: "The essence of a myth [is] that it should not have a taint of allegory to the maker and yet should suggest incipient allegories to the reader".[11]

By applying this distinction to the questions here discussed many seeming ambivalences can be resolved, especially Tolkien's own paradox wordings quoted above. Those statements do indeed originate from a time before Tolkien had come up with the term "applicability". As far as the published corpus goes, this term makes a first appearance in 1957, in a letter to Herbert Schiro, when Tolkien is already 65 years old. But when he expresses his views on allegory to Stanley Unwin (1947), Milton Waldman (1951) and W.H. Auden (1955), he does not yet have a suitable distinction at hand and thus writes:

> "I dislike Allegory — the conscious and intentional allegory – yet any attempt to explain the purport of myth or fairytale must use allegorical language. (And, of course, the more 'life' a story has the more readily will it be susceptible of allegorical interpretations: while the better a deliberate allegory is made the more nearly will it be acceptable just as a story." (*L* 145)

This describes exactly the concept of applicability – just without naming it. The same thing can be said about a statement made in *L* 212: "In a larger sense, it is I suppose impossible to write any 'story' that is not allegorical in proportion as it 'comes to life'". We can see that Tolkien had developed his attitude long before he had words for it. He could

---

[11] Tolkien manuscripts, quoted according to Carpenter, *Inklings* 30.

therefore express himself only in paradox way, until he came up with a second term to distinguish it from "allegory". This is indeed a dialectical process in the classical sense: something first occurs as a contradiction in terms and only gradually coagulates into differentiated terms. Therefore it is unfair to chide Tolkien for his paradoxes and wrong to conclude from them that his attitude is ambivalent.

But what exactly is applicability, as opposed to allegory? This sometimes seems to be not very clear. Tom Shippey, for example, just substitutes "applicability" where we would usually say "allegory" when he asks "Is there any ‚applicability' in this?" (Shippey: *Author* 173). He here ignores one characteristic that Tolkien emphasizes:

1. Applicability *originates with the reader* and not with the author. It is therefore not an objective feature of the text and pursued only at one's own peril ("You can *make* the Ring into an allegory of our own time, *if you like*", *L* 121; my emphasis)

There are, however, two other important characteristics:

2. Applicability is *versatile*. There is not just one solution (as in allegory). By application texts can be made fruitful for new situations, even if the author could not have known or thought of them. This is what all viable myths and religions have in common.
3. Applicability is only an extrapolation ex post. Applying a narrative to a situation means extracting a specific trait from the complexity of the story as such. The extracted principle then often seems to be more fundamental than it actually is. But indeed it is just *poorer* than the actual story.

## Priority

The latter point shows a very important aspect of Tolkien's attitude. He writes: "When they have read [*The Lord of the Rings*], some readers will (I suppose) wish to 'criticize' it, and even to analyze it, and if that is their mentality they are, of course, at liberty to do these things - so long as they have first read it with attention throughout" (*L* 414). The sequence that Tolkien describes here is not just chronological. Of course it is preferable that one should read a work before discussing it, but the decisive thing in Tolkien's statement is that immediate fascination should antecede analysis. We should first be enchanted by the secondary reality of a story before we start reflecting on it. This demand is grounded in the conviction that fascination has not only *chronological* but also *logical* priority over interpretation. Interpretation is always retrospective – even for the author himself (see *L* 211, *L* 246, *L* 238pp). Tolkien does not write a narrative out of an allegorical state of mind, but out of immediate fascination for what is actually going on inside the story. He remains entirely within the secondary reality of the narrative and develops it further, step by step.

This attitude can also be inferred from Tolkien's tendency to *quote* himself or others when he discusses his *own* work: "It is to me, anyway, largely an essay in 'linguistic aesthetic', as I sometimes say to people who ask me 'what is it all about?'" (*L* 220); "one critic (by letter) asserted that the invocations of Elbereth, and the character of Galadriel as directly described (or through the words of Gimli and Sam) were clearly related to Catholic devotion to Mary." (*L* 288); "I was primarily writing an exciting story in an atmosphere and background such as I find personally attractive [...] Though it is only in reading the work myself (with criticisms in mind) that I become aware of the dominance of the theme of Death" (*L* 267). By describing it in such a mediating fashion, Tolkien emphasizes that even those things that can be said *correctly* about *The Lord of the Rings* are nevertheless said in retrospection only.

This explains the Tolkien's frequent use of Lord-of-the-Rings-metaphors. They are nothing else than a later application and not an allegory lying at the heart of the narrative.

The priority of immediate fascination is especially directed against an attitude very common in academia. Where quick reading of heaps of books is an every-day chore, reading degenerates to merely pinning down a few general facts about what is read before turning to the next book in line. This often fosters the attitude that a story is fully decrypted (and disenchanted) once we have named its sources, topics and allegorical implications - as if these facts were prior to and more fundamental than the story itself and would show its true essence. From this perspective the actual narrative becomes secondary: only an arbitrary manifestation of a "message", just another instance of general topics (topoi), or an eclectic composition of various older sources. All unique aspects of the very story in question (and thus any possible merit of the story as such) become arbitrary, random and irrelevant.

Tolkien also attacked this attitude in his allegory at the beginning of *Beowulf. The Monsters and the Critics*[12], which I will discuss below: that the essence of a story is not what we can interpret into or out of it, but the story itself, as it is, and the secondary reality it creates[13].

## OBJECTIVITY

It is however not entirely correct to say that applicability lies in the freedom of the reader, just because it extrapolates ex post and allows several different readings. If that would be the case, every application of a text would be arbitrary: we could read into the story whatever pleases us and

---

[12] It is irrelevant that Tolkien himself wrote a full-fledged allegory in this case, since his aims are argumentative and not literary here.

[13] Thus Tolkien does not criticise the clumsiness of allegories (that is caused by their contingent aspect), as it has been criticised in the debate over allegory and symbol. Tolkiens critique is more radical because he generally denies any reference to any extranarrative idea.

there would be absolutely no measure by which we could tell whether one reading was more appropriate than another. The text could serve as a carrier even for contradictory ideas. Someone could identify Sauron with Hitler, while another one would identify Sauron with Jesus Christ. I do not want to deny the possibility of the latter. But certainly we do need a much greater creativity in reading to make it plausible than for the former association. So even though there is not a single correct reading, there is still an objective aspect in applicability.

That there is such an aspect we can also see in the word "applicability" itself. Just as "inflammability" or "invisibility" refer to the (potential) property of an object, "applicability", taken literally, refers to the narrative and not to the reader or his reading. And this is not just quibbling with words, but shows something that lies at the heart of the issue: works must be suitable for a particular interpretation. This suitability is not absolute, but at least a gradual one, and it depends in part even on the author, his interests and values. That is why there are good and bad, or to be more precise: myths that are applicable better and worse. The eventual success of a work of this type is therefore not completely dependent on the chances of reception. The work itself, as it is, and the ways in which we *can* read it, play a certain part in its success. Tolkien himself mentions that it is "the test of the consistency of a mythology as such, if it is capable of some sort of rational or rationalized explanation." (*L* 261). This consistency is an objective indicator – and yet the issue is much more complex than any 1:1-parallelism. Because of this fact, Shippey was indeed right to substitute "applicability" for "allegory". And the same thought lies in Lewis' remark quoted above, that describes the narrative itself as the active part: "[a myth] should suggest incipient allegories to the reader".

## Subcreation

The objective aspect of applicability is closely related to the idea of subcreation, as Tolkien describes it in *L* 188pp; *OFS* 138pp, or 155pp. This theory, as we can see from the word itself, describes the man's creations (Tolkien means especially mythical narratives, but also works of art in general) as mirroring and at the same time completing God's own creation: "We make still by the law in which we're made", as Tolkien writes in *Mythopoeia*. This idea now provides an ontological reason for the claim that interpretation is secondary in every sense. As a subcreator, man participates in God's creation and by drawing on its elements (=his knowledge and experiences) he catches in his works of art at least a spark of God's primal truths. These truths are not there because the artist deliberately puts them into his work. They are contained in the materials he uses and the use he makes of them – and they are much finer and more versatile than he could consciously make them.

The problem is that many will not find the theory of subcreation very attractive, since it presupposes the existence of a heavenly creator. However I think that this theory could be rephrased in a secular way, since it is essentially more (neo)platonic than genuinely Christian. The basic idea is simply that plausible characters and plots and a dense and finely crafted secondary world participate in ideas and facts that are also true in the primary reality (because of that known to the author in the first place)[14]. The author can of course only grasp a fraction of this reality and he is directed and limited by his own interests. But whatever he grasps contains the logic of reality, just like the ring and its effects mirror some truths about the psychology of power. Therefore we find many patterns applicable *to* reality when we read a well-done narrative: not because the author symbolized these patterns in allegories, but because

---

[14] See also "each of us is an allegory, embodying in a particular tale and clothed in the garments of time and place, universal truth and everlasting life." (*L* 212) or "far greater things may colour the mind in dealing with the lesser things of a fairy-story." (*L* 288)

he completely remained in a state of mind where he did nothing but develop a secondary reality[15]. We could perhaps say that hereby natural allegories appear, as opposed to artificial (=intended) ones.

## THE DENIAL OF MEDIATION

At last we arrive at a non-ambivalent concept of Tolkien's attitude towards allegories. After all, his aversion is not a contingent characteristic of his personality, just as other people may dislike cabbage, jazz or pink socks. Tolkien does not dislike allegory as a single literary tool, but his aversion is part of a more general conviction that includes several topics and forms a part of Tolkien's overall theory of literature: *he denies all kinds of mediate approaches to literature*, especially if they pretend to bring out something essential about a narrative.

Tolkien's approach to both writing and reading is immediate: fascination antecedes analysis and application, and both of them remain optional tasks. This view is not peculiar to Tolkien. It is not even confined to literature, but has frequently been held in the history of the arts. For example, it is very similar to the quarrel between absolute music as opposed to program music in the 19th century. While protagonists of the latter made music a vehicle to convey extra-musical feelings and ideas, protagonists of the former insisted on music being an aim in itself, following its own aesthetic logic, that could only be spoiled by tying it to something outside music.

This is the same idea that Tolkien expresses in the analogy in his *Beowulf* essay (*BMC* 7ff). Here he compares the author of *Beowulf* with a man who builds a tower from stones of various older sources. Later historians and critics take his tower apart and chide its creator for mak-

---

[15] See "And, of course, the more 'life' a story has the more readily will it be susceptible of allegorical interpretations: while the better a deliberate allegory is made the more nearly will it be acceptable just as a story." (*L* 145), and the remarks in *L* 232, or to Auden (*L* 212, quoted above).

ing a building to his own liking instead of reconstructing the older sources properly. The creator however, says Tolkien, could view the sea from the top of his tower. The tower has a distinctive quality of its own, and is not to be taken as a vehicle for understanding something else. It allows its creator an immediate aesthetic experience. This is exactly what the critics, who tend to forget the work itself over its analysis, refuse to see. It is, however, not important from where the elements are taken but what an author has done with them. This is a claim that Tolkien frequently makes in his theoretical works[16].

## AND YET...

... there is still a problem. Even if the attitude here described is consistent and not ambivalent: *Leaf by Niggle* does not match it. I myself, at least, do not manage to remain on the level of secondary reality when I read it. At best, it takes a few pages until I have associated Niggle's journey with death. Otherwise it would remain entirely enigmatic why Niggle has to go, why he does not know where he is going, and why all this has the flavour of conclusiveness (since he obviously cannot hope to return one day to finish his work). All these questions cannot be answered from the information given by the story. But all makes sense when we read "death" for "journey"[17].

It could of course be said that all stories leave certain matters unanswered. It is one of Tolkien's most potent literary tools, especially in

---

[16] See especially *OFS* 119ff; see also "I fear you may be right that the search for the sources of The Lord of the Rings is going to occupy academics for a generation or two. I wish this need not be so. To my mind it is the particular use in a particular situation of any motive, whether invented, deliberately borrowed, or unconsciously remembered that is the most interesting thing to consider." (*L* 418)

[17] All the more since the metaphorics of "departure" has had a long tradition in the Western history of ideas. And there are also other indicators for an intended metaphysical background: the description of Niggle's Parish as an "introduction to the Mountains" (*LN* 143), – or the use of capital letters for "Mountains" or the "Tree". All this makes sense only if it refers to more than just trees and mountains.

*The Lord of the Rings*, to merely allude to many explanations and background stories, like Gandalf's origin or the details of the fall of Númenor. These questions are answered in the wider Legendarium, but here again many threads leave room for speculation, like if there are halls for dwarves at Mandos, or how Beren and Lúthien died. Nevertheless we can assume that these questions in principle can be answered within the secondary reality Tolkien created, even if he was not able to or did not want to answer them. There are informational gaps, but they do not challenge the plausibility of the the secondary reality.

In *Leaf by Niggle*, however, this is not the case. Here the entire composition lacks coherence on the level of the secondary world. It is impossible to have a comprehensive view of Niggle's world, as we have of Middle-earth or Arda. It remains unclear why the village episode is followed by the scene in the workhouse, and it is yet more unclear what the tree's becoming real has to do with it, or why the doctors know Niggle's private thoughts. In particular situations there is a plausible picture of a reality, but no systematic coherence that would allow including all these scenes into one integrated idea of a world. This is why I cannot read *Leaf by Niggle* as a story alone: because it requires extranarrative elements in order to make sense.

## AN ATTEMPT AT RECONCILIATION

So do we finally end up with another ambivalence? Or at least with Tolkien's misjudging of his own story? One might be inclined to say that shorter works automatically tend to extrapolation (cf. Adorno: *Essay*). Single short stories, as opposed to novels or full-fledged mythologies, have to remain crude and have to emphasize some aspects over others. They cannot help conveying a much clearer message than greater narratives. In spite of this argument, however, we must admit that *Farmer Giles of Ham* oder *Smith of Wootton Major* do not seem allegorical to the same degree as *Leaf by Niggle*. And they are not as incoherent either.

But then how can we explain the fact that *Leaf by Niggle* is so close to allegory without contradiction? True, though not entirely satisfying, would be to say that *Leaf by Niggle* is not a *systematic* allegory – as opposed to, for example, Lewis's *The Pilgrim's Regress* – because the allegoric elements amount to only a fraction of the narrative's structure. There was a starting-point for *Leaf by Niggle* – Tolkien's neighbour "maiming" the tree in front of her house (*L* 321). This is not an allegory but an inspiration, as described above: a trigger without further influence. Another inspiration is that Tolkien once knew a gardener named "Parish" and the name incidentally fit well into the story (ibid.). Then there is, as in all narratives, a lot of special and general knowledge about characters and the world. And then there are the two allegorical aspects: the theological and the biographical one. The latter one is in fact optional: the story can still be read without a (further) lack of coherence if the reader does not know anything about Tolkien's life and character. The theological aspect is not optional to the same degree. However it does not require any special knowledge. The basic pattern can always be inferred, even if we only know the fact that human life is finite. *Leaf by Niggle* would indeed even be a suitable didactic narrative: a story that teaches the ideas of purgatory and paradise rather than referring to them as something already known. The theological aspect as such however does remain scattered. It draws only on certain elements, but other elements that are just as central in the story do not have a theological meaning. Besides the general ideas of death, purgatory and paradise and perhaps the two voices, there is hardly anything that has theological implications. In order for the story itself to make sense, there does not have to be an implication in the roofer not showing up or in the conversations of the other members of the community. All this is plain secondary reality, even though it can be applicable at the same time.

As we have seen in the beginning, the allegorical traits become diffuse once we go beyond the first points. Instead of teaching us further details, like systematic allegories do, *Leaf by Niggle* is almost fully exhausted once it has been recognized as an allegory at all. Therefore the theological allegory works itself only as a mere *inspiration*: it kicks off the story, but does not further guide its elements.

This is very similar to the development in Tolkien's other works, especially the *Notion Club Papers* and many parts of the *Silmarillion*. Tolkien started off with well-defined allegories – the associations between Eressea and England, Kortirion and Warwick, Tavrobel and Great Haywood (*LT* 1 24pp). In the latter case, there are the associations between the protagonists of the story and particular members of the Inklings in the former (*SD* 150) – but all these clear references are gradually given up during the further development of the manuscripts. What remains is a kind of white noise made up of half-dissolved allegories that do not constitute the essence of the story any more. In the *Notion Club Papers* the protagonists retain character traits of the Inklings, but these are newly combined[18] and also the later versions of the *Silmarillion* still draw on general aesthetic experiences from the spring of the romance of Ronald and Edith. But these are vague and not easy to pin down. Similar processes can also be observed in Tolkien's use of literary materials like the Kullervo and the Atlantis myths.

The final product of these processes is now very similar to the non-systematic allegory *Leaf by Niggle*. There are well-defined allegories in *Leaf*, but they cannot be pursued further and dissipate within the narrative flow of the story. *Leaf* may thus be allegoric, but it is not essentially an allegory. Allegoric it is in some respects, but secondary reality lies in every aspect and this reality often directs the story

---

[18] See "I beg of the present company not to look for their own faces in this mirror. For the mirror is cracked, and at best you will only see your countenances distorted, and adorned maybe with noses (and other features) that are not your own, but belonging to other members of the company if to anybody" (*SD* 148pp).

independently from the logic of analogy. Therefore *Leaf by Niggle* is much richer than a systematic allegory, much more independent from its allegorical implications, and it is thus also more applicable – both along the lines of the intended allegories and against them[19]. Even Niggle can thus be described as "meant to be a real mixed-quality person and not an 'allegory' of any single vice or virtue" (*L* 321) – and he is not simply to be identified with Tolkien himself, though they have a lot in common. It is therefore right to call *Leaf by Niggle* "not really or properly an 'allegory'" as Tolkien describes it in a letter to Jane Neave (*L* 320). In fact Tolkien keeps himself out of trouble by using the narrow concept of allegory here. But this is unnecessary in this case – because the statement would hold true for the wider concept as well. Tolkien wants to emphasize that the immediate life of the narrative and its fascination are the crucial things. This alone constitutes the genuine value of literature as such. Any mediate approach makes literature obsolete, because it could be replaced by what it is mediated by. Or, more polemically: if the essence of a story were the message it is meant to express, the author should write down the message directly and not waste so much effort on telling a story.

FABIAN GEIER, born 1976, studied Philosophy, English Literature and Linguistics, Theory of Music, and Education at the Universities of Würzburg, Warwick and Heidelberg; PhD in Philosophy in 2006; lecturer for philosophy at various institutions (Heidelberg, Mannheim, Witten-Herdecke, Essen-Duisburg); deputy secretary of the Gesellschaft für Philosophie und Wissenschaft e.V.; board of editors at the portal www.philosophie.de; author of a Tolkien biography (Rowohlt-Monographien-series, forthcoming).

---

[19] In the end every allegory is applicable and richer than the mere parallels that constitute it, but in general the difference is not as much as in this case.

## Works Cited

Adorno, Theodor W. "Der Essay als Form". *Gesammelte Schriften Bd. 11.* Darmstadt: Wissenschaftliche Buchgesellschaft, 1998. 9-33.

Carpenter, Humphrey. *J.R.R. Tolkien – A Biography.* New York: Houghton Mifflin, 2000.

---, *The Inklings. C.S.Lewis, J.R.R.Tolkien, Charles Williams and their Friends.* London: HarperCollins, 2006.

---, *The Letters of J.R.R. Tolkien.* London: HarperCollins, 1995.

Hammond, Wayne G. and Scull, Christina. *The J.R.R.Tolkien Companion and Guide. Reader's Guide.* New York: Houghton Mifflin, 2007.

---, *The Lord of the Rings. A Reader's Companion.* London: HarperCollins, 2005.

Kurz, Gerhard. *Metapher, Allegorie, Symbol.* Göttingen: Vandenhoek und Ruprecht, 2004.

Murray, Robert. "Sermon at Thanksgiving Service, Keble College Chapel, 23rd August 1992". *Proceedings of the J.R.R.Tolkien Centenary Conference 1992.* Ed. Patricia Reynolds, Glen H. GoodKnight. Milton Keynes: Mythopoeic Press, 1995.

Shippey, Tom. *J.R.R. Tolkien – Author of the Century.* London: HarperCollins, 2000.

Spahn, Andreas. "Rationalistische und traditionalistische Hermeneutik". *Perspektiven Philosophischer Forschung.* Ed. Fabian Geier, Andreas Spahn, Christian Spahn. Essen: Oldib Verlag 2007. 19-41.

Tolkien, J. R. R. "Beowulf: The Monsters and the Critics". *The Monsters and the Critics and other Essays.* Ed. Christopher Tolkien. London: Allen and Unwin, 1983. 5-48.

---, *The Book of Lost Tales I.* Ed. Christopher Tolkien. London: HarperCollins, 2002.

---, "Leaf by Niggle". *Tales from the Perilous Realm.* London: HarperCollins, 2002. 119-144.

---, "On Fairy-Stories". *Beowulf and the Critics.* Ed. Christopher Tolkien. London: Allen and Unwin, 1983. 109-161.

---, *The Lord of the Rings.* New York: Houghton Mifflin, 2004.

---, *Sauron Defeated.* Ed. Christopher Tolkien. London: HarperCollins, 2002.

# Redefining the Romantic Hero: a Reading of *Smith of Wootton Major* in the Light of Ludwig Tieck's *Der Runenberg*

## MARTIN SIMONSON

### ABSTRACT

In his literature, Tolkien presented several versions of fictional heroes that are torn between a love for a particular place and a longing for a different reality, deeper and more meaningful than prosaic everyday life is able to offer. While these heroes share some basic motivations with especially (though not exclusively) Romantic antecedents, they differ substantially from the Romantic hero's approach to the conflict. In this paper, I will take a look at some similarities and differences between *Smith of Wootton Major* and Ludwig Tieck's *Der Runenberg*, in order to see if Tolkien's deviations can be explained with reference to the latter's particular theory of fairy stories.

### INTRODUCTION

Ever since *Smith of Wootton Major* was first published in 1967, the question of what to make of it has been subject to an ongoing polemic, which in later years has been upheld mainly by Verlyn Flieger and Tom Shippey. While Flieger, in *A Question of Time* (227), adopted the stance of Roger Lancelyn Green as the latter explains it in an early review of Tolkien's tale[1], namely that to search for any deeper meaning in the tale is to "cut open the ball in search of its bounce", Shippey believes that the tale may be read as an allegory of Tolkien's own life and career, an interpretation that he first offered in *The Road to Middle-earth* and elaborated further on both in *J.R.R. Tolkien: Author of the Century* (296-304) and in the revised edition of *Road* (271-280). Altogether, the tale's

---

[1] *The Sunday Telegraph*, 3 December 1967.

meaning has been considered somewhat elusive, and few attempts have been made to put it in a critical context outside of allegorical readings. However, things appear to be changing. Flieger, for instance, now seems ready to admit another set of possibilities for critical interpretation. In her new, annotated edition of the tale she writes that she believes it may be read as an enactment of Tolkien's essay 'On Fairy Stories' (*SWM*, 60), hence obviously admitting that the tale serves to elucidate the aspects discussed in that essay – that is, theory exemplified by the actual art of fairy-story telling. If this holds, as I believe it does, it would invest Tolkien's tale with further layers of meaning. It would then be possible to explore the critical context of the ideas exposed in that essay and compare the artistic outcome, *Smith of Wootton Major*, with that of previous writers concerned with similar issues. In this paper I will concentrate mainly on the concept of 'Recovery' – the idea that custom blinds us to the miracles of our everyday experience of the world, and that we need to recover an older, more intuitive vision of the (natural) world that surrounds us in order to appreciate its full, original meaning – and match *Smith of Wootton Major* against Ludwig Tieck's *Der Runenberg*, in order to see what the comparison may tell us about Tolkien's particular approach.

As for Tolkien's views on the subject, when discussing the idea of recovery in 'On Fairy Stories', he claims that "we need recovery. We should look at green again, and be startled anew (but not blinded) by blue and yellow and red [...] We need, in any case, to clean our windows; so that the things seen clearly may be freed from the drab blur of triteness or familiarity – from possessiveness" (*The Tolkien Reader* 77).

For Tolkien, fairy-stories, if they are well told, may be an excellent tool to promote this awareness and to help us achieve a recovery of previous, more meaningful, perceptions of reality. This was apparently what he tried to do when writing them himself. The idea as such, however, was far from new. Apart from the views of Neoplatonized Christianity – that fallen Man has lost contact with Oneness, which is represented by God, and lapsed into a state of multiplicity, confusion and Evil, from which only a process of reintegration would lead to redemption – the notion of recovery also echoes important strands of Romantic thought. For instance, among the British Romantics Coleridge expressed in *Biographia Literaria* the idea that a poet's genius depended on his ability to portray "familiar objects as to awaken in the mind of others a kindred feeling concerning them and that freshness of sensation which is the constant accompaniment of mental, no less than of bodily, convalescence." (50) This conception was later echoed by several highly influential nineteenth-century writers such as Carlyle in *Sartor Resartus*, and the American transcendentalist Ralph Waldo Emerson in *Nature*.

One of the reasons why this concern appears in much of Romantic and Transcendentalist philosophy and literature is that it constitutes a criticism of the Enlightenment's mechanistic world-view, against which the Romantic movement was, on the whole, a protest (Abrams 170-171). In the Enlightenment mind frame, inspired by a long-standing tradition of Western philosophical thinking from Aristotle on to Descartes, science is supposed to be able to explain the universe by breaking down all phenomena to their most basic parts, while the human mind is considered an entity totally separate from the outside world. For the Romantics, such an approach to the natural world has distorted our awareness of the deeper, transcendental dimensions of nature. As a consequence, the Romantic hero, whether in the shape of artist, prophet or fictitious hero, often fought actively against Enlightenment-derived social, linguistic and philosophical barriers, attempting to break free from these constraints in pursuit of a more intuitive contact with both God and the natural world – a deeper reality. However, as Enlightenment standards constituted the very axis on which the whole of Western civilization turned, they were fighting a losing battle. This tragic circumstance was acknowledged by many Romantic artists, and the Romantic hero is often doomed to alienation, madness or premature death.

I will argue that Tolkien, in *Smith of Wootton Major*, offers a redefinition of this pessimistic Romantic hero by adding the ingredients of Escape and Consolation to the Romantic notion of recovery. A comparison between *Smith of Wootton Major* and Ludwig Tieck's *Der Runenberg*, which was written in the early nineteenth century and articulates a more purely Romantic expression of the concept, will show this with more poignancy. Curiously enough, as far as I know neither Tieck's story nor the author himself have previously been studied as possible sources of inspiration for Tolkien's own theories or writings, in spite of the intriguing similarities between the two tales. The nearest we come is Douglas Anderson's inclusion of another story by Tieck, *The Elves*, in his anthology *Tales Before Tolkien*.

Perhaps this is as it should be, since there is no evidence that Tolkien ever read Tieck. Consequently, the aim of the present paper is not to establish any obscure analogues derived from speculations about Tolkien's possible awareness of Tieck's writings, but rather to compare a fairy tale of the Romantic era – *Der Runenberg* – with *Smith of Wootton Major*, in order to find out what the *deviations* may reveal concerning possible layers of meaning in Tolkien's perhaps most enigmatic and elusive tale, and to see whether the idea of this story as an enactment of 'On Fairy Stories' has anything to do with it.

## DER RUNENBERG

Briefly summarised, Tieck's tale is about a young man named Christian who, wishing to escape from the tedious routines and traditions that dominate life in his native village on the plains, settles in a forest among the mountains to become a hunter. When the tale begins, Christian has already been away from his hometown for some time and he is feeling melancholy and frustrated about not being able to understand the voice of nature. As he ponders the possibility of returning to the plains, he meets a mysterious stranger who, after listening to the young man's laments, recommends him to pay a visit to a legendary mountain called 'Der Runenberg' (the Mountain of Runes).

Guided by the moonlight, Christian climbs the steep hillside and reaches a sort of cavernous dwelling, adorned with crystals and brilliant stones, where he glimpses a woman through the distorting image of a window. The woman is performing a strange ritual with a lamp, walking back and forth in the room while chanting a rhyme. Taking off her clothes, she holds up a board encrusted with fiercely shining stones. Christian is spellbound by incomprehensible visions and cannot to take his eyes off the board's brightly shining silhouette. The woman then hands it to him, and the silhouette penetrates into his body and stays there, while the other lights gradually fade.

Dawn finds him on the mountain with the board in his hands. He is deprived of any clear distinction between the marvellous and the commonplace, memories and dreams, having both realities swirling around inside of him, and he descends the mountain in a state of shock.

When Christian finally reaches the plains, he attempts to forget about the disquieting experience, settling in a village and beginning a new life marked by conservative conventions and traditions. He marries into a well-to-do family of farmers and relies on husbandry to feed his humble earthly desires, enjoying a slowly but steadily growing fortune and family. On a journey to search for his parents he finds his long-lost father, a gardener, and brings him to his new home to prosper with him.

The years go by in this carefree atmosphere, until a stranger appears in the village. The stranger stays with Christian's family for some time, becoming a popular character among old and young alike. Then he suddenly goes off again, allegedly in search of a vision that has enchanted him in the mountains. He leaves Christian in charge of a considerable amount of gold that will be his if the stranger should fail to return.

Once the stranger has left, Christian becomes obsessed with the shining metal, taking it out to look at it during the nights and dwelling on its importance during the days. Memories of the visions he once had in the Runenberg come back to him with full force, and the powerful light blinds him to the virtues of the traditional farming life on the plains. His ambitions now focus on an all-consuming desire to dissect, extract and possess the secrets and fortunes that he believes are hidden in the depths of the earth – rejecting the surface-world of the ephemeral plants that must die and disappear at the end of each passing year, he begins to yearn for new visions of the eternal stony essence that he once glimpsed in the Runenberg. The desire is so strong that he is ready to sacrifice all that he has achieved during his years in the village. Abandoning everything that has kept him attached to the human community he embarks on a quest to recover his lost visions, descending into an old mine.

At the very end of the tale, Christian briefly returns to the village as a human wreck. His clothes are torn, his looks savage, and as proof of his madness he carries a sack of materially worthless stones in a bag, supposedly containing an inner light and incredible secrets which he is unwilling to share with anyone else, not even his wife, whose life has been marked by misfortunes ever since he left. Poor, mad and lonely, he leaves the village for the last time and nobody ever sees him again.

## SIMILARITIES

Reading *Der Runenberg*, it should be fairly obvious to anyone familiar with *Smith of Wootton Major* that there are several similarities – and rather striking ones – between the two tales. In the first place, both works are essentially about individuals in search of a reality more profound than that the superficial rituals of their native village are able to offer. Both stories rest on the fact that the traditions in the village have been drained of their deeper significance, which has led the inhabitants to adopt an attitude of unquestioning complacency, however humble it is supposed to be. That in turn results in faded creativity and a generally decadent atmosphere. In Tieck's tale, this decadence is emphasized by having the plants – the cornerstone of the village economy – scream[2] in Christian's mind when they are uprooted, as evidence (for the protagonist) of the rotting wound they stem from – in turn interpreted by Christian as the remains of previous and magnificent though dead worlds. In Tolkien's tale, Wootton Major also shows signs of past but decaying splendour, such as the Great Hall which, though well-kept, is "no longer painted or gilded as it had been once upon a time" (*SWM*, 6).

However, both tales also emphasize the dangers implied by becoming separated from one's native village and all that it implies in terms of cultural and family bonds, by having animate, primordial powers of the natural world warn the two protagonists about the potential dangers of their errantries. In Tieck's tale, the possibility that Christian actually misinterprets the screams of the plants – which would be consistent with his general misinterpretation of the natural world, as we shall see – allows for a different reading, namely that they scream in order to make him aware of the fact that his erroneous approach to the natural world is alienating him from the human community of the village. Similarly, a birch in Faery, which has been harmed by Smith when he clings to it during a terrible storm, explicitly tells him to go back to his own world, at a point in the narrative when his excursions in the deeper realm have become more and more extended and he runs the risk of becoming cut off from his life in Wootton Major.

---

[2] The explicit reference, at the beginning of the tale, is to the mandragora that according to an old legend wails when taken from the earth. This sound was supposed to bring madness to the one who heard it.

Thus, Christian's initial impatience with the cultivation of plants, his general aversion to life on the plains and his subsequent obsession with the mineral world of the mountains, all spring from an inherent desire for some deeper, eternal reality closely linked to the wildness of the natural world. In a similar fashion, the Cake becomes, in the first part of Tolkien's tale, a faded shadow of its own self – a symbol of a tradition which used to enrich the community life by performing a ritual aimed at keeping the memory of Faery alive, which has been spoiled by the villagers' lazy attitude towards tradition and a general lack of interest in keeping open the old connection with the deeper reality of Faery, itself profoundly embedded in the natural world. The eternal, primordial ingredients have been forgotten by the new Master Cook, himself a prototype of this unreflective and arrogant complacency (it actually takes an active intervention from the King of Faery, in the shape of Alf the Prentice, to bring them out of their old hiding place and reintroduce them in the Cake).

In both tales, a shining object coming from a transcendent realm – the board encrusted with jewels which is given to Christian by the mysterious woman in the Runenberg, and the Star, found by Smith in the Cake through the subtle mediation of the King of Faery – becomes physically and psychologically integrated into the protagonists and allows them to enter a reality that lies beneath or beyond the world of conventional perceptions and appearances.

Furthermore, the two authors explore the question of whether or not it is possible, or desirable, to combine the two realities that now dwell inside of both Christian and Smith. Smith, when wearing the star, is inspired by his experiences and journeys in Faery to create objects that are both beautiful and useful for his community, enriching the life of his fellow villagers by bringing traces of the old connections to Faery back to them. At the same time he tends to become a bit aloof – while he fulfils his basic social duties, his mind seems to be elsewhere and he is always eager for more time in Faery, wishing to travel further and further towards the innermost regions of this perilous realm in order to explore its secrets.

As for Christian, he manages to repress the experiences in the Runenberg for several years, prospering as a diligent follower of the accepted conventions and traditions of the village, but the memory still lingers at the back of his mind. When he sets out to find his parents he is powerfully attracted by the towering mountains, the stony essence of the earth that breaks the surface in all its might, and though he is conducted back to the village by his father's moral authority, it is not long before the stranger appears with the gold and tempts him to recover his lost visions.

Another similarity between the two tales is that both Christian and Smith are heavily influenced by guides in order to come to terms with the purpose of their particular relationship to the realm of the deeper reality. It is the stranger who beckons Christian on to the Runenberg and leaves him a sack of gold that triggers in Christian a feverish desire to journey beyond the borders of the conventional, prosaic and seemingly ephemeral reality in order to find, dissect and possess the eternal truths of deeper reality. Similarly, it is Alf's shrewd interventions that enable Smith to find the Star, and it is the same Alf who later explains the full meaning of his presence in Faery, putting him on the right track (back towards the village) and urging him to pass on the Star so that future generations may benefit from it.

Finally, both tales feature female figures that are intimately related to the deeper reality, portrayed as a kind of spirit that inhabits the very centre of the natural world's transcendental dimension. In Tieck's story, this figure takes on the shape of the mysterious woman in the Runenberg, who later on appears changed into the "Lady of the Woods". The second encounter, in which Christian sees her as an ugly old woman, only vaguely recognizing her, significantly takes place after a prolonged sojourn in the village, something that has, it is implied, blunted and distorted his early, more intuitive perception of the deeper reality.

In Tolkien's tale, the Queen of Faery also changes in shape depending on the eyes of the beholder, from her representation in sickeningly sweet sugar of a dancing little fairy that merely *adorns* the Cake without conferring any deeper meaning to the ritual, to the dancing fairy that Smith encounters after having travelled for some time in Faery, and, finally, to the powerful, shining presence that Smith finds at the very heart of Faery once he has journeyed far and wide there.[3]

### DIFFERENCES

The above-mentioned similarities, however, are almost entirely overshadowed by the particular and significant twists that Tolkien confers to his tale, which set a different course for the protagonist. To begin with, the purpose of the guide-figure is markedly divergent. Alf is an active agent of Faery, whose aim is to reintegrate both realities so that the mythic, transcendent dimension shall reinvigorate the traditions in Wootton Major and invest the prosaic village life with a more profound meaning. He is clearly concerned about the spiritual welfare of the inhabitants,[4] urging Smith to pass on the Star so that others may continue to benefit from the permeability between the two realities made possible by this object.

---

[3] Shippey says of the evolution in Smith's perception of the Queen that these different images "are avatars of the Queen of Faërie, representing successively the tawdry images of former fantasy which are all the modern world has left [...]" (*The Road to Middle-earth* 277).

[4] Tolkien himself points out in an essay on the tale that "[...] the Elven folk, the chief and ruling inhabitants of Faery, have an ultimate kinship with Men and have a permanent love for them in general. Though they are not bound by any moral obligation to assist Men, and do not need their help (except in human affairs), they do from time to time try to assist them, avert evil from them and have relations with them [...]" (*SWM*, 93)

The stranger, on the other hand – who significantly is a stranger both in the Mountains *and* on the Plains[5] – incites Christian to adopt an attitude towards the deeper reality based on dissection and selfish possession. Christian becomes an easy prey to both madness and alienation from the human community that he is obliged to leave in order to pursue his visions and engage fully in the exploration of the stony "essence" hidden beneath the living earth. As opposed to Alf, the stranger offers no guidance back to a gratifying life in the village and disappears as soon as he has put Christian on the road to perdition.

Smith is able to make more productive use of the inner tension between Faery and Wootton Major that the star has brought him. Consciously or not, he takes on the role of a mediator, making objects in the smithy that apart from being useful are also artful and reminiscent of the past intimacy between the two realms – the connection invests his craft with a more profound dimension. Christian, for his part, cannot find a synaesthesia that works for him in order to fruitfully channel his energies, and the tension is so strong that he must neglect one side of himself in order for the other to function satisfactorily. In the village, Christian represses the visions he acquired at the Runenberg, but the stranger's gold brings the fatal tension back. In the end, Christian voluntarily sacrifices his ties to the human community and everything related to it – family, religion, profession, wealth, and social rank – as he embarks body and soul on a quest into the realm of the mineral world, where he believes he will find transcendent, eternal truths.

However, the mythic reality he is searching for is not the same as Smith's. The subtle influence of the stranger has instead made him interpret the female natural spirit at the Runenberg as the enticing myth of science, the Enlightenment's vision of the world in which all phe-

---

[5] This adds further weight to my reading of this character as an embodiment of a misleading and dangerous approach to the natural world, an idea that I will elaborate further on in the following section.

nomena may be explained by a method of analytic divisiveness. He is also swept off his feet by a wish to keep the visions to himself, jealously hiding them from the rest of the human community. While Smith was able to overcome this desire with the help of Alf, the stranger, rather than to temper the possessive impulse actually encourages Christian to follow it by leaving the sack of gold in his care. As a result, Christian's exploration of the underground world is not only useless for the human community, it is also profoundly negative for his family, and in the end he is left to poverty, madness and alienation.

As for Smith, he is bereft of Faery when he yields up possession of the Star. As he does so, however, he also releases himself from the inner tension and can engage in a more personal dialogue with his family and the rest of the human community in the village. His son, for instance, is partly relieved to hear that he is back for good, implying that Smith has neglected to teach him all that which he needs to know in order to completely shoulder his role as village smith and continue his father's inspired labours. He contributes with songs at the following Twenty-four Feast, and he enjoys the sight of the children, all of whom appear, in his eyes, to be suitable inheritors of the star. In his old age this life in the community partly makes up for the personal loss of Faery he has suffered, especially as he sees that the village has been enriched both by his previous efforts and final sacrifice.

## CONCLUSIONS

These differences map a fundamental deviation from the evolution described in Tieck's tale, a twist that can be explained with reference to the main features of fairy stories, as outlined by Tolkien in his essay on the subject: the notions of Recovery, Escape, and Consolation (*The Tolkien Reader* 75-87). Escape, as Tolkien sees it, is an unwillingness to accept a negative and generally impoverishing – spiritually or otherwise – state of affairs and a willingness to search for a more positive, fruitful and creative existence.⁶ Such an escape, Tolkien implies (though the order of exposition is inverted in his essay), may be found if we achieve a form of recovery of an older, more intuitive perception of reality, in which simple things were enjoyed for their inherent value and for what they might tell us about ourselves and our relationship to the rest of the world – both human and animal. In this way, Recovery will invest our lives with a deeper meaning, which, in turn, will bring us a certain measure of 'Consolation'. It is one of the main points of the essay that fairy tales can help us achieve this. Now, contemplated in the context of *Smith of Wootton Major*, the imperatives of 'Recovery', 'Escape' and 'Consolation' necessarily imply a redefinition of the tragic, self-destructive Romantic hero who follows his inner voice in search of visions and fulfilment of eternal ideals, but who is ultimately defeated and driven into alienation, madness, or death – or all of them.

The quests, both Christian's and Smith's, may be considered Romantic in the sense that they mainly deal with an idealistic search for deeper truths that have been hidden beneath customs and empty rituals which only retain surface and echo half-forgotten memories of the original unity with a deeper, transcendental dimension of the natural world. The quests are also typically Romantic in that the protagonists are so bent on achieving a more solid contact with the deeper reality that they are ready to sacrifice their contact with the human community from which they start – indeed, their entire earthly lives.

As we have seen, the process described in Tieck's tale is twisted towards the opposite pole in Tolkien's,⁷ and the two stories end up pre-

---

[6] Tolkien (*The Tolkien Reader* 80) stresses the *individual's* right to protest and choose other alternatives in order to enrich *community* life: "[…] he might rouse men to pull down the street-lamps. Escapism has another and even wickeder face: Reaction."

[7] In both tales, this process is framed by a changing portrayal of the village rituals and of the female spirit. For Christian, the first of the traditional rituals (the mass to celebrate the harvest that takes place upon his return to the plains) seems to him to offer authentic depth and a profound meaning, while the second mass exposes the emptiness of the ritual for the protagonist. This second harvest celebration convinces Christian of the futility that lies in blindly accepting traditions that supposedly reveal the mysterious na-

senting distinctly different responses to the question of whether or not both realities may engage in a symbiotic relationship and enrich the human community. Tieck's tale offers no hope for a successful combination, the pessimism presumably being based on the premise that an Enlightenment-oriented approach poisons the inherently Romantic quest, making it self-destructive and useless for the human community. This failure can be seen as a result of Christian's misinterpretation of the natural light: invited by the stranger to the Runenberg, he is given glimpses of a fragmented, shining reality and he later tries to possess the light, separating it from its natural source in order to understand the voice and the visions of the transcendent realm hidden beneath the ordinary natural world. Thus, while the attempt to gain insights into a deeper reality through the contemplation of nature may be Romantic, Christian's interpretation certainly isn't – it is a scientific impulse and analogous to the approach to reality and nature offered by Enlightenment standards, in which the pursuit of knowledge becomes an end in itself. This is portrayed as anti-natural and harmful. However, Christian's – the name is surely no coincidence – Christian upbringing may also have something to do with it. In Tieck's rendering, the Christian community of the village, which offers only rituals empty of meaning, is also to blame, because it lacks resources to fruitfully moderate or integrate the modern impulse.

Christian refuses to "die in sweet sorrow", like the plants do for love of humans according to his father (who recommends such an atti-

---

ture of human existence, without a profounder exploration of the mysteries of Nature. The children he saw playing when he first arrived now sit as grave adults in the church, having lost all traces of their former *joie de vivre* due to a blind acceptance of superficial traditions that do not reach down to the essence of things, producing nothing but lame reactions to its potential brilliance. Similarly, Christian's first vision of the female spirit is that of a vigorous young woman with strong limbs, while in the second apparition she is described as an old, ugly, bent hag. In Tolkien's tale, the ritual of the Cake and the Twenty-four Feast is portrayed as almost drained of any deeper meaning at the beginning of the tale, but it becomes full of it at the end. The images of the Queen of Faery follow a similar scheme – they become successively less vulgar and feeble, and increasingly more noble and powerful, as Smith learns more of Faery.

tude to his son as proper and fitting in order to ensure a rewarding life in the village). Having been "contaminated" by a confused hotchpotch of Romantic and Enlightenment desires, there is no turning back to humility and quiet resignation, and the Christian religion's present weakness cannot make up for such a loss.

In Tolkien's tale, an (implicitly) Christian tradition and upbringing[8] will not necessarily give rise to deficient mental health when faced with modern dangers, as it does in Tieck's – rather does the tradition, however diluted, serve as a backbone for the imaginative visions to rest on, making the transcendental experience of the natural world even richer. The predominant note is the *fusion* between imaginary vision and traditional community life, in which imagination provides the stable (though somewhat lifeless) village existence with a fresh, novel, beautiful and inspiring element, and where tradition moderates the Romantic impulse, which would otherwise, at least potentially, lead to madness and alienation, even for Smith. In this way, the bitter-sweet death of the plants which in Tieck's tale is rejected by Christian is, in Tolkien's story, portrayed as the necessary, perhaps even desirable, outcome of an imaginative life. For Tolkien, imagination is not oppressed by tradition if the deeper aspects of this tradition may be recovered through Art – *recovered*, not dissected and used for any specific purpose. Even if the artist loses the imaginative vision, the same, enriched tradition may still offer consolation. Smith *accepts* the fate of dying in sweet sorrow without direct access to Faery, partly because a human community previously enriched by the influence of the deeper reality can offer enough consolation to make it worthwhile. He has been able to play an active role in the process of recovery because he has been inspired by his contact with Faery to adopt a humble, respectful, imaginative and crea-

---

[8] Tolkien himself establishes the allegory between the Great Hall and a village church, while the Master Cook is "plainly the Parson and the priesthood." (*SWM*, 100)

tive[9] attitude. Furthermore, he has not been tempted into any scientific approach towards an understanding of the natural world. In Tolkien's essay on the tale, he writes of the creatures of Faery that

> their good will is seen mainly in attempting to keep or restore relationships between the two worlds, since the Elves (and still some Men) realize that this love of Faery is essential to the full and proper human development. The love of Faery is the love of love: a relationship towards all things, animate and inanimate, which includes love and respect, and removes or modifies the spirit of possession and domination. Without it even plain 'Utility' will in fact become less useful; or will turn to ruthlessness and lead only to mere power, ultimately destructive. (*SWM* 94)

The spiritual education offered by a prolonged contact with Faery is thus intimately related to the concept of recovery, as explained by Tolkien in his essay, whereby Smith's explorations of Faery come to represent a growing insight in these fundamental matters. And though Smith is not redeemed from the instinct of possession, being human and therefore essentially flawed (or fallen), Alf does not have to *force* him to pass on the star; Smith gives it back to him voluntarily. Christian, on the other hand, is unable to integrate the Romantic search for transcendence in the reality of the village, not because of the actual idiosyncrasy of the village itself but rather as a result of the overarching influence and temptations of scientific and commercial outlooks upon life and the world – exactly the dangers that Tolkien depicts in his essay and that have befallen Wootton Major at the beginning of the story (*SWM*, 92). Christian is also incapable of sharing his visions with others.

---

[9] These are four qualities that Christian lacks. Christian has not *recovered* a previous, transcendent vision of the natural world, rather has the vision been made *distorted* by his scientific and possessive approach to Nature.

Hence, Smith performs the deed that Christian cannot – he renounces direct contact with the deeper reality and settles down in the village to die in sweet sorrow. Granted, Smith has never engaged in any profound dialogue with scientific or capitalistic ambitions, and though they are supposed to be present in Wootton Major, at least to some extent, the tension seems less dramatic than the one Christian has to endure. However, this criticism becomes quite redundant if we look at the tale in the (extended) context of the theoretical framework that supports it. The narrative was obviously addressed to contemporary readers, who knew full well what kind of a world-vision the Enlightenment had created for them, being thoroughly immersed in it. The issue at stake is *not* to offer yet another portrayal of a dreamy individual bashing his idealistic head bloody against the implacable world of hard fact and survival of the shrewdest and most ruthless. That would have been an attempt to escape in the wrong direction, so to speak. For Tolkien, we may be engaged in a losing battle, but if we are able to Recover a true contact with the mythic reality (through escape, as Tolkien understands it) and thus retain a sense of wonder, at least we will be offered consolation. As he argues, fairy stories, as he conceives them, can help us achieve just this, in spite of the many pitfalls of modern life. In this sense, *Smith of Wootton Major* is an enactment of the essay – and through the *art* of fairy story, the tale clarifies with much more immediacy than any essay Tolkien's corrective to the pessimistic and self-destructive Romantic stance.

MARTIN SIMONSON studied English philology and translation at the University of the Basque Country in Vitoria, Spain, and holds a Ph.D. from the same university with a dissertation on the narrative dynamics of *The Lord of the Rings*. He has contributed with several essays on Tolkien's work for previous WTP publications and *Tolkien Studies*, and will soon publish a full-length study on the interaction of narrative genre in *The Lord of the Rings*. Martin's current research is focused on American nature writing and literary myth-making in the context of the Great War. He is currently teaching Swedish language and literature at the University of the Basque Country.

## Works Cited

Abrams, Meyer H. *Natural Supernaturalism: Tradition and Revolution in Romantic Literature.* New York and London: Norton, 1973.

Anderson, Douglas A., ed. *Tales Before Tolkien: The Roots of Modern Fantasy,* New York: Ballantine Books, 2003.

Carlyle, Thomas. *Sartor Resartus. Victorian Prose and Poetry.* Eds. Lionel Trilling and Harold Bloom. New York, London, Toronto: OUP, 1973.

Coleridge, Samuel T. *Biographia Literaria.* 1817. Oxford: Oxford University Press, 1965.

Emerson, Ralph W. *Nature. The Essential Writings of Ralph Waldo Emerson.* Ed. Brooks Atkinson. New York: Modern Library, 2000.

Flieger, Verlyn. *A Question of Time.* Kent: Kent State University Press, 1997.

Shippey, Tom. *The Road to Middle-earth* (revised and extended edition, first edition 1982). Boston and New York: Houghton Mifflin, 2003.

---, *J.R.R. Tolkien: Author of the Century.* Boston and New York: Houghton Mifflin, 2000.

Tieck, Ludwig. *Der blonde Eckbert; Der Runenberg, Die Elfen: Märchen.* Stuttgart: Reclam, 2001.

Tolkien, J.R.R. *The Tolkien Reader.* New York: Ballantine Books, 1966.

---. *Smith of Wootton Major.* London: George Allen & Unwin, 1967. Extended edition prepared by Verlyn Flieger. London: HarperCollins, 2005.

# *Smith of Wootton Major*, "The Sea-Bell" and Lothlórien: Tolkien and the Perils of Faërie

## Maria Raffaella Benvenuto

### ABSTRACT

In this paper I aim to explore the topic of the 'perils of Faerie' as it is presented in *Smith of Wootton Major*, the poem "The Sea-Bell" and the Lothlórien episode of *The Lord of the Rings*. Although vastly different, these three texts share their treatment of the motif of mortals who manage to enter Faërie and experience its 'otherness' in different ways. In doing so, I will draw upon both literary and folklore sources, as well as some of the most important critical contributions on the subject.

### INTRODUCTION

At a superficial glance, Tolkien's shorter fiction may seem to be mainly aimed at children; the same applies to his collection of poems, *The Adventures of Tom Bombadil*. Therefore, to the inexperienced observer, or even to those whose knowledge of Tolkien is limited to his major works of fiction, the concept expressed by the title of this paper might sound odd, to say the least. In our politically correct times, we often think that children's literature should not be disturbing, though to all intents and purposes it is very often so; or even to provide the kind of intellectual stimulation that should be more appropriate for adults.

On the other hand, it was Tolkien himself who, in the opening words of his essay "On Fairy-Stories", stressed the ambiguous nature of Faërie', which is "a perilous land, and in it are pitfalls for the unwary and dungeons for the overbold"(*OFS* 109). As Tom Shippey aptly points out in his seminal volume *The Road to Middle-earth*, there is much more to Tolkien's so-called 'minor' works than meets the eye.

Among the "childish" poems and the funny, light-hearted children's tales lurks a rather disturbing streak, which is mainly related to the interaction between humans and the fairy world.

## AN IRRESISTIBLE LURE

The eighth chapter of Shippey's *Road*, which deals with Tolkien's minor works, bears the title "On the cold hill's side" - a direct quotation from one of the most celebrated poems about a mortal trapped in Faërie, John Keats's "La Belle Dame Sans Merci". Originally written in 1819 in the style of medieval ballads, the poem tells the tale of a knight enthralled and ultimately destroyed by a beautiful fairy. The story is reminiscent of well-known folk ballads such as "Tam Lin" and "Thomas the Rhymer", which was its most likely source (Kroeber 66), together with the legend of the German poet Tannhäuser and his imprisonment in the underground abode of the goddess Venus[1].

As a matter of fact, the theme of a mortal's entrapment by a fairy is a common feature of European folklore, appearing in both songs and tales. Though the "victim" is usually a man, there are also examples in which the captive is a woman, as in the Bluebeard-like tale of "Lady Isabel and the Elf-Knight"[2]. The topic seems to be more frequent in ballads than in fairy tales, at least as concerns the absence of a traditional "happy ending": Tam Lin is freed from the fairy queen's spell by his mortal lover, Janet of Carterhaugh; while Thomas the Rhymer is forbidden to utter even a single word during his seven-year stay in Elfland, and must promise never to reveal its secrets to the outside world.

---

[1] The derivation of Keats's poem from the legend of Tannhäuser is maintained, for instance, by Mario Praz in his book *The Romantic Agony* (1976). "La Belle Dame Sans Merci" is seen as the prototype of the Decadent *femme fatale*, to whom Galadriel's figure is undeniably related.

[2] In this ballad, common all over Europe, the heroine kills the elf-knight who has lured her into a wood with the intent of killing her like he did with other six maidens.

In fairy tales, the mortals who marry supernatural creatures are never actually held captive by their fairy spouses, but rather held to a promise of not revealing the latter's true nature, or not boasting about them. Breaking the promise inevitably means the disappearance of the magical spouse: in Antti Aarne and Stith Thompson's fundamental work of classification, *The Types of the Folktale*, originally published in 1928, the type AT 420 is designated as "The Man on a Quest for His Lost Wife"[3]. In many of those tales, the bride, who is lost and found again by her spouse after a series of trials, can transform herself into an animal, usually a bird, as in the widespread Scandinavian tale of "The Swan Maiden" (Tatar 72-2). To quote Tatar's words, "some female animal brides lure their mortal husbands into a hermetic world of timeless beauty, a world in which the husbands revel in pleasure yet never feel completely at home" (31-2).

Most examples originate from Northern Europe (including England and Scotland), and Tolkien's familiarity with them should not come as a surprise. His fascination with the subject is further borne out by his two Anglo-Saxon poems about "trapped mortals", included by Shippey in one of the appendices to *The Road to Middle-earth*. The first of those poems, which first appeared in the collection *Songs for the Philologists*, privately printed in 1936, "Ides Aelfscýne", adds a romantic element to the topic treated in "The Sea-Bell". In the other, "Ofer Widne Garsecg", the same story is presented with a happier ending, though from the closing lines it is evident that, according to common medieval belief, those who consorted with fairies and other such creatures were eventually damned[4]. As Shippey states,

---

[3] Type AT 425, "The Search for the Lost Husband", can be considered AT 420's feminine counterpart. Its earliest known written version is Apuleius's tale of "Cupid and Psyche" (Tatar 25).

[4] This belief is central to Oscar Wilde's "The Fisherman and His Soul" (1891), which was clearly inspired by Hans Christian Andersen's "The Little Mermaid" (1837). In both tales, the inhabitants of the sea are stated to have no soul, but in Wilde's tale the inevitable damnation of those who consort with them is explicitly mentioned.

> It seems that, at times at least, Tolkien thought that getting involved with Faërie was deeply dangerous. Though *Smith of Wootton Major* offers a reassurance that imaginative visions are true, it also declares, in private images, that mortal men cannot wander in these visions all the time, without danger. They must give up and make their peace with the world (*Road* 318).

Earlier in his book, Shippey says that "the allure and the danger are mixed" (67). In "Ides Aelfscýne", the affair between the elf-lady and the mortal knight ends in desertion and despair, leaving the young man "alone and palely loitering" like the knight in Keats's poem. Even in the absence of a romantic or sexual element, the consequences for mortals interacting with Faërie can be extremely serious. As seen in "The Sea-Bell", the mortals who manage to reach Elvenhome will never be the same again: "it is traditional […] for the people the elves reject to be unable to return to society, often because everyone they once knew is dead" (*Author* 281). This is another widespread motif in European folklore, though the main character of the tale often travels to the underworld rather than Faërie[5]. When he returns to the land of the living, he drops dead shortly afterwards, after having realised that centuries have passed since he set out.

We can thus conclude that Tolkien's attitude to Faërie seems to be rather ambivalent, as it is clearly shown by most of his life's work. In *The Hobbit*, the presence of the Elves in Mirkwood feels attractive and disturbing at the same time:

> At times they heard disquieting laughter. Sometimes there was singing in the distance too. The laughter was the laughter of fair voices, not of goblins, and the singing was beautiful, but it sounded eerie and strange, and they were not

---

[5] In the Aarne-Thompson classification, this motif is featured in type AT 470, *Friends in Life and Death*.

comforted, rather they hurried on from those parts with what strength they had left (*H,* 138).

Later in the same episode, when Bilbo and the Dwarves accidentally stumble upon a party of Elves feasting in a forest glade, those disappear as soon as they are approached, leaving the company alone in the utter darkness. This episode echoes the way Elves are portrayed in "The Seabell", where the inhabitants of the enchanted land only appear as disembodied voices – one of the main reasons for the narrator's unease and anguish. On the other hand, the Elves at Rivendell are friendly, harmless and even a bit silly, as their initial song shows quite clearly. Rivendell itself, while a very pleasant place, has none of the otherworldly characteristics associated with Elvish dwellings elsewhere in Tolkien's work.

### INSIDE THE DREAM

It is, however, in the Lothlórien episode of *The Lord of the Rings* that the image of Faërie appears in all its ambiguity. The Fellowship's stay in the Elven realm proves to have positive effects for most of the people involved, though it can also be seen as a life-changing experience in a number of ways. While Gimli, in spite of his initial misgivings, literally falls under Galadriel's spell, Boromir, when forced to reveal his innermost thoughts to her, reacts with distrust and hostility.

Most importantly, the members of the Fellowship experience that feeling of being "out of time" that seems to be one of the most distinctive features of Faërie. As Verlyn Flieger points out in her excellent study on the subject, *A Question of Time*:

> Without a doubt it [Lórien] is meant to be a real place. It is on the map. Travelers arrive by the road and on their own two feet. And yet it is extraordinary in some way. It is isolated from the ordinary world not just by its inaccessibility,

but also by that indescribable quality that Sam calls Elven magic and that Tolkien called Faërie – an air of enchantment, an atmosphere, an ambiance. We are told that Lórien has a strange reputation, that people are afraid to go in for fear they will be changed when they come out. It is most certainly, in some indefinable but recognizable respect, 'in there'. But until Sam raises the question there is little to suggest that 'in there' is outside natural law. (91)

In spite of its otherworldly beauty, Lothlórien is made as much of shadow as of light, as Marjorie Burns points out: "shadows, 'deepening' or looming, persistently intrude, and the green hill of Cerin Amroth is in the shape of a burial mound." (121) Galadriel herself is described as beautiful yet daunting: her eyes reveal her immense age, and can read into people's minds. However, it is in the episode of her "temptation" before the Mirror that she appears most dangerously. Her exclamation, "all shall love me and despair!", would not be out of place in the mouth of one of the many fatal women of late Romantic and Decadent literature. On that occasion, Sam and Frodo realise the full extent of her power, as well as the sacrifice she is willing to make for the sake of Middle-earth.

As Shippey observes, beauty is in itself dangerous; this is what Sam tries to explain to Faramir during their encounter in Ithilien:

> 'Then she must be lovely indeed,' said Faramir. 'Perilously fair.'
> 'I don't know about *perilous*,' said Sam. 'It strikes me that folk takes their peril with them into Lórien, and finds it there because they've brought it. But perhaps you could call her perilous, because she's so strong in herself. You, you could dash yourself to pieces on her, like a ship on a rock; or drown yourself, like a hobbit in a river. But neither rock or river would be to blame.' (*LotR* 664-5)

Beautiful, powerful and immortal, Galadriel is a distant figure of awe and fear even to Elf-friends like Faramir, or enemies of Sauron like Éomer. However, Sam seems to be the only character in the book who understands the true nature of her danger to those who meet her: she is a catalyst, bringing out the hidden flaws or qualities in people's characters. As Gimli undergoes a positive change, leaving most of his suspicious, introverted Dwarvish nature behind, so Boromir must come to terms with the temptation of the Ring, which he will eventually give in to.

### FROM DREAM TO NIGHTMARE

Though "written" by a Hobbit like the rest of *The Adventures of Tom Bombadil*, "The Sea-Bell" is nowhere as light-hearted in tone as the other poems for the most part are. In fact, it sees Tolkien's vision of the relationship between mortals and Faërie at its most pessimistic. The narrator of "The Sea-Bell", often identified with Frodo, feels estranged and ultimately rejected by the mysterious land he has reached by chance; his return to his own land is so traumatic that he will feel alienated from his fellow men until the end of his days. The shell (the titular "sea-bell") he finds on the strand lures him away towards the land of the Elves, but at the end it goes "silent and dead" – unlike what happens in the poem's earlier version, the revealingly-titled "Looney", written thirty years before, between 1932 and 1933.

A whole chapter of Flieger's *A Question of Time* is dedicated to a thorough analysis of the poem, whose importance in Tolkien's body of work has long been overlooked. In her opinion, the picture presented by both "Looney" and "The Sea-Bell" is that "the journey to the otherworld is unchangingly and unrelievedly bleak. Desolation verging on despair may be the fate of the visitor who would rashly venture into Faërie" (216). The final verse of the poem indeed conveys all the horror of the narrator's plight:

> Houses were shuttered, wind round them muttered,
> Roads were empty. I sat by a door,
> And where drizzling rain poured down a drain
> I cast away all that I bore:
> In my clutching hand some grains of sand,
> And a sea-shell silent and dead.
> Never will my ear that bell hear,
> Never will my feet that shore tread,
> Never again, as in sad lane,
> In blind alley and long street,
> Ragged I walk. To myself I talk,
> For still they speak not, men that I meet. (*ATB*, 60)

Not surprisingly, both Flieger and Christine Davidson draw parallels between the fate of the poem's protagonist and that of Coleridge's Ancient Mariner. In both cases, the traveller is shunned by those who meet him; the former's situation, however, is even worse, since, unlike the Mariner, he cannot find any listeners for his tale. According to Flieger, this condition is comparable with Coleridge's Death-in-Life: "he is changed forever, taken out of his time, lost to the otherworld and estranged from its own, very much as Frodo was after his return from Mordor to the Shire, not just 'falling asleep again', but caught in a nightmare from which he cannot awaken" (216). Keats's knight-at-arms suffers much the same fate:

> And there she lullèd me asleep
> And there I dreamed – Ah, woe betide! -
> The latest dream I ever dreamed
> On the cold hill's side. (401)

His dream of love and passion quickly changes into a nightmare: he will be forever held in thrall by "La Belle Dame Sans Merci", pale and anguished, drained of life, though not truly dead.

Even though the poem's protagonist has committed no crime like the Mariner's shooting of the Albatross, he is nonetheless guilty of *hybris*, as Davidson points out (17): after having "invaded" the unknown land, he proclaims himself its king – only to find out he is not welcome, and to see the land's beauty suddenly turn cold and hostile. Even at the beginning, a sense of darkness and danger underlies that otherwordly beauty – an unheeded warning to the intruder: "but under cliff-eaves there were glooming caves/weed-curtained, dark and grey/a cold air stirred in my hair/and the light waned as I hurried away" (*ATB* 57-8). He has brought his own peril into Faërie by presuming too much, and is therefore severely punished.

## RECONCILIATION

The story narrated in *Smith of Wootton Major* comes across as Tolkien's highly individual twist on the traditional tale of a mortal who manages to gain access to Faërie. In it, acceptance is mixed with rejection, though, unlike what happens in "The Sea-Bell", the titular character ends up more or less unscathed. However, there is a very significant difference between the two texts: while in the poem the protagonist is an intruder, in the short story he receives a sort of formal invitation. The fay-star he finds in the cake at the age of ten allows him to enter Faërie whenever he likes, while preventing him from suffering severe consequences: "he was welcome there; for the star shone brightly on his brow, and he was as safe as a mortal can be in that perilous country. The Lesser Evils avoided the star, and from the Greater Evils he was guarded" (*SWM* 24). Though we never really learn what those evils are, we get several glimpses of disturbing events and situations.

At the same time, as the Fairy Queen makes it clear to him, the star is not a "passport to go wherever he wished" (*SWM* 33). In fact, after a long series of visits to Faërie, Smith gets suddenly rejected from the enchanted realm, though only on a temporary basis. In spite of his shock at this unexpected occurrence, he summons the courage to go back again; on this occasion he meets the Queen for the first time, though disguised as a young maiden. She dances with him and puts a flower in his hair; after this meeting, he appears somewhat transformed, almost an object of awe, so that his son tells him he looks "like a giant" (*SWM*, 34). The flower itself is clearly a magical object, never fading or withering; in a way, it represents Smith's romantic involvement with the Queen, which nevertheless does not interfere with his family life or his relationship with his wife, Nell, nor does it bring him any of the devastating consequences discussed earlier.

However, his second meeting with the Queen, whom at last he manages to see in all her beauty and glory, also signals the end of his welcome in Faërie. Though she makes him her messenger, at the same time she sends him back to "weariness and bereavement" (*SWM* 48) – that is, to a life forever deprived of the light and excitement of the hidden realm[6]. On the other hand, after surrendering the star back to Alf, and consequently giving up his visits to Faërie for good, Smith is able to go on with his life, pretty much unscathed by his experience. Unlike the narrator of "The Sea-Bell", he understands when the time to give up his privileges has come, and accepts his lot.

This is what enables Smith to resume his life as a blacksmith, a family man, and a member of his community. The story ends with his choice of the next holder of the star, a sort of joke he plays on the prosaic-minded Nokes, who sees the Fairy Queen as no more than a little doll wielding a magic wand. In spite of his obvious loss, Smith has reconciled himself with the limitation of his human nature, and thus with being only a short-term guest in the enchanted land. Through his acceptance, he avoids becoming an outcast among his peers - unlike the nar-

---

[6] Similarly, in "The Last Ship", the poem's main character, Fíriel, who cannot board the Elven-ship because she was "born Earth's daughter", goes back to her dreary everyday life, symbolised by darkness, shadow and the fading of the sunlight (*ATB* 63-4).

rator of "The Sea-Bell", who is so blinded by what he sees that he forgets himself, forever destroying his own life.

CONCLUSION

The following quotation from Paul Kocher's *Master of Middle-earth* is, to my mind, a more than fitting conclusion to this paper, as well as a source of ideas for further development of the subject:

> Because of Tolkien's unvarying idea that the paths of elves and men are sundered, in none of his fairy lands or elven homes can a mortal man be more than a temporary guest. [...] Such, then, Tolkien seems to say, is the tragic homelessness of the man who lives and creates fantasy in a rationalistic age. (Kocher 200-1)

However, in spite of the many dangers lurking beneath its timeless beauty, and of the "weariness and bereavement" that inevitably come with its loss, mortals will always find the lure of Faërie hard to resist.

MARIA RAFFAELLA BENVENUTO, born and based in Rome, Italy, is currently completing a Ph.D. in Comparative Literature on the subject of Finnish fairy tales. Her interest in Tolkien dates back from the early '80s. In the past three years, she has worked as editor and translator of the Italian editions of Tom Shippey's *The Road to Middle-earth* and Verlyn Flieger's *Splintered Light*. She has also contributed four articles to *The J.R.R. Tolkien Encyclopedia,* and written several articles on Tolkien and fairy tales.

## Works Cited

Aarne, Antti, and Stith Thompson. *The Types of the Folktale: A Classification and Bibliography.* Helsinki: Academia Scientiarum Fennica, 1961.

Burns, Marjorie. *Perilous Realms. Celtic and Norse in Tolkien's Middle-earth.* Toronto: The University of Toronto Press, 2005.

Coleridge, Samuel Taylor. *The Rime of the Ancient Mariner. The Oxford Book of English Verse.* Ed. Christopher Ricks. Oxford: Oxford University Press, 1999. 357-73.

Davidson, Christine. "*The Sea-Bell.* A Voyage of Exploration". *Tolkien, the Sea and Scandinavia*, Proceedings of the 11th Tolkien Society Seminar. Telford: The Tolkien Society, 1999. 11-18.

Flieger, Verlyn. *A Question of Time. JRR Tolkien's Road to Faërie.* Kent (OH): The Kent State University Press.

Friedman, Albert B. (ed.). *The Viking Book of Folk Ballads of the English-Speaking World.* New York: The Viking Press, 1968.

Keats, John. "La Belle Dame Sans Merci". *The Oxford Book of English Verse*, cit. 400-1.

Kocher, Paul. *Master of Middle-earth. The Achievement of JRR Tolkien.* London: Pimlico, 2002.

Kroeber, Karl. *Romantic Fantasy and Science Fiction.* New Haven and London: Yale University Press, 1988.

Shippey, Tom. *JRR Tolkien: Author of the Century.* London: HarperCollins, 2000.

---, *The Road to Middle-earth.* 3rd ed. London: HarperCollins, 2005.

Tatar, Maria. "Introduction: *Beauty and the Beast*". *The Classic Fairy Tales.* Ed. Maria Tatar. New York: W.W. Norton & Company, 1999.

Tolkien, J.R.R. *The Adventures of Tom Bombadil.* Illustrated by Pauline Baynes. Boston: Houghton Mifflin, 1963.

---, "Smith of Wootton Major". *Smith of Wootton Major and Farmer Giles of Ham.* Illustrated by Pauline Baynes. New York: Ballantine, 1985. 6-59.

---, "On Fairy-Stories". *The Monsters and the Critics and Other Essays.* London: HarperCollins, 1997. 107-61.

---, *The Hobbit.* London: HarperCollins, 1999.

---, *The Lord of the Rings.* London: HarperCollins, 2002.

# A Star Above the Mast:
# Tolkien, Faërie and the Great Escape

### Anna E. Slack

#### ABSTRACT

This paper begins with the notion that man has at his core a desire to make 'the Great Escape' into another world. This paper posits that by reflecting the eternal world, the secondary world of Faërie holds echoes of what man seeks in that escape, and that it is this that prompts him to venture into the Perilous Realm. By examining some of Tolkien's minor works (*Smith of Wootton Major, The Sea Bell, Leaf by Niggle* and *Bilbo's Last Song*) in conjunction with Tolkien's theory of eucatastrophe, this paper explores how men in Tolkien's works relate to Faërie. In turn, these relationships are assessed to see how they may shed light onto Tolkien's own views both of dealing with Faërie and the Great Escape itself.

The glimpsing of other worlds is at the heart of Faërie (*TL* 41), but at the heart of man is a deep-seated yearning for more than a glimpse; at the heart of man lies the desire for 'the Great Escape: the escape from Death' (*TL* 68). This escape is figured in Faërie by what Tolkien calls the sundered paths of the two kindred; to man is given the gift of death, and to the elves the gift of deathlessness. Tolkien posits that, just as our own storytelling traditions speak of the quest for eternal life and escape from death, the stories of the elves are filled with escape from deathlessness. This notion was given concrete form in Tolkien's own mythology in the tale 'Of Beren and Lúthien', where the pivotal point of the myth is found in the escape from deathlessness chosen by Lúthien in the halls of Mandos.

That Lúthien's farewell to the world of Faërie is at the beating heart of Middle-earth tells us something about how Tolkien viewed the Great Escape and the relationship between man and Faërie.

Before we may venture to Faërie, we must consider the assumption that man seeks a Great Escape even in our own time, and examine how faith and Faërie may be linked.

Matters of faith have always dominated man's view of the world. If you look to the consolation provided by the great religions you will find the Great Escape presented mostly as the afterlife; the place where, according to the Christian mythos, there will be 'no more mourning or crying' (Rev. 21.4). This escape ultimately entails leaving the world through death. But man has always sought other ways to reach the eternal world. In the Middle Ages many entered into the anchoritic life. These men and women felt that withdrawing from the world was a gesture of responsible fugitism which brought them closer to the Great Escape; seclusion from the world was best sought swiftly so as to come more quickly to the New Jerusalem. This style of life – rejecting the world by closeting oneself in a cell to contemplate the divine – could not be taken on lightly. Anchoritic 'guides' like the *Ancrene Wisse* figured the novice's withdrawal from our world as a battle against spiritual forces. In this, authors borrowed language from both the Bible and popular romances; the latter heavily influenced by the traditions of Faërie. Long before Tolkien wrote, faith and Faërie were intertwined. Visions of the afterlife were touched by Faërie, and vice versa.

So to Faërie. You will find the Great Escape offered by faith foreshadowed in the perilous realm in the countless journeys of men who fall asleep upon a mound. Here, the fleeting (and at times joyous) escape is marred by farewells, both to the world on leaving it, and to Faërie on returning. When travellers return, it is often to find that the long years of their lives have passed along with all whom they have known. The returned wanderer becomes doubly outcast; none can know him in his own world and he can never return to the realm of Faërie where he once resided. Think for a moment of the fate of Keats's knight in *La Belle Dame sans Merci*, left 'alone and palely loitering' (*Belle Dame*

2) by the withered sedge; his rest on a mound leaves him 'in thrall' (*Belle Dame* 39-40), along with the dozens of kings, princes and warriors who have been beguiled before him. Having tasted the raptures of Faërie he becomes a prisoner in the historical world, bereft of all his joy. The knight enters into a kind of involuntary anchorage, with his memories of the *Belle Dame* making his cell walls; rather than passing his time in prayer, he passes it pining for the eternal world that was shown to him in the guise of Faërie.

We can compare this to the experience of the dreamer in the Gawain-poet's *Pearl*, a work later edited by Tolkien and E.V. Gordon. In this poem, the boundaries of faith and Faërie cross, co-existing in a way reminiscent of the mixed elements of paganism and Christianity in the epic poem *Beowulf*. The poem's dreamer, sleeping on a mound, does not encounter a belle dame nor even descend to Faërie, but rather ascends in a vision to the New Jerusalem where he meets again his 'pearl', posited to represent a daughter lost to him in death. The Pearl expounds the substance of this vision – a kind of catechism wherein the dreamer slowly grasps the promises of heaven – but the joy and consolation which he reaps are countered by his sudden reawakening into the primary or historical world where his grief returns to him in force. The dreamer can speak about what lies beyond the Faërie-like 'crystal cliffs' (*Pearl* 3.174) and the river of his dream, but he must still live out his years on earth. Although he closes by enthusiastically expounding the theological essence of what he has learned, his farewell to his vision is a troubled one; his attempt at escape has been thwarted.

In *Pearl* we can see traces of Tolkien's theory of eucatastrophe; that Faërie can be a means of highlighting faith, as the Pearl does when she speaks to the dreamer about the New Jerusalem. Though Faërie cannot, as Tolkien observed, be 'the road to heaven' (*TL* 5), it possesses a haunting echo of that escape. So man, seeing (though not always recognising) in Faërie aspects of the greater journey, ventures after it. Some are wounded in the search, others are enriched. What a man finds when he crosses the threshold is determined not so much by the realm where he travels, but what he takes with him.

It is this taut relationship between man and the perilous realm that Tolkien explores in so many of his minor works. In charting possible relationships between men and Faërie, Tolkien tries to demonstrate the inherent value of Faërie to men, and to reconcile it via eucatastrophe to the eternal world of the Great Escape.

So how does Tolkien illustrate these relationships? We may begin with a word of caution: 'while [a traveller] is [in Faërie] it is dangerous for him to ask too many questions, lest the gates should be shut and the keys be lost' (*TL* 3). Tolkien knew, perhaps better than most, that the realm of Faërie is called 'perilous' for good reason. Even (or especially) in childhood, we are well aware that Faërie is high and deep, with creatures in its borders who purpose both good and evil. These stories teach us that those who travel into Faërie with 'the heart of a little child' (*TL* 44), with humility and innocence, succeed in their trial, whatever its nature. But those who are arrogant – the hordes of elder princes and princesses whose youngest siblings outdo them – never come to a good end. For them, Faërie is the idle realm of children.

In the minor works on which I have chosen to focus, Tolkien presents us with several types of people who approach Faërie: first, those who don't believe in Faërie; second, those that hold false beliefs about Faërie and its nature; third, people for whom Faërie can be detrimental despite their knowledge of it; and fourth, figures who both believe in, and know, Faërie. For this last group, knowledge of the perilous realm affects the kind of recovery, escape and consolation that Tolkien clarifies in 'On Fairy Stories'.

Characters with no belief in Faërie hold that Faërie is better spelt *ai* than *ae*, and that the stories are fit only for the entertainment of children. *Smith of Wootton Major* presents us with just such a character: Nokes. If Nokes ever believed in Faërie at all he has been disabused of it, and actively seeks to diminish its influence on others. His notions of wands and pink icing, not to mention his sidelong snickers, clearly seek to relegate Faërie to the nursery (for 'it amuses the children' *TPR* 152). This is an activity that we know Tolkien found detestable, attributing it particularly to academics and critics; this disregard of Faerie by relegating it to the nursery Tolkien compared to the cutting off of other 'adult' arts like science. (*TL* 35). In 'On Fairy Stories', Tolkien writes that 'the fear of the beautiful fay that ran through the elder ages almost eludes our grasp. Even more alarming: goodness is itself bereft of its proper beauty' (*TL* 65). This bereavement is a result of deeming Faërie childish, and results in losing any sense of awe. Nokes understands neither awe-full fear nor awe of goodness; for the characters in which we, as readers, see these attributes, Nokes has only patronising words: Smith is a 'quiet, slow boy' (*TPR* 173), Alf is 'nimble' and 'artful' (*TPR* 178). Nokes deprecates Faërie itself at every turn, as when he snidely asks Alf to tell him if, among the raisins for the cake, he notices any 'special, fairy ones' (*TPR* 152). Nokes, unlike Smith, feels a pitiable, grovelling fear when confronted with the King of Faërie in his proper guise: he can only beg not to be harmed. His encounter with Faërie does not clear Nokes' sight; he attributes his vision to bad food.

For Nokes, everything has been disenchanted. Yet whilst he pours scorn on Faërie, he still reaches for its creative power although he does not apprehend its source: in the matter of the cake, he must rely on what he has garnered surreptitiously from Prentice to satisfy his 'severe critics' (*TPR* 150). He claims a creative and inventive superiority to Prentice, saying that it is '[his] place to have ideas, and not [Prentice's]'

(*TPR* 153), but he can only palely copy Prentice's genius. Nokes has dethroned Faërie, and seeks to be a 'master of arts' in its place.

We can easily apply to Nokes many of Tolkien's comments about those who advocated 'real life' over 'fantasy' (*TL* 63): factories and railways would be more real to Nokes than centaurs and dragons. In demeaning Faërie and his dogged preference for 'real life', Nokes suffers a long-term bereavement which he cannot see himself, but which is represented in the pomposity of his character. His joy at the end of the tale that Prentice is 'gone at last' (*TPR* 178) rings deadeningly in the reader's ears. For Nokes, there is no Great Escape; the greatest achievement in Wootton Major is the great riddance of Alf.

*Smith of Wootton Major* reveals Tolkien's anxiety at the critical treatment of Faërie; Nokes's attitude expresses Tolkien's feeling that Faërie was being reduced to nursery rhymes by critics who saw only escapism, not the Great Escape, in its borders. That Nokes's voice dominates the end of the text reflects this, and creates a feeling of bereavement. It is of note that this keen sense of loss appears in one of Tolkien's last works, at a time when his own thought was 'weighted with the presage of 'bereavement'' (*Letters* 389). Tolkien's concern that the didactic qualities of Faërie will be lost as the world fills with Nokeses is clear. It is just this bereavement that Nokes has suffered without knowing it.

Holding no belief in Faërie is, as we have seen, bad enough. As a younger man, Tolkien had also studied what happened to men who held false beliefs about the perilous realm. His poem *The Looney* was first written in 1934, and later revised and republished in 1962 as *The Sea Bell*. In both poems we can see Tolkien exploring another bereaving aspect of Faërie, this time the result of seeking Faërie and the Great Escape, but with that trademark of the great tragedies: hubris.

The most notable change between the two versions of Tolkien's poem is in terms of framing; originally, like Keats' *La Belle Dame*, the piece represented the speech of the titular Looney, who has returned from Faërie and is recounting his misadventure to an interested party. But the later version has no comparable narrative frame. Instead, in the added introduction, it is noted that the poem (subtitled 'Frodo's Dreme'), is 'of hobbit origin' (*TPR* 64). As Tom Shippey has noted in his book *Tolkien: Author of the Century*, this notation calls our attention to an alternative ending (282) for Frodo where there is no great escape to Valinor.

Like Firiel in *The Last Ship*, *The Sea Bell*'s traveller encounters an empty ship. His call that 'it is later than late' (*TPR* 110), brings to mind the Great Escape. The 'forgotten strand' (*TPR* 110) where he disembarks, and to which we can compare later descriptions of the white shores of Valinor, is beautiful but deserted. To the traveller's horror, the landscape is not paradise regained but rather threatening; there are 'hidden teeth' (*TPR* 110) in it, the willows weep, the flowers are like fallen stars, and the ford is guarded by 'gladdon swords' (*TPR* 111). The traveller finds no one and wherever he goes, everything that he expects from Faërie, figured in distant singing, flees from him. In response to this, the traveller makes himself a mantle and wand, claiming kingship for himself over the land. Having crowned himself with flowers he stands on a mound to make his proclamation of lordship, declaring himself master of the land.

Though the traveller may have begun well by wishing to journey on the empty ship to seek the Great Escape, this gesture is obviously hubristic and misguided. Its arrogant nature is enhanced by the fact that in this deed the traveller effectively tries to force a second entry into Faërie on his own terms; his mocking crown is an attempt to gain access to the hidden world which is frustratingly just beyond his reach. But when he tries to master Faërie he becomes like a mole, bent to the ground. Instead of an escape his claim produces a shroud of night, and brings to him a kind of death that touches everything about him; Tolkien vividly describes the dead trees, filled with spiders and beetles. The traveller, unsurprisingly, wanders 'in wit' (*TPR* 112) in this period where Faërie lies dead all about him.

The traveller at last makes the long journey home. Returned from his escape, he casts away everything, including the sea bell which he will never more hear. The object has become a shell in more senses than one, and represents the hollowness of Faërie for the traveller. His desperate experience in Faërie was the result of forsaking or neglecting the first image and true form of Faërie (represented by the threatening sea and caves) for one closer to his own ideas of what Faërie should entail (hares and singing on the hill). These he never finds, even though Faërie encompasses them. The traveller's hubristic experience makes him an outcast both from Faërie and from his own world upon his return; the ships standing in the port are 'laden with light' (*TPR* 113), at peace and fulfilled, while the returner is 'dark as a raven' (*TPR* 113), unfulfilled and bereft.

Tolkien's concern about having a correct attitude to Faërie is clear; neither the realm nor tales of it may be trifled with, especially by means of adaptation or domination. The traveller seeks a very tame Faërie and in his disappointment his farewell to it is bitter. He returns unable to speak of his journey to anyone, because, just as in Faërie, none will speak to him. That Tolkien revised this poem later on in his life may illustrate some of Tolkien's own fears regarding his work. Had he obscured the Great Escape in what he wrote? Had he trifled with Faërie and rejected its true nature? *The Sea Bell* becomes an anti-Faërie story. The arrogant rejection of the Great Escape and the true realm of Faërie robs the traveller not just of Faërie, but also of the real world. The Great Escape has passed him by, the glimpse is lost as the sea bell ceases to ring.

So trying to master Faërie is a perilous business. How can we reconcile our visions of Faërie to the real world, and all that the real world represents? Our world is full of business, toil and duty that cannot easily be set aside to search for Faërie. For *The Sea Bell's* traveller, that search entailed the loss of both Faërie and of society in his own world. Is the risk one worth bearing, when we have so many duties and the price of adventure can be so high? Surely it is safer to be like Nokes, and allow Faërie to pass.

Tolkien did not hold this view. In *On Fairy Stories* he expresses at length his notion that involvement with Faërie was vital in facilitating and deepening ties to the real world rather than the opposite. We can compare this idea to that hinted at by C. S. Lewis in his Narnia stories, where the children gradually grow 'too old' (*Prince Caspian*, 188) for the Faërie realm of Narnia, but must take the lessons they have learned there back to their own world. So the experience of Faërie, unlike that of *The Sea Bell's* traveller, can be made a part of the real world. But the transition and reconciliation are not easy; for some, the perilous realm itself becomes dangerously greater than the escape that it mimics.

This concern is vividly expressed in *Leaf by Niggle*. In *Niggle*, Tolkien lays before us the unenviable position of a man unconvinced of his ability, and perhaps unable, to reconcile Faërie and his duties in the primary world in his own lifetime. Faërie, and the Great Escape itself as figured in Niggle's journey, become distractions rather than a source of recovery or reflection of the eternal world.

Niggle is afraid of the great journey due to his fascination with Faërie and the knowledge that he often struggles to complete all the tasks allotted to him. Like the traveller in *The Sea Bell*, Niggle is possessive of his time in Faërie; he spends a good deal of time painting, setting, for example, great importance on a single leaf at the expense of others. This obsession with Faërie is never allowed to go so far that he does not participate in the real world, but he does so with the kind of heavy heart that: makes 'him uncomfortable more often than it [makes] him do anything' (*TL* 3). Niggle constantly feels pulled away from his love of Faërie by the hindrances of the real world, whereas his love of Faërie should actually fuel his involvement in it (just as, we might add, a looking forward to the 'Great Escape' should sharpen our taste for our own world).

Unlike *The Sea Bell*'s traveller or Smith, Niggle is not offered a journey to Faërie: the journey offered to him is death itself. It is little wonder, then, that he is trying to put it off as best as he can, reasoning that once dead, his own voyage to Faërie, figured in his painting, will be concluded. He sees no link between Faërie, his world, and the Great Escape. For Niggle, Faërie is both a distraction and a frustration. It is not until he learns to place the beauty of Faërie and the real world together during his purgatorial sojourn with the mysterious voices and subsequent work with Parish that his connection to Faërie bears real fruit. It is then that his painting reflects part of the great journey, becoming the very landscape in which he travels: *Niggle's Parish*.

Here, Tolkien very clearly states that the subcreation of those who can describe Faërie can also reflect the great journey. The conclusion to Niggle's story is an antidote to the despair at the end of *The Sea Bell*. Tolkien also suggests that those who long for Faërie, like Niggle, look for the Great Escape in another guise. For many, we are told, Niggle's painting 'makes the best introduction to the mountains' (*TL* 118); that is to say, the crystal cliffs of the eternal world.

In Niggle's story we can see that it is possible to come to some kind of understanding with Faërie, and that Faërie itself can be the connection between the historical and eternal worlds. This connection is also at the heart of Tolkien's eucatastrophe, the moment when the eternal world strikes through into the historical one. According to Tolkien, Faërie was the best kind of setting for this occurrence, and it goes without saying that Tolkien hoped that his own work could have a similar effect. Niggle only comprehends this aspect of his painting after his journey has begun; his relationship with Faërie is retrospective. We can posit that the ideal would be to be reconciled to Faërie whilst in the historical world, allowing it to enrich and prepare us for the greater journey. Interestingly, the minor work that best demonstrates this positive relationship with Faërie is also the one that speaks most clearly about the loss that accompanies Faërie: *Smith of Wootton Major*.

Smith is able to pass freely between the real world and Faërie (a feat making him nigh unique in literature) thanks to the fay star. This star enriches Smith deeply. Compare, for example, Smith's ability in song, and the beauty of the practical things that he makes, to Niggle's frustrated efforts at a double life. Smith travels in Faërie and sees things both terrible and lovely, but, unlike Nokes or *The Sea Bell*'s traveller, he remains in awe of them, does not flee from them, and does not attempt to claim lordship over them. He seeks the King of Faërie, rather than seeking to become the king, and in return for his modesty is guarded from the 'greater evils' (*TPR* 157). He remains a learner and explorer, and his encounters with Faërie give him a great shadow, noted by his son as the true measure of his character. He grows beyond his stature in Wootton Major, but does not outgrow the village. He is at peace both in Faërie and at home, respected in both places.

The greatest moment of Smith's journey is when he is greeted by and recognises the Queen of Faërie. But this moment, which shows the depth of Smith's connection to Faërie, also highlights his bereavement from it:

> So he seemed to be both in the World and in Faery, and also outside them, and surveying them, so that he was at once in bereavement, and ownership, and in peace. When after a while the stillness passed he raised his head and stood up. The dawn was in the sky and the stars were pale, and the Queen was gone [...] and he knew that his way now led back to bereavement. (*TPR* 164).

Here Tolkien summarises the double-nature of knowing Faërie, highlighting at once the way that Faërie figures the Great Escape, but also how it is not, and cannot be, that escape. The paradox of being both in bereavement and ownership is something that reaches beyond the scope of experience in the primary world, and is heightened by Faërie. Smith's true bereavement is in attaining for a moment the clarity loaned to Faërie by its echo of the Great Escape, and knowing that he cannot keep it, just as he cannot keep the star. He must bid it farewell.

Like Bilbo giving up the Ring, Smith gives up the star of his own volition, knowing that some things are not given as heirlooms. Thus, he renounces the possessiveness of the sea bell's traveller, and in so doing he demonstrates a nobility which is akin to Faërie. His return to Wootton Major is similar to that of Sam in *The Lord of the Rings*; Smith will do much good to the world by being back in it. Smith's son notes that Smith has much to teach besides the working of iron, but a shadow of the journeys that he made will always lie over him, making him more than what he would otherwise have been. Smith keeps the hall gilded in memory of Alf, just as Sam keeps the Red Book.

In Smith we see the epitome of a man touched by Faërie, but we see also that Faërie must always be left. For Smith, unlike Frodo and even Sam, there is no last crossing to Elvenhome, though he likely longs for it. Like the dreamer in *Pearl*, Smith must content himself with the memory of his journey while awaiting the greater one. Smith in many ways represents an ideal link to Faërie, but his farewell to it does not yet entail the complete reconciliation between Faërie and the historical world that Tolkien longed for. It is the sorrow in parting from Faërie having glimpsed, but not attained, the Great Escape that creates the sense of 'an old man's book' (*Letters*, 389) in many of Tolkien's minor works.

We have seen how possible relationships with Faërie can vary from arrogance and blatant disbelief, to eventual understanding of and acquiescence to bereavement and farewell. It is at the point of farewell that the true nature of the relationship is put to the test; for some, the mimetic nature of Faërie offers escape, recovery and consolation so as to effect a fruitful return to our own world. Tolkien's theory of eucatastrophe puts both reader and author in the place of the king who, after long and wild adventures in Faërie, returns to his kingdom with clear and deepened sight because he has glimpsed the eternal in his journey. The manner of our return reflects the nature of our journey, and our deepened sight should give us the vision to look forward to the journey for which Faërie has been a kind of testing ground. Like Smith, we should have the courage to keep the hall gilded in a world beset with Nokeses.

Tom Shippey views *Smith* as a 'valedictory address' (*Author of the Century*, 303), and certainly there is in Smith much that bears comparison to Tolkien himself. There is the long history of travel in Faërie, the illustration of its scope in the dark elves, the dancing queen, and the weeping birch. In Smith himself many of Niggle's worrying faults have been remedied; his participation in the life of Wootton Major is enhanced by his sojourns in Faërie, and perhaps Tolkien felt able to say the same of his own work. After Smith's return to Wootton Major it is difficult to know what the village's future will be, but it is at least encouraging that any of the children seem 'fit to find the star' (*TPR* 176). Perhaps one of the consolations of Tolkien's own farewell lay in the notion that his journeys would help to encourage a correct attitude towards Faërie, and through that towards the Great Escape.

For Tolkien, Faërie was a place where the Great Escape to the eternal world was foreshadowed. But in many of Tolkien's works, both major and minor, there is a tone of despair, as travellers are forced to return to the historical world, some without learning the lessons that Faërie had to teach them. There is, however, one of Tolkien's minor works where faith and Faërie collide at the very departure point of the Great Escape: *Bilbo's Last Song*.

The poem has at its beginning the weight of impending bereavement figured in the familiar motif of the ending day, except in Bilbo's case it has already ended, and his eyes are 'dim' (*BLS* 1). The singer bids farewell to his friends; like many before him, he can hear the call of a world beyond his own, and the stanza moves between literal descriptions of the harbour (the stony wall and the salt-sea) to visionary statements of going 'beyond the sunset' (*BLS* 6). The stanza's focus on what the singer can hear, compounded by the emphasis on dimness of sight, enhances the capacity for vision that reaches beyond the world, just as those who go to Faërie see beyond it. But, on the cusp of the great journey, this vision can no longer be sneered at.

The second stanza returns to literal descriptions of the moorings fretting (perhaps with a desire to begin the journey). Yet as the stanza moves on, the searing vision of the first stanza settles into a kind of travelogue, charting the road that must be taken through shadows to 'west of West' (*BLS* 15). In the final line we are told that in these lands, night 'is quiet and sleep is rest' (*BLS* 16). This draws on the biblical assurance of a future where there will be no more weeping; the visionary world, enhanced by Faërie, is beginning to echo the eternal one[1].

In the third stanza the poem mentions the Lonely Star, in which we can see the crossroads both of Faërie and eternity. This star is now

---

[1] This echo of the eternal world would perhaps have been influenced by the writing of this poem so close to the end of Tolkien's life. Bilbo, although related directly to Middle-Earth in name, seems now to be an allegorical representation of Tolkien himself. Although Tolkien does not speak directly about faith in his poem the matching of the appearance of the star with his comments in *On Fairy Stories* about how eucatastrophe (the cornerstone of Faërie) is, in Tolkien's mind, intrinsically related to the cornerstone of his faith (Christ, also biblically represented as the morning star), the star here seems to stand for faerie and faith in connecting to the themes of journeying into the West. Indeed, *Bilbo's Last Song* affords interesting comparison with Tennyson's *Crossing the Bar*.

no longer a passport as it was for Smith; it is the guide, and the true measure of the journey is where the singer, whose eyes had previously been dim, cries to the ship 'I see the Star above your mast!' (*BLS* 24). Up to this point, the poem has been a vision of the Great Escape and the way to the West, but now, in this eucatastrophic moment, the Star itself is seen. Faërie and the Great Escape are unified as the star, laid down in old age, returns as a guide to lead the singer home.

That the Star at this point of farewell stands for both faith and Faërie is a fitting conclusion to Tolkien's long life. This double-facet of the Star also ties *Bilbo's Last Song* to Tolkien's essay 'On Fairy Stories', where he states that Faërie stories moved closest to the eternal world in their capacity for eucatastrophe. For Tolkien, who struggled in many of his works to reconcile Faërie to the real world, the long-sought Great Escape shows that both Faërie and faith unite at last 'west of West', in the Star above the mast. He finds himself gazing at the very core of eucatastrophe: an 'especially beautiful fairy-story' that is 'primarily true' (*TL* 72). What greater escape could there be?

ANNA SLACK is a teacher of English Language at a private language school in Palermo, Sicily, known for waxing lyrical about Tolkien in general (and Eucatastrophe in particular) at the slightest excuse. She graduated with a first class degree in English Literature from the University of Cambridge in 2005. Whilst at Cambridge, Anna spent two years editing the tri-annual journal of the Cambridge Tolkien Society, *Anor*, and a year as the society secretary. She helped pioneer and partook in the acclaimed performance of the BBC Radio Adaptation of *The Lord of the Rings* in aid of the National Trust. Anna has written and delivered several papers on Tolkien at the universities of Birmingham, Oxford and Jena, and is currently preparing a contribution for the forthcoming conference on *The Hobbit* to be held in Jena in 2008.

## Works Cited

Carpenter, Humphrey, ed. *The Letters of J. R. R. Tolkien*. London: HarperCollins, 1995.

Gordon, E. V., ed. *Pearl*. Oxford: Clarendon Press Oxford University Press, 1980.

The Holy Bible: *New International Version*. London: Hodder and Stoughton, 2000.

Keats, John. "La Belle Dame Sans Merci" *The Poems of John Keats*. Ed. Miriam Allcott. London: Longman, 1970. 500 – 506.

Lewis, C. S., *Prince Caspian*. Harmondsworth: Penguin, 1962.

Shippey, Tom, *J. R. R. Tolkien: Author of the Century*. London: HarperCollins, 2001.

Tolkien, J. R. R., *Tree and Leaf, including the poem Mythopoeia and The Homecoming of Beorhtnoth*. London: HarperCollins, 2001.

---, *Tales from the Perilous Realm, including The Adventures of Tom Bombadil, Leaf by Niggle, Smith of Wootton Major and Farmer Giles of Ham*. London: HarperCollins, 2002.

---, *Bilbo's Last Song*. London: Hutchinson, 2002.

# Journeys in the Dark

MARGARET HILEY

### ABSTRACT

This paper will focus on two of Tolkien's shorter texts: the story *Smith of Wootton Major* and the poem "The Sea-bell". Both story and poem can be interpreted as belonging to a genre typical of fantasy literature: the quest. However, they are not traditional quest tales, but rather serve to illustrate a statement Tolkien makes in "On Fairy-Stories": their heroes are "hardly more than wandering explorer[s] in the land, full of wonder but not of information." As their journeys progress, they fail to gain knowledge of the perilous realms they have entered, remaining always strangers and outsiders. While this same condition of strangeness and alienation can also be seen in Tolkien's longer works such as *The Lord of the Rings*, it is particularly marked in these two texts.

Here, Tolkien can be seen as starting an innovation that was to become typical of modern fantasy: the hero sets out not to discover and master a new world, but to realise that the fantastic world is and will always remain unknowable. As the quest tale is also traditionally seen as constituting self through the gaining of knowledge, the failure to do so results in a fundamental questioning of identity and can end in its utter collapse. We can see this in both poem and story, which each show a different way of how the journey into the unknown can end: Smith returns to his home and family after giving up the star, his passport to Faërie, saddened by its loss but content to know that it will pass on to a worthy successor; the speaker of "The Sea-Bell", by contrast, through his journey has become an outsider in his own world too, and the result is disorientation and madness. Both *Smith* and "The Sea-Bell" conclude (again like *The Lord of the Rings*) with the loss of the strange and wonderful fantastic world.

Thus both texts give different and to a certain extent complementary answers to the question of what happens when one reality is exchanged for another, and how one can cope with the loss of the fantastic. While these themes are also central in Tolkien's longer works, both poem and story necessarily focus on them more directly and thus they can be read as representative of his *oeuvre* as a whole in this regard.

## FANTASY AND QUEST

This paper will focus upon one of Tolkien's short stories and one of his poems: *Smith of Wootton Major* and "The Sea-Bell", and its aim will be to examine them in terms of how each of them represents a Quest: the Quest for Faërie. In this respect, the two texts can be seen as representing two sides of a coin. Smith, the hero of *Smith of Wootton Major*, travels to Faërie and can yet return home "unscathed", if not "unchanged" (cf. *FR* 329). The speaker of "The Sea-Bell" in contrast returns back to mortal realms well-nigh destroyed by his quest. One might be led to assume that the one represents a "successful" quest and the other a "failed" one. Yet I believe that in fact *both* journeys are "failed" quests in the traditional sense.

A couple of general words upon the centrality of the quest motif in the genre of fantasy. Fantasy is particularly concerned with space, and the spatial is its defining dimension. Fantasy relies on the strangeness and unfamiliarity of its worlds to entrance its reader into wonder, and the settings of fantasy novels, their landscapes, cities, and realms, form a central part of the stories told. One of the most famous definitions of the Fantastic[1] also relies on spatial terms. Tzvetan Todorov defines the Fantastic as "a frontier between two adjacent realms" (44); it is the frontier between the natural and the supernatural, the known and the unknown.

It follows then that the central form of fantasy narrative must be one that accommodates the importance of space. This narrative form is, of course, the quest: the tale of a journey across the fantastic world. According to W.H. Auden (on whose seminal article "The Quest Hero" I largely base my definition of the quest), "to go in quest means to look for something of which one has, as yet, no experience" (40). It is thus a

---

[1] Although I am aware that the terms "Fantasy" and "The Fantastic" do not necessarily denote the same thing, I am going to use them as interchangeable here as for this paper the distinction between them is irrelevant.

journey into the unknown, and most fantasy novels (and films, and games) are about such journeys. In this respect the chapter title, "A Journey in the Dark", taken from the Mines of Moria sequence of *The Fellowship of the Ring*, which forms the title of the present paper, can be seen as representative of the fantasy genre.

So what is it "of that [we have], as yet, no experience"? Of course, the quest can simply be to explore an unknown country of which we have no experience – somewhat the way Smith does on his first voyages into Faërie. However, in fantasy literature a quest is only rarely purely about exploring and charting an unknown country. According to C.S. Lewis, man enters Faërie "in search of [...] beauty [and] awe", but also of "terror" ("On Science Fiction" 90) – he (or she) goes in search of aesthetic and emotional experiences of an intensity not usually found within the Primary World. And these can be both of a good or bad nature – or even both at the same time. For Tolkien's other name for Faërie is of course the "Perilous Realm". Thus, the geographical dimension of the quest is also tied to a spiritual or psychological dimension – sometimes so much so that we interpret the spatial dimension as being purely symbolic of the psychological.[2]

Traditionally, there is an object to the quest – a magical artifact to be won (or destroyed, as in *The Lord of the Rings*), a beautiful princess to be found and married, a fearful beast to be vanquished (cf. Auden 44-45). Through the achievement of these tasks, the hero establishes himself: his (hidden) virtues are made clear and / or his hidden identity is revealed, and his position in society is secured. Then, we have our traditional ending: "and they all lived happily ever after."

This is the model for texts such as C.S. Lewis's *The Horse and His Boy*, where the fisher-boy Shasta leaves his supposed father to run away

---

[2] C.G. Jung's works are of course important here; for example in *Archetypes and the Collective Unconscious* he discusses the importance of journeys in the dark and the confrontation with one's shadow.

to Narnia, and in the course of travelling through the countries of Calormen and Archenland discovers that he is really the long lost son of King Lune of Archenland. Shasta also encounters both beauty and terror hitherto unknown to him in the person of Aslan.[3] This is also the kind of model Tolkien follows in *The Hobbit*, where Bilbo embarks on his quest, which brings out hitherto unsuspected qualities in him, and afterwards returns home again – "There and Back Again". However, we know that actually this is not the end of Bilbo's tale.

In *The Lord of the Rings* we find out that Bilbo does not remain in Hobbiton happily till the end of his days. The Ring sets to work on him, and the wide world calls him, and in the end he sets out on another journey – one that we as readers do not really see concluded. In the sequel to *The Hobbit*, Tolkien's depiction of the quest is far more ambiguous – as we know, Frodo's quest ultimately succeeds but only at great cost to himself. This then is a quest that ends ambivalently to say the least; indeed, I would not be sure whether we can call it a truly successful quest or whether in certain respects it is actually rather a *failed* quest. For the object, the destruction of the Ring, is achieved; but in the end it is not the quest hero who manages to destroy the Ring, and far from Frodo being established in society through his deeds, he is actually cut off from it through his quest and in the end decides to depart from Middle-earth altogether. There is no "happily ever after" in *The Lord of the Rings*.

In this regard Tolkien's works are typical of the twentieth-century re-imagining of the quest. When the quest motif is adopted – as it is for example prominently in works such as Joyce's *Ulysses* or Eliot's *The Waste Land* – it is ironised or depicted as fruitless. You can't be J. Alfred Prufrock, or Leopold Bloom, or indeed Frodo Baggins to achieve the

---

[3] Cf. Lewis, *Horse*: "[Shasta] turned and saw, pacing beside him, taller than the horse, a Lion. [...] It was from the Lion that the light came. No one ever saw anything more terrible or beautiful." (177).

Holy Grail. Looking at twentieth-century fantastic writing, which has produced works as varied as David Lindsay's *Voyage to Arcturus*, or the more recent *Farseer* trilogy by Robin Hobb, most fantastic quests do not have a happy ending – or even an ending at all!

## WANDERERS AND TRESPASSERS

Tolkien's short works demonstrate the same problematisation of the quest that can be found in his longer works. Indeed, perhaps of necessity they focus more directly upon this problem, as their form is more condensed. Looking at the examples of *Smith of Wootton Major* and "The Sea-Bell", we will now examine more closely in which ways these works conform to the definition of a quest, and in which ways they challenge and differ from that definition.

In both texts, there is no obvious "object" (such as the destruction of the Ring) to the journeys the protagonists make. Thus the exploration of Faërie itself, the "search for beauty and terror", is the main "object" of their voyages in the Perilous Realm. In Smith's case one could take the desire to see the Faery Queen as the object of Smith's journeys; after all, she says to him "Ever since that day [when Smith received the star] you have desired to see me, and I have granted you your wish" (28). However, the Queen can be taken as representative of the heart of the land of Faery and thus the desire to behold her is also the desire to see the Perilous Realm itself.

One traditional aim of the quest story is for the hero to explore the new realms he has entered and to a certain extent make them "his" (I am purposely using the male pronoun here: by the time we have female quest heroines in fiction, the quest as a motif has already been questioned and is no longer portrayed in a traditional way). This might occur by, for example, killing the evil wizard who rules over them and appropriating ("liberating", to use our current politically correct jargon) his realm, or marrying the beautiful princess to whom the country belongs. In "On Fairy-Stories", Tolkien problematises this, stating that we mortals are but "wandering explorer[s] (or trespasser[s])" (109) in the Perilous Realm. Faërie is *not* a place to be conquered and appropriated. Thus Smith in *Smith of Wootton Major* is called "a learner and explorer, not a warrior" (17). He does not seek to subdue Faërie and make it his own; indeed, the story makes it very clear that he would be most foolish to do so, and that his humility is one of the reasons he can visit Faërie for so long (and his failure to observe his boundaries, passing into Inner Faery, results ultimately in the star being taken from him). In "The Sea-Bell", of course, the speaker does attempt to make himself the ruler of Faërie:

> Of river leaves and the rush-sheaves
> I made me a mantle of jewel-green,
> a tall wand to hold, and a flag of gold;
> my eyes shone like the star-sheen.
> With flowers crowned I stood on a mound,
> and shrill as a call at cock-crow
> proudly I cried: "Why do you hide?
> Why do none speak, wherever I go?
> Here now I stand, king of this land,
> with gladdon-sword and reed-mace.
> Answer my call! Come forth all!
> Speak to me words! Show me a face!" (*ATB* 58-59)

The consequence is disastrous: the speaker is surrounded by a dark cloud, driven mad, loses track of time, and almost never finds back to his boat that can carry him back to mortal lands.

One of the key differences between the speaker of the poem and Smith is that Smith is a legitimate "explorer"; he received the gift of the fay-star that acts as his passport to Faërie (a bit like the white stone given to Frodo by Arwen, that acts as his token by which he may enter Valinor – or, on a grander scale, the Silmaril enables Eärendil to reach Valinor). The speaker of "The Sea-Bell" does not have such a passport;

he appears to find the mysterious "shell like a sea-bell" by chance. And even if he was meant to receive the shell, he squanders the chance he is given by attempting to crown himself king of Faërie. He is thus, according to Tolkien's definition, a "trespasser" in Faërie, one who is not there by right.

However, as mentioned above, even Smith becomes a trespasser when he passes through the encircling mountains that guard the "heart of the kingdom". His encounter with the dancing maiden (who is later revealed as the Faery Queen) makes this clear:

> She laughed as she spoke to him, saying: "You are becoming bold, Starbrow, are you not? Have you no fear what the Queen might say, if she knew of this? Unless you have her leave." He was abashed, for he became aware of his own thought and knew that she read it: that the star on his forehead was a passport to go wherever he wished; and now he knew that it was not. But she smiled as she spoke again: "Come! Now that you are here you shall dance with me"; and she took his hand and led him into the ring. (23)

Forgiven as Smith is on this occasion, we can see that the possession of such a token does not guarantee possession of or belonging in the magic world. A further episode in Smith's wanderings makes this very clear:

> [...] a breeze rose to a wild Wind, roaring like a great beast, and it swept him up and flung him on the shore, and it drove him up the slopes whirling and falling like a dead leaf. He put his arms about the stem of a young birch and clung to it, and the Wind wrestled fiercely with them, trying to tear him away; but the birch was bent down to the ground by the blast and enclosed him in its branches. When at last the Wind passed on he rose and saw that the birch was naked. It was stripped of every leaf, and it wept, and tears fell from its branches like rain. He set his hand upon its white bark, saying: "Blessed be the birch! What can I do to make

amends or give thanks?" He felt the answer of the tree pass up from his hand: "Nothing," it said. "Go away! The Wind is hunting you. You do not belong here. Go away and never return!" (20 – 21)

*"You do not belong here."* If there is one quote that I personally would take as epitomising modern fantasy (and science fiction too, for that matter), this is it. This is confirmed for example by Lucie Armitt in her study *Theorising the Fantastic*: "If fantasy is about being absent from home [...], then the inhabitant of the fantastic is always the stranger" (Armitt 8). This foreignness and sense of "not belonging" is a central feature of modern fantasy. This is also mentioned by Ursula Le Guin, who puts it as follows: "the point of Elfland is that you are not at home there. It's not Poughkeepsie. It's different" (71).

Thus neither Smith nor the speaker of the Sea-Bell can achieve belonging in the realms they explore or trespass upon. In general, we can observe that the protagonists of twentieth-century fantastic writing are not settled characters, integrated into their society or world; they are strangers, sojourners, who travel through different places only to leave them again, often enough to find that when they return to what was once their home, they can no longer or only with difficulty be part of it again. This represents a fundamental questioning of the traditional quest motif.

## KNOWLEDGE AND IDENTITY

Another particularly modern trait of fantasy is that, besides denying its protagonists a home, it denies them any real possibility of gaining knowledge through their travels. As we have seen, a fantastic journey is not a (colonial) exploration and mastering of foreign regions. Tolkien states that the traveller in Faërie is "full of wonder but not of information" (*OFS* 109). Or to bring in another example, the protagonist of

David Lindsay's *A Voyage to Arcturus* is told: "You came to carve a strange world, and now it appears you are carved yourself" (112).

The Perilous Realm must always remain beyond the understanding of the strangers passing through it. Thus Lucie Armitt notes that "the type of strangeness noted here is not one of former ignorance which can be transformed into knowledge. Here we are dealing with the always/already unknown and the unknowable, the world of alien beings who will always be 'other'" (25).

In this sense also, *Smith* and "The Sea-Bell" can be seen as representative texts. Although Smith journeys many times to Faery over many many years, he still never is able to work out the geography of the fairy country; he discovers there is an "Outer Faery" and an "Inner Faery", but little else. For example, he is unable to rediscover the "King's Tree": "He never saw that Tree again, though he often sought for it" (20). Also I feel the way the narrator states that he "believ[ed] he was in an island realm beleaguered by the Sea" (18) implies he is mistaken about this fact. The speaker in "The Sea-Bell" also loses his way and is unable to find his way back to where he came from. This lack of geographical information corresponds to a lack of understanding of the ways of Faërie. The speaker of the poem cannot gain understanding of his surroundings as he can never make contact with the inhabitants of Faërie (as he should not be there), and he also misinterprets the warnings given him (for example by the "cold wind" that stirs in his hair). Smith also cannot fully grasp the sights he sees in Faery: "he had seen things of both beauty and terror that he could not clearly remember nor report to his friends, though he knew that they dwelt deep in his heart. But some things he did not forget, and they remained in his mind as wonders and mysteries that he often recalled" (18). Even when he meets the Faery Queen he at first does not even realise who it is he is speaking to, and when he does recognise her it is only to lose her almost immediately; it is hardly "knowledge" we can speak of here.

Julia Kristeva, in *Strangers to Ourselves*, claims that strangeness and foreignness are "the hidden face of our identity" (1) – what we perceive as strange is actually that part of our identity which we hide from ourselves, projected onto others. What happens, then, when all that is perceived is strange, and there is no home to go to? If this strangeness is, as Armitt claims, "the always/already unknown and the unknowable", then we can never come to know ourselves: self-knowledge becomes an impossibility.

Traditionally, as we have heard, a quest is seen as something that constitutes self – the hero sets out to discover his true worth or his hidden identity. However, most twentieth-century fantastic works are more ambiguous in their approach to journeying into the unknown as a means of discovering identity. The Perilous Realm is forever beyond our ken, and thus voyages in it can lead to neither knowledge nor self-knowledge. Fantastic journeys destroy identity rather than constituting it, as the travellers are taken out of their society and even their world.

Thus the speaker of "The Sea-Bell" significantly exclaims at towards the end of the poem *not* "I have lost my way" but "I have lost myself" (the utterance "I know not the way" follows afterwards; *ATB* 59). He is an outsider in Faërie, and upon his return to the land of men he finds he is still an outsider. Tolkien in the poem expresses this through language: in Faërie, he hears "never a greeting", and no one replies to his significant command "Answer my call! [...] Speak to me words!". At the tragic end of the poem, even the sea-shell is "silent and dead", and all communication is turned inwards in a vicious circle as the speaker concludes: "To myself I talk; for still they speak not, men that I meet" (*ATB* 60). His quest for knowledge and for identity has failed disastrously.

Smith appears luckier. He is, after all, a legitimate wanderer in Faërie, and even has a guide in the form of Alf (of course, a significant name as it is Anglo-Saxon for Elf), who is later revealed as the King of

Faery. He has a firm foothold in the outside world, a profession and a family, which the speaker of the poem has not. Yet he does, after all, lose at least part of himself: the part of himself called "Starbrow" – part which seems more important to him than his role as a husband or head of a family. I think it is quite significant that on his final return from Faery, the smith is not welcomed by his wife and children (as he is on his return after the dance with the Faery Queen). Instead, he is welcomed only by his son (both men are conspicuously absent from a family celebration), and we have a final picture of consolation in male companionship – even if it is the special bond between father and son that is emphasised here – rather than in the bosom of a complete family. His voyages in Faery have threatened, if not destroyed, his identity in the mortal world.

## MAELSTROM REALITIES

This lack of identity and self-knowledge is the cause of particular dangers lurking in the Perilous Realm: those that are part of the traveller and that he brings with him. That this is the case is made clear for example in *The Lord of the Rings*. When the Fellowship approaches the Elven land of Lothlórien, Boromir is loath to enter, finally agreeing only "'Then lead on! [...] But it is perilous.' 'Perilous indeed,' said Aragorn, 'fair and perilous; but only evil need fear it, or those who bring some evil with them" (*FR* 329). This is repeated by Sam: "I don't know about *perilous* [...] It strikes me that folk takes their peril with them into Lórien, and finds it there because they've brought it" (*TT* 665).

While this particular point may not be so relevant to Smith, who shows only a small degree of hubris, it is most certainly the case that the speaker of "The Sea-Bell" brings peril with him to Faërie. The cause of his disaster in Faërie lies only within himself – in his pride and possessiveness. He is confronted with himself and his flaws, not with any external threats. There is perhaps a parallel in the fiery lake scene in Smith

– it is when he oversteps his boundaries that he is in the greatest danger, and we might read the wind that seeks to destroy him as an externalisation of his own faults (coincidentally – or not – the speaker in the poem is also chased by a "withering wind" *ATB* 59). However this threat is not as explicit as in the poem, where as a consequence of the peril brought with him into Faërie, the speaker loses his mind and must "sit, wandering in wit" for the traditional fairy-tale period of a year and a day. He is trapped ultimately by the conflict between his own perception of reality and the reality of the Perilous Realm.

This problem of negotiating the shifts between different realities is a central concern of modern(ist) literature as well as fantasy. In the early twentieth century, external reality seemed increasingly overwhelming and incoherent; instead of one grand master narrative of reality, we are presented with individual perceptions of it (stream-of-consciousness technique of course springs to mind); Tolkien's and Lewis's friend and fellow Inkling Owen Barfield describes "the man of today [as] overburdened with self-consciousness, insulated from Reality by his shadowy, abstract thoughts, and ever on the verge of the awful maelstrom of his own fantastic dreams" (126). I for one cannot think of a better way to describe the speaker of "The Sea-Bell" than this. (We should not forget that in some of the instances where stream-of-consciousness is employed most effectively, it is used to depict the thoughts of a madman, such as in Woolf's *Mrs Dalloway*.)

This maelstrom is perhaps one of the greatest dangers of the Perilous Realm: the traveller can lose his way back to our world, or as Tolkien puts it: "while [the traveller] is [in Faërie] it is dangerous for him to ask too many questions, lest the gates should be shut and the keys be lost" (*OFS* 109). The exchange of one reality for another can result in being trapped in madness, as the quester runs the risk of being caught forever in "his own fantastic dreams". This is exactly what happens to the speaker of "The Sea-Bell".

This ties in with another point made by Todorov. In his study *The Fantastic*, Todorov claims that in the twentieth century, it is not monsters, nor vampires, but "'normal' man [who] is precisely the fantastic being" (173). When mortal man enters the Perilous Realm, the strangest and most threatening being he can encounter on his quest will always be himself. Fantasy fiction, even "minor" works such as *Smith of Wootton Major* and "The Sea-Bell", makes it clear that man himself is fantastic; he is a foreigner, he is a stranger to himself, and carries within himself dangers that threaten to annihilate him.

## Conclusion

Thus *Smith* and "The Sea-Bell" to a certain extent give complementary answers to how the Quest for Faërie can end: on the one hand we have Smith, who is deeply saddened by the loss of his star but appears content that it has passed to a worthy successor of his choosing; on the other, we have the speaker of the poem, whose quest ends in disorientation and madness.

However, both texts evince a fundamental questioning of the traditional quest motif. Neither protagonist can gain possession of Faërie (for it is not something that can be "possessed", as much as we may desire to do so). Neither can he gain true knowledge of that realm (knowledge again representing a form of mental possession that is impossible). Their identities, far from being constituted through their travels, are threatened and in the case of the speaker of "The Sea-Bell", even destroyed completely. In this sense, like Frodo's Quest, they are "failed" quests.

Margaret Hiley holds a Ph.D. from the University of Glasgow dealing with the Inklings and their controversial relationship to literary modernism, and she has published and lectured on various aspects of fantasy and science fiction. Between 2005 and 2007 she was a Visiting Lecturer in English Literature at the University of Regensburg, Germany, and now is Lecturer in English at the Regional College in Peterborough, U.K., where she is proud to have introduced fantasy and science fiction to the English degree programme!

## Works Cited

Armitt, Lucie. *Theorising the Fantastic*. London: Arnold, 1996.

Auden, W.H. "The Quest Hero" In: Isaacs, Neil D. and Rose A. Zimbardo (eds.). *Tolkien and the Critics*. Notre Dame: U of Notre Dame P, 1968. 40 – 61.

Jung, C.G. *Archetypes and the Collective Unconscious. The Collected Works of C.G. Jung*, Vol. 9, Part 1. London: Routledge, 1966.

Le Guin, Ursula. "From Elfland to Poughkeepsie" *The Language of the Night*. London: The Women's Press, 1989. 70 – 82.

Lewis, C.S. "On Science Fiction" *Of This and Other Worlds*. Glasgow: Collins, 1982. 80 – 96.

---, *The Horse and His Boy*. London: Collins, 1998.

Lindsay, David. *A Voyage to Arcturus*. London: Gollancz, 2003.

Todorov, Tzvetan. *The Fantastic*. Transl. Richard Howard. New York: Cornell UP, 1975.

Tolkien, J.R.R. "On Fairy-Stories". *The Monsters and the Critics*. London: HarperCollins, 1997. 109 – 161.

---, *Smith of Wootton Major*. London: Allen & Unwin, 1967.

---, *The Adventures of Tom Bombadil*. London: Allen & Unwin, 1962.

---, *The Fellowship of the Ring*. London: HarperCollins, 1997.

---, *The Two Towers*. London: HarperCollins, 1997.

---, *The Return of the King*. London: HarperCollins, 1997.

# *Smith of Wootton Major* Considered as a Religious Text

MARTIN STERNBERG

ABSTRACT

*Smith of Wootton Major* and the texts belonging to it can be seen as Tolkien's last published thoughts on Faery and its relation to and function for human primary reality. This relation can be classified as religious, but is not limited to the Christian faith. Smith's experiences in Faery resemble numinous and mystical experiences, and his travels into and within Faery widely follow traditional mystical ideas and motifs. But as these religious contents of the story are not directed towards some transcendent deities, but towards material and particular things and beings, the mysticism of *Smith of Wootton Major* may also be related to a "godless mysticism" directed not towards God but the world, an idea that developed in modernity alongside traditional mystic concepts. Faery represents a world beyond human physical as well as mental domination to which man must reconnect in order to regenerate himself and his world, and in this is equitable to the holy time of creation as defined by Mircea Eliade. This religious reading implies for the relation of primary and secondary realities that they stand in a polar opposition that cannot be dissolved by interpretations. Instead, this opposition drives a human oscillation between them as distinct conditions that is necessary both for realizing the full human potential and for motivating a careful and sparing attitude to the non-human environment.

Tolkien's defence of the fantastic is derived mostly from his essay *On Fairy Stories* and the story *Leaf by Niggle* as its illustration, and as such it is ultimately based on religion. Man as subcreator follows the model of God the creator in whose image he is created, and in its happy ending, the fairy-story follows the example of the salvation history of mankind that has been brought to a good ending by the incarnation, passion and resurrection of Christ.

These ideas are obviously rooted in Tolkien's Christian faith, but founding a legitimation of fantasy on religion may follow from an inner necessity independent of specifically Christian thoughts. In many theories on religion, the object of religion is defined as lying outside the observable everyday reality. For Rudolf Otto and Mircea Eliade, it is the sacred separated from the profane (Otto 28-35; Eliade, *Das Heilige und das Profane* 14 pp). For Niklas Luhmann, the object of religion is the underdefined environment of a society seen as a system. The constitution of a system is always a process of selection and limitation in which, of a potentially infinite amount of elements, certain elements and certain aspects and qualities of these elements are linked up into a system. The remaining environment of elements that are not linked up in any way into the system may however still affect it. In Luhmann's view, religion provides chiffres that try to encompass this underdefined environment, chiffres that, in the process of being applied to it, also obscure it (Luhmann 18-20, 33-38). With these theories in mind, it is likely that a kind of literature that takes place outside observable reality has its place, object and function in this "outside" and man's relation to it, and may thus show characteristics of religion and perform some of its functions.

In contrast to *Leaf by Niggle*, *Smith of Wootton Major* has been regarded mostly as an autobiographical text. Paul Kocher sees it as Tolkien's farewell to his art (195-204), while Tom Shippey reads it as an allegory about the relation of Tolkien's profession as a philologist and his writing of fantasy, coloured with a certain remorse for his perceived neglect of the former (296-304).

But *Smith of Wootton Major* developed out of a foreword to George MacDonald's *The Golden Key* in which Tolkien tried to explain the nature of Faery. Now that Verlyn Flieger has edited that foreword and the other texts related to *Smith of Wootton Major*, especially the essay Tolkien wrote about it afterwards, it becomes apparent that this compound of texts represents in fact Tolkien's last thoughts on the nature of Faery and its relation to and functions for the human existence. The following paper shall therefore explore the question whether these thoughts can be classified as religious, and do so in three steps: the consideration of Smith's experiences in Faery as religious experiences, of his journeys into and within Faery as a religious way, and of the relation of Faery to the human world as a relation comparable to the relation between the sacred and the profane.

## RELIGIOUS EXPERIENCES IN FAERY

The classification of Smith's experiences in Faery as religious experiences is possible both by criteria drawn from Tolkien's own work and from writers on the science of religion, in this case from Rudolf Otto's *The Idea of the Holy* and the characteristics of the holy as the numinous described therein. In Otto's view, the holy has to be kept separate from conceptions of ethical or religious perfection, as it precedes them and is independent of them. He therefore calls it the numinous. The numinous is an emotional stirring that is irrational in the sense that its experience cannot be adequately related in language, it is ineffable (Otto 5-8).

Bearing this limitation in mind, the experience of the numinous can be described as the concurrence of conflicting emotions in a kind of "contrasting harmony". It is at the same time a *tremendum*, something instilling fear, dread, and awe (15-20), and simultaneously a *fascinans*, attractive and blissful (42-45). Alongside these attractive and repellent aspects, the experience of the numinous contains the *augustum*, the experience of the majesty and superiority of the numinous object or being that contrasts with the virtual and objective worthlessness of its beholder (66-69).

While *tremendum*, *fascinans* and *augustum* leave their traces in the texts of those who relate their experiences of the holy, its fourth compound leaves its traces in their lives. As an *energicum*, the numinous is powerful, dynamic and motivating (27). It may lead to radically changing the course of one's life, the rejection of the world or the undertaking of special tasks and burdens.

But this is only an approximation, for the numinous above all is *mysterium*, a mystery that can only be known by experience, not by description (30-31).

Smith's travels in Faery fit these criteria quite well: "In longer journeys he had seen things of both beauty and terror that he could not clearly remember nor report to his friends, but he knew that they dwelt deep in his heart" (*SWM* 26). Its marvels are *tremendum* and *fascinans*, and they are *mysterium* to such an extent that they not only cannot be told to others, but not even remembered by Smith himself. The superiority of value of Faery as *augustum* displays itself when Smith does not kneel before the Queen, as "for one so lowly all gestures were in vain" (37), and in the Living Flower that is untouchable by the forces of decay in the human world, for it neither fades nor grows dim (35). Finally, Faery as *energicum* affects Smith's life profoundly in his smithcraft, his attitude to manufacturing weapons and the importance travels into Faery have for him.

Of special significance is the experience of Faery as *mysterium* because Otto has repeatedly stressed that the numinous experience must not be confused with other contrasting harmonies of conflicting emotions (Otto 56-60). The emphasis Tolkien puts on the *mysterium* of Smith's experiences allows to qualify them as genuine numinous experiences of great intensity.

Another hint of a religious nature of Faery lies in the King's Tree that grows in the centre of Faery. Like the tree in *Leaf by Niggle*, it is a tree bearing a multitude of leaves, flowers and fruits, none two being the same. But it is not only its larger dimension that sets it apart from Niggle's tree, it is its root: a great hill of shadow (*SWM* 28). We are used to seeing shadow and darkness as images of evil in Tolkien's work, as the absence of light (Shippey 128-135). There is another tradition however where darkness describes the condition before creation. In ancient Egyptian thought, darkness meant the undifferentiated One "when there were no two things" from which creation in a process of differentiation sprang (cf. Hornung 170-171). A more important notion that is likely to have crossed Tolkien's path in his studies of medieval texts is (Pseudo-) Dionysius Areopagita's idea that God can be described as darkness because God is above all thinking and perceiving; God is *hidden* by the light in the world of being. His light is brighter than the human eye can perceive, he seems dark because he is brighter than bright (Pseudo-Dionysius Areopagita, *Mystische Theologie* 74-77). In this reading, the King's Tree is an image of (divine) creation, and it is bright like the sun at mid-day because in the Tree, the bright creation flows into the world out of the overbrightness of God. In consequence, this is a first hint that Faery is not a secondary reality, but in fact a primary reality rather more prime than the world of men.[1]

The religious dimension of Faery can also be inferred from a kind of experience found also in *Leaf by Niggle*. Upon entering his picture that has turned into a real country in what is some kind of hereafter, Niggle notices as the first difference to his former experience of the world that approaching something does not diminish the charm that distance laid upon it. Instead, overcoming successive distances leads to an addition of the successive enchantments conveyed by them (*TL* 89). In *On Fairy Stories*, Tolkien stated that the splendour of things is lost, that we cease to really see them once we take them into mental or physical possession (53-54). In the afterlife of *Leaf by Niggle*, things remain untarnished by the appropriation that implies approaching them.

It is exactly this quality that Tolkien in *Smith of Wootton Major* confers on the Living Flower that Smith brought with him out of Faery. Despite lying directly before the eyes, it still looks as if seen from a great distance. It is immune from the "triteness of familiarity", as Tolkien

---

[1] This image of light flowing out of darkness as its source seems to be an interesting deviation from Tolkien's more often expressed idea that creation is a process of refraction of a primordial single white light, see Flieger, *Splintered Light* esp. 46-48, 59-60. But this contradiction can be solved by regarding light as an *emanation* of God.

called it, that accompanies proximity and possession. And it is immune from the wear of the time passing in the human world, as it neither fades nor grows dim (*SWM* 35).

In his essay on the story, Tolkien describes this quality of Faery as follows:

> "Faery represents at its weakest a breaking out (at least in mind) from the iron ring of the familiar, still more from the adamantine ring of belief that it is known, possessed, controlled, and so (ultimately) all that it is worth being considered - a constant awareness of a world beyond these rings. More strongly it represents love: that is, a love and respect for all things, 'inanimate' and 'animate', an unpossessive love of them as 'other'. This love will produce both *ruth* and *delight*." (101)

This characterization of Faery as a world outside the iron rings of familiarity, possession, knowledge and control means that Faery is different from everyday reality not alone by the things in it, but mainly by man's relation to them. Faery is wonderful because it is a world that stands outside the normal human relation to the world aiming at possession, subjugation and understanding (and that includes language as a most important means to these ends), because it is *incommensurable* with them.

In religion, incommensurability with human understanding is the domain of mysticism, its basis being that God and his mysteries cannot be disclosed by rational human thought, but can only be experienced when God discloses himself in mystic vision, *visio*, and mystic union, *unio* (Langer 28, 200 pp.). And for many mystics, the precondition for the mystic experience is that all assumptions about God be abolished beforehand. As the author of the *Cloud of Unknowing* puts it, not only any thoughts of created beings, but also all conceptions about God and his qualities must be forgotten, because the latter will block the ascent to

God as well as the former (*Cloud* 33-35; ch. 9). The eye looking for God must be cleansed of all assumptions about him.

This view equals Tolkien's breaking out of human understanding and preconceptions in Faery, though its aim is not God, but particular and finite things and beings. Alongside the traditional concept of mysticism, however, there has arisen in modernity a concept of mysticism no longer defined by its object, but by a specific mode of experience incommensurable with rational thought and everyday perception (cf. Berensmeyer 142). Uwe Spörl has described examples of this kind of mysticism in German literature around 1900 for which he coined the term *neomystic*. According to him, a neomystic experience resembles structurally the *unio mystica*, the union of the mystic with God, and yet is not directed towards a god or any other transcendent entity. Instead, it consists in an exceptional understanding of and highly emotional nearness to things in the world. In the neomystic union, the separation of subject and object is overcome. It is set apart from everyday perception and cannot be adequately described in everyday or scientific language (Spörl 26). In this way, Faery as the realm of the incommensurable and incommensurably Other can well be called a (neo)mystic realm.

Tolkien's "unpossessive love" in the paragraph quoted above presents another parallel to mysticism, because the chief instrument in its approach to God is not reason, but love. According to the *Cloud of Unknowing*, God may be loved, but cannot be thought. The contemplative shall therefore incessantly beat with his love at the cloud of unknowing that is between him and God, to receive in rare cases a ray of divine light in which God reveals his mysteries (*Cloud* 24-28, ch. 5-7). This mystic love is often called pure or chaste love, as it longs for the beloved in itself, and not as a means for other ends, especially worldly ones (*Cloud* 51-52, ch. 20; cf. Langer 204).

As in mysticism, love is the basis of the "faerian condition", and it is a pure love, for loving something "as other" means loving it for itself and not as a means for furthering one's own objectives.

The pairing of ruth and delight that this love will produce is already prefigured in the concept of mystic love as well. For the mystic cannot always be in the exalted states of *visio* and *unio*, mystical ecstasy is soon followed by the bereavement of God's absence. "Mystics call such oscillations the 'Game of Love' in which God plays, as it were, 'hide and seek' with the questing soul" (Underhill 273-275). The *Cloud of Unknowing* gives a very interesting reason for this oscillation: by withdrawing himself, God ensures that the mystic does not grow proud and attributes his mystic experiences to his own abilities (which would ultimately mean that he can have God at his disposal), or that he may rejoice in future visions all the more (*Cloud* 131-132; ch. 75). The dangers of possessiveness, pride and the triteness of familiarity are thus known to the author even in man's relation to God, as is a love in ruth and delight as a remedy against them.

Although Tolkien's critique of possessiveness seems to square well with the traditional view in mysticism that the absence of material as well as mental possessiveness is essential for the mystic, an important difference must be stated. In mysticism, possessiveness is detrimental either because it attaches man to other things than God or tries to subdue God to the human will, which God answers with his withdrawal. And in Meister Eckhart's view, all ways of "having God", even in the traditionally accepted ways of *visio* and *unio*, presuppose that the beholder and the beheld are separate entities. Who "has God", even in the sense of Augustine's "deum habere", cannot reach union with him (Eckhart 1: 560-563; Sermon 52, cf. Langer 331-334)[2]. Both ways, possessiveness prevents closeness to God.

---

[2] For Meister Eckhart, the contemplative remains distinct from God as long as he sees God as the creator and himself as his creature. Only if he loses all kinds of attachment, even to God as creator, can complete union with or in God be achieved.

For Tolkien, in contrast, both *Leaf by Niggle* and *Smith of Wootton Major* stress as the precondition of the faerian version of the mystic vision not closeness, but distance, a distance that normally is destroyed in the approach of appropriation. This stress on distance instead of closeness forms an interesting parallel with Rainer Maria Rilke's *Ein Erlebnis*. Here things seem at the same time more distant and more true, and there is even an echo of Tolkien's love in ruth and delight when Rilke says his enjoyment of the being of these things, separated from him, gathers a sweet taste as if everything were seasoned with the bloom of goodbye (668).

The paradigm for this kind of vision is therefore seeing something for the first time, when no familiarity and no preconceptions stand between the beholder and the beheld. Frodo's neo-mystical experience of the world on Cerin Amroth is described as beholding shapes and colours as if for the first time (cf. Hopp 143-144). Such a first encounter is also a moment of creation: not of the outside world by a deity, but of its image in the human mind.

Beside mystic vision, mysticism strives for mystic union, the *unio mystica* between the mystic and God. This union must not, upon theological reflection, be thought of as a complete fusion of man and God in nature and person, but as sharing something with God, most notably the will (Langer 207).

In this way, Smith's encounters with the Queen of Faery can be regarded as successive mystic unions of increasing intensity, a development however that at its climax in Faery deviates from traditional notions of mystic union. But it is exactly this deviation that ensures consistency with the "worldly mysticism" of *Smith of Wootton Major*.

The first of these unions is Smith meeting the Queen, unrecognized by him, in the Vale of Evermorn. Dancing with her, he experiences what it is "to have the swiftness and power and the joy to accompany her" (*SWM* 33). This expression suggests that he lacks these capabilities under normal conditions, and attains them only by joining hands with the Queen while dancing. And as is the nature of experiences of mystic union, it passes all too quickly for Smith: a first but fleeting touch. Interestingly, the ring dance is not only associated with fairies, but occurs frequently in mystical literature as an image of closeness, ranging from dancing with the saints or virtues to dancing with Christ who leads the ring or performs as minstrel (cf. Banz 99-100, Riehle 77-79). It can even be regarded as a traditional image for the condition of the soul in mystic union (Lüers 267-268). For Mechthild von Magdeburg, Christ leads the soul in a dance of engagement that is preceding full mystic union (Mechthild 60-61; book I, ch. 44), an idea that fits the place of the unifying dance in *Smith of Wootton Major* quite well.

Smith's second meeting with the Queen on the high place under the stars is on an altogether higher level both in duration and quality. Now he recognizes the Queen, and they do not join their hands, but their thoughts and minds (*SWM* 37). Thus a union takes place by sharing the knowledge and wisdom of the Queen.

The next and final step on the mystic way would be a kind of union that consists in complete passivity, a death-like resting in God that is the apex of the traditional mystic way (Bonaventura 106-111; ch. 7, Riehle 190-194). But this kind of union does not take place – with the Queen. She can, as she says herself, give him no more. Instead, Smith's travels in Faery culminate in him resting in the cosmos: "Then he knelt, and she stooped and laid her hand on his head, and a great stillness came upon him; and he seemed to be both in Faery, and the World, and also outside them and surveying them, so that he was at once in bereavement, and in ownership, and in peace" (*SWM* 38). It is a union that comprises the whole world and all modes of existence Smith may have therein.[3]

## THE WAY INTO FAERY AS A RELIGIOUS WAY

As has been demonstrated, the experience of Faery can be classified as a kind of religious experience, and Faery is thus a religious, or holy and sacred, space. But how can man access it? Faery is, as Tolkien stresses repeatedly, a material world like ours, but with a different spatial and temporal mode of existence. There are entrances into Faery in the Wood west of Wootton Major, and they can be passed also by ordinary humans, not only bearers of the star (86-87). The King of Faery created the star only to protect humans from the dangers of Faery so that they could travel deeper into it (95).

Neither does the Star confer the leave to walk at will in Faery. This is made explicit when the Queen remarks to Smith on his entering the Vale of Evermorn that he is becoming bold to go there without the Queen's leave, and when the birch tells him to go away because he does not belong to Faery (30-31). In consequence, Smith has to be guided on his journeys to the greater marvels of Faery, often on ways hidden by mist and shadow (28, 36). The vision of Faery is thus not at the disposal of man, he can see Faery only so far as it chooses to reveal itself. Even the casket Smith makes for the Living Flower echoes this, as the time of its closing cannot be influenced by the beholder.

Thus the vision of Faery is grace, and this idea is another connection to mysticism. The mystic cannot force *visio* and *unio* to happen by any action of his own, for this would mean to force God, which is naturally impossible. *Visio* and *unio* are always acts of grace by God for

---

[3] This deviation is all the more significant as God touching the soul is a common image for mystic union or more generally God's direct action on the mystic, cf. Riehle 160-162.

which the mystic can prepare the ground in himself, but nothing more (Langer 281, 328-331).

To these preparations belongs entering into oneself in contemplation, because the soul of man, being created in the image of God, can provide an image of God. The three capacities of memory, reason and will are a reflection of the Holy Trinity, and realizing this aids the further progress to God (Bonaventura 51-63; ch. 3).

In *Smith of Wootton Major*, the human mind seems likewise to contain an image of the ultimate aim of its neo-mystical progress, and it is the memory of Faery that occupies this place. The birdsong on the morning of his birthday reminds Smith of Faery (*SWM* 19-20), and that this memory is not a gift of the star is shown later on when his son remarks on the scent of the silver bells Smith brought with him on his last errand in Faery: "A scent that reminds me of, reminds me, well, of something I have forgotten" (50).

There is a memory of Faery in everyone that is waiting to be woken (Kocher 198), even by an undignified representation of it like the puppet of a dancing Fairy Queen, "for some the only glimpse. For some the awaking" (*SWM* 38). This innate memory that is meant to guide man on into Faery provides thus another link with mysticism and the mystic way.

This mystic perspective allows us to address Christopher Williams's criticism of Tolkien's story as an elitist one where access to Faery as access to imagination is a gift bestowed upon the fortunate few and not the "right and possible prerogative of every child" (see Flieger, *A Question of Time*, 233-234). But if access into Faery is grace, it cannot be anyone's right and prerogative. The only right man has to Faery is the memory of it, and that indeed lies hidden in everyone. Whether it is allowed to wake depends on each person, as the negative example of Nokes shows. William's comments can still bear out as a critique of religion as such, a critique however that in this context depends on an anthropocentric world-view where man is entitled to everything, a view which Tolkien explicitly rejects, as we shall see in the next section.

The idea of access into Faery as dependent on grace may also explain the fact that there is a strong stress on heredity in the story, as Tom Shippey has pointed out, but that this heredity of star and the office of Master Cook passes Smith and his family by, a fact that according to Shippey makes Smith's life end in multiple disappointment (Shippey 300-301). Yet disappointment can arise only where appointment has been presumed, and if access into Faery is grace, such a possessive presumption is wrong, however human such desires may be. One may rather argue that the idea of heredity actually needs to be stressed in the story precisely so it can be refuted.

## THE RELIGIOUS RELATION

If Faery is a space for numinous experiences and a neomystical vision of things different from everyday perceptions, the question arises where the border to that everyday reality lies, and how it is drawn. Moreover, if Faery can be equated to a holy and sacred space that is separated from the profane world of man, how are these two entities related to one another? For religion presupposes the difference between the sacred and the profane, but exists to overcome that separation, to link up the profane world to the sacred for the benefit of the former. According to Mircea Eliade, the sacred releases and creates the profane reality, its forms, structures and orientations and is the source of its life-force (Eliade, *Das Heilige und das Profane* 15 pp.). Religious practice must therefore reconnect the profane with the sacred. Likewise for William James, whose theory of religion is founded entirely on religious experience, the core of religion is the connection to a superior "source of life" (James 382).

As for the border with Faery, Tolkien makes it quite explicit that this border does not run between the visible and invisible, reality and unreality or physical reality and imagination. Faery begins where human domination, by whichever means, ends. Tolkien locates the entrances into Faery in the Wood west of Wootton Major, because for him the wood is a region still untouched by human activity. To proceed further from these points into Faery means to go further and further away from the "familiar and anthropocentric world" and to recognize that Faery is limitless and "mainly involved in vast regions and events that do not concern men and are impenetrable by them" (*SWM* 86-87). This defining characteristic of Faery is borne out by the way of experiencing it: It cannot be looked on at will, but has to reveal itself, it cannot adequately be spoken of, for it cannot be subdued by human language, and not even be clearly remembered, for it is too vast and too different for the human mind to grasp. In Hoffmansthal's *Ein Brief*, the mystic vision of things brings with it the inability to speak and think about them coherently (Hoffmansthal 55-59), and justly so. While speaking or thinking of the "incommensurable other", this "other" is not present and cannot help man by revealing itself.

In consequence, the borderline between Faery and the world of men is also a borderline between human activity and passivity: Faery as the place of Smith's passively received visions and the human world as the place of his own creativity. For Tolkien the contact with Faery is nonetheless essential for the human wellbeing:

> "This 'love' [of Faery] will produce both *ruth* and *delight*. Things seen in its light will be respected, and they will also appear delightful, beautiful, wonderful even glorious. Faery might be said indeed to represent Imagination (without definition because taking in all definitions of this word): esthetic: exploratory and receptive; and artistic; inventive, dynamic, (sub)creative. This compound – of awareness of a limitless world outside our domestic parish; a love (in ruth and admiration) for the things in it; and a desire for wonder, marvels, both perceived and conceived – this "Faery" is

as necessary for the health and functioning of the Human as is sunlight for physical life: sunlight as distinguished from the soil, say, though it in fact permeates and modifies even that." (*SWM* 100).

The effects this experience of the otherness of things and their love in ruth and delight has on the human behaviour towards the world can be easily demonstrated on man's passively receptive relation to them: If things are not loved for their usefulness for human aims or their conformity with certain human concepts, but for their otherness, they are loved for themselves. Their value lies already in their existence, and the prospect of the ending of that existence will provoke ruth, mental pain in Tolkien's own interpretation of that word in his *Middle English Dictionary*. This mental pain can induce human counteraction to avoid the destruction of the beloved, and in many cases, this action may be a decision not to act that leaves things as they are. Patrick Curry has pressed this point very strongly in *Defending Middle Earth*: "The things, places and people we love will either be saved for their own sake, or not at all, and that is ultimately a religious valuing" (Curry 119).

The influence of Faery on human creativity is more complex. Tolkien describes Wootton Major as a village not of farmers, but of craftsmen whose products are famed for their quality, a quality that stems from the formerly intensive contacts with Faery. But commercial success led to smugness and coarseness. The villagers forget about their indebtedness to Faery. They banish song, dance and storytelling, arts related to Faery, from their festivities in the Great Hall, and the practitioners of such economically unprofitable arts abandon their professions. The Great Hall itself is kept structurally sound, but its ornaments and paintings are neglected. This development leads to a lessening in the artistic quality of their products and their skill, so that the economic decline of Wootton Major is imminent.

In this situation, the King of Faery devises the "missionary plan" to save Wootton Major by granting to some humans the opportunity of exploring Faery more deeply than ever before, and he creates the star as a safeguard against its dangers (95).

Tolkien considers three possible reasons for the King's interest in the fate of the village. Because Faery exists independently from the human world, this interest must be founded not on necessity, but on love. Thus the humans themselves become the object of the love of Faery. Secondly, this interest could be rooted in an ultimate kinship of elves and men. Thirdly, although Faery exists independently from the human world and men cannot aid the elves in their affairs, the destruction of the human world would affect Faery detrimentally, so that the elves have an enlightened self-interest that mankind treats its part of the world well (*SWM* 93-94).

The King of Faery is thus part of two religious traditions: The survival of the world is the shared responsibility of elves and men as it is in cosmotheistic religions, where the preservation of the cosmos is the central aim of religion, an aim in which the gods need to be assisted by human religious practice like prayers and rituals (cf. Assmann 232-235). In *Smith of Wootton Major*, the elves take on the functions of gods, and the supporting actions of men do not consist in religious practices, but in a kind and sparing behaviour towards their world and in their sub-creational productivity. By kindling the love of Faery in men again, the elves rekindle in them a relation to the world in ruth and delight. The second tradition is the Christian one. The motivation of the elves and the King by love reminds of the Christian idea that the creation and God's incarnation in it are acts of God's love (Pseudo-Dionysius Areopagita, *Die Namen Gottes* 49-50; ch.4 § 10, Beinert 1: 423-428).

But how can the experience of Faery help to achieve these aims? The first possibility is that, as man in Faery is cleansed from his possessive and dominating attitude to the world, he is also freed from a view of things that reduces them to certain and especially static human concepts and to definite uses which, by being definite, by necessity always omit certain aspects and possibilities, leading ultimately to a petrifying of human life and culture. The dissolution of static definitions in Faery thus allows the perceiving of something new and the possibility of creating something new. This idea squares well with Tolkien's frequent critique on attitudes of static preservation, e. g. of the elves of the third age, who began nothing new (*RK* 456, appendix B), or in Faramir's description of Gondor's decline (*TT* 352). It also corresponds well with Robert Musil's thoughts on what he called the "other condition": Whereas in everyday perception an object is perceived only in certain aspects and therefore only a limited amount of its possibilities, in the other condition, the human mind encompasses it as a whole, all its possibilities light up, providing starting points for creating something new (Reinhard 50-52). To put it in Niklas Luhmann's terms, the *other condition* would mean stepping outside the system and its limitations and be thus truly ecstasy, ek-stasis, a standing outside of the world as it is known. From a religious perspective, this is reminiscent of the mystical idea that God is continuous creation, so that overcoming human mental possessiveness allows man to be part of that stream of creativity again.

And indeed, the first draft of *Smith of Wootton Major* showed signs of such a stress on the new: Smith's grandfather Rider originally brought new recipes with him out of Faery that were not well received by everyone because of their newness (*SWM* 105), and the effect of losing the star on Smith originally was that he could still enter Faery, but not see something new (121).

Yet Tolkien abandoned these passages in the final version of the story, and with good cause. To start with, this fixation on the new does not address the problems of Wootton Major as a whole. Tolkien speaks here not only of petrification, but decline: Not only the artistic quality of the products is lessening, which could be attributed to a lack of innovation, but also the traditional manual skill. There is not only a dearth of new designs, but also old ones are no longer carefully executed. There is a lack also of attention and devotion to the known. In fact the sole stress on discovering and creating something new would not overcome possessiveness, but deepen it: The known would not longer be looked on and cared for simply because it is known, and the unceasing hunt for the new would just serve to augment the hoard of human possession of the world with aspects and possibilities formerly free from it; would be a love solely of the new delights in acquiring mental possessions and in exerting the power of one's creativity. It degrades the other to mere material for human ends, whereas delight in the otherness of things rejoices in the other as an end in itself. And there is no ruth in this love of the new for that which is already there, and so no power for *preserving* things for their own sake. The stress on the new and the creative is not only romantic. It lies also at the core of Joseph Schumpeter's famous dictum on the "creative destructivity of capitalism". It has serious side effects, and therefore, it should be handled with care.

In contrast, recovery in its full sense allows for seeing the other in all its aspects both known and new. Tolkien said in *On Fairy Stories* that especially the things untouched by fantasy regain their splendour in secondary realities, "made luminous by their setting" (*TL* 55). This can happen because the fantastic elements of Faery signal to the traveller in Faery or, for that matter, the reader, that he has left the realm of human domination. This may lead to surrendering a dominant and possessive attitude to the world, so that even simple and familiar things are freed from the triteness of familiarity and can become objects of wonder and a love in ruth and delight. The recovery of sight leads to recovered human activity that can result in both new creation and the careful execution of already known designs, which may be attributed to remembering the experiences of Faery: the image of the tree as seen in Faery feeds further human creativity involving the tree.

From a mystical perspective, another explanation also exists for the regenerative effect apart from Faery generating specific images and notions. Both the author of the *Cloud of Unknowing* and Meister Eckhart say that the suppression of any thoughts on created beings or of attributes of the creator will be difficult at first, but become easier with increasing practice until it has become a *habitus*, a habit that no longer needs any straining of the will (*Cloud* 62; ch. 26, Eckhart 2: 350-353; tract. 2 no. 6).

Transferring this idea to the possible effects of Faery, this means that the traveller in that realm will return not only with memories of distinct perceptions, regenerated images, but also a regenerated mode of perceiving, a regenerated imagination. His way of perceiving the world will have acquired a different habitus that allows him, in Tolkien's words, to see things of the human or primary world in the light of Faery. Not just distinct ideas and notions in his consciousness, but his consciousness as a whole is thereby transformed.

All these effects of Faery can be amply demonstrated by Smith. Most of the things he makes belong to everyday life, tools, pans and firehooks, "they were strong and lasting, but they also had a grace about them, being shapely in their kinds, good to handle and to look at" (*SWM* 21). This excellence is not due to having visited an ironmonger's shop in Faery, but the ability acquired there to see things outside fixed concepts and to pierce the veil of familiarity. He is therefore able to attend to them beyond the measure required by their use and market expectations. That ultimately is a kind of grace, and it is therefore that these things have quite literally, in the double meaning of that word, a grace about them.

Moreover, the connection with Faery has conferred on Smith the ability to shape iron, the metal of utility and power, into delicate forms that yet retain the strength of iron. Such things he makes "for delight", and he is singing when forging them (21); song always being a sign of a connection to Faery or a "faerian mood". Now these are things hitherto unknown in Wootton Major. Here, the contact with Faery leads to the creation of something new.

But why, if the contact with Faery is so beneficial, does Tolkien call Faery the "Perilous Realm"? He is entitled to do so not only by the beings and powers in Faery that are actively hostile to humans, but precisely because of the effects described so far. For man can only exist by limitation, by linking up selective aspects of the elements in his environments into a system of preconceptions that allow him to act. If these preconceptions are loosened too much or permanently dissolved, if the traveller in Faery cannot recreate them on his return into human reality in order to reconnect to it, an inability to live, a kind of madness must ensue. In this, Faery displays in concordance with its numinous nature what Eliade called the "ambivalence of the sacred", for in many languages, the word for "sacred" means also "cursed" or "impure" (Eliade, *Die Religionen und das Heilige* 38-39).

Returning to the positive effects of Faery, they become finally apparent in Smith's giving up the star and the choosing of its next bearer. And it is in this act that he reaches what did not happen in Faery: a mystic union with the Queen and the King. A notion widely held about the mystic union is that it consists in the mystic exchange of the individual's own will (*voluntas propria*) for the will of God. This does not mean a submission to the will of God in the sense of "listen and comply", but a sharing of the will of God and is therefore called *voluntas communis* (Langer 200-201, 207, 336-341).

Such a shared will starts to unfold when the Queen sends Smith to the King with the message "The time has come. Let him choose" (*SWM* 40). As far as her share in the choice of the next bearer goes, she cedes it to Smith. And although Smith chooses the child already selected by the King, the King would have accepted a different choice by Smith. Here indeed we find a common will, *voluntas communis*, of Queen,

King and Smith, without any kind of subordination on any part. And again, the love of Faery informs this choice, for it is neither based on Nokes of Townsend's Tim's kinship with Smith, nor hindered by his kinship with Nokes: "Nokes of Townsend's Tim is quite different. [...] But apart from the kinship I love little Tim. Though he is not an obvious choice" (48). Smith's choice is motivated neither by kinship nor obvious qualities, but by love and the qualities its more careful look will discover.

In Tolkien's words, Faery represents a specific kind of love, and it represents imagination. But what is the connection between love and imagination? As this is not the place to reflect on the implications of different theories on love, especially the creative aspect of love, may have on imagination, an answer shall be provided by following Tolkien's essay quite closely.

When Tolkien says the love of Faery will produce both ruth and delight, he is differentiating between love as an action of the will and the emotions flowing from it. This complies with the traditional idea that love is not simply a feeling, but a special kind of directing the will at an object so that love and the will may even be equated (Augustinus 122-123, 216-217). And there are two kinds of love or two faces of it: the love that wants to have the beloved and the love that wants to give to the beloved, often called in theology by the names of *eros* and *agape* (Nygren 135-148).

The love of Faery means that man craves the other for its own sake ("love of things as other"). Because this love, as *amor purus*, has its reward in the beloved itself, it can liberate the beloved from human preconceptions and subjugation under certain uses. For the receptive imagination, it provides thus fresh and more complete images of things already existing. But this love of the other is not limited to perceiving, cherishing and preserving the other already present, but can exert itself also by creating a new, previously non-existent other. Love is thus the engine, the hot kernel in imagination that drives the transformation of the perceived into the produced.

But images fade. Human activity is forced to analyse things, to subject them to reason, to certain uses, to reduce them to certain aspects in order to be able to handle them creatively, which leads ultimately to repossessing them. The veil of familiarity descends on the eye again, the habitus of Faery is lost. Then it becomes necessary to return into Faery or, in religious terminology, to return into the primeval condition of the first beginning and to regenerate oneself in it.

For this reason, an oscillation, a commuting between Faery and the human world is necessary, and in consequence, *Smith of Wootton Major* is structured by cycles centred on man's relation to Faery: the Feast of Good Children every twenty-four years, Smith's commuting between Faery and the world and finally the necessity of passing on the star to a new bearer, to allow the intensive contact with Faery to continue. Faery is a functional equivalent of the mythical time of creation that in many religions must be cyclically re-entered by means of ritual to regenerate a world worn out by the passing of time (Eliade, *Das Heilige und das Profane* 70-75)[4]. This is also true when the interpretative step is taken from Faery as a world to Faery as a story. As has been pointed out above, the specific vision of things in Faery corresponds to seeing some-

---

[4] Eliade's concept of sacred time may also help to solve the apparent inconsistency of Tolkien's treatment of "Faery time". Tolkien says that the rulers of Faery may arrange the re-entry of travellers in Faery into the human world in such a way that their existence in the human world is not negatively affected. A week of absence in the human world can be equivalent of a stay in Faery maybe even of years (*SWM* 85-85). This is difficult to accept rationally (Flieger *Question of Time* 252). But if Faery time is seen as an eternal now, re-entry into human time could happen at any given point of time. And if Faery time is seen not as another time in a fixed relation to human world time, like two clocks ticking at different speeds, but as Other Time, a return into Human Time could happen at any given point where Human and Faery time are contagious, in the same way as a traveller into Faery may leave by another entry than the one by which he entered. In any case, the parallel of Faery time both with reading time (SWM 85) and sacred time is fitting: A reading time of an hour may span actions that need years in the secondary world of the story, and a ritual performed in an hour may re-actualize a myth that, could it be measured in profane time, would take much longer.

thing for the first time. Entering Faery as a story means for the reader not a re-actualization of the mythical creation of the world, but of the time when he created his first image of it.

But before *Smith of Wootton Major* can be classified as a defence and definition of Fantasy by means of religion, a qualification must be made, an obstacle overcome and a vacancy filled. The qualification is that classifying the experience and function of Faery as religious does not mean that Faery can take over *all* functions of religion, especially the Christian one. In contrast to *Leaf by Niggle*, for example, *Smith of Wootton Major* does not deal with the question of death. There are also hints at a transcendence beyond both the world and Faery in the way Smith is touched by the beauty of Even-star and moon after giving up the star, or in Tolkien's remark: "Also another point is that visions of imagination are not enough; they are only pictures and intimations. When wisdom comes the mind though enriched by imagination, having learned or seen truths only perceptible in this way, must prepare to leave the world of man and of Faery" (*SWM* 81).

On the other hand, the amount in which religious experiences flow from experiencing the material world that Faery is and the amount in which Faery and its Queen become objects of mysticism cannot be ignored. The possible conflicts become apparent when comparing this religious reading of *Smith of Wootton Major* with the one proposed by Jane Chance. She sees the story as an exposition of abstract Christian ideas and ideals and e. g. quotes approvingly the statement of the *Ancrene Wisse* that the love of worldly things taints the eye in such a way that it cannot recognize or rejoice in God (Chance 99-110). But as we have seen, the story as well as Tolkien's essay are chiefly concerned with the human ability to love and rejoice in earthly things and its restoration[5]. If e. g. Smith's travels into Faery can be compared to the Chris-

---

[5]     It should be noted that the *Ancrene Wisse* belongs to that strain of mysticism that is highly critical of anything visual and regards visions as errors or sent by the devil (42).

tian's quest for the Heavenly Jerusalem and the King's coming to Wootton Major to the Incarnation of Christ, the question arises how such an extensive occupation of Christian imagery in the service of Faery can be justified. Whether this exalted role of Faery can be fitted into traditional Christian religion must be left to a separate study, however.[6]

The obstacle to overcome is the opinion on the religious nature of Faery held by Tolkien himself. For him, Faery is not religious. Instead, the Great Hall is an allegory of the village church, the Master Cook an allegory of the parson, domestic cooking of private prayer and the cooking at feasts an allegory of religious festivals and divine service (*SWM* 99-100).

But this opinion of the lack of religious import of Faery is based on Tolkiens narrow view on religion, defined by him as the propitiating, thanking or supplicating of higher powers by certain ceremonies (100). Judged from outside Tolkien's work, this view of religion is much too narrow since it neither takes account of religious experience nor the relation of the sacred and the profane. And judged from within Tolkien's story, it is inconsistent. For if the Great Hall is the village church and the master Cook the parson, what does it mean when the King of Faery becomes the parson and reintroduces elements connected to Faery like song, dance and storytelling into the church and its service? Whom, in this allegory, does the King of Faery represent? If Faery indeed is not religious, *Smith of Wootton Major* would be a story of how the world takes charge of or infiltrates religion, or, in the terms of a differentiation from *On Fairy Stories*, the magical infiltrates the mystical (*TL* 28).

A way to bridge this gap could be that the Great Hall is not any church, but a reformed church. Verlyn Flieger has pointed out that especially Puritan reformation meant discouraging decoration in churches,

---

[6] Because Faery and God are a different kinds of good, Hopp (150-152) doubts such a compatibility on the basis of Augustinian theology.

a sobering of religious service and a clampdown on secular celebrations like music and dance as well (*SWM* 147). And given Tolkien's high regard for the sacrament of communion (*L* 338-339), his description of the festivities in the "reformed" Great Hall as "public assemblies for talk assisted by eating and drinking" is an irreverent but apt description of worship in Protestantism which rejects the idea of transsubstantiation in the Eucharist. With this in mind, the King of Faery's taking the office of parson becomes a kind of faerian counter-reformation in which the love of images, the emotionality and a certain world-friendliness of Catholicism infiltrate Protestantism and re-form it into an older form of faith.

But bridges can be crossed both ways. Among the things Protestantism developed against was what it regarded as an inappropriate worldliness of the church, not only the often too worldly behaviour of the clergy, but also what it regarded as the worshipping of images and justification by works. Reformation for the reformers meant a re-formation to the original form of the Christian faith. For Protestant Christians, Tolkien's counter-reformation by the King of Faery could be further proof that what distinguishes Catholicism from Protestantism and is presented as attractive in this story is in fact worldly, non-Christian, even heathen. *Smith of Wootton* Major is therefore a necessary reminder of the fact that classifying something as Catholic does not mean that it is necessarily undisputedly Christian, especially if it is not specifically Christian and thus accessible to other religious convictions as well.

Nevertheless, Tolkien's remarks on the place of religion in Wootton Major point to the vacancy still to fill: So far, we have encountered religious experiences and their objects, religious structures and functions, but no equivalent to religious institutions and practices that in real-world religions intermediate between the sacred and the profane or, in the terms of the story, between Faery and the world of men. This was not necessary because Smith had direct access to Faery and an unmediated experience of it. What about the ones that had not? It may even be said that the first stage of the King's plan failed because Smith's experiences in Faery made him an excellent example of the beneficial effects of Faery, but not an example for others to follow. There was no way of sharing his experiences with them even if, given the general mood of the village, they had wanted to. Smith is an artisan, not an artist, he creates things that enter other people's lives and enrich them, but he is no sub-creator in the strict sense of one who creates secondary realities into which others can enter. In the same way that Faery is a real world of its own and no secondary world or sub-creation, the imagination that takes place in Faery is, as far as Smith is concerned, of the receptive kind.

For most of the story, Smith seems not to represent the writer, but the reader. This changes only at the very end after Smith has given up the star and comes back home to his son who looks forward to his father teaching him many things beside the working of iron (51-52). Tolkien elaborates on this that unlike his mother and sister, Smith's son Ned neither has contact with elves nor is he an occasional traveller in outer Faery and is thus "one precisely of the practical and plain normal men and workers whose enlightenment and vivification was one of the objects of the King's plan" who could receive Faery only by the lore and companionship of his father (99). For his son, Smith will have to sub-create Faery in tales. He will also have to sub-create Faery in his memory for himself, because he no longer has access to it as a primary reality. But even here, Smith's truly sub-creational activity remains in the confines of his family.

Being a subcreator is not the job of a smith in Wootton Major, after all. In the village, the surnames of people describe their hereditary professions. Giving glimpses of Faery was the job of the Sedgers (tale-tellers), Sangsters (singers) and musicians with names like Piper and Harper, many of whom had given up their craft and become hired men of the commercially more profitable professions, which also grew in power in the village council (92-93). So there were no suitable and suitably respected "multiplicators" for the cause of Faery in the village, and it became necessary for the King to come in person and work from the generally respected position of Master Cook for a change in attitudes. This the King seems mostly to do with children. Smith notices at Alf's last Twenty-four Feast that the children invited are more beautiful and lively than in his boyhood, and attributes this to Alf's activities in his spare time (60). We may assume that the glimpses of Faery Alf provided were by means of telling stories, providing secondary realities into which the children could enter. The Great Hall, with its paintings and carvings restored, and the festivities with storytelling, song and dance taking place therein are the necessary intermediate institutions between Faery and the human world, and insofar, Tolkien's allegorical identification with church, parson and religious festivals is fitting.

The existence of such institutions has a further consequence: In *Smith of Wootton Major*, Faery is present both as primary (as experienced by Smith) and secondary reality (in the tales told about it). When it comes to applying the story to our world, the interpretative effort is thus very slim because our situation where Faery is only accessible as a secondary reality is already contained in the story. Furthermore, Tolkien said that a secondary reality is experienced similarly to a primary reality, author and reader enter it to the satisfaction of their senses, with the Author as guide (*TL* 49, cf. *SWM* 74). In the moment of experiencing it, there is no difference between Faery as a primary or a secondary reality. It is only afterwards that our experiences will be coloured (or tarnished) by the knowledge that this Faery was only a story. But again, this is not different from the reality of religions. What for the believer is the re-enactment of an occurrence of the mythical past as a re-actualisation that has an effect in this world is for the ethnographically minded onlooker a "theatrical performance" that has a meaning. Indeed, differing ideas about the Eucharist are just such a case.

To sum it up, the relation between Faery, and thus the secondary reality of fantasy, and the world or primary reality, is an oscillating relation between the sacred and the profane, passivity and activity, regeneration and consumption. It has a religious structure, and the contact with Faery performs similar functions attributed in cosmotheistic religions to contacts with the divine sphere. The states of being in Faery and being in the human world cannot be fused into a third condition that encompasses them both and unites their capabilities *at the same point in time.* And although a story of Faery can be interpreted in the same way as any story of the human world, the *specific* effects of being in Faery cannot be grasped by any interpretation, because an interpretation is made up of (rational) language, in which, as Smith demonstrates, the (neo-)mystical experience of Faery cannot be adequately related. The tension between Faery and the world is not to be dissolved in thought, but released into action, not in interpretations, but in the works of those who perform this oscillation by living it. It is only in works that Faery and the human world can coexist: in their effects.

This oscillation pervades even the texts surrounding the story. Tolkien sets out from writing a foreword *about* Faery, then, finding this approach insufficient, he devises a story to lead the reader *into* Faery, and swings back to a planning approach *outside* the story, devising possible endings to express specific meanings. Then it is back *into* Faery again with the finished story. In the essay about *Smith of Wootton Mayor*, the frequency of this oscillation increases, Tolkien giving in turns additional details of the story as "feigned history" and his interpretations, until he arrives at the definition of Faery he set out for – on the last page of the essay –, a definition given in dualities: Our domestic parish and the world outside it, ruth and delight, imagination receptive and creative, sunlight and soil.

Meister Eckhart once said that a mystic should forsake the greatest ecstasy if necessary to prepare a soup for a sick person (Eckhart 2: 363;

tract. 2 no. 10). With Tolkien, who had a certain fondness for similes involving cooking himself, one may answer regarding the religious functions of Faery that a traveller in that realm should enjoy his ecstasy thoroughly to the end – in order to be able to prepare a nourishing soup afterwards.

MARTIN G. E. STERNBERG studied ancient and medieval history, history of art, philosophy and law at the University of Münster / Germany. He works as a lawyer in the telecommunications industry.

## Works Cited

*Ancrene Wisse.* Ed. Hasenfratz, Robert. FEAMS Middle English Text Series. Kalamazoo, Michigan. Medieval Institute Publications 2000.

Assmann, Jan. *Ägypten. Eine Sinngeschichte.* Frankfurt am Main: Fischer Taschenbuchverlag 1999.

Augustinus. *De trinitate.* Kreuzer, Johann ed. a. transl. Darmstadt: Wissenschaftliche Buchgesellschaft 2001.

Banz, Romuald. *Christus und die minnende Seele.* Breslau: Verlag von M. & H. Marcus 1908.

Beinert, Wolfgang (Ed). *Glaubenszugänge. Lehrbuch zur Katholischen Dogmatik.* Paderborn, Wien, München, Zürich: Ferdinand Schöningh 1995.

Berensmeyer, Ingo. „Aufbrüche nach Anderswo. Zum Verhältnis von Rationalität und Mystik in der Literatur der Moderne". *Jenseits der entzauberten Welt.* Ed. Vondung, Klaus and Pfeiffer, K. Ludwig. München: Wilhelm Fink Verlag 2006

Bonaventura. *Itinerarium mentis in Deum – Der Pilgerweg des Menschen zu Gott.* Ed. a. transl. Schlosser, Marianne. Münster: LIT Verlag 2004.

Chance, Jane. *Tolkien's Art. A Mythology for England.* Rev. Ed. Lexington: University Press of Kentucky 2001.

*The Cloud of Unknowing and the Book of Privy Counselling.* Ed. Hodgson, Phyllis. London: Oxford University Press 1944.

Curry, Patrick. *Defending Middle Earth.* London: Harper Collins Publishers 1998.

Eckhart von Hochheim (Meister Eckhart). *Werke.* Text and Translation. Ed. Largier, Niklaus. Frankfurt am Main. Deutscher Klassiker Verlag 1993.

Eliade, Mircea. *Das Heilige und das Profane.* Frankfurt am Main: Insel 1998.

---, *Die Religionen und das Heilige.* Frankfurt am Main: Insel 1986.

Flieger, Verlyn. *A Question of Time.* Kent and London: The Kent State University Press 1997.

---, *Splintered Light. Logos and Language in Tolkien's World.* Rev. Ed. Kent and London: The Kent State University Press 2002.

Hoffmannsthal, Hugo von. *Der Brief des Lord Chandos.* Stuttgart: Reclam 2004

Hopp, Martin. "Das Heilige und das Andere. Weltbild und Weltbindung in Tolkiens Herr der Ringe." *Hither Shore* 2 (2005), 137-155.

Hornung, Eric. *Der Eine und die Vielen.* 4th ed. Darmstadt: Wissenschaftliche Buchgesellschaft 1990.

James, William. *The Varieties of Religious Experience.* Cambridge und London: Harvard University Press 1985.

Kocher, Paul. *Master of Middle earth.* Boston: Houghton Mifflin Company 1972

Langer, Otto. *Christliche Mystik im Mittelalter.* Darmstadt: Wissenschaftliche Buchgesellschaft 2004.

Lüers, Grete. *Die Sprache der Deutschen Mystik des Mittelalters im Werke der Mechthild von Magdeburg.*München: Ernst Reinhardt 1926.

Luhmann, Niklas. *Funktion der Religion.* Frankfurt am Main: Suhrkamp 1977.

Mechthild von Magdeburg. *Das fließende Licht der Gottheit.* Ed. Volmann-Profe, Gisela. Frankfurt am Main: Deutscher Klassiker Verlag 2003.

Nygren, Anders. *Eros und Agape.* 2nd ed. Gütersloh: Bertelsmann.

Pseudo-Dionysius Areopagita. "Über die Mystische Theologie". Über die Mystische Theologie und Briefe. Introd.,transl and annot. By Ritter, Adolf Martin. Bibliothek der Griechischen Literatur vol. 40. Stuttgart: Anton Hiersemann 1994. 74-80.

---, Die Namen Gottes. Introd., transl and annot. by Suchla, Beate Regina. Bibliothek der Griechischen Literatur vol. 26. Stuttgart: Anton Hiersemann 1988.

Otto, Rudolf. *Das Heilige: Über das Irrationale in der Idee des Göttlichen und sein Verhältnis zum Rationalen.* München: C. H. Beck 1987.

Reinhardt, Ursula. *Religion und Moderne Kunst in geistiger Verwandtschaft.* Marburg: N. G. Elwert Verlag 2003.

Riehle, Wolfgang. *Studien zur englischen Mystik des Mittelalters unter besonderer Berücksichtigung ihrer Metaphorik.* Heidelberg: Carl Winter 1977.

Rilke, Rainer Maria. "Erlebnis I". *Werke.* Ed. Engel, Manfred, Fülleborn, Ulrich, Nalewski, Horst, and Stahl, August. Frankfurt am Main and Leipzig: Insel Verlag 1996. Vol. 4, 666-668.

Shippey, Tom. *J.R.R. Tolkien – Author of the Century.* London. Harper Collins Publishers 2001.

Spörl, Uwe. *Gottlose Mystik in der deutschen Literatur der Jahrhundertwende.* Paderborn u. a.: Ferdinand Schöning 1997.

Tolkien, John Ronald Reuel. "A Middle English Vocabulary". Sisam, Kenneth ed. *Fourteenth Century Verse and Prose.* Oxford: Clarendon Press 1959.

---, *Letters.* Ed. Carpenter, Humphrey. London: George Allen and Unwin 1981.

---, *The Lord of the Rings.* 4. Aufl. London: Unwin Hyman 1988

---, *Smith of Wootton Major.* Extended Edition. Ed. Flieger, Verlyn. London: Harper Collins 2005.

---, *Tree and Leaf.* 2. Aufl. London: George Allen & Unwin 1988.

Underhill, Evelyn. *Mysticism.* 11th ed. London: Methuen & Co. 1926.

# Metaphysics of Myth:
# The Platonic Ontology of "Mythopoeia"

FRANK WEINREICH

ABSTRACT

There are some places in Tolkien's fictional work which express the ontological beliefs of the author and in which his personal convictions about creativity and human (sub-)creational powers can be described and identified. "Mythopoeia", the poem which he dedicated to C.S. Lewis in order to show him that myth does not consist of lies, but instead conveys facts and deeper truths, is the most important place of these. For this is what the poem really is about – it is the quintessence of Tolkien's ontology, which is, as will be shown, at the core a Platonic one. To demonstrate this the following article will take a look at the circumstances of the origin of "Mythopoeia", it will examine the form and content of the poem and the opinions expressed therein or lying behind its metaphors.

*Poetry ist the blossom and the fragrancy of all human knowledge.*
(Samuel Taylor Coleridge: *Biographia Literaria*)

*Those who know poetry whence poetry is,*
*and the need that man has for song,*
*or know any one of the fifty branches of magic,*
*have little time to waste on such things as science.*
(Lord Dunsany: *The King of Elfland's Daughter*)

"Mythopoeia" is a powerful as well as an enigmatic poem which can be described as the creed of Tolkienian ontology.[1] In wording and metre "Mythopoeia" recalls romanticism, whereby particularly John Keats's "Lamia" may come to mind. Regarding content one is on the other

---

[1] To understand the poem in this sense, it is essential to keep in mind the famous essay *On Fairy Stories*, which points in the same direction as "Mythopoeia", though the poem uses all the poetic emphasis which a scholarly paper like *OFS* would not allow itself.

hand also led to Classical antiquity, since the poem shows didactic qualities and ambitions like *Peri Physeos* by Epicurus or Lucretius' *De rerum natura,* both of which were textbooks on natural sciences. This impression is amplified by the subtitle and the dedication Tolkien gave to his poem.[2] What is the meaning of this mix of romantic speculation and scientific statements found in two very differing poetic ancestors, and what can be derived from it regarding Tolkien's fictional work? A first look shows the history of "Mythopoeia", and we see that the entrance to the Professor's ontological beliefs opens with a dispute between friends.

## CAUSE

Humphrey Carpenter reports the reason why *Mythopoiea* was written in the first place (*Biographie,* 169pp).[3] According to Carpenter, Tolkien had a heated discussion with Hugo Dyson and C.S. Lewis one night in September 1931. The topic: Tolkien and Dyson tried to enlighten Lewis about the true meaning of myths. According to Lewis himself, he was a theist at that time but still had not found his belief in the Christian faith (Lewis 1998, 275, cf. also chapters 14, 15). During the discussion Lewis is reported to have said that myths – the focal myth discussed that evening was the Christian myth – were lies although they might be of the highest artistry (therefore Tolkien spoke of "lies, breathed through silver"). Interestingly myths, according to Lewis – an author who later wrote *Perelandra* and *Narnia,* works which are overloaded with myth – are lies, no matter how artfully they might be wrapped up.

---

[2] "Mythopoeia" is dedicated to C.S. Lewis with these words: "To one who said that myths were lies and therefore worthless, even though 'breathed through silver'." Furthermore the poem is subtitled "Philomythus to Misomythus" e.g. lover of myths to sceptic of myths (line 0; from here on the count is "You look at trees and label them just so" = line 1, and so on).

[3] What happened that night was also confirmed by Walter Hooper, Lewis' biographer, who gave Joseph Pearce in an interview an account of the evening which tells the same story (Pearce 57p).

That caused Tolkien to intervene at once. He denied the opinion of myths being lies and is reported to have said, as early as on that occasion, that myths convey truth.[4] In the weeks following this evening "Mythopoeia" came into being as a condensed and artistically embroidered version of the arguments Tolkien held against Lewis's accusation of myths being lies. That was the occasion that led to *Mythopoiea* being composed six years before *On Fairy Stories*, the famous statement of the relation between human artistic creativity and reality, which indeed must be read with and against "Mythopoeia" for a full understanding of Tolkien's convictions about creativity and ontology.

## FACTS

Some remarks on verse, metre and other facts are in order. "Mythopoeia" is neologism,[5] a creation stemming from the Greek words "mythos" and "poeisis". "Mythos", of course, means myth[6] while "poiesis" stands for acting as well as creating. Creation in the case of "Mythopoeia" is used in an artistic sense, and this artistic sense is related by Tolkien to the human ability of sub-creation, which he outlines in *On Fairy Stories*, though there he uses it more carefully and presents it with a lesser ontological status than in "Mythopoeia" (*OFS* 25), six years before writing *OFS*. "Mythopoeia" therefore means myth-making, and the

---

[4] A conviction which also sheds light on the status of Tolkien's own writing: "In expounding this belief in the inherent *truth* of mythology, Tolkien had laid bare the centre of his philosophy as a writer, the creed that is at the heart of *The Silmarillion*." (Biography 147). Hooper speaks of Tolkien describing myth as a "way of conveying truths" (Pearce 58).

[5] The OED cites an example from 1927. The adjective "mythopoeic" is first attested in 1846. More significantly, there is an example from 1875 from the philologist Sayce, in *The Principles of Comparative Philology*, a publication that Tolkien is more than likely to have read.

[6] Myth does not need to be translated, otherwise an excursion would become necessary which would not be appropriate for this article and in which in greater detail explanations about myth, a word which originally just meant "narration", and its variety of meanings would have to be discussed. For explanations on myth and its meanings cf. Schneidewind and Weinreich *Fantasy*, Chap. 3.

title taken together with the dedication to Lewis – see above: "To one who said that myths were lies …" – depicts the program of the poem, which was composed to explain what myth-making is and thereby show the ontological status of myths in general.

The poem consists of 148 lines in 12 stanzas of differing length. It is written in so-called "heroic couplets", rhyming pairs of lines in iambic pentameter:

> You *look* at *trees* and *la*bel *them* just *so*,
> (for *trees* are '*trees*,' and *gro*wing *is* 'to *grow*')
> (lines 1f.)

The origin of the heroic couplet is unknown. In English poetry it was used at least from the 14th century onwards. Geoffrey Chaucer was the first poet to make extensive use of it. In the 17th century its usage reached its peak and it became the dominating metre in English dramatic poetry. Its best known examples are the works of John Dryden and Alexander Pope.

The formal structure of "Mythopoeia" therefore differs from the poetry usually found in Tolkien's works. Clive Tolley supposes that the reason for that lies in the assumption that Tolkien not only wanted to answer C.S. Lewis with "Mythopoeia" but tried to go much further and write the poem as a critique of Alexander Pope's "Essay on Criticism" and "Essay on Man" – by using the same literary form as Pope to correct the weltanschauung in Pope's poems into what Tolkien believed to be true (Tolley 82-84). Pope composed his two poems in heroic couplets (Pope 1711, 1734), which made it fitting to answer him using the same verse form. But a possible conflict between Pope and Tolkien is not the topic of the following considerations on "Mythopoeia".

## INTERPRETATION

In the context of the following considerations the content of the poem is much more important than verse and metre. Nonetheless it will not be necessary to examine the poem line by line. The intentions and the meaning of "Mythopoeia" can be derived from a close look at a selected number of stanzas and lines, as is done in the following.

The poem itself does not begin at once. The dedication to C.S. Lewis[7] is not part of the poem, although it clearly belongs together with it since it stands as an outline of what is to come – a refutation of the claim that myths are lies. Before the first line Tolkien inserted a subtitle "Philomythus to Misomythus", marking the poem as a message from one who loves myths to one who is at least sceptical about myths, but may even be hostile to them and the stories they convey. It is very unlikely that Tolkien wanted to characterise Lewis in earnest as someone hostile towards myth, even though "Mythopoeia" dates from a time when neither *Perelandra* nor *Narnia* were even thought of. Tolkien only points to Lewis's incredulity concerning truth in myth. The prefix "mis-" means "wrong" as well as "bad" and is used, I think, in both senses by Tolkien. Lewis did not want to mark myths as defective, neither in a moral nor in an aesthetic sense, when he said that they were lies. The reference to silver, through which myths might be breathed, even points to the aesthetic value and possibly the moral value myths can have, as artistic delight or morally inspiring tale. Like Tolkien, Lewis was simply referring to their truthfulness, which he denied but Tolkien emphatically defended[8]. Seen in this light it is more likely that Tolkien did not address Lewis as Misomythus but instead thought of the materialists, people who believe in (natural) sciences and empirical knowledge only. This sort of knowledge is discussed in the first stanza.

---

[7] The dedication of the published versions of the poem does not name Lewis explicitly and only says "To one who said ...". But Carpenter mentions a manuscript that also carried the remark "For C.S.L." (Carpenter, 170).
[8] As Carpenter and Hooper stated, cf. footnote 4.

It is Misomythus, the materialist, about whom the poet is talking when he begins with the lines "You look at trees and label them just so, / (for trees are 'trees' and growing is 'to grow')" and so on. This is the materialistic world view pictured in poetic terms, and in particular the world view of the empirical sciences: looking (i.e. examining) and labelling. The materialist and the empirical sciences recognise phenomena in the perceptible world and classify them according to an explanatory system which attaches labels like 'tree', 'earth', 'globe' and so on. Even a star, once a celestial phenomenon which was the topic of countless mythical and romanticising interpretations, is now nothing more than "some matter in a ball" (line 5), which runs on fixed trajectories, purposelessly and dumb (i.e. "inane", 7), which might better be translated as mindless, in the sense of de-spiritualised. What Misomythus sees is a universe with unbreakable natural laws, inescapable and without transcendental purpose.

Line 8 appears to be of special interest in this context; there physical matter in this universe is described with the words "where destined atoms are each moment slain" – so even atoms have an inescapable fate which threatens to destroy them at any moment. My interpretation is that line 8 refers to the model of atomic structure established by the Danish physicist Nils Bohr in 1913. This model points out the rules of atomic properties and indeed allows a view that describes atoms as 'fated', though in physical terms that is, of course, nonsense. In 1931 the basics of thermodynamics were well known, as was Bohr's model. An educated man with a wide range of interests like Tolkien surely was familiar enough with it to embed, as I think, the picture of fated atoms in "Mythopoeia" in the way he did. One can assume that Tolkien was familiar with the model of atomic structure and that he knew that an atom cannot easily be destroyed or 'slain'. Why then did he choose the picture of slain atoms? That atoms can indeed be destroyed might have been an idea that in 1931 was under discussion among theoretical physicists such as Bohr, Fermi or Heisenberg. But it is highly unlikely that Tolkien had an idea of the then merely theoretical concept of nuclear fission. I think it is much likelier that Tolkien here in line 8 refers to a pre-empirical concept of atoms derived from the ancient records of Leucippus and Democritus. They were the first thinkers who in ancient Greek had developed the idea of atoms being the basis of all physical matter. And while it is unlikely that Tolkien was aware of the most recent speculations of theoretical physicists of his time, it is on the other hand very probable that he, especially as philologist, knew the ancient Greek writings of presocratic philosophers, which had been completely reconstructed by 1930. But in "Mythopoeia" a connection between ancient beliefs and modern nuclear physics is established, if only to the better known basics laid out by Bohr and not to upcoming theories of nuclear fission. The term "destined atoms" therefore stands for two concepts. First, it stands for atoms as the basis of all matter and all material things the way Democritus and Leucippus assumed, who, of course, could not have the slightest idea of the theory of relativity and the equivalence of energy and matter. Second, it stands for the modern concept of atoms as described by Bohr in his model of the structure of atoms. The connection to modern physics can be found in the word "destined", which relates to the structure of atoms in the form of a nucleus and orbiting electrons. Ancient thinkers on the other hand had excluded atoms, for them the basis of all matter, from fate and fatal developments; they were convinced that atoms were indestructible (cf. Capelle 291f, 397p) and aimless as well as purposeless (cf. 405). But according to "Mythopoeia" this foundation can be destroyed. How? Why? That remains unknown in the first stanza, so we have to go on.

The second verse reports the development of time, cosmos and earth, "from dark beginnings to uncertain goals" (line 12). Interestingly the concept of evolution is mentioned without critique here: in lines 15 and 16 it says "an endless multitude of forms appear, / some grim some frail some beautiful, some queer" which according to lines 17 and 18 stem from one source, "one remote Origo". That is nothing less than a poetical short version of the concept of evolution. But while these four lines do not contain criticism, the next line states without doubt that God created earth and the life on earth: "God made the petreous rocks, the arboreal trees" (line 19). Lines 20 and 21 then state that God also created the wide universe ("tellurian stars") and man himself. At first glance this means that there is no evolution whatsoever. But from a conemporary point of view the concept of creation poses no problem. Evolution and belief in God are not exclusive. Even without the aid of a questionable concept like the so called 'intelligent design', findings on evolution and various religious beliefs are compatible.[9] But back in the first half of the 20th century the mention of God's creatorship in the same context as evolutionary theory can only be read as an objection against evolutionary theory.[10] Therefore a critical remark on the findings of modern natural science must be noted when reading verse 2 of the poem.

Stanza three then for the first time provides a hint of the superior role that language, names and the giving of names might have for man himself, particularly man in his role as witness of the existence of all things ("trees are not trees until so named and seen", line 29): trees are not trees before someone gives them a name ("named) and acknowledges ("and seen") them as trees henceforth. Acknowledging and naming can only be done after an observer has come into being who possesses the ability of conscious observation and language as grounds for the naming – mankind. Man, who does not become man until he possesses language and the ability to speak, as is said in line 31 ("who

---

[9] Cf. the documentation *Zum Kreationismus und zur Theorie des intelligenten Designs* of the Evangelische Zentralstelle für Weltanschauungsfragen and my own introductory summary of intelligent design and creationism: www.polyoinos.de/philstuff/intelligent_design.html.
[10] A short summary of the problems of evolutionary theory in the context of history can be found in Weinreich *Evolution*.

speech's involuted breath unfurled"). Man discloses himself as man only at the point when he uses speech: speech which is but a faint echo and cloudy picture of the world and everything in it, not in the sense of a recording or a photograph. It is not easy to unfold what is hidden in this meaningful third stanza. And since it is so important for the whole poem, we will have to examine the stanza and line by line.

1. Trees become trees only when they are acknowledged for what they are and, which is even more important only when they are given the name "tree". I think that tree in this line stands for every phenomenon of the living world, and perhaps also of the non-living world, since in line 19 tree and rock were equated as products of a creational act. That can be carried further to the assumption that, if this is right, the whole world and everything in it comes into its true being only when it is given a name. That is a prerequisite which could not happen before man appeared and used his special ability – speech. A convinced materialist must find this nonsensical since for him world, universe and matter are given things which possess reality independent from any observer. But in a non-materialistic, in a dualistic world view, which is definitely the one Tolkien held, this is in no way nonsensical but makes all the sense one can possibly think of. Why? Because the process of acknowledgement by sentient beings, and foremost the act of name-giving, is a first strong hint for the existence of a second level of being. One can imagine this also as a second plane of being in the ontological sense, besides the material universe which then would be counted as the first plane of existence or the Primary World, to use a Tolkienian term.[11] The

---

[11] A certain problem with levels, planes or worlds arises in the special case of Tolkien's ontology. As a man of deep Christian faith he believed in an afterlife and in a spiritual level of existence. One could call the material plane, on which we live together as humans, the real world or universe. But that would suggest that the spiritual level is not real, that it might be a fancy of imagination. But at least for Tolkien, and it is his ontology we are discussing here, the spiritual level was as real as the material world, perhaps in a sense even more realistic than reality and in every case more important than the world where our bodies reside. Tolkien was also the author who in *On Fairy Stories* coined the terms of Primary and Secondary Worlds, meaning the 'real' world on the

second plane or level perhaps can be found in the characteristic circumstance that this second level is a level which specifically depends on man and his ability to think and speak: trees become real trees when a sentient being acknowledges them and gives them the name which is the necessary condition for becoming real trees. In terms of the two differing planes or levels of existence – the material level of the real world and the second level where objects and beings are united with their designating names – there are two trees. The first one is the evolutionary product descended from a chaotic soup of carbohydrates and amino acids; it is one of the "forms" mentioned in line 15, "an endless multitude of forms appear". The second tree, the real tree, is the one which has been observed and which carries a name – tree. But in the Primary World the first cannot be distinguished from the second tree – not through touch, nor by biochemical and microscopic analysis. So where is it that the true being of the second tree exists, the true being of the real tree? That is a question we will put later in this essay at Plato's feet.

2. Line 31 then tells about the name-giver, albeit in a poetical way which is not readily comprehensible. A form of language which is difficult to understand discloses him as what he is ("who speech's involuted breath unfurled"). This disclosure means that through his faculty of speech man becomes man. That is a topic which is familiar to every philologist and philosopher, that is the ancient Aristotelian zoon logon echon, the animal that has language at his disposal. From ancient times

---

material plane in the first case and sub-created worlds of literary fiction in the latter. But we cannot just use these terms, since the Primary World is the real world, certainly, but the spiritual level, where trees get their names from (see below), is not a Secondary World but something else (when counted the spiritual level would be prime; or perhaps 'proto-', as would be fitting for the following involvement with Platonic thought). Secondary Worlds in Tolkien's sense are fictional worlds whose process of creation is inspired by God's act of creating the Primary World and therefore has a connection to the spiritual level, but must not be confused with it since all it receives directly from there is an inspiration, mediated through the agency of the author, a man or woman of the Primary World. These explanations notwithstanding I will use the term Primary World for purposes of comprehensibility in some places in the following text, when the physical world is meant.

the ability to speak was held to be the "differentia specifica" which distinguishes man from all living beings.

3. The following lines can be read as a first characterisation of language. It is not important whether man or language are meant in line 32 when it is said that speech is a "faint echo and dim picture of the world" because man and speech are held to be identical in the motif of the zoon logon echon. Then, why is it that speech is thought of as dark and faint in its ability to reproduce the phenomena of the world? The poem insists that language is "neither record nor a photograph" (line 33). One explanation comes to mind. If speech and the declaration of names were nothing more than a photograph, they would also be nothing more than one of the "multitude of forms" line 15 presented. But this is not what words do – that is the unambiguous statement from line 33. What words do is instead circumscribed in line 32 – they produce a faint echo and dim pictures of reality, thus providing an imperfect portrait of the world. This means that they portray another world than the one which a tape-recorder and camera would picture, hence another world than that of pure matter. That can then only be the world (or universe or plane or level of existence) which is the home of the tree which received its name, the one mentioned in line 29. So this is the home of the real tree, the tree which, through receiving a name, is designated as the true tree, far more than an assembly of woody fibers sprung from matter. Otherwise the poet should have given further explanations.

What we find in lines 29 and 30 is the belief that there must in fact be a level of existence besides the mere material level where our bodies reside and where the deficient instruments of empirical sciences are used for the scrutiny of 'reality'. And this spiritual level must have something to do with language, with the human faculty of speech and thought. This makes the assumption most likely that the Aristotelian zoon logon echon is in possession of a key which allows him to enter the second level.

The poem goes on to describe processes of thought. Lines 39 to 44 say that man digs out foreknown things from memory and thus produces spiritual ideas and thoughts. Especially the "elves" with their extraordinary artistic abilities and "dark secrets", secrets which probably also stem from faërie as do the elves, are topics of this remembrance. Two things are important in this context.

First the word "foreknown" from line 39. The knowledge is not of the kind that man has learned but possesses even before subjective experiences. That indicates the possession of knowledge from before the beginning of his life on earth, since experiences begin from conception onwards. Assumptions of this kind are not unknown and reach down into history at least to Greek antiquity. Ancient Greek philosophy would not use the term "digging" (line 39) but instead speak of birth and of the art of a midwife who assists in giving birth, in this image not to a child but to a memory, to foreknowledge. That is the so-called Socratic method, which helps (re-)produce the remembrance of a knowledge with which men are born and which they only need to remember. Socrates's role, then, was to help give birth to these things like a midwife. The memories are incarnated in man and can be known anew, if man begins to remember them. The concept of remembering incarnated and immortal truth is explained in detail for the first time in Plato's *Phaedo*. But where does the knowledge Socrates and Plato postulate come from? It comes from another plane of being, from the world of ideas, which, according to Plato, is in an ontological sense the level where the true being or the essence of all things resides.[12] So we here

---

[12] Plato postulated a clearly divided dualistic cosmos. He was convinced that there is a second level of being, a superior level which exists beside and independent of our reality (whereas our reality does not exist independent of the second level, from which it receives all form as Aristotle would have said). The superiority of the second level is grounded in its being the home of the essences of all things, i.e. the 'ideas of things', where a circle can really be a perfect circle as it never could in the material world. The

find another reference to the transcendental plane or world (of ideas, as Plato would have it).

Furthermore these lines provide the first indication of the special role art and creativity play. What does man remember from foreknown knowledge? The elves and their looms and forges (lines 42 – 44). Those are the same elves about whose 'magic' Tolkien was later to write in a famous letter to Milton Waldman: "its object is Art not Power, sub-creation not domination and tyrannous re-forming of Creation" (*L*, 146). The elves and their forges and looms, which, according to "Mythopoeia" work their art in the heads of man, serve as a metaphor for art and the worth of art and creativity, which man remembers. And it should be noted that art is equipped with "great power" (line 41).

Stanza 4 then describes in beautiful and poetical words the magic one can also recognise in the material world if one sees it with elvish eyes, which, with regard to the letter to Waldman, translates into observing the world with the eyes of an artist. Stanza 5 talks about man in the order of things in our world. He is fallen from grace, but God has not given up on him. Instead he still grants him wisdom, he has just to be capable of recognising it (lines 55 – 58). He is man, sub-creator and he refracts the white light in order to combine it anew in countless variations.[13] And this ability has not ended with the fall. Still man is required to practise his powers as sub-creator: "We make still by the law in which we're made", it says in line 70, with which stanza 5 closes. Stanza 5 is the strongest link to *On Fairy Stories*, which Tolkien was to write 6 years later and which is rightfully brought into close connection with "Mythopoeia", the scholarly article and the poem forming two sides of Tolkien's view of art.

---

[13] theory of ideas forms the core of all Platonic philosophy and cannot be discussed in the current paper. A good introduction to Platonic thought can be found in the papers which compose *The Cambridge Companion to Plato*, edited by Richard Kraut.
Thereby "mak[ing] manifest fragments of original truth" (Flieger 47).

Stanzas 6 – 9 tell of the perils of the Primary World and make clear that evil is a fact: "of evil / this alone is dreadly certain, evil is" (lines 79f.). The latter is a thought which a materialist would find hard to believe because a metaphysical evil is meant, a force which Tolkien later in Middle-earth will embody in Melkor/Morgoth. But a force that is also a constant threat to our lives and souls in the Primary World. It is the purpose of the myths to warn against this evil. People who are aware of this and hold on to their courage are blessed (verse 8). Especially blessed are the ones who raise their voices and tell about evil, perils and the rewards of courage in mythical stories: "blessed are the legend-makers with their rhyme" (line 91). Line 92 then again hints at the transcendental spiritual plane, saying, that the "legend-makers" are telling the truth though they are not reporting scientific facts since they speak of "things not found within recorded time". In all humbleness Tolkien then in verse 10 expresses his wish to be allowed to sing with the bards for once in order to also raise his voice like the blessed legend-makers. Well, this was in 1931 and we can say that this wish was definitely granted.

Stanza 11 is of special interest because of the picture it shows of the natural sciences. Line 119 speaks about "progressive apes", which is a dig at the theory of evolution and its founder Charles Darwin, which Tolkien presumably felt to be first of all an insult to the belief that man was created as an image of God. More important for the understanding of "Mythopoeia" and Tolkien's stance on the sciences is the abyss that gapes before the apes, i.e. man; which means it gapes before progress and technological advancements. It is well known that Tolkien was very sceptical about technological progress. But technology depends on scientific findings, and therefore the question arises as to what Tolkien thought of science?

Attacks on science are not as easy to recognise as are Tolkien's objections to technology and modernity, of which he once said that it was

"Mordor in our midst" (*L* 165). Still, it is only consistent to assume a critical position also towards the pure sciences, perhaps even to other branches of scholarship since for example the Positivism of Auguste Comte likewise stands in opposition to the view of man that Tolkien sketches in "Mythopoeia" (and elsewhere) and it also is part of the success of technocratic societies, just as the invention of flight by Daedalos led to the great aircraft that carried the bombs in World War II (cf. *L* 88). Also in Middle-earth some signs of hostility towards scientific thought can be traced. When Gandalf reports the betrayal of Saruman, he also tells about the changing of his white cloak into a multicoloured cloth – a kind of refraction of the white light that Newton discovered and which marks an important point in scientific progress (cf. Vanderbeke 146).[14] Another lead can be found in the portrayal of Fëanor as a Faustian character who puts his craft above all other things. This makes it important also to note the dig at Darwin in line 119.

Lines 125 to 130 are the unmistakable expression of the refutation of modernity with its lack of spirituality. And they are an expression of Tolkien's objections to the materialism of modern societies, which he seems to have experienced as overwhelming. This is definitely not the way the poet will take; he will not bow before the iron crown, nor will he lay down his golden sceptre of creativity (lines 129f.).

Of special interest is line 126 before the poet paints the impressive pictures of the iron crown and sceptre. Here, I think, we have another hint of his relation to science, though quite hidden this time. Line 126 says the poet refuses to "denot[e] this and that by this and that" with no special reference to a particular fact. This means, I think, that the poet refuses to use the basic approaches to scientific understanding: induc-

---

[14] Footnote 13 mentions Flieger and her approach of understanding the refraction of light as discovery of "original truth" beyond the material world (cf. Flieger 46p). That is a plausible reading in the context of lines 61 – 64 of "Mythopoeia". In the context of Saruman's appearance before Gandalf I nonetheless think that the refraction of light refers to natural sciences and their "artificial intervention into nature" (Vanderbeke 146), which in fact is what Saruman is about to do in the following course of the Ringwar..

tion and deduction. To denote something by another thing and vice versa stands for the reasoning that obtains or discovers general laws from particular facts or examples, induction, or for reasoning the other way round, when conclusions are drawn from general principles to particular cases, i.e. deduction. Together with experiment and observation, induction and deduction are the basic principles of discovering new findings like "a star's a star, some matter in a ball" (line 5) and "destined atoms" (8); they, and with them the whole corpus of scientific thinking and empirical sciences [research?], are the basis of all sciences. The principles of induction and deduction were first fully developed in Aristotelian logic (cf. Hankinson). Tolkien would not be the first to criticise Aristotle – who began his *Metaphysics* with the words "all men desire to know" (980a21) and who believed that his set of principles and syllogisms could indeed lead to such knowledge (981b25-27) – for disenchanting the world and eventually allowing the rainbow to become unwoven. Aristotle was often attacked this way, directly or indirectly, by critics who attacked the principles which are owed to his epistêmê: for example, Coleridge, Years, and Keats. "Philosophy will clip an angel's wing", John Keats says in "Lamia".[15]

The suspicion that the philologist Tolkien seems to have been hostile to sciences is growing stronger. But why are his opinions hidden?

---

[15] John Keats: "Lamia", line 234; the argument is directed at Isaac Newton. "Philosophy" in Newton's time, and it is Newton's *Philosophiae Naturalis Principia Mathematica* that Keats refers to, was a term which in the first place meant all natural sciences, not the discipline of philosophy as part of the corpus which form the humanities we think of today. Therefore it is the sciences, the empirical world view, which cut off the wings of the angel. The Romantic poets in opposition to this claimed that it was their works which described eternal truths (cf. Coleridge 179). They put their works in opposition to the empirical and mathematical knowledge of the scientists and believed that their findings and inspirations were superior. This is shown for example in the poem "*Wenn nicht mehr Zahlen und Figuren*" by the German Romantic poet Novalis (Georg Friedrich Philipp Freiherr von Hardenberg, 1772 – 1801; the title translates "When numbers and figures no longer ...") which ends with lines that state, after the belief in scientific truth has been wiped out, "then "before a secret word, the whole wrong being will vanish" ("dann fliegt vor einem geheimen Wort / das ganze verkehrte Wesen fort"; Novalis *Zahlen*, lines 11f.):

Could it be that Tolkien, an Oxford professor, was a member of the scholarly community and he did not want to discredit them openly? Maybe. But another reason, I think, was that he was not in the least opposed to knowledge, not opposed to acquiring understanding and gaining wisdom. Tolkien was searching and researching all his life, and so he can only have objected to certain approaches to knowledge. Maybe the critique of science in "Mythopoeia" is hedged in because he was trying to differentiate. Another reason for his formulations is, of course, due to the poetic form of the whole argument.

But how great, then, is the terrain that knowledge can cover? What is it that man can come to know? Tolkien has shown what he objects to, he has shown what a myth is and that myths can convey truth, even though they are but faint and dim truths. Also human creative powers, even when they become 'Elvish', can show only reflections of truth. This is the point where an old image of thought springs to mind – faint pictures, dim sounds, reflections? Does not that remind one of Plato's Cave?

According to "Mythopoeia", so far the transcendental second plane cannot be brought onto earth. And it stays this way. Lines 131 – 136 in the last stanza make it clear that the true essence of all things can only be experienced on the second plane – though even that not with certitude ("perchance the eye may stray", line 131) – which in the poem is then equated with Paradise (131). In Paradise man's eye now has the chance "to see the day-illumined, and renew" (133), thereby leaving the triteness of the earthly light behind him. The formulation is also reminiscent of Plato; it takes up a picture from the allegory of the sun. There the sun, an object that provides the brightest light, is equated with the idea of good – a good that is necessary to view the truth that can only be seen in the brightest light (*Republic* 508a-d). Following the allegory of the lines (509d – 511a), the possible view of truth depends on the angle at which sunlight shines upon the objects of knowledge. Line 133 is reminiscent of the Platonic parables of sun and lines. But more important is line 134: the day – illuminated and renew[Again, something is strange here.] – there (on the other plane!) shows "from mirrored truth the likeness of the True"[16] – this means objective knowledge. This view makes it possible to look on the blessed land as it is, "made free", a liberation which then extends to the spectator.[17]

What is it that the poet and reader are "made free" from? The mistaken assumptions of an empiricism which does not allow other modes of acquiring knowledge.[18] The important point is that it is possible in Paradise to renew the sight of truth, because "renew" again takes up the topic of remembered, 'Socratic', foreknowledge which was mentioned above. Therefore the key terms of verse 12 are "renew", which refers to knowledge gained from the second plane, and "mirrored truth". Mirrored truth is again a Platonian picture. It refers to the allegory of the cave, the most influential idea of Plato's philosophy (*Republic* 514a-515c). The parable tells the story of people who are chained inside a cave. They are looking upon a wall before them, unable to turn around. They can only see shadows on the wall and hear sounds originating from outside the cave. The shadows are faint, the sound is dim, both are but a reflection of the real world outside the cave. These people will never come to know reality but only experience incomplete reflections if they are not freed (or free themselves), stand up and look at what is really outside their cave. The meaning of the parable is that the real world, the only world which the materialist believes in, only allows us to see reflections from the second plane, just like the reflections the prisoners in Plato's cave can see and hear. The possibility "[to] see that

---

[16] Note the capitalized "True" - meaning the 'one truth' or essence of being which on earth, with its different modi of reasoning and observing, cannot be found.

[17] The lines 131 to 136 in context: "to see the day illumined, and renew / from mirrored truth the likeness of the True. / Then looking on the Blessed Land 'twill see / that all is as it is, and yet made free:".

[18] Tolkien certainly does not go so far as to object to any empiricism. But he objects to a certain kind of empiricism which rules out all other forms of gaining knowledge.

all is as it is" (lines 135f.) exists only on the second plane, in the Platonic world of ideas, in the "Mythopoeian Paradise". Even the liberation in Paradise – "all [...] as it is, and yet made free" – connects "Mythopoeia" to Plato since the view of truth, which man experiences by leaving the cave, constitutes an act of liberation.

## Conclusion

What are the most important points of "Mythopoeia"? For Tolkien there is something wrong with an exclusively materialistic world view. But observing the world as it appears there is something which touches man ("nerves that tingle touched by sound and light" it says as early as in line 22). With this first indefinable tingling the realisation of something deeper begins, which in the end points to another plane or level of existence, a plane which transcends our physical world. The importance of this plane, as we can deduce from the critique of the material world, lies in the assumption that in it things appear as they really are, perhaps best described in Greek as "kath auto", the essence of a given thing which Kant called the "Ding an sich".[19] This is especially true for everything belonging to knowledge of the religious kind. But man cannot enter this plane, at least not directly and unmediated while living. But words can mediate between the Primary World and the transcendental plane. Words can transport inklings of the deeper truth, they can be the "blaze of light in every word" that Leonard Cohen postulated in his song *Hallelujah* (Cohen, lines 20f.). And these inklings can be found in myths, which therefore cannot be lies. But myths are not told in professorial circles, possessed of Positivism, in Vienna and in their Cambridge lectures, but by poets who remember their Elvish crafts and whose creativity proves that there are many more things one can speak of than

---

[19] "Ding an sich" or "kath auto", also known in Latin as "per se", is roughly translatable as "thing-in-itself", a key term of the *Critique of Pure Reason*, which is defined in the *Transcendental Aesthetics* (Kant 78).

tivity proves that there are many more things one can speak of than the contemporary philosopher believes possible.

What do these things mean in philosophical terms? It is quite easy to summarise that: the beliefs and expressions which make up "Mythopoeia" are pure Platonism! The whole poem is a (very) short version of the theory of knowledge developed in *Phaedo, Phaedrus* and *The Republic* because that is what Platonic ontology is about: dualism, the belief that knowledge is to be found in the light (of reason),[20] the assumption that whoever is searching for knowledge only in the material world looks upon the walls of a cave, seeing nothing but mere reflections of what really is going on while the authentic 'things-in-themselves' are hidden behind their backs. Not until man gets up, turns around and leaves the cave is he able to see "from mirrored truth the likeness of the True" (line 134). For Tolkien the situation is even more dramatic than it is for Plato, because he sees mankind not just looking at the walls of a cave but standing before an abyss. It is the abyss of modernity, including modern science, that leads to the conclusion: "I will not walk with you progressive apes, / erect and sapient. Before them gapes / the dark abyss to which that progress tends" (lines 120 to 122).

Of course there are a number of possible objections to what I have said. For example, one could argue: 'He was of the Christian faith, a true Catholic. Plato's thoughts could not have had this importance for him.' Or: 'It is well known that Tolkien, while composing "Mythopoeia", was heavily influenced by Owen Barfield's *Poetic Diction.*' To this I can only say – both are right ... in a sense; certainly the Christian faith was much more important for him than Plato's speculations on metaphysics, and Barfield's Gnostic anthroposophy was perhaps more

---

[20] The light of reason is, of course, a topic taken from the Enlightenment which Romanticism and poets like Keats or Yeats, in whose succession I have put Tolkien in this paper, were opposed to. But they, like their Romantic German counterparts in philosophy – J.G. Fichte, the brothers Schlegel, F. Schleiermacher – also clung to reason, albeit for their own purposes and finding reason in speculative thought. Educated metaphysical speculations are far from being unreasonable, as Plato and Aristotle have proved.

appealing to him than ancient Greek book lore. Gnostic disparaging of the material world would have affected him more than the quiet irony of Socrates, I think. But to understand theories *and* beliefs one has to examine the sources they stem from in order to understand what the theories and beliefs mean and what their agents and followers see in them. The source of Gnostic beliefs, the source of anthroposophical theories and the bases of developed Christian theology are Platonic and depend on Plato's writings[21] and dialogues, they are ingrained with Platonic thought. A famous dictum of the philosopher Alfred North Whitehead says that all philosophy is but a footnote to Plato's teachings.[22] In a sense that is right, and "Mythopoeia" is a witness to it.

What should one make of it? Theory of ideas and second plane of existence? Creativity and sub-creation? First of all it is speculative and can be nothing more until God or the second plane prove their existence by direct intervention. These are questions of faith and belief, which, by the way, is also true for Plato's metaphysics. My aim was not to attack or defend the speculations described in this article but to explain what stands behind "Mythopoeia" and to remind Tolkien's readers that the roots run deep and that you have to follow them in order to gain an understanding of Tolkien's convictions.

FRANK WEINREICH studied philosophy, communication sciences and politics in the early Nineties and holds a PhD in philosophy from the University of Vechta. He has worked as an independent scholar, freelance author and editor in Bochum, Germany

---

[21] Only Plato's dialogues are extant, and even in the case of some of these it is disputed whether Plato really wrote them. It is known that Plato, like Aristotle (of whom only writings are extant while the dialogues he is said to have written are lost), also published theoretical papers, of which not one is known nowadays but to which the Gnostic thinkers of antiquity might have had access.

[22] "The safest general characterization of the European philosophical tradition is that it consists of a series of footnotes to Plato. I do not mean the systematic scheme of thought which scholars have doubtfully extracted from his writings. I allude to the wealth of general ideas scattered through them" (Whitehead, Ray 39).

since 2001. His interests focus on ethics, bioethics, media ethics, technology assessment, education, new media, fantasy and science fiction, myths and mythology, and, of course, the works of Tolkien. He has published numerous books, articles and essays, including a well received Introduction to fantasy literature (Famtasy. Einführung. Essen 2007). He is co-editor of *Hither Shore*, the Scholarly Journal of the German Tolkien Society, and co-editor of *Stein und Baum*, a German source for fantasy literature and works on fantasy. He can most easily be contacted through his professional web site www.textarbeiten.com (mail: fw@textarbeiten.com) or via his private Tolkien-page, which at the moment carries more than forty articles, essays and stories on Tolkien, Middle-earth and fantasy literature: www.polyoinos.de/tolk_stuff (mail: fw@polyoinos.de).

## Works Cited

Aristotle. *Aristoteles' Metaphysik*. Hamburg: Meiner 1989.

Barfield, Owen. *Poetic Diction*. A Study in Meaning. Middletown: Wesleyan University Press 1973.

Capelle, Wilhelm (ed.). *Die Vorsokratiker*. Stuttgart: Kröner, 1968.

Carpenter, Humphrey. *J.R.R. Tolkien. A Biography*. London: Allen & Unwin, 1977.

Carpenter, Humphrey (ed.). *The Letters of J.R.R. Tolkien*. London: Allen & Unwin, 2000.

Cohen, Leonard. "Hallelujah". *The Essential Leonard Cohen*. [Audio-CD] Track 13.

Coleridge, Samuel Taylor. *Biographia Literaria*. Or Biographical Sketches of My Literary Life and Opinions. London: J.M. Dent & Sons, 1965.

Evangelische Zentralstelle für Weltanschauungsfragen. "Dokumentation: Zum Kreationismus und zur Theorie des intelligenten Designs." *Zeitschrift für Religion und Weltanschauungsfragen* 9/07 (2007). 337 – 342.

Flieger, Verlyn. *Splintered Light*. Logos and Language in Tolkien's World. Kent, London: Kent State University Press 2002.

Hankinson, R. James. "Philosophy of Science". J. Barnes (ed.). *The Cambridge Companion to Aristotle*. Cambridge: Cambridge University Press 1995. 109 – 139.

Kant, Immanuel. *Kritik der reinen Vernunft*. Werkausgabe, Vols. III and IV. W. Weischedel (ed.). Frankfurt/M: Suhrkamp 1968.

Keats, John. *The Poetical Works of John Keats*. London: Warne 1884.

Kraut, Richard. *The Cambridge Companion to Plato*. Cambridge. Cambridge University Press 1993.

Lewis, Clive Staples. *Überrascht von Freude*. Giessen: Brunnen, 1998.

Novalis [Georg Friedrich Philipp Freiherr von Hardenberg]. *Werke*. München: Beck 2001.

Pearce, Joseph. *Tolkien: Man and Myth*. London, HarperCollins, 1998.

Plato. *Sämtliche Dialoge*. Otto Apelt (ed.). Hamburg: Meiner, 1993.

Pope, Alexander. *Essay on Criticism*. 1711. [http://www.gutenberg.org/dirs/etext05/esycr10h.htm, cited 12.12.2007]

---, *Essay on Man*. 1734. [http://www.gutenberg.org/dirs/etext00/esymn10.txt, cited 12.12.2007]

Rehn, Rudolf. *Platons Höhlengleichnis*. Das Siebte Buch der Politeia, gr.-dt. Exzerpta Klassika, Band 23. Mainz: Diethrichsche Verlagsbuchhandlung, 2005.

Sayce, Archibald Henry. *The Principles of Comparative Philology*. London: Trubner 1874.

Schneidewind, Friedhelm. *Mythen und Phantastik*. Essen: Oldib 2008.

Shippey, Tom. *The Road to Middle-earth*. Boston, New York: Houghton Mifflin, 2003.

Tolley, Clive. "Tolkien's 'Essay on Man': A Look at Mythopoeia." In: *The Chesterton Review*. J.R.R. Tolkien. Mythos and Modernity in Middle-earth. Vol. XVIII, Feb./May 2002. 79 – 95.

Tolkien, John Ronald Reuel. *Tree and Leaf*. Including the Poem Mythopoeia. London: Grafton, 1992.

Vanderbeke, Dirk. "Language, Lore and Learning in *The Lord of the Rings*." *Reconsidering Tolkien*. Thomas Honegger (ed.). Zurich, Bern: Walking Tree Publishers.

Weinreich, Frank. *Die Evolution*. Bochum 2005 [http://www.polyoinos.de/philstuff/evolution.html, cited 12.12.2007]

---, *Eine Notiz zu den Gefahren des sogenannten intelligent design*. [http://www.polyoinos.de/philstuff/intelligent_design.html, cited 12.12.2007]

---, *Fantasy*. Einführung. Essen: Oldib 2007.

Whitehead, Alfred North/ Griffin, David Ray: *Process and Reality*. An Essay in Cosmology. New York: Free Press 1979.

# Walking Tree Publishers

Walking Tree Publishers was founded in 1997 as a forum for publication of material (books, videos, CDs, etc.) related to Tolkien and Middle-earth studies. Manuscripts and project proposals can be submitted to the board of editors (please include an SAE):

Walking Tree Publishers
CH-3052 Zollikofen
Switzerland
e-mail: info@walking-tree.org
http://www.walking-tree.org

## *Cormarë Series*

The *Cormarë Series* has been the first series of studies dedicated exclusively to the exploration of Tolkien's work. Its focus is on papers and studies from a wide range of scholarly approaches. The series comprises monographs, thematic collections of essays, conference volumes, and reprints of important yet no longer (easily) accessible papers by leading scholars in the field. Manuscripts and project proposals are evaluated by members of an independent board of advisors who support the series editors in their endeavour to provide the readers with qualitatively superior yet accessible studies on Tolkien and his work.

*News from the Shire and Beyond. Studies on Tolkien*
Peter Buchs and Thomas Honegger (eds.), Zurich and Berne 2004, Reprint, First edition 1997 (Cormarë Series 1), ISBN 3-9521424-5-X

*Root and Branch. Approaches Towards Understanding Tolkien*
Thomas Honegger (ed.), Zurich and Berne 2005, Reprint, First edition 1999 (Cormarë Series 2), ISBN 3-905703-01-7

Richard Sturch, *Four Christian Fantasists. A Study of the Fantastic Writings of George MacDonald, Charles Williams, C. S. Lewis and J.R.R. Tolkien*
Zurich and Berne 2007, Reprint, First edition 2001 (Cormarë Series 3), ISBN 978-3-905703-04-7

*Tolkien in Translation*
Thomas Honegger (ed.), Zurich and Berne 2003 (Cormarë Series 4), ISBN 3-9521424-6-8

Mark T. Hooker, *Tolkien Through Russian Eyes*
Zurich and Berne 2003 (Cormarë Series 5), ISBN 3-9521424-7-6

*Translating Tolkien: Text and Film*
Thomas Honegger (ed.), Zurich and Berne 2004 (Cormarë Series 6), ISBN 3-9521424-9-2

Christopher Garbowski, *Recovery and Transcendence for the Contemporary Mythmaker. The Spiritual Dimension in the Works of J.R.R. Tolkien*
Zurich and Berne 2004, Reprint, First Edition by Marie Curie Sklodowska, University Press, Lublin 2000, (Cormarë Series 7), ISBN 3-9521424-8-4

*Reconsidering Tolkien*
Thomas Honegger (ed.), Zurich and Berne 2005 (Cormarë Series 8),
ISBN 3-905703-00-9

*Tolkien and Modernity 1*
Frank Weinreich and Thomas Honegger (eds.), Zurich and Berne 2006 (Cormarë Series 9), ISBN 978-3-905703-02-3

*Tolkien and Modernity 2*
Thomas Honegger and Frank Weinreich (eds.), Zurich and Berne 2006 (Cormarë Series 10), ISBN 978-3-905703-03-0

Tom Shippey, *Roots and Branches. Selected Papers on Tolkien by Tom Shippey*
Zurich and Berne 2007 (Cormarë Series 11), ISBN 978-3-905703-05-4

Ross Smith, *Inside Language. Linguistic and Aesthetic Theory in Tolkien*
Zurich and Berne 2007 (Cormarë Series 12), ISBN 978-3-905703-06-1

*How We Became Middle-earth. A Collection of Essays on The Lord of the Rings*
Adam Lam and Nataliya Oryshchuk (eds.), Zurich and Berne 2007 (Cormarë Series 13), ISBN 978-3-905703-07-8

*Myth and Magic. Art According to the Inklings*
Eduardo Segura and Thomas Honegger (eds.), Zurich and Berne 2007 (Cormarë Series 14), ISBN 978-3-905703-08-5

*The Silmarillion - Thirty Years On*
Allan Turner (ed.), Zurich and Berne 2007 (Cormarë Series 15),
ISBN 978-3-905703-10-8

Martin Simonson, *The Lord of the Rings and the Western Narrative Tradition*
Zurich and Jena 2008 (Cormarë Series 16), ISBN 978-3-905703-09-2

*Beyond Middle-earth: Tolkien's Shorter Works. Proceedings of the 4th Seminar of the Deutsche Tolkien Gesellschaft & Walking Tree Publishers Decennial Conference*
Margaret Hiley and Frank Weinreich (eds.), Zurich and Jena 2008 (Cormarë Series 17)

*Constructions of Authorship in and around the Works of J.R.R. Tolkien*
Judith Klinger (ed.), Zurich and Jena, forthcoming

*Tolkien's The Lord of the Rings: Sources and Inspirations*
Stratford Caldecott and Thomas Honegger (eds.), Zurich and Jena, forthcoming

Rainer Nagel, *Hobbit Place-names. A Linguistic Excursion through the Shire*
Zurich and Jena, forthcoming

### Tales of Yore Series

The *Tales of Yore Series* grew out of the desire to share Kay Woollard's whimsical stories and drawings with a wider audience. The series aims at providing a platform for qualitatively superior fiction with a clear link to Tolkien's world.

Kay Woollard, *The Terror of Tatty Walk. A Frightener*
CD and Booklet, Zurich and Berne 2000 (Tales of Yore Series 1),
ISBN 3-9521424-2-5

Kay Woollard, *Wilmot's Very Strange Stone or What came of building "snobbits"*
CD and booklet, Zurich and Berne 2001 (Tales of Yore Series 2),
ISBN 3-9521424-4-1

Ossie felt the back of his neck go prickly....

www.ingramcontent.com/pod-product-compliance
Lightning Source LLC
Chambersburg PA
CBHW070717160426
43192CB00009B/1222